The Cruising Life

Second Edition

Jim Trefethen

INTERNATIONAL MARINE / McGRAW-HILL EDUCATION

Camden, Maine • New York • Chicago • San Francisco • Lisbon • London • Madrid
Mexico City • Milan • New Delhi • San Juan • Seoul • Singapore • Sydney • Toronto

1 2 3 4 5 6 7 8 9 0 QFR/QFR 1 0 9 8 7 6 5

ISBN 978-0-07-182321-0
MHID 0-07-182321-2
eISBN 978-0-07-182193-3
eMHID 0-07-182193-7

Library of Congress Cataloging-in-Publication Data is available from the Library of Congress.

All photographs courtesy the author. Line illustrations are by Dick Gagner.

McGraw-Hill Education books are available at special quantity discounts to use as premiums and sales promotions or for use in corporate training programs. To contact a representative, please e-mail us at bulksales@mcgraw-hill.com.

Questions regarding the content of this book should be addressed to www.internationalmarine.com

Questions regarding the ordering of this book should be addressed to
McGraw-Hill Education
Customer Service Department
P.O. Box 547
Blacklick, OH 43004
Retail customers: 1-800-262-4729
Bookstores: 1-800-722-4726

Contents

CONTENTS

CONTENTS

CONTENTS

List of Sidebars

Preface to the Second Edition

The Cruising Life was first published in 1999, right after SV *Sultana* and crew (me, my wife, Susan, and our two children, Sarah, age 12, and Phillip, age 10) completed a leisurely and event-filled cruise from our previous home in Marblehead, Massachusetts, to the lovely port town of Nelson, New Zealand. Unknown to us at the time, this was to become our home for the next 20 years.

Seven days out of Nuka'lofa in Tonga, *Sultana* had been badly damaged in a storm, damage that took three years to repair and led to a much-needed complete refit. And by the time the boat was ready to leave, we weren't. Sarah had emerged like a butterfly from her chrysalis of childhood into a lovely young woman, headstrong and independent, and was off to college in California. While Phillip came along on a year-long tour of the South Pacific after the refurbished *Sultana* was launched, at 17, he was tugging at the reins ready to gallop off on his own life of adventure and romance. Thus, Susan and I returned to New Zealand from Australia by ourselves, tied *Sultana* to the dock, moved ashore, and made the painful transition from being active cruisers to shore-bound boatowners.

Life in New Zealand was good, but after 10 years we yearned still for the land just over the horizon with the winds whispering promises of adventures unknown and destinations undetermined. We had sold *Sultana* when we decided that we were too old for cruising, then decided that, hell no, we weren't too old at all, not yet anyway. After a 3-year search, we found *Vicarious* tied to a dock in North Carolina with owners who had changed life's direction and were ready to sell. Within a few months we were back where we belonged: far from shore, first headed north to the Arctic, then, when the weather didn't cooperate, east across the Atlantic, then, when that didn't work out, south to the Caribbean and through the Panama Canal, and then on to wherever the fickle winds and currents of fate took us next.

We left the life of a typical retired couple in a cottage in a lovely little town in New Zealand to become a couple of grouchy old farts on a boat; we became people normal people think should grow up and act their age. Our first trip on *Vicarious* was a marvelous five-day sail up the Gulf Stream from Cape Lookout, North Carolina, to Block Island, Rhode Island. At the end of the first day at sea when the stars came out to guide the way and the full sails were sighing in contentment (the way they do), it was a lot like coming home—no, amend that—it was coming home.

To say that a lot has happened in the world since *The Cruising Life* was first published is an egregious understatement. In the short span of 14 years we have suffered through two major recessions (one of which is with us still); mind-boggling military actions in Iraq and Afghanistan; terrorists attacks in New York and Boston; a quadrupling of fuel prices; global warming on an unprecedented scale; major shifts in weather patterns and political systems in countries popular with cruisers; burgeoning population growth with a billion more of us devouring an ever decreasing store of resources; a sharp increase in the frequency of deadly pirate attacks that has altered the circumnavigation plans of a generation of cruisers; and (tragically) a precipitous reduction in the size of both Big Mac and Whopper hamburgers.

Thus, when it was first suggested by International Marine editors that I might want to look at writing an updated version of *The Cruising Life*, my first reaction was, "Dang, I'll have to rewrite the whole bloody thing." But, being the true cruiser that I am, I resolved to soldier forth and confront the task with determination and optimism. I procured a working copy of the original manuscript for review, and as I read through the words I had written all that long ago, I was pleasantly surprised to discover that, in spite of social, political, and economic upheavals on a monumental scale, not that much has actually changed in the cruising community. Much of what I had written was as valid today as it had been 15 years ago.

People everywhere at every socioeconomic level still want to go cruising, and for all the same reasons. If anything at all has changed in the collective desire to cast off the lines and take to the seas, it is in the degree of urgency with which some of us feel the need to get gone. No doubt, this increase in desperation is caused by steady increase in angst that trying to live a tranquil life in today's demanding society entails. The number of people who want to go has increased by a lot, but ironically, there has not been an associated increase in the number of people who are actually doing it. The sluggish economy has been hard on a lot of us in the middle classes, and many of us have suffered a loss of earning power for reasons we have no control over. Reduced income and job security have naturally raised anxiety levels and taken a toll on relationships with a corresponding rise in the number of people who fantasize about running away in a boat. Trying to escape our troubles by sailing away from them is still not a great idea, and we will expand on the reasons why in Chapter 3.

Yes, lots of us still dream of cruising the world in a sailboat, and lots of us are still not going because we are making the same well-intentioned-but-wrong decisions that we were making 15 years ago. We are still focusing on finding the perfect boat more than we are on getting our personal affairs in order; we still fail to realistically assess the sacrifices that world cruising involves, both on a personal and financial level; and we continue to buy boats that we think will impress our neighbors instead of ones that will realistically do the job we need done with a minimum drain on our limited resources. (If your resources aren't limited, you are reading the wrong book.) If anything, we are now buying even bigger boats than ever before and still going into debt to do it. Debt remains the same sure-fire killer of the cruising ambition that it has always been.

The upshot is that, except for a few editorial changes and an update here and there, the first five chapters of this rewrite remain basically unchanged. I have added a few appropriate anecdotes here and there and rewritten a few parts that really needed to be rewritten. A few other paragraphs have been revised more from a desire to engage with fresh material the readers who are familiar with the original book so they won't feel that they have been here before.

There has been, in the last few years, a noticeable increase in the number of rather affluent retired cruisers, as more and more of the baby boomers who were employed by large corporations and the state and federal governments in the go-go decades of the seventies and eighties take advantage of the generous retirement plans offered during that wonderful time. Many in this fortunate group end up in the Caribbean, on the Intracoastal Waterway (ICW), or in the South Pacific aboard expensive condominium-style yachts with little interest in being more than a day's sail from the next party; many are over-reliant on mechanical and electronic devices and under-reliant on basic seamanship skills; more than a few are trying long ocean passages on boats more suited to coastal rather than offshore cruising; and many grow quickly disillusioned with the cruising life and move back ashore to become golfers and RVers. There is nothing wrong with cruising the Waterways, the Caribbean, or the South Pacific (or, for that matter, with golf or RVs), of course, and what cruiser doesn't like a great party now and then. So throughout this book we will try to offer hints to these happy folks on how to better enjoy their retirement by making it more like real cruising and less like

an extended bare-boat charter with the gang from the office.

If you are among the above group of retired-yuppie cruisers and I point out that the expensive central air-conditioning that you recently installed on your boat doesn't really add that much to the overall cruising experience, that the power-hungry unreliable bow thruster you use to dock your boat is unnecessary if you would only practice a few basic maneuvering tactics, and that the fully enclosed Conestoga-wagon-like tent (probably also air-conditioned) you have permanently installed over your cockpit can destroy sailing performance and be downright dangerous in a blow, please don't take it personally.

One thing that cruisers do best is help other cruisers, and if I can convince you to stop trying to make your boat into a copy of your house and make it instead into a comfortable and livable vehicle for the true adventure and freedom that real cruising offers, these humble efforts will have been amply rewarded.

One interesting development, which I have confirmed with several boat-broker friends, is in the psyche of potential cruisers looking for cruising boats. Undoubtedly influenced by the gorgeous displays in boat shows and the cavernous interiors of the present crop of production boats, the requirement for a walk-around queen-sized bed is now near the top of the list of must-have items for many wannabe full-time nautical gypsies, right after central air-conditioning. On *Vicarious* we call the place where we sleep a "bunk." Who ever heard of a full-size walk-around bunk? No matter how you say it, mate, unless you are talking about side decks, "full-size walk-around" just doesn't sound salty and if it ain't salty, it won't work on a real cruising boat. There are lots of other things that you don't really need to commence cruising, and I will try to point these out (tactfully, of course) wherever I encounter the opportunity.

A lot has changed in Chapters 6, "The Cruising Kitty: How to Get One," and 7, "The Cruising Kitty: How to Feed It After You've Got It," mostly because of the financial turmoil of the past few years. Funding a cruise with a second mortgage on your house is no longer as easy as it was a decade ago. And while the long-term plan of buying a house to sell for a profit when you are ready for departure still works under the right circumstances, extreme caution and a greater degree of experience and sophistication are required to make it work. Intimate familiarity with the local real estate market is also more critical than it once was because the differences in the residential property markets in different areas have grown vast and are still changing rapidly. As a result of the massive upheaval in the social and economic environment of the last decade, nearly all of the material in Chapter 6 has been discarded as outdated, and the entire chapter has been rewritten and expanded. Also, with the real estate market still bubbling like a witch's cauldron, we will explore a few easier-to-understand and less-risky alternatives to growing a fat and sleek kitty.

While all the original material in Chapter 8, "Planning for Departure," and Chapter 9, "Living Aboard and Acquiring Skills," is as valid today as when it was written, both these chapters have been expanded and updated to reflect the reality of today's cruising environment.

At this point, I have introduced an entirely new chapter on what is arguably the most important technological and social revolution that the cruising community has seen since the ancient Phoenicians invented galley slaves. We are talking here, of course, about the composting toilet: a marvelous device that greatly simplifies the cruising life and substantially reduces the cost of living it.

OK, OK, just kidding. I'm not really going to subject you to an entire chapter on naturally biodegrading heads. In fact, the jury is still out on this relatively new device for processing human waste, and it is too early to make any recommendations. At the moment, composting toilets are a good way to get around laws requiring holding tanks, but their practical use for cruisers is still unproven. We do, however, have an all-new chapter on the Internet: the second most important development in the cruising world. (Any reader wanting to argue that the Internet may be slightly more important than the potential of effective composting toilets is encouraged to read the rest of this book. I am sure I can convince you otherwise.)

Hardly anybody today goes cruising without a smartphone, a laptop or tablet computer, a reliable means of connecting to the Internet when a signal is available, and a dependable means of exchanging emails from the high seas. The Internet has done more to change the way the world looks at us seaborne vagabonds, and the way we look at the world, than any invention since the printing press, and the effect on the cruising world has been profound. Sending and receiving personal communications both written and verbal; navigating across the bay or around the world; staying in touch and up-to-date with advice on destinations, equipment, and the daily news; running a profitable business from a boat (and an unprofitable one, as I can personally attest); buying equipment and supplies (and just about anything else you want); paying bills; being entertained; searching for a new boat or the best fuel prices; and expressing our opinions, prejudices, and observations in real time—these are all as easy as a finger on a touch screen can make it. And it hasn't stopped yet. Thus, Chapter 14, "Electronics," is completely rewritten . . . Chapter 10, which is now Chapter 11 replacing the old Chapter 11, which is now . . . . oh well, forget it and just enjoy the book.

Another important development in the electronics and communications revolution is the rapid increase of the number of cruising-oriented forums that are popping up on the Internet and in the number of people who participate in them. Cruisers Forum (www.cruisersforum.com), Sail Net (www.sailnet.com), and Sailing Anarchy (www.sailinganarchy.com) are three of my favorites, but there are lots more. These forums are excellent ways to get up-to-date information and advice from experienced cruisers from around the world. Once you join the forum, you can post questions and participate in discussions. No matter how silly or deeply technical your query, you are guaranteed to get a least three or four valid answers. Some emotionally charged questions dealing with such issues as "guns on board" and "project boats" will generate dozens, if not hundreds, of responses. The problem is, of course, that all these responses represent the opinions of individuals who can be experts in their respective fields or complete phonies who respond with answers to every question posted regardless of their knowledge of or experience in the topic. Unless you already know something about your subject, you can get bombarded with ridiculous solutions to simple problems and with authoritative-sounding advice that is just plain wrong. Most of these forums are controlled by a few (sometimes as many as a dozen or as few as one or two) individuals (called *moderators* in forum-speak), a few of whom can be highly opinionated, a bit inflexible, and often dictatorial.

Frequently these moderators are quite knowledgeable, but sometimes not. There is one prolific poster with thousands of posts on several popular forums whose cruising ground (according to his long and detailed "profile") is a 300-acre man-made lake in Iowa. There is no indication that this person has ever seen an ocean much less cruised on one. But the interesting thing is that most of the information and advice that this person dispenses in his multitudinous posts is spot-on correct, valid to a fault,

usually very helpful, and always entertaining. I suspect that he reads a lot. Anyway, we will talk more about the important subject of how to gather information (correct information) from the Internet in this new and updated chapter.

While we are on the subject of the Internet, we will also delve into the art of running your own blog, which is essentially a personal website that you can use to keep friends, family, and anyone else who stumbles across it, informed on the progress of your cruise, political perspective, photographic proficiency, poetic prowess, or anything else you might want to share with the cyber universe. Running a proper blog (blogging, if you will) is time-consuming but also rewarding, so a substantial number of cruisers are doing it. Setting up a blog can be as easy or as complex as you would like it to be, so we will show you several alternative ways to quickly get your blog online and taking hits like an amateur boxer.

Old Chapter 9, "OK, Let's Buy a Boat," (now Chapter Something Else located somewhere else) has been completely redone to reflect the exciting (from a buyer's perspective) changes in the current used-boat market. Interestingly, while inflation at the average annual rate of approximately 2.5 percent has reduced the value of a 1999 dollar to a mere 70 cents, the actual dollar amount we can expect to pay for a good cruising boat remains about the same, indicating a useful (to us) drop in used-boat values.

The lower price we can expect to pay for a good used sailboat is a great opportunity for wannabe cruisers like you and me. There are also a lot more good boats available from a larger number of builders that are now in the budget-cruiser price range than there were at the beginning of the century. Thus the makes and models that are recommended here have changed as the lower price of boats that were in the premium category just a few years ago bumps out some of the great old classics that are becoming hard to find in cruise-worthy condition.

Buying the right boat at the wrong time, the wrong boat at the right time, and the wrong boat at the wrong time are three mistakes that remain in the top five killers of the cruising dream. We want to buy the right boat for us at the right time for us, so we will dwell on this subject with the care and sensitivity that it deserves.

The old Chapter 10, "Commence Cruising," (who knows where it is now—oh, my editor does—it is Chapter 12 now) is pivotal to this entire book so all the subject matter has been updated (with a few embarrassing typos corrected) and greatly expanded. It is even more important in today's environment to have or acquire skills on the care and maintenance of your cruising yacht than it was a decade ago. Nothing can strangle a cruising kitty quicker than an unscheduled visit to a boatyard for professional repair or service. The overall boating market has shrunk ("retracted" in economic gobbledygook) at a frightening rate since the onset of the 2008 recession. And rather than lower prices to attract more customers, many boatyards are raising prices drastically to extract more money from their existing customers.

Manufacturers of marine products are also caught in the vortex of shrinking demand for ever-more-expensive-to-make products, and they are raising their prices accordingly, far faster than the official inflation rate. I predict (and my predictions, like those of Nostradamus, are never wrong—just frequently misinterpreted) that as we continue to emerge from recession, the surviving manufacturers will continue to raise prices to cover historical losses. Even if this doesn't happen, there isn't much good news on the horizon for the cost of maintenance and equipment upgrades, making the do-it-yourself

approach for the budget-minded cruiser even more critical than it was before.

Except for a major revision in the paragraphs on the cruising galley sink, necessitated by a hostile and unjustified rejection by the majority of my readers of my dry-sink concept, the old Chapter 11, "The Cruising Galley," remains unchanged, although it is now Chapter 13. There are a few more tips and tricks on electric apparatus (toasters and such) that reflect improvements in the 12-to-120-volt inverter technology, and a major review of the new stand-alone energy-efficient refrigeration units that have become popular alternatives to the traditional cold-plate-and-icebox units of the past.

OK, so contrary to the opening statement, the art of cruising the world in a small boat has changed a lot in the past 13 years, but not nearly as much as the rest of the world has changed. Sailing away to destinations undetermined is still a sure-fire way to break free of the anxiety and constraints heaped upon the shoulders of our shore-bound brethren by a crowded and consumerist-oriented society.

Americans have always been the world's most vocal champions of personal freedom, and we remain so today, but now a new freedom has emerged, one that experienced cruisers the world over are expressing as among the most wonderful of all the various perks unique to the cruising life—that is the freedom from the despotic tyranny of our accumulated possessions.

As a result of the ever-increasing pressure on American public to buy more and more stuff that we surely don't need and probably don't even want, one of the most profitable growth industries, recessions notwithstanding, has been the personal-storage-unit business. The average new-home size of 4,028 square feet with a full basement and an average 2.67-car garage (I just made those figures up, but hey, they sound about right) is no longer large enough to hold all of our stuff. In desperation, we are resorting to external storage units by the millions to hold the overflow—that is, if we can find an empty one, which we can't in many places.

The cruising life isn't for all of us. It isn't even for most of us, but it is for some of us, and for a few of us it is essential to survival. If you are one of the chosen who believes that you can be happiest in a very small space that is constantly bouncing about trying to fling you off your feet or to chuck you into the sea, and if you want to live a vigorous, healthy life with few material distractions, no traffic jams, and unlimited adventures, then perhaps you too should sell all your stuff, buy a boat, and steer for the distant horizon.

Like the magical end of the rainbow, the far horizon is hard to reach, and it can take a long time to get there. But unlike the rainbow, the pot of gold isn't at the end; it is collected along the way. And so what if we never arrive? In our quest for the unreachable destination, the journey is all that matters, and if that isn't a real pot of gold, it will suffice.

1

So You Want to Go Cruising

*And we are the dreamers
of dreams,
Wandering by lone sea
breakers.*

**—ARTHUR WILLIAM EDGAR
O'SHAUNGHNESSY**

There are those among us who would be cruisers and those who would be dreamers of cruising. There are those who will go cruising on a whim, with hardly a second thought or backward look or even a clear idea of what they are doing or where they are going—they are going cruising and that is enough. And there are others, lots of others, who plan and save and dream and scheme most of their lives about the glorious day when they are finally ready to leave on that trip around the world or across the lake to the other shore—but they never leave because ready never comes. Still others amass huge fortunes in banks and on balance sheets against the day when they will throw off the fetters of toil, stress, and worry to sail away to freedom and adventure, only to find that the very fortunes that were to buy their freedom have become their shackles. Others sail the oceans of their dreams without a dime in their pocket—with naught but a grip on the tiller and an eye on the horizon. And there are the few among us who plan carefully and act cautiously. But act they do and cruising they go, while others watch from shore.

And this is as it should be because ocean voyaging isn't for everyone. Those who stay ashore are also lucky because that is where they belong, as surely as the ones who go belong in a small boat upon the sea. Those who stay ashore envy the adventure and excitement of sailors' lives at sea; those who sail envy the stability and predictability of those who stay ashore. Whether our dreams are lucid plans or ridiculous fantasies depends not on the nature of the dreams but on the nature of the dreamer.

Which sort of dreamer are you? A little honest introspection and a few hundred pages of reading should yield the answer, so

Day Dreamer

Beware the dreamers of the day. "All men dream: but not equally. Those who dream by night in the dusty recesses of their minds wake in the day to find that it was vanity: but the dreamers of the day are dangerous men, for they may act their dreams with open eyes, to make it possible." —T. E. Lawrence. OK, so this famous quote is a bit Victorian and a lot sexist (women daydream about cruising even more than men do—just ask Susan). Making it PC destroys the poetry, but it remains true any way you read it.

let's go take a look. We'll cover the fantasy first and save the hard parts for later.

Fantasy Versus Reality

It is amazing how many people think they want to go sailing on the oceans of the world on a small boat. You are one of them or you wouldn't be reading this book. Go ahead and admit it. The desire to go cruising is nothing to be ashamed of, and it might help you to know that you are in good company. Later, I will tell you about ordinary people for whom the dream of cruising in a sailboat—whether for a few months, for a few years, or for a lifetime—has become a reality. I will also tell you that it is an amazingly easy thing to do—once you make up your mind to really do it, that is. And I will tell you that nearly everyone who makes up their mind to do it, can.

First, though, I will ask you to think a bit, to ponder the ramifications of a major change in your life and to consider all the effects that change will have on you and on those whom you care about the most. Sure you'd like to quit your job, sell your possessions, buy a boat (an old fishing schooner or a retired Baltic trader will do), and sail away from the rat race with all its pretensions and injustices and demands that you live your life in a way that you would, perhaps, rather not be living it. You can envision a land where the breezes blow warm, where the sky is always blue, where people are judged by the kind of people they are rather than by the size of their bank accounts, and where the only clothing you'll need is a T-shirt, shorts, and a pair of shower clogs for those rare days when you want to dress up. To pay for it all, you can . . . well, let's see . . . you can write that novel you've been thinking about for the past 10 years and live off the royalties and the residuals from the sale of the movie rights, or maybe you can win the lottery, or perhaps some unknown relative will expire and endow you with more wealth than you can spend in one lifetime.

Lots of people have done it before you. Old Joshua Slocum did it all by himself (and he didn't even have a GPS). Sir Francis Chichester did it. Eric Hiscock did it. Lin and Larry Pardey did it (without an engine in their boat, for Pete's sake). Robin Lee Graham and Tania Aebi did it when they were only kids. The list goes on and on. Even the likes of your humble but intrepid author did it, and God only knows that if he can do it, anyone who can eat soup with a spoon can do it.

Ocean voyaging, or what I prefer to call the "cruising life," is within reach of anyone who really wants to do it. The idea of selling everything we own, buying a boat, and sailing off into the sunset is one of the world's most popular fantasies. In fact, as fantasies go (or at least those we can discuss in a family-oriented book), the cruising fantasy is among the Big Three—right up there with writing the great American novel and becoming a rock/movie/sports star.

Not everyone who wants to be a rock/movie/sports star can do it, of course, and even though every new great American novel that is written can now be instantly published online, only a tiny percentage of them ever sell more than a few dozen copies, and an even smaller percentage of them ever make it to the bestseller lists. The cruising fantasy, however, is achievable—it simply needs to be tempered with a dose of reality.

Images of the cruising life are universal: white sand beaches, sunsets, and piña coladas under the stars. We envision days on end of bounding through gentle seas with a billowing main and flying jib pulling us to lands of adventure and romance. We don't see the loneliness of separation from friends and family, the terror of a storm at sea, the humiliation of being ignored by an arrogant port captain, or the drudgery of rowing out a kedge at 3 a.m. while the rain is falling and the wind is rising.

I never fail to be amazed at how many people say to me, "I've always wanted to cruise, but Mabel doesn't like boats," or "Sidney gets seasick" (where Sidney is the dog), or "That's just what I'm going to do after the kids leave

Picnic

We read the sailing magazines and see the glossy photos of sleek yachts lying at anchor, of cookouts under the stars, and of smiling cruisers shopping in exotic markets. We see what the magazines want us to see or, perhaps, what we want to see. When we look at the cruising life in this light, it isn't surprising that so many people adopt it. What's surprising is that so many don't.

home and I can divorce George," or my personal favorite: "I was going to do just what you're doing, but then I got lumbago (or a trick knee, married, or promoted)."

Everyone Wants to Go

No one knows for sure just how many cruisers are out there plying the world's oceans in sailboats (and this slightly disreputable anonymity is one of the things about the cruising life that appeals to many of us), but the consensus seems to be that the world's population of active cruisers has stabilized at about 25,000 people. (Note: Any competent mathematician will call the following figures "backdoor statistics" and tell you that the numbers and any conclusions drawn from them are hopelessly invalid, but what the hell, we'll use them anyway.)

For the sake of my argument, let's say that for every 1,000 people who dream of the cruising life, only 1 ever buys a boat. And for every 100 people who buy a boat in which to pursue their dream, only 1 ever does it. That means that with a little creative extrapolation, we can deduce that about 2,500,000 people worldwide have bought boats in which to go cruising, but for one reason or another they haven't gone, and a whopping 250,000,000 people (that's more than 4 percent of the population of the world) wanted to buy a boat in which to go cruising but didn't.

More Reality

Bluewater cruising is a difficult lifestyle that involves hard work, sacrifice, risk, and yes, even danger on a scale that most rational people aren't willing to accept. Those white sandy beaches often turn out to be black slimy mud banks or insect-infested swamps. Our dreams of billowing sails and gentle seas disappear as we wallow in leftover swells while the empty sails slat and slap in the airless heat. Even those cookouts on the beach get rained on once in a while.

Life on a cruising boat is hard work—much harder than most noncruisers can imagine. In fact, Susan and I never worked as hard in our lives as we did during our first year on *Sultana*. People often ask if we get bored on the long passages, and the answer is always the same: never. There is always more work to do than there is time to do it. And when we finally do reach safe harbor, there is a week or so of toil and labor, much of it dirty and unpleasant, that

needs to be done before we can begin to relax and enjoy ourselves.

The physical and psychological comforts that a cruiser forfeits when shoving off to sea are many, but the financial sacrifice of leaving a steady job and the emotional sacrifice of leaving friends, family, and a comfortable home are the hardest for most people to bear and often the reasons that, as the fantasy starts to become a reality, it also begins to lose some of its luster and appeal. A lot of wannabe cruisers plan to take off after they retire, when money won't be a problem, and many do indeed go cruising then. Others, though, find that when they retire, they've aged a bit, and the idea of adventure on the high seas is less attractive than a country house with an easy chair and a view of the lake.

A lot of people are used to owning a lot of insurance. Upon learning that most active cruising boats are uninsurable and that most owners of insurable boats can't afford the premiums, would-be cruisers are troubled. The thought of loading all their worldly possessions onto a frail craft and sailing off into dangerous waters quails many otherwise-stout hearts.

What about those who do decide to sell up and sail out? Do their stories usually have happy endings? And do they usually find the paradise of their dreams? The answer to these questions is a reserved yes. "Reserved" because few find the life they expected to find, but "yes" because those who try cruising find one of the healthiest and most rewarding ways to live available. But the news here isn't all good. For every successful cruiser, there are probably two who give up after a year or two and go home, discouraged and disillusioned.

The reasons for failed cruises are many and complex. Some new cruisers are unable to overcome the fear and anxiety of sailing a small boat far from land in stormy seas; others with large complex boats are surprised at the cost and amount of work required to keep going; while even more give up when "nothing ever seems to go right" and they never quite understand why. The answer often is that they just haven't been at it long enough to develop the basic skills in seamanship and economical living that make life aboard so easy for others. Others miss their families and friends and the safety, comfort, and familiarity of the life they left behind. And, although they seldom admit it, even more find life without a three-bar cell phone signal, lightning-fast Internet, and a Walmart within driving distance just too much to bear.

Eschew Delusion Through Enlightenment

Cruisers and would-be cruisers tend to be optimistic folks. (I can recall meeting only one man living on a cruising yacht whom I would consider a full-time pessimist.) Optimists are doughty souls who remain sanguine in the face of adversity and blasé in the shadow of misfortune. They are prone to hear and see only what they want to hear and see, and this predisposition to self-delusion, along with lack of preparation for a major change in lifestyle, are the two major reasons that the dream of the cruising life sometimes turns sour.

I recall one delightful couple we met on the Intracoastal Waterway in the Carolinas. They had worked diligently for five years growing their kitty and preparing their 40-foot Beneteau for their dream cruise: a five-year circumnavigation that would hit all the great spots that they had been reading about. They had done everything right: they had read all the books (including the first edition of this one), they had chartered a boat in the Virgin Islands on three separate occasions, and they had grown

their cruising kitty to more than double the amount they anticipated spending.

Alas, when we met them, their cruise had ended after only a year. They never got farther than the Bahamas, and their boat was for sale. When asked what went wrong, they responded, "It just wasn't anything like what we thought it would be like." But a few diplomatic queries uncovered more specific reasons for the premature demise of their dream cruise.

It seems that Robin and Bobbin (not their real names but close) had, on several occasions, chartered a Beneteau Oceanis 36 with a center cockpit and a 4-foot draft. They liked this boat because of the commodious interior and the fact that they found it easy to sail. The Oceanis is, I believe, an ideal charter boat. But for most of us, it would be totally wrong for a world cruise.

The boat they bought for their adventure was a Beneteau First 40 with an aft cockpit and over 6 feet of draft. They figured that if the Oceanis was a good boat for them, the monstrous First 40 would be that much better. But, while the Oceanis would have been a bad choice for them, the First 40 was a horrible one. "But we got such a good deal on it, we couldn't turn it down," confided Robin after I tactfully pointed out a few inherent problems with novices trying to cruise in a lightweight performance boat (squirrely handling on passages and constantly running aground in the Bahamas, just to name two of many).

The second problem that Robin and Bobbin faced was more generic and should have been easy to avoid. They didn't have the money problems that most of us face, so they spent a fortune trying to turn their new boat into a copy of their house. They installed a full-sized refrigerator, a heavy-duty washer and dryer, air-conditioning (AC) throughout, a big generator to run the AC, and a host of electronic gadgets including an ice maker, custom carpeting everywhere, built-in vanities and storage units, and two custom-made 8-inch-thick innerspring mattresses that the Queen of Sheba and a brace of eunuchs would have found comfy. In the end, the interior was so chopped up and cluttered that there was hardly any room left for the cruisers. In their efforts to make their dream boat as comfortable as possible, they made it unlivable. The dreary, overcrowded interior doomed their cruise to early failure without their ever realizing why.

The sad part of the Robin and Bobbin saga is that it is not at all unusual. Many people who sacrifice everything to go cruising without preparing properly find they have made a very costly mistake and return home disappointed. Our intent in writing this book is to see that this doesn't happen to you.

One of the first steps anyone can take toward making the cruising fantasy become reality is to read everything there is to read on the subject. But, as Robin and Bobbin discovered, danger lies there too. Books on the cruising life are, for the most part, a celebration of cruising. Good cruising books—from Joshua Slocum's *Sailing Alone Around the World* to David and Daniel Hays's *My Old Man and the Sea*—are written by good cruisers. Except for life-raft sagas, which always seem to find a ready audience, few readers are interested in gloomy stories about failed or disastrous voyages, and few publishers are interested in printing them. Thus, inexperienced and impressionable readers with optimistic bents might get the idea from the world-cruising literature that the cruising life is all a bed of roses. And that just ain't so.

Cruising Isn't What It Used to Be

A yacht should expect the unexpected while cruising in developing countries. Politics and finances can change rapidly, leaving cruising guides outdated as soon as they are printed. For example, when the first edition of this book was written, Venezuela was a cruiserly destination of choice noted for safe harbors, friendly people, good labor rates, and cheap fuel. Then after the anti-American Cesar Chavez was elected to the presidency, the entire country became hostile and even dangerous to Americans. Now, two years after Chavez's death, the attitudes are starting to soften a bit, although things still have a long way to go to get back to normal. And when Mexico suddenly devalued the peso in 1994, the Yucatan almost immediately became an inexpensive place to visit. Except, of course, for those cruisers who were already there with pocketfuls of pesos. These unlucky souls dubbed their financial setback "the tequila crisis" as they watched their cash dwindle to half its former value, and they weren't the least bit happy about it.

In all but the most remote islands, cruising boats are no longer unusual, and many new cruisers are astonished when no one even looks up as they drop anchor in a harbor where Slocum, Chichester, and Hiscock each received royal welcomes. Some cruising books tell of chiefs on small islands who welcome boats with open arms and a pig roast, but today you are much more likely to be greeted with an open palm and a roasting for anchoring too close to the chief's black-pearl farm. Of course, you can still partake of a welcoming feast when you arrive at many popular Pacific islands—the only difference is that the hāngi has become a profitable commercial venture, and you'll pay a hundred bucks a head for the privilege. (But it's not to be missed at twice that price.) The one we attended in the Vava'u Island Group of Tonga was complete with the kava ceremony, native dancing, and a roast pig with all the trimmings.

No, cruising isn't what it used to be—it's better. And in many ways, it's much better.

Cruising Mythologies

Many cruising books and nearly all the online cruisers' forums are shamelessly fostering cruising mythologies. My favorite myth is the almost universal belief among cruisers that Joy dishwashing detergent possesses some magical properties that make it the sole detergent capable of cutting grease or producing suds in salt water. Actually salt water is terrible for washing anything (except teak decks), and it doesn't make a prune pit's worth of difference what kind of soap you use. Detergent suds are produced by phosphates, and although manufacturers might have used unlimited amounts of phosphates 40 years ago, in Canada, the United States, and the entire European Union, they are now strictly regulated. Thus, most detergents produce about the same amount of suds. I don't have anything against Joy, but the idea that it is dramatically different from any other detergent is silly. If you really want suds, wait until you get to South America, then buy some Axion dishwashing detergent. It's sold in sticks, like dynamite, and without FDA regulations, you'll see plenty of suds.

By the way, the cruising myth that shampoo makes a fine dishwashing detergent isn't a myth at all. Liquid dishwashing detergents and shampoos are essentially the same thing—only their colorings, fragrances, and a few other benign additives are different. The next time you run out of dish soap, a little shampoo will make a fine substitute, and if you need a truly exotic shampoo, try some of that Joy. (Don't use Axion as a shampoo though. That stuff will dissolve anything organic, including your scalp.)

Another common fable related to the Joy myth is the idea that all cruising boats need a saltwater tap in the galley. This is nonsense, but every cruising boat that Susan and I looked at while searching for *Vicarious* had one. We even had one on *Sultana*, but I took it out during the refit simply because in five years we used it no more than a few times. Even if you do find salt water a handy addition on the galley, please consider what you have to do to get it there; for my money, the additional plumbing, through-hull fittings, and pumps just aren't worth any perceived benefit.

Saltwater taps on deck are another matter. *Vicarious* has a faucet in the cockpit and a high-pressure saltwater wash-down on the bow, and I don't know how we got along without them on *Sultana*.

As another example of how cruising literature has influenced our actions, take those silly little wooden plugs that nearly every cruising boat has safety wired to all its seacocks. These plugs have an interesting history that goes all the way back to the very first through-hull fittings that were used to direct cooling water to the first internal-combustion engines used in small boats. Often, these fittings didn't have seacocks, and the plugs were insurance against the fairly common failure of the early hoses. Today, though, they have no practical purpose. Even so, nearly every cruising book that has been written in the past 30 years says that these plugs are a necessary safety item, and many racing rules require them, but no one says how to use them. The most common cause of leaks at seacocks is hose failure—which often results from an overly enthusiastic application of hose clamps, in which case closing the seacock stops the leak.

In the unlikely event that a seacock is ripped from the hull, the hole would be far too big to be stoppered by a plug, and if a seacock were to snap off at the flange (another astronomically unlikely event), an old sock or piece of T-shirt stuffed into the opening would make a far better stopper than a wooden plug. In over 60 years of messing around in boats, I have never used one of these plugs to stop a leak, nor have I ever heard of anyone else using one.

Let me shoot down one more egregiously misleading cruising myth. (This one is important, folks.) Forget about turning over your eggs every few days while you're cruising. That practice is even less necessary on a boat than it is at home because, except in California, houses seldom jump around the way boats are inclined to do in a seaway. Oh yeah, don't bother slathering them with vaseline or other disgustingly viscous materials either. Just cook 'em and eat 'em the way normal people do. If they get a little green, eat 'em anyway. With my considerable egg-eating experience, I have discovered the hard way that it is practically impossible to eat a bad egg (or even get close to one, for that matter). Do cook them thoroughly though.

Cruising Can Be Economical, but It Isn't Cheap

A lot of cruising literature and all the online forums foster the idea that cruising is a cheap way to live. Once upon a time it was possible to live on a boat and spend very little money, but today, living on a boat is becoming more costly all the time, and world cruising is a rather expensive undertaking for most people.

Annie Hill, in her delightful book *Voyaging on a Small Income*, champions a cruising lifestyle that cost the author and her husband only a few thousand pounds a year. It was an austere life that reminds me of the glorious back-to-nature movement of the 1960s. I knew three families then who bought separate plots of land in New Hampshire and planned to return to nature and the good life, building a little cabin, chopping their own firewood, and eating their own organically grown vegetables. Unfortunately, they failed to consider the rigors of New England winters and the fact that woodchucks and deer also like organically grown vegetables. Two of the families quit

halfway through the first winter, and the third lasted about two years.

Of course, it is possible to live in the woods and eat nuts and berries. Our ancestors did it, and they were happy for the chance to do so, but today most of us demand at least the minimum of modern comforts, and the appeal of a life without them wears thin with the first hunger pangs.

The ascetic cruising life described by Hill is certainly within the grasp of anyone willing to make the sacrifices to live it; *Vicarious* has met several boats with crews who were living on pasta and spunk. But cruising seems to lose some of its objectives when you are forced to avoid attractive destinations because of expensive clearance fees (for the privilege of entering a country) or because you can't afford to rent a car for a country tour or because you can't eat at a local restaurant.

Yes, there are still many countries that charge low fees (although the number is shrinking rapidly), and yes, the very best way to see many countries and meet local people is by riding the local bus, and yes, indeed, the tastiest food most often comes from the smallest shops and sidewalk vendors. But even riding buses and eating local food requires money. People in developing countries who once viewed yachts as curiosities now see them as a source of revenue and are charging accordingly.

Back when we started cruising, the total clearance fees (customs, immigration, and the like) for *Sultana's* international stops, excluding bribes that are unavoidable in some places, came to a little less than $200 in each country we visited. Now fees and taxes average well over $300 and often way over. Panama charges over $600 just to check into the country, and that has nothing to do with a canal passage, which now is several thousand dollars. On a three-year, 50-country cruise then, which is a healthy world tour, required fees alone will run way over $10,000—or more than half of Annie Hill's entire cruising budget.

The Costs Continue to Climb

Boat maintenance, labor, moorings, provisions, and entertainment are more expensive today than they were yesterday no matter where you go. Even if you do most of the work on your boat yourself, the cost of materials seems to continue on an upward spiral, and the 2008 recession didn't help things a bit. As this is written (mid-2014), boatyards in the United States are starting to get busy after five years of dreary sales and empty parking lots. Unfortunately, this is having the effect of raising prices even further as boatowners clamor for repairs that have been delayed because of the economy.

However, the news isn't so bad for international cruisers. The dramatic increase in the availability of goods and services in places that were once remote and isolated means that supplies and services are increasingly available, often at reasonable prices, where there were none before. The Rio Dulce in eastern Guatemala has several new high-tech boatyards, and Thailand is becoming a destination for cruisers in the South Pacific looking for reasonable prices on all boating services. We haven't been to Thailand yet, but we are on the way. We'll let you know what we find when we get there.

A reverse example is our home base in New Zealand. When we got there in 1991, boatyards were enjoying a major increase in business for new cruising boats and major refits of old ones. Boatbuilding was booming because of a favorable exchange rate (the kiwi was worth less than US$0.50 and about EU$0.25). Budget-minded cruisers were attracted by the quality of the workmanship in the New Zealand yards as well as the prices. When we finished our refit of *Sultana* in 1999, the new-boat business was all but stagnant, but the refits were still going great guns.

Now, 15 years on, New Zealand has become a rather expensive place to live. Boating costs are about the same as in the United States and Europe, primarily because of the exchange rate. Fortunately, the boatyards are now busy with refits of megayachts attracted by the high standards of the Kiwi workforce. Megayacht owners could give a stuff about the prices, but us little guys are best advised to do the work ourselves or find another destination. Such alternatives are increasingly found in Southeast Asia.

Once you have your boat, it will cost a lot more to equip it than it did just a few years ago. Not only do individual items cost more but also advances in technology mean that there are a lot more things to buy. Some cruisers still choose to sail without a single-sideband (SSB) radio or a good life raft because of their substantial costs, but for some radar has become a must-have item; most cruising boats now have several computers aboard plus at least one iPad tricked out with any number of charting programs (or aps); and a satellite phone is found on about a quarter of the boats we surveyed. Only fools venture offshore without a GPS, and most of us who plan on sailing the surface of the sea for even a few more years wouldn't go without a 406-MHz emergency position-indicating radio beacon (EPIRB).

If you think you would like to try a cruise on the cheap, be forewarned that truly economical cruising is much more difficult now than it used to be, and as the global economy warms up, that trend will continue. Overly optimistic expectations of cost—often followed by disillusionment—are one of the major problems faced by new cruisers.

The Boat Isn't as Important as You Might Think

What's the most important element in the successful cruising equation? "The boat, of course," is the obvious and most resounding answer. But it's also wrong—dead wrong. Successful cruisers are out there in the most incredible assortment of boats that can be imagined. There are new boats and old boats, fat boats and skinny boats, big boats and little boats, fast boats and slow boats. In any popular cruising port, you will see custom-designed-and-built floating palaces costing millions of dollars moored next to cement-and-chicken-wire tubs that some lubber has thrown together in a backyard. In Bora Bora we were anchored between a brand-new ocean-racing catamaran and a lovely old Dutch sailing barge from the Zuider Zee. The proud crew of the catamaran claimed that, on a reach, it could sail 25 percent faster than the wind. I suspect the Dutch barge would sail downwind about 25 percent faster than a log would float. Yet in spite of their differences, they were both lovely boats and good sturdy sea vessels in which their respective owners took a great deal of justifiable pride.

A Study in Contrasts

In Panama we met a couple from Russia who were sailing around the world with a baby in an engineless 25-foot sloop. In Rangiroa in the South Pacific, we met a couple from the United States with two kids on a custom-designed 60-foot Deerfoot ketch with every electronic gizmo and gadget known to man, including a commercial satellite link and electronic sail furling and reefing. They too were sailing around the world.

You could, I suppose, make an argument that the family from the United States was learning more and having more fun than the couple from Russia, but if that were true, it was hard to tell. The American captain was furious because his satellite link was down (again), and he spent three days in an expensive resort hotel faxing his displeasure to the equipment manufacturer. The obvious difference between the two families, except for the size of their boats

and the ages of their kids, was the amount of money they were spending. If dispensing cash makes a person happy, then the Deerfoot crew were ecstatic. These two boats represent the extremes in family cruising. The only quality that successful bluewater cruising boats have in common is that they are sturdy and seaworthy—beyond that, anything goes.

A Logical Conclusion

Although I know I risk the ire of boat lovers and lifelong cruisers by saying so, the type of boat you go cruising in doesn't matter anywhere near as much as most people would like to believe. The cruising boat is a means to an end—the freedom of the cruising life—and as such, it's one of the last things you need to worry about. True, we have seen several long-planned voyages come to grief because the inexperienced and ill-advised sailors bought the wrong craft, but Susan and I have seen far more cruises ruined because the right boat ended up with the wrong cruisers. Thus, the most important element in the cruising equation is you. Boats can sink and burn and disappear in the night, but a captain and crew with a positive attitude go on forever.

Don't Buy a Boat Until You Must Buy a Boat

Buying a boat too early in the planning process is one of the most common mistakes made by potential cruisers. Unless you have a lot of experience with bluewater craft and many years of coastal cruising, it is unlikely that you know just what you will want or need in a cruising boat. There is also a hidden risk in paying too much attention to what self-proclaimed experts tell you in the printed press and on the Internet. Many cruising authorities don't really have that much offshore experience and will often promulgate a specific point of view. "Catamarans are the only way to go" or "If your boat can't make 150 miles a day to windward, you are wasting your time" are just two extreme examples. By waiting until the last minute to buy your boat, you give yourself time to think things over, try out the options, and get it right the first time.

When Susan first decided that the cruising life was the life for us, we were convinced we wanted a catamaran. We had a growing family, and catamarans have lots of room, they are safe and easy to sail, and their shoal draft promised access to the small harbors and out-of-the-way anchorages we have always favored. But after looking at every catamaran on the East Coast that was for sale in our price range, we changed our mind. Cats were a lot more expensive to buy than monohulls; the best are built to flimsy scantlings that make them sensitive to weight (and we were never very good at traveling light); the bridge can pound unmercifully in a heavy sea, the motion in even a moderate sea is squirrely and unpleasant; and they are cumbersome and awkward at anchor—which is where cruising boats spend most of their time. If we had bought one of the first few boats we looked at, we would have been stuck with the wrong boat.

Here I must quickly assume a defensive posture against the legions of catamaran lovers who are going to slam this book shut with disgust, write a nasty Amazon.com review, and fire off a vitriolic email to my already beleaguered editor (it is astounding how some folks become indignant when I say anything bad about Joy dishwashing detergent). I will state here, unequivocally, that catamarans make fine cruising vessels. Catamaran owners are, it seems, the fastest-growing segment of the cruising community and among the most vocal. Obviously twin-hull cruising has its appeal; it's just not for Susan and me.

The previous owners of *Vicarious*, Spencer and Kathleen, were fans of two hulls. For years,

while planning their world cruise, they chartered a succession of catamarans in both the Pacific and the Caribbean. They found the stability, easy sailing qualities, and interior comforts of the cats to be very much to their liking. But when it came time to actually buy a boat, they chose instead a heavy (at nearly a thousand pounds per foot), quite tender (due to round bilges), and cramped monohull motorsailer. Who knows why they didn't buy the boat of their dreams—perhaps it was the economics because catamarans cost about 25 percent more, on average, than similarly equipped monohulls. Whatever the reason, after 18 months of cruising in the Caribbean, they returned to the mainland, sold the motorsailer to Susan and me, then bought a catamaran.

Spencer and Kathleen are an excellent example of my case in point: the type of boat you cruise in actually makes little difference, but it is critically important that the boat is the right one for you. And it is nearly as important to delay the purchase of your boat for as long as you can before leaving the dock. By waiting a few years to buy, you will get just the right boat for you because the longer you wait, the more you will know just what you want, and you will save a pot full of money in the process.

Buying a boat early in your planning means you have to pay for and care for the thing while you are getting ready to leave, and although this sounds like a logical thing to do, it's often a serious mistake. Boats, especially boats sturdy enough for ocean cruising, are expensive to buy and maintain, and the newer ones depreciate faster than fish rot. If you own one during the years you are preparing to leave, you will be spending a huge amount of money on the boat that would be better off going into your *cruising kitty* (the cruiserly equivalent of a bank account), and you will be spending a lot of time sailing and working on the boat that is better spent working for cash that will further fatten that kitty.

I know that a lot of would-be cruisers justify the purchase of a boat early in the planning stage by saying they need the time to get the boat ready to go and to learn to sail it well, but this sort of reasoning is rationalization, and all it will get you is broke. Unless you've done it before, no matter how much you try to get everything sorted out on your boat before you leave, you are going to find dozens of changes you want to make once you've been under way for a year or so simply because you have no way of knowing what will work for you until you try it.

Of course there are some advantages to owning the boat before you try cruising in it—a lot of them in fact—but few of them are worth the time and money that boat ownership will detract from your cruising kitty. Concentrating on the boat while ignoring the critical tasks of developing a new cruiserly attitude, living a more austere lifestyle, and accumulating cash is the big reason so many people who buy cruising boats never go.

If you have a boat that you are convinced is just what you want to start your cruising life in and your departure is imminent—say, within the next two years—sure, hold on to it. But if you won't be leaving for at least two or three years or if you own a mortgaged boat, selling the boat now and buying another when you are ready to go might make sense.

Dreams make the impossible possible, dedication makes the possible probable, and work makes the probable happen. Modern cruising is a difficult way to live. It requires hard work and sacrifices, but for many who crave personal freedom, adventure, and a simple life, it's worth it. The trick is to realize what you're getting yourself into before you cast off the lines and head out to sea.

2

The Cruising Community

*The sea speaks a
language polite people
never repeat.*

—CARL SANDBURG

Looking for Brian Lecur

A long time ago, as I sat at my desk in a Boston office building, a singular event occurred that would pound my complacent rock of a life into sand. It was a frigid day in January, and the Montreal Express was howling down Congress Street piling the snow in drifts everywhere, when I looked up to see a man approaching. He had long brown hair tied in a knot at the back of his head and a friendly smile on his bearded face. He appeared to be about 40 years old or a little more, and he said his name was Brian Lecur.

He plopped a substantial toolbox on the floor next to my chair and asked in a polite, soft-spoken voice if he could stand on my desk while he made some adjustments in the electrical apparatus that resided behind a panel in the suspended ceiling over my head. It's not every day that a large hairy person asks to stand on your desk so, lacking any reason why he shouldn't and welcoming the diversion, I agreed.

The electrician and I hit it off right away, and at the end of an hour or so, we were chatting away like old buddies. As he worked, I handed him tools, and he told me his tale.

Brian, as it turned out, was an adventurer. He had spent his life on the road living where he felt like living, going where he wanted to go, doing what he felt like doing with whomever he wanted to do it. He had lived in Australia and Tierra del Fuego and Afghanistan. He met his Bavarian wife, Greta, while hiking in the Sierra Leone, and for three years they lived in a cabin they built from logs on the sunny side of the Brooks Range in

13

Alaska. They shot moose for meat and trapped animals in the winter for fur. They moved south to Idaho when she became pregnant, and he worked on a dude ranch teaching school teachers and accountants how to ride horses and guiding hunters from the city after elk. They moved to Berkeley when his daughter, Sally, was born, and with his master's degree from MIT, he got a job teaching high school science and math. Sally, now nine, was being homeschooled by Greta, who was also debugging software for the local computer industry. Brian spoke five languages and was now working as an electrician in Boston because it paid better than teaching and involved "fewer hassles." They were saving all the money they could and in the spring would head to California, where they had an old Westsail 32 waiting for them at Marina del Rey. They were going to move aboard and set sail for the South Pacific. Their first stop would be Hawaii.

"It's time to settle down," Brian said. "I can't live this crazy footloose life anymore—too hard on my little girl."

"You call sailing the South Pacific in a 32-foot boat 'settling down'?" I asked without expecting an answer.

That noontime we shared sandwiches from his ample lunch pail. "Why Hawaii?" I asked, unable to drop the subject.

"Because we wanted to start the little girl off on an easy one," he answered.

Brian's work in the ceiling over my head ended up taking most of two days, partly because the job turned out to be more complicated than it first appeared and partly because we spent most of the time talking about such things as hunting wild pigs in Australia, hiking through Greece, and trout fishing in Argentina. As bits of wire and scraps of insulation rained down from above, I bombarded Brian with questions. Some were rather blunt.

"Do you ever think of getting a regular job?"

"Sure," answered Brian. "I worked at teaching four years straight after my girl was born."

"Why'd you quit?"

"Well, a friend owned a shrimp boat down in Louisiana and needed some help, so we went down to give him a hand. Besides, I needed some air. I worked there for two years."

"Why'd you leave that?"

"Boat sank."

"Oh, but what about your daughter? Isn't it tough on her traveling around and never going to school?"

"Nope. Greta's a good teacher, and Sally's the smartest nine-year-old there is—smarter than any kid in regular school."

"But isn't it hard on her not having any friends?"

"Sally has plenty of friends. She's real popular with her church group, and there are plenty of kids her age where we live now."

"Church? You go to church?"

"Sure, every week. Wouldn't miss it. You meet great folks at church."

"What kind of church?"

"Small ones."

"But what denomination?"

"Doesn't matter. Whatever's handy. We're going to a Baptist church now. Went to a synagogue in Berkeley."

"Isn't that kind of cynical?"

"Naw. My parents were Jewish, and Greta was born a Catholic. Same God. He doesn't care."

"You know that for sure?"

"Yep."

"But what about health insurance? Don't you get a little nervous not having any insurance?"

"Nope. Don't get sick."

"But what if you broke a leg or something?"

"Don't do that either."

"What about money? Doesn't it get tough not having any money?"

"We've got plenty of money. We always keep enough in the bank to live for a year just in case."

"How much is that?"

"Oh, probably about what you make in two months."

"OK, but what about major expenses? What do you do when you need a new car or television?"

"Well, we never pay more than $500 for a car, and I haven't owned a television set since the bastards took Perry Como off the air."

And so it went. Sitting at my desk in my business suit, I initially felt superior to Brian in his overalls and carrying his toolbox, but once I got over that feeling, I was a bit shaken. Brian put away his tools and left when the job was done. I never saw him again, but I never forgot him either. I ended up sitting at that desk or one just like it for eight more years, and as I sat, I would often think of Brian and wonder what trails he was hiking or which ocean he was sailing. I compared his lifestyle to mine, and with time, a clear picture of two simple but divergent philosophies emerged.

Brian lived a life that was dictated by his interests, and he did whatever he had to do to support those interests. Of course, many people would call him an irresponsible bum, but he always voted at election time and always paid his taxes. Some people might call him selfish, but he was devoted to his family, and I doubted if he would ever want to do anything they couldn't do together. He owned neither a new car the way I did nor a spacious house in the suburbs like mine, and while he didn't seem to begrudge me these things, he didn't seem to want them either. Brian wasn't irresponsible or selfish—he just refused to play the game the rest of us were playing, and I somehow found that unsettling.

When I compared my life with Brian's, the contrast was remarkable. Even though this was in the freethinking 1970s, there was no way I could wear my hair long and tied in a knot the way he did. I dressed the way the

company wanted me to dress, lived in a house I knew they would approve of, and drove a car that looked like the cars driven by every other young management employee where I worked. I attended all of the company parties and other social functions that I felt would further my career. My life was driven by my job—and it wasn't even a great job. It was a dull and boring job that I was good at, and it paid well. I consoled myself with the knowledge that I was soon due for a promotion, but then I realized that my boss's job was even duller than mine and his boss's job was even worse. And I also realized that, although Brian had not made any attempt to denigrate the way I lived or to convince me that his lifestyle was better than mine in any way, he lived the way he wanted to live, and I was free to do the same. It was the freedom to choose how we lived that was the most unsettling. I was living the way my parents and my company and the local authorities and IRS and the advertisers of the products I consumed wanted me to live. I was a paragon of the young urban wage earner, and fortune was smiling on my efforts even though I was not. I realized that my role model was no longer some high-level executive in the marketing department. It was a bearded guy in overalls who had spent two days getting footprints and wire scraps all over my desk.

After our children, Sarah and Phillip, were born, the image of Brian Lecur worked itself into my psyche, and eventually, with a major push from Susan, it prevailed. In 1993, Susan quit her job, and I closed my small-but-profitable yacht-repair business. We rented (and eventually sold) our house in the trendy Boston suburb of Marblehead, rescued a broken-down sailing yacht from under a pile of plastic tarps and pigeon guano from a barn in Maine, moved aboard, and sailed away.

Slowly but surely the pervasive arguments of an itinerant electrician who, 25 years earlier, had stood with his feet on my desk and his head in the clouds prevailed. Brian taught me that it was OK to be a dreamer and that it was possible to render dreams into reality once you learn to trust your instincts and ignore the sheepdogs of convention that are determined to keep humanity running together as a flock. Now when anyone asks me why it is we are doing what we are doing, I answer that we are looking for Brian Lecur.

Types of Cruisers

Brian Lecur has come to represent, for me, the paragon of the cruising sailor. The freedom for which he worked so hard allowed him to make his own rules yet thrive in the face of a society that was determined to force ever more of its own rules upon him. He lived his life in a way that many, perhaps most, would scorn as being irresponsible and indifferent—yet there remains a vestige of begrudging admiration in all of us for the few among us with the courage to jump the track and head off in a new direction. The rugged individualism of the American pioneer is the stuff of folklore and legend. It is elevated to ever higher plateaus with each telling of stories that are so embellished that we can't possibly know which actually happened and which were invented by our collective imagination. But Brian is real and he is now, and there is nothing that he has done that the rest of us couldn't do if we wanted. Who cares if the track we follow has been worn broad and deep by all the Brians that have gone before us, and that the appellations of "pioneer" and "adventurer" have been replaced by "proselyte" and "disciple"? The cruising life is there for those of us who want it.

But the cruising life doesn't appeal to everyone. It's not that the cruising community is exclusive or that ocean voyaging is overly difficult. It's just that when the actual cost of cruising in dollars, personal sacrifice, and hard work are considered, the majority of us bow out and find some less disruptive activity closer to home. Others find that their personal commitments, relationships, and fondness for the shoreside life won't allow them to chuck it all and sail away.

This is fine and as it should be. There are, after all, many advantages to a conventional shoreside life that can't be denied: your house is unlikely to drag anchor in the middle of the night; if your basement fills with water through some misadventure of the plumbing system, you will at least be spared the agony of watching your home slide beneath the waves; and even if your house were to sink, the local emergency services (fire, police, ambulance, and such) wouldn't need to home in on an emergency locator transmitter (ELT) beacon just to find you. The cruising life isn't necessarily better than the shoreside life, but it is different—a lot different. One reason why I'm writing this book is to help you decide, rationally and systematically, if the cruising life is for you. Remember that it's OK to have your head in the clouds as long as you keep your feet on the ground, and I'll try to show you how you can do just that.

For now, let's assume that you are one of those fortunate few to whom the cruising life, after close scrutiny, retains its exotic allure. Although cruisers as a whole are maddeningly hard to categorize, what follows is a rough grouping of the types of people for whom this lifestyle is often most appropriate.

Retired Cruisers

The cruising life has undeniable and natural appeal to people who have worked a full and rewarding life, who are looking for more than shuffleboard tournaments and mall prowling, and who shudder at the prospect of living in a retirement community in Florida or Arizona. Retirees with a moderate pension supplemented by social security can live quite well on a boat. But please note: Just because you have retirement income doesn't mean you don't have to tend to your cruising kitty. In Chapter 5 I'll discuss a few principles that can help you stretch a meager retirement income.

Many retirees keep going well into their seventies, and I've even encountered the occasional oceangoing octogenarian. In fact, if there is a problem with retired cruisers, it is that a few of them don't know when to quit—and I say that with fond admiration for their perseverance. The vigorous and healthy cruising life seems to keep older people going longer.

Age, however, is a reality that we must all deal with sooner or later, and as with most things, it is better and easier to deal with it earlier. If you intend to cruise well into your retirement years, be aware that your cruising skills and abilities will change with your advancing years, and plan accordingly.

Middle-Aged Retirees

The rash of forced early retirements and corporate layoffs in the 1980s and early 1990s resulted in a flood of retirees in their forties and fifties with a steady income and nothing to do. Many of them bought sailboats and tried cruising. In addition, there are more and more cruisers in their early fifties who have decided to step out of harness with less retirement income just so they can start cruising while they have the health and stamina to enjoy it. For them the financial sacrifice of not working an extra 10 years until the common retirement age of 65 is worth it many times over. This observation is reinforced by the most prevalent comment we hear from cruisers who didn't get started until after age 65: "If I'd only known how wonderful it is, I would have quit the job and started earlier."

We have also met retired people who are even younger, a fortunate few of whom are in their thirties. Many of these folks have family money to draw on, have sold a business, invented something profitable, or otherwise accumulated enough cash to allow them to relax and enjoy life at an early age.

Although there are many ways to finance a retirement cruise, we have yet to meet anyone who was able to sail away because of a killing in the stock market or a winning number in the lottery, which leads me to believe that while there are sure to be notable exceptions, stock market killings and lottery winnings are probably not reliable ways to finance the cruising life.

Before we leave the subject of retired cruisers, I can't resist the temptation to mention another social phenomenon that has slightly tragicomic overtones—tragic if it happens to you, comic if it happens to someone else. That is, the current trend of adult children returning to the nest, often with grandkids in tow. We have several shoreside friends to whom this very thing has happened. I met a guy in Florida who was building his own boat and making all the bunks 5 feet, 8 inches long because his son-in-law, a strapping lad who had just moved with his bride back into dad-in-law's house, was 6 feet tall. I'm not sure if cruising is a good way to avoid this sort of thing (assuming it's something you want to avoid), but I do think that a small boat in a big ocean might have less appeal to clingy offspring than the posh family homestead.

Sabbatical Cruisers

Susan and I have met a lot of cruisers who have interesting and rewarding careers ashore that they have no intention of abandoning or even neglecting long enough to do anything as frivolous as casting off on a sailboat for the rest of their lives. But they do have a powerful urge to experience the romance and adventure of a high-seas voyage. They want something more than a few weeks or months in the tropics, but they don't want to devote their lives to living on a boat. Most of these temporary cruisers are in the fortunate position of being able to take off for a few years while they sail around the world, do the Intracoastal Waterway or the Inland Passage, or just sail away from the world of cell phones and traffic jams long enough for the steam to evaporate from their pressure-cooker lives. Tenured professors are naturals for this type of cruising, of course, but we have also met successful physicians, stockbrokers, and business consultants.

The typical cruisers in this category have a lot of money and influential positions where they can dictate their own terms and return to a life pretty much as they left it. While we may admire or even envy these cruisers, most of us cannot emulate them, so we'll give them a friendly wave as they blast by in their Deerfoots and their Hinckleys, then return to our task of forging an interesting life on a somewhat smaller anvil.

The Ultrarich Cruisers

The next rung up on the socioeconomic cruising ladder takes us to the truly absurd level of the ultrarich cruisers. Typically, these cruisers own huge boats manned by a professional crew who sail the boat to whatever port the owner dictates, at which point the owner flies in to do some "cruising."

The ultrarich owner is often a celebrity, like the late William F. Buckley, Jr., or the head of a large corporation. Fans of Buckley knew him as an avid sailor and have most likely read *Airborne*, his account of his circumnavigation on his schooner *Cyrano*. That he was able to complete the trip without interrupting his busy TV and editorial schedule is quite remarkable, but I doubt if he could have done it without his crew.

We have met a surprising number of ultrarich cruisers in the course of our travels.

I recall a large motoryacht with a full-time husband-and-wife crew anchored in Honduras awaiting the arrival of an owner who had invented a popular type of charcoal grill, and a huge catamaran that we first met in the Marquesas belonging to the owner of a large restaurant chain. One of the biggest and loveliest private yachts that we've encountered was a 160-foot three-master that belonged to the owner of a huge running-shoe company (no, not that running-shoe company—the other one) and that was manned by a full-time crew of four young Kiwis.

There is also a newer group of cruisers in the ultrarich category. For most of us, the recent recession has been a time of reduced income, shrinking savings accounts, and lost jobs. But some of us, particularly those of us working in the finance and insurance industries, have done quite well by the economic drop-off. This isn't the place to discuss social issues, but the inequity between the top 10 percent of incomes and you and me continues to spread. The result is a plethora of superyachts that have joined the cruising fleet in the last 10 years or so. Fortunately, most of these megaboats have professional crews who ferry them between posh marinas and luxury resorts leaving the rest of us alone. But when one does decide to anchor out, it can be a disaster.

The worst example that I have encountered was while we were anchored off the posh Jean-Michel Cousteau's Fiji Islands Resort (www.fijiresort.com) just outside of Savusavu on the island of Vanua Levu in Fiji. We had been there for only a day when a huge yacht (150 feet or so) dropped anchor about 50 yards off our starboard side and immediately started unloading jet skis and a Cigarette Gladiator speedboat. While half the crew busied themselves making large wakes and as much noise as possible with the environmentally unkind watercraft, those who remained on board cranked up the stereo and proceeded to get stoned and roaring drunk. The party went on all night, but when we pulled the anchor at first light for a premature departure (we had planned to be there for a week), the great white megayacht was deathly quiet. I couldn't resist pulling alongside and giving our new friends a 10-second departure salute with *Sultana*'s oversized fog horn. A mean and vindictive gesture? You bet. Satisfying? Right again.

As discouraging as the foregoing tale might be, it shouldn't deter you from a visit to this famous resort the next time you are cruising in Fiji. When we were last there (admittedly over 10 years ago), the entire resort was graciously open to any visiting boats, and the restaurant was among the best in the country.

Working Cruisers

What about those of us who don't want to wait until we retire to go cruising, those who are unencumbered by a business or family fortune, or those who haven't invented a computer chip or heart valve that will produce enough royalties to pay the way? In other words, what about most of us? Well, the working cruise is an attractive option for a lot of people, so let's take a look at it.

The working cruise is best defined as a work-as-you-go affair where the cruisers sail into an attractive port, arrange a semipermanent live-aboard slip or mooring for the boat, then seek employment ashore. This sort of arrangement is often the best option for younger people who don't have children, who don't have a good start on a large kitty, and who don't want to wait around long enough to accumulate one either. The working cruise also appeals to highly trained professionals with esoteric skills that are easily marketed in diverse locations. Most of the people we met in this category had engineering backgrounds (civil, structural, electrical, and even agricultural), but we also met diesel mechanics, welders, computer programmers, and teachers. In Pago Pago, we met a young cruiser who was making decent money as an airline pilot.

Short-Term Cruisers

Many people, of course, yearn to cruise but don't want to or can't make it a lifetime commitment, and they lack the resources of sabbatical cruisers. For these cruisers, working for 5 to 10 years to accumulate a kitty is not an attractive option. They want to do more than coastal cruising on weekends and holidays, and they can save or borrow enough for a one- or two-year cruise. We have met many cruisers who are doing just that. Quite a few of these people just quit their jobs, went sailing, and then went job hunting when the kitty ran dry. This tactic works particularly well for professionals such as computer programmers and engineers, for people between jobs, and for self-employed individuals—particularly those in the building trades.

Although it isn't as easy to do or as common as it was before the most recent recession, borrowing money, often as a mortgage on the family home, still seems to be a popular option among short-term cruisers. Then, after the money is gone, they go back to work to pay for the cruise. Although many people get to go cruising quickly by borrowing money, I constantly argue against doing so. Taking out a loan to finance a cruise is financial lunacy and a good way to wreck your life. I'll talk more about this later, but for now, keep foremost in your mind that, if you want to go cruising, work first, cruise later. Ignore the "do it now" pundits in the Internet chat rooms who, for the most part, aren't cruising either.

Commuter Cruisers

When we were commissioning *Vicarious*, I bought a set of outsized winches (to replace the diminutive ones that a previous owner had installed) from an interesting bloke named

Otto who worked at a major boatyard in New England. Otto and I hit it off right away as he was a dedicated cruiser who liked to talk about his travels, and I was a dedicated listener. Otto made a good living working on superyachts and expensive sailboats, but he loved the freedom of the cruising life. Unfortunately, he and his wife had a certain standard of creature comfort that they were unwilling to compromise and couldn't afford without their combined substantial income. They solved this dilemma by working like bilge rats during the five-month New England boating season and cruising for the rest of the year wherever the winds and currents took them. When I last heard from Otto, they were off to Turkey with plans to move their Shannon 38 cutter to the Canary Islands where they would leave it for another season of kitty-fattening work.

Commuter cruising is becoming increasingly popular with people like Otto and his wife who for various reasons aren't prepared to embrace full-time voyaging. Perhaps they can't afford to leave their jobs just yet, or family commitments preclude their sailing off forever. More likely though, they just don't want to commit themselves to living on a boat year-round.

A lot of these don't-wanna-be-full-timers are answering the call to the cruising life with the commuter-cruiser option. They follow the seasons from place to place, just like the rest of us, but when they get there, they secure the boat and return home to work on kitty building. The time that they spend in each activity varies from a few weeks—as with our friends Jack and Trudy *Heart's Content*—to a few months, like Otto and his wife, to several years, like Bill and Jane on *Conquistador*.

For many cruisers, the commuter option is a precursor to living full-time on a boat, but just as often it seems to be a way of holding on to the cruising life when full-time is no longer tenable. When we get old or broke or just plain used up, commuting between the cruising life and the shoreside life can sometimes keep us going when others have to hang up the paddles and go home.

Unemployed Cruisers

I wouldn't bother to mention these cruisers except that we have met several who were collecting unemployment benefits while cruising. On the Okeechobee River adjacent to the Everglades, we met a young man on a 27-foot sloop who claimed to be cruising the East Coast and financing his trip entirely with an emotional disability benefit from social security. He was a bit emaciated, and the boat was a long way from being a nautical showplace, but otherwise he seemed to be doing fine.

On the island of Aitutaki in the Cook Islands, we met another young man who had lost his accounting job in Paris and was sailing around the world in his beautifully built 32-foot steel cutter on the two years of full unemployment compensation offered by his government. To top that, the unemployment agency deposited his monthly check directly into his bank for him. Now that's what I call benefits.

Noncruising Cruisers

A lot of people are cruising through life, living a low-impact existence, getting by the best they can on what they have without credit cards, computers, or fancy cars, with naught but a kind word for their fellow travelers and a helping hand for the less fortunate souls they meet. These are people who embody all of the very best attributes found in cruisers but don't know the first thing about boats, and they have no interest in learning about them. Perhaps you are lucky enough to know a few of these lifestyle cruisers. I'm lucky enough to know several—in fact, there are a few in my family, and they are among the most valuable of my friends.

My late pal Jerry lived his entire life as an educator without regard to material gain or self-aggrandizement, and in the 30-odd years I knew him, he never failed me when I needed a helping hand or a kind word. A list of Jerry's friends would be longer than the phone book for many cities.

Another cruiser without a boat is my brother-in-law, Eddie. Many years ago, Eddie gave up the life of a union machinist to live in the woods and cut trees for a living just because he likes living in the woods and cutting trees. He lives year-round in a trailer far back in the Maine woods where moose nibble the vegetables in his garden and bears regularly feast from his garbage pit. But Eddie is not your average logger; he owns no giant log skidder of the kind that most woodcutters use to harvest thousands of board feet of lumber in a single day. He cuts his trees one at a time and transports the logs to the road in an old Jeep. Most logging areas look like war zones once they are completely cut, but when Eddie finishes a job in a forest, the deer and the squirrels hardly notice he was there. Eddie doesn't make a lot of money, but he makes enough to do what he wants to do the way he wants to do it.

The third member of my rogues' gallery is a hermit named Dale who lives with his dog in a hollow log in the New Zealand bush. Dale survives on optimism, the occasional generosity of his friends, and a diet of wild pigs and feral goats he harvests with a fearsome-looking crossbow that he traded for a bale of possum skins. (Feral bushtail possums, imported from Australia a hundred years ago, are a plague in New Zealand, and their hides and hair make an environmentally friendly cash crop.) Ten years ago, Dale abandoned a lucrative career as a sound and lighting technician for rock groups touring Australia. He knows nothing about boats, but he remains the most cruiserly cruiser of all the cruisers I know, on or off the water.

"Dale"

My friend Dale lives with his dog, Hatook, in a hut deep in the bush on the South Island of New Zealand where he is so far off the grid that it is a 5-mile walk to the nearest lightbulb. Dale and Hatook live by their wits off the land with a carbon profile as light as a shadow in the dark. Even though they don't have a boat and wouldn't know what to do with one if they did, they are living the cruising life in every sense of the word.

Dale lives life wholly by his own standards, uninfluenced by the demands of a materialistic society. He doesn't really live in a hollow log—I just made that up—but he would be just as happy if he did.

Cruisers Like You and Me

One of the best ways to participate in the cruising life, and the one championed in this book, is to work your butt off while limiting your expenses over a long period of time so you can accumulate a cash reserve (the kitty) that you will squirrel away in a judicious and profitable manner so that when you need the cash to pay for all or a substantial part of your cruising expenses, you will have it. Earlier we argued that the cruising life is less stressful than life ashore, but don't for a moment get the idea that it is stress free, and the stress of not having enough money to pay bills is a major source of anxiety on a boat just as it is ashore. The only way to eliminate economic stress is by living a basic life and maintaining a fat kitty. I'll talk much more about the care and feeding of the cruising kitty in Chapter 6, but for now all that is required is a willingness to work hard, a few major and a lot of minor changes in your lifestyle, a slight shift in your value system, and time.

How long it will take to get you cruising depends on your earning power, your willingness to cut out frills, and your cruising requirements, but 5 to 10 years is a good average. Although this may seem like a long time, most successful cruisers I have talked to have spent about 10 years in the planning and preparation process. Naturally, this assumes that you will be young enough to enjoy the cruise once you accumulate your kitty. However, we did meet a man in South Carolina who was in his eighties when he started building his cruising boat. As I've said before: cruisers are optimists.

Common Traits of Successful Cruisers

The international cruising society is made up of a diverse and disparate group of colorful and stimulating people from all walks of life, from many countries, and from all social and economic strata—but we share several traits. Cruisers are:

- Optimists who view life as a stroll from the shade into the sun.
- Rainbow chasers and magic-bean buyers who often have unrealistic expectations of

the worlds that are about to be conquered and the dragons that are about to be slain.
- Idealists who believe that life should be a little better than it is and who work to make it so.
- Fatalists who accept life as it comes, know that there are a few jokers in every deck, and realize that fate doesn't always deal a winning hand.
- Realists who know that someday the sun will set on the final anchorage and who can sail on to whatever comes next without regrets, remorse, or a glance at the wake.
- Loners who thrive on solitude and understand when another boat just wants to be left alone.
- Gregarious and friendly to a fault and always ready to dinghy for miles through a swamp on a rainy night to attend a potluck supper or to come to the aid of a fellow cruiser.
- Inclined to gossip like fishwives at every cruiser gathering (cruisers call it the "coconut telegraph," and it is one of the most efficient grapevine communications systems on earth).
- Suckers for a good sea story or yarn, who are always ready to sail off in search of some rumored perfect harbor or pristine anchorage.
- Able to find the material for great stories in ordinary circumstances.
- Independent and self-reliant to a fault.
- Free-spirited (sometimes to the point of capriciousness).

Not all of these traits are positive, of course, but they are as much a part of cruising as rusty anchors and sunsets, and they combine to make life afloat a little more simple and basic than life ashore, to make it easier to accept the bad things that happen while emphasizing the good things, and to carry on into the storm when noncruisers come about and head for harbor. The fact that you are reading this book is evidence that you already have a few of these traits.

Cruising: The Simple and Basic Life

There are vast differences between life ashore and life on a small boat. Life is simpler on a boat in that you are free from shoreside stresses, anxieties, and pressures wrought by the largely artificial environment we have constructed for ourselves above the tide line. Few cruisers worry about getting to work on time, almost none give a thought to the color of their power tie or fret about the stylishness of their new business suit, and it's been years since I have been caught in a traffic jam. The social and economic stratification endemic to most shoreside neighborhoods disappears when you move aboard and sail away, and those who live on actual boats are all in the same metaphorical boat regardless of wealth and position.

More subtle differences also exist. People on boats tend to be more friendly and open than when they are ashore. Often they even allow themselves to be more vulnerable to disappointment and rejection. I have no way of knowing if cruising changes a person's personality or if it simply appeals to those with a certain disposition, but I suspect it is, like a good confection, a subtle blend of many ingredients that makes boat people more aware of their surroundings and more sensitive to the feelings of others than when they were house people. If these differences are small—tiny, really—then so be it. By its simplicity, life in the cruising community can be a bit closer to fundamental and real than any other way we can live; thus, it is just slightly closer to being human. And if that isn't a step in the right direction, then what is?

But, as in all things, you get what you pay for, and if the rewards of the cruising life are high, then so too can be the price. Our nanny society provides cops, ambulances, hospitals, marriage counselors, and teachers for our children. We have grown to expect and even demand these things and to expect our society to take care of us when we are ill or old or poor or crazy. But when we sail away, we sail into a life where a kidney stone or a slip on the deck can be fatal, where exotic diseases and ignorance proliferate, and where there are few schools or hospitals to correct or cure them. If we become ill or old or poor or crazy, we are left to look after ourselves and each other.

The shift to the cruising life can be traumatic. Ashore we live our lives according to schedules. We have schedules for our education, our career advancement, servicing the family car, and getting our hair cut. Afloat we live by the winds, the tides, and the seasons, and any attempt to schedule anything is frustrated. Ashore we have rules, regulations, laws, and nosy neighbors to monitor our behavior and keep us from doing things we ought not to do. But afloat, and especially in developing countries where corruption, thievery, and chicanery are a part of everyday life, there are few laws and regulations, and our behavior is guided by our moral turpitude and our character. Ashore, when we want something, we go to the store, whip out our credit card, and buy it. Afloat we agonize over every item that comes aboard: Do we really need it? Can we afford it? Will it do the job? Do we really need it? Is there room for it in the forepeak? Will it stand up to salt water? Do we really need it? Do we really . . . ?

Most of us are used to a pretty easy life— no, let's be realistic: most of us are as soft as wet bread. But the cruising life is a rigorous physical life with no Sunday football marathons and no daytime talk shows to fill the empty hours of sedentary days. Afloat, your feet are almost always your sole means of shoreside transportation. Cruisers walk a lot—to post offices, grocery stores, chandleries, boatyards, and laundromats. Recreation often means a game of volleyball on a beach, a brisk row around a harbor, or diving for dinner. Exercise and fresh air prevail in the cruising life, and obese cruisers are rare.

The constant physical activity and the reduction of stress and anxiety are important reasons why cruising is a healthy way to live, but there are other conditions intrinsic to the lifestyle that make it a healthy existence. For one thing, cruisers tend to eat well. In most popular cruising locales, fresh vegetables and fruits are readily available and cheap, and they are nearly always organic because the native farmers usually can't afford expensive fertilizers and pesticides. At the same time, beef, pork, and other red meats are scarce, expensive, and of poor quality; chicken or other fowl not killed and dressed on the spot is always suspect. Thus, a cruiser's diet usually drifts away from meat and shifts almost automatically to the more beneficial fruits and vegetables—a move that health professionals have been begging us to adopt for years. Many cruisers even become de facto vegetarians, not by intent but by default, as their diet gradually shifts from fat- and sugar-laden foods to a healthier and more practical diet of natural foods.

If you think you would like to adopt the cruising life, you should start now to alter the way you think and live, to start becoming simple and basic in all things, and to learn to depend on no one but yourself and your family. I'll show you how you can alter a few of your basic beliefs and routines by making small and periodic adjustments in your lifestyle and attitude so you can avoid drastic and unsettling changes. The shift from the shoreside life to the cruising life can be a gradual but steady movement away from the objective world of material goods and status you will be leaving toward the more subjective world you will be entering. The transition is a lot easier than you think, and even if you never do go cruising, it will be one of the most rewarding things you have ever done.

Here we are, for the second time in this book, at the end of an important chapter, and once again I will admonish you to think carefully about your decision to embrace (or not embrace) a life of voyaging to distant lands on a small boat. The cruising life isn't for everyone. If you try it and don't like it, you are likely to not like it a lot. It's much better to be sitting at home wishing you were cruising than to be cruising wishing you were sitting at home, so before you head out on your adventure, make sure that you are really a candidate for the cruising life and haven't just been listening to too many Jimmy Buffett songs.

3

Should You Go Cruising?

For my part, I travel not to go anywhere, but to go. I travel for travel's sake. The great affair is to move.

—ROBERT LOUIS STEVENSON

We often hear the cruising life described in evasive generalities like "It's anything you want it to be" or the (slightly) more poetic "The cruising life is as diverse as the sunsets cruisers sail off to find." But this is a cynical cop-out because the life of those of us on boats on the sea has a code of conduct that is as structured as the lives of most of our shoreside friends, and even more so than some. We wear our shorts and battered Topsiders instead of a company tie and wing-tip shoes; we have the common goal of avoiding common goals; we foster among ourselves a universal disdain for officious authority and those who pretend to wield it; and we hold ourselves to a lofty set of principles that shoresiders (especially those working for banks or insurance companies) would find restrictive.

Before you spend a major portion of your earthly wealth on anything as capricious as a boat, make sure you know what you are getting yourself into. Once you realize that the cruising life is a simple and basic way of living on the fringe of normal society rather than being an escape or departure from society, you'll be on the right track. If you are aware from the beginning that cruising is a lot of work, that it is often scary and sometimes terrifying, but nearly always rewarding, you won't go too far wrong. And once you get the idea that cruisers are like normal people, only a bit crazier and a lot more passionate, you will be almost ready to go.

Start Now to Develop Your Plan for Departure

Schedules don't work in the cruising life, but you should establish a rough plan for your departure. After all, if you've read this far, you're serious about it. First, determine what type of cruiser (retired, working, commuter, short-term, or combination as described in Chapter 2) you plan to become. Doing so will allow you to make a careful analysis of your financial resources and lead to a realistic estimate of how long it will take you to improve them enough to shove off. Modify your plan based on an honest assessment of your personal situation and that of anyone you expect to accompany you. Your age, health, responsibilities to children and other family members, and your personal resolve and fears are all things to consider in addition to your ability to raise a fat kitty (see Chapter 6).

Next—and this is important—think about the living standards you expect to maintain while cruising. We have met cruisers living on tattered old boats kept afloat with love and seizing wire, eating boiled noodles and rice three times a day, earning money any way they could, and loving every second of it. And we have met cruisers on floating palaces equipped with every modern convenience who never missed an opportunity to voice their displeasure with their boat, their surroundings, the guidebook, the port captain, and life in general. There is a very real and interesting correlation between the size and luxury of cruising boats and the inability of their crews to handle the rigors of the cruising life.

I will discuss this irony a bit later, but for now if you think you want to try an austerity cruise, you have to realize beforehand what life without all the luxuries and comforts that you are accustomed to will be like. Similarly, if you know you require a certain minimum lifestyle, and this applies to nearly all middle-aged and older cruisers (including your aging-but-able author), then make sure you are providing for enough of a financial cushion so you can achieve this lifestyle without worry or anguish. If you are forced by circumstance to live below your minimum standards, you run the risk of making yourself

and those around you miserable and wrecking your cruise.

Conversely, we have seen several cruises come to an early end because the cruisers added so many expensive shoreside features to their boats (air-conditioning is the favorite, but big freezer/refrigerators are a close second) that the boat becomes untenable as a practical vehicle for adventure. Often these condo/yachts simply remain in a marina where the would-be cruisers revert to the live-aboard life simply because they don't want to unplug their 60-inch flat screen from shore power. Just as often they simply trade the boat for a gigantic ("She's a fiver, mate, with four sliders and dual air; the tow machine is a deuce-and-a-half with the big option") RV camper. (Oops, there I go again dumping on RVs. I love RVs, honest.)

Once you have completed a painfully realistic initial assessment of your requirements, you should be able to come up with a preliminary time for departure. If you don't have a substantial start on your kitty, or if you don't receive a retirement income or some other continuing cash flow and you are starting from zero, you can plan on about five years of hard work and lean living (more or less depending on your earning power and the living standards you expect).

Five years is long enough for most people who are serious about cruising and not building their own boat to plan on getting under way—some can do it in as little as two years; others will require more time. The average seems to be closer to 10 years from the time the idea first takes hold to when the dock lines are cast off, but this usually involves about 5 years of hemming and hawing. You are way past this stage or you wouldn't be reading this book. But beware: we have met more than one would-be cruiser who has spent a lifetime planning a cruise never taken. Don't let yourself become so engrossed in the planning process that you never leave.

Who Is Going with You?

For most married couples or those involved in some other permanent relationship, the decision about which person you are going to cruise with is an easy one—you'll cruise with each other—and further discussion on the matter is moot. On the other hand, many otherwise-sound relationships have ended when one partner wanted to go cruising so badly that the cruising life was more attractive than the continuation of the relationship. We have some good friends who faced this problem just before we left Marblehead. He wanted to go cruising, and she wanted to move to the Berkshires and raise Saint Bernards. Today, he is cruising, and she is in Chicago as an important executive with a huge multinational drug company (funny how some things work out), and they send each other cards at Christmas. It's a sad story, but when the desire to cruise is stronger than the desire to continue a relationship, it is much better to work things out early on than to suffer the agony of trying to dissolve a relationship while living on a boat.

Poor George

If you are single, but you would rather not try to sail alone, you are advised to find your cruising companion well in advance of the time you leave on your cruise. Consider the following tale.

When Susan and I were looking for a boat in which to pursue our dreams of the cruising life, we heard from many sources that Charlotte Amalie Harbor in the U.S. Virgin Islands was chock-full of cruising boats for sale at bargain prices. So I took a couple of days off and flew down to take a look. There were, indeed, dozens of boats on the market, and I spent three days checking them out, but only one of the many boats I looked at sticks in my mind.

It was a lovely CSY 44 of the older "walk-over" type that had been rebuilt from Windex to worm shoe by professional boatwrights. She was owned by a man named George who had dreamed his whole life of cruising around the world. Unfortunately, his wife didn't share his dream, so they separated, and George sailed off alone looking for the sun and a new mate with whom to share his boat and his life. He dropped the hook in a small harbor on the back side of St. Thomas and began dating every single woman on the island. He advertised for female crew in all the cruising magazines and on every adult dating site on the Internet. He even answered an ad that read "Meet Hundreds of Lonely Russian Women Online. Satisfaction Guaranteed." Alas, either his standards (or, more likely, those of the ladies he met) were too high or his luck was bad, because after two years of diligent searching, George gave up and went home to his wife's geranium farm, leaving his for-sale boat as a memento of his failure.

The sad ending to this touching tale holds a simple lesson for all single men and women who yearn to cruise: the cruising life is ready-made for lovers of life and dreamers of romance, but unless you really want to sail alone, select your cruising companions before you go, and then leave enough time before departure to get to know each other.

In our travels we have been lucky to meet many singlehanded cruisers, but we've met only one or two who were really happy about sailing alone. Off the top of my head, I can name four successful singlehanders whom I came to respect for their formidable sailing skills and strength of character. Two were men and two were women, but all four were remarkable people; three of the four would rather not have been sailing alone (and two of those three subsequently got married in Tahiti).

Singlehanding is romantic and exciting, but it is also dangerous. Of the five boats lost while *Sultana* was crossing the Pacific, two were singlehanders. And, of course, singlehanding, like bumblebees' flying, is technically impossible. International conventions require a constant watch when sailing on the high seas, and singlehanders just can't provide one. Common sense and an instinct for self-preservation also require a constant watch in heavy-traffic areas, and singlehanders can't do that either.

If you get the impression that I'm not comfortable with singlehanded cruising, you're right.

Family Cruising Is the Way to Go

The overwhelming majority of successful cruisers we have met are married couples or family groups. Couples with small children are particularly good at adapting to the cruising life because, I think, with their focus instinctively on the welfare of their children, they are motivated to make all the right decisions and choices. They tend to be much more cautious in choosing when and where to sail than are couples without children, and they are more careful with the kitty. All of these are factors that make for a happy and successful cruise.

Right after married couples with children in the hierarchy of cruising success stories come married couples without children, then unmarried couples who have known each other for a while, and finally come same-sex crews.

Mixed Crews Can Be a Disaster

Several years before we left on our cruise, a young woman friend from Boston came to me all aflutter with exciting news. She had accepted a position as cook on a 50-foot cruising yacht that was being moved from San Diego to Sydney. In addition to Tiffany, the experienced but nonprofessional delivery crew would be made up of the owner's college-age

Phillip

Families cruising with children enjoy one of the highest success rates of all cruisers, probably because the focus is on the children and every decision made has their safety and welfare in mind. Children raised on boats are similar to children raised on farms in that they mature at an alarming rate and are often ready to take on responsibility far ahead of shoreside children. At the age of 10, Phillip could safely operate the dinghy with a 25-horse outboard and could row for miles without tiring.

son and two of his friends. It would be a dream cruise through the South Pacific with no time or budgetary constraints to detract from an entire sailing season of fun in the sun. I sent her off with best wishes and a smile, but if I had known then what I know now, I would have begged her not to go.

I heard through the grapevine that the cruise ended in disaster after only two months. It seems that all three of the lads had fallen madly in love with Tiffany, and their rivalry for her favors came to a head in Papeete. Fisticuffs erupted, two of the lads were hauled off by the gendarmes, and the third went for a brief stay in the hospital. Tiffany flew home in tears, and the owner had to fly in a professional crew to complete the voyage.

Mixed crews can and do work very well—we have met several that were efficient and effective—but they seem to work best in a professional environment with a strong and resourceful captain at the helm.

Mixed crews made up of two cruising couples can also work, but here too there is a danger of discord. I haven't met any crews where two couples were sharing the cost of a boat to go cruising, but I understand that the practice isn't uncommon and that it has a mixed level of success. I do, however, take every opportunity to talk to the crews and service people in the charter yacht industry, and these folks all have juicy tales about mixed-couple crews who embark as friends and return bitter enemies. Of course, boat charterers aren't cruisers (I'll discuss why later on), and though the lesson here is neither salient nor profound, it is clear: if you are contemplating a mixed-couple or mixed-sex cruise with other than family or life companion, be careful.

And Why Are You Going?

I never miss a chance to make the acquaintance of any cruiser who anchors within hailing distance of *Vicarious*'s cockpit. As soon as the opportunity arises, and it always does, I'll ask him or her what it was that motivated the big jump from shoreside life to cruising, and the answers I get are as varied and fascinating as the cruisers themselves. Some have dreamed all their lives of sailing off on a boat to see the world, and many of them are living their dream on a vessel they built (and often designed) themselves, having spent 10 or even 20 years

in the process. Others have sailed on impulse, having been shocked into a realization of their own mortality by a close call with a dangerous illness or the untimely death of a close friend. Probably the most common answer to my question "Why did you do it?" is this: "When I turned 40, I realized I wasn't going to live forever and that there was a lot more to living than sitting at a desk shuffling papers."

Many others, however, honestly don't know the answer to this most basic question. "I often wonder about that myself" is the usual response, while others seem to have never thought about it. To them cruising is something that they just had to do so they did it. Just as often we will meet a couple who took time off from the shoreside life to face the challenge of a year long cruise across an ocean or to some far-off land only to find that they liked it so much that they didn't go back. Sometimes they do return to the shoreside life but only so they can work on fattening the kitty and make cruising a lifestyle rather than an adventuresome interlude.

I think there is a romantic notion that many people go cruising for the same reasons that people used to join the Foreign Legion or seek solace in the bottom of a whiskey bottle—to escape a troubled life or the heartbreak of a lost love. This is nonsense, of course, and I have yet to meet a successful cruiser who is cruising to avoid some unpleasantness. Cruisers are seekers, not runners. Nearly everyone I talk to is looking for something, not running away from it—a fuller life, perhaps, or adventure, or the infectious camaraderie of the high seas. But often the reason people give is even more mundane: they cruise simply because they love boats and sailing; others cruise just to see the world. The two exceptions are Johnny X who was hiding out in on the *Isla de Provedencia* in Colombia to avoid a New York felony warrant (his boat was named *Onthelam*—pronounced *onth-elam*) and my friend Dave who is stuck in Fiji until a certain sheriff in Miami toting a major civil summons in his pocket either dies or gives up and goes home.

There are hundreds of good reasons for choosing the cruising life; let's review a few of them.

It's an Alternative to the Rat Race

Cruising full-time is one of the last great alternatives to the pressures and influences of modern society. In fact, it may be the only remaining alternative to the overregulated and controlled existence that most of us lead ashore. It seems that everywhere we go on shore there are rules, laws, and regulations that govern every detail of our daily lives. In Bundaberg, Australia, I went into a sporting goods store to buy a pocketknife to replace the one that I had dropped overboard (it's always a bad day when that happens). Once I had made my selection from the many on display and paid for it, the owner of the store, with a fatherly tone and authoritative expression, advised that I wasn't allowed to take the knife out of the store. It seems that it is illegal to carry a knife in Queensland but not illegal to sell or buy one. I advised the chap that I had no intention of carrying it anywhere, but I would keep it safely stowed in my pocket where it would do no harm to anyone. The store owner looked like he would happily set the coppers on his mum, so I left quickly walking directly away from the docks where *Sultana* was tied.

I later read that Australia has more regulations and controls on personal behavior than China or Russia. True or not, Australia is still a great place to visit. Just stay as far away from the wabbies as you can, mate, and don't spit the dummy on the footpath (or toss a wobbly) unless you can handle hard time in the chokey.

That doesn't mean that cruising doesn't come with its own pressures and anxiety-inducing situations, but it is fascinating to see how many cruisers come from high-intensity

business careers or from law practices or the advertising industry. Wherever cruisers congregate, you will find a lot of people who led Type A lives ashore: doctors, lawyers, dentists, accountants, computer programmers, stockbrokers, and writers—lots of writers. To many of these formerly highly paid denizens of the pressure cooker, the laid-back easygoing pace of the cruising life is a welcome relief; it can even be a lifesaver. We've met several cruisers who gave up their frantic lifestyles on their doctors' orders, and I've often heard the comment, "I hadda get away from sales (marketing, advertising, Wall Street, Fleet Street, etc.)" or, "The doc said my blood pressure was going to do me in for sure."

That said, there seems to be plenty of room for the Type A personality in the cruising community. Many cruisers are sailing on schedules—indeed, many people can't seem to get by without them. There are people frantically sailing from harbor to harbor trying to see as many places as possible within some arbitrarily established time frame, and there are others, a lot actually, who are sailing around the world in a year or two. Some need to get back to jobs before their leave of absence or sabbatical expires, while others need to get home before their welfare runs out (really), and others are doing it just for the challenge of beating the clock. But even the most frantic Type A, if exposed to the cruising life long enough, will gradually and painfully come to endorse the *mañana* principle—that pervasive and universal belief among residents of the tropics that there is nothing so important that it can't wait until tomorrow—and learn to stop and smell the banana blossoms, kick back, and relax.

Cruising Is a Cheap Way to See the World

Modern men and women are great travelers, and the tourist industry is one of the largest service industries we have. Multitudes of workers look forward to their week or two in the sun on the beaches of the Caribbean every year, cruise liners attract millions of others, and organized groups travel to the ancient cities in Greece, Mexico, and Israel or to the great capitals of Europe. Lately, the concepts of adventure travel and ecotourism have taken hold, and we find dental assistants from Vancouver digging Inca artifacts in the mountains of Peru and schoolteachers from Dallas studying pelagic fishes in the Bering Sea.

But these activities are expensive, and for many of us a week on Maui isn't enough to satisfy a yearning for adventure and faraway places. Bora Bora, in French Polynesia, was one of the

loveliest places *Sultana* visited on her voyage across the Pacific, and we stayed there nearly a month, scuba diving, snorkeling in the lagoons, and hiking and bicycling around the island. It was easy to imagine the gloom of those who save and then spend thousands of dollars to get there, only to have to return home shortly after recovering from jet lag.

Many places aren't accessible to even the most dedicated tourist. The outer islands of the Marquesas in French Polynesia and the Kermadecs that lie between Tonga and New Zealand aren't served by the normal tourist industry and can be reached only by horribly expensive special charter or by cruising sailboat.

The extensive harbor behind the sand dunes of Cape Lookout on the Outer Banks of North Carolina is a popular destination for local weekenders and vacationers, and the starting price for a small cabin nearby is over $1,000 per week. The Vicarious *crew lived here on the hook for over two weeks, fishing, snorkeling, walking the dunes at sundown, and generally enjoying life, all for a total cash expenditure of the replacement cost of the ship's stores we lived on. The cruising life isn't necessarily a cheap way to live, but when compared with the costs of other ways to travel to exotic and interesting places, it can be a bargain.*

And even places closer to the United States, like Colombia's lovely San Andres Island (about 300 miles north of Panama) and the uninhabited and desolate Vivario Banks just off Cabo Gracios a Dios in Nicaragua, aren't readily accessible to American tourists. San Andres is a favorite destination of tourists from Colombia and other South American countries, but to get there from North America, you must first fly to Bogotá. The Vivario Banks are two days against the wind from the Bay Islands of Honduras, and none but the cruisers and shrimp boats that use them for refuge ever get to see them.

Leisurely voyaging by boat is one of the few practical ways for those of us who aren't wealthy to travel the world, and it is one of the major reasons many of us give for adopting the cruising life.

The Cruising Life Is an Adventurous Life

Who among us hasn't thrilled to the thought of trudging to the top of the Himalayas at the head of a column of trusty Sherpas? On a less vicarious level, adventure sports like parasailing and white-water rafting are attracting an ever-growing cadre of aficionados and participants, while mountain-bike racing and heli-skiing are attracting thousands of others. If you play by the rules and use your head, you can participate in these sports without undue risk to life or limb and still derive all the excitement that any normal person would ever want.

Many people love adventure, but real adventure is getting hard to find. Well, how about buying a boat and sailing around the world? Sure, thousands of people have done it, and sure, it's not even unusual anymore, and sure, it's easier today than ever before and bound to get even easier, but ocean voyaging is still an adventure in every sense of the word. In fact, it's one of the last true adventures open to most of us.

It Can Even Be Dangerous If You Want It to Be

Did you ever wonder what attracts people to extreme sports like rock and ice climbing and base jumping? (*Base* is an acronym for "buildings, antennae, spans, earth." It is an insane activity too extreme to be called a sport. To participate, one flings oneself off the tops of high places with nothing more than a parafoil to prevent oneself from splattering the landscape. It enjoys a casualty rate only slightly lower than the Normandy invasion.) Psychologists tell us that humans as a species (or at least many of us) seem to have a high requirement for risk and uncertainty in their lives, and many of us find participating in these ultrahazardous activities to be quite satisfying.

Anthropologist Ruth Benedict, a contemporary of Margaret Mead's, argued in her 1934 classic book *Patterns of Culture* that a society free of any dangers to its members will always find a way to inject it artificially—and she used several South Sea island cultures with no indigenous hazards as examples. These islands were isolated from any belligerent neighbors, they offered plenty to eat without the inhabitants' having to work for it, and there were few dangerous or poisonous creatures to worry about. The inhabitants compensated for this boring lack of natural peril in a unique manner: they had a shaman, or religious leader, who was empowered to sneak up behind anyone at any time and bash their brains out with a large ceremonial club.

A more pertinent example might be in New Zealand, which has constructed one of the safest societies on earth. Here too there are no dangerous animals, and the islands' isolation has all but assured their safety from nearby enemies. New Zealanders enjoy lifelong security with free medical care for everyone and a welfare system that is one of the most generous on earth. "No worries, mate," could well be a national slogan rather than a beguiling bit of vernacular slang. Yet it is New Zealand that has developed and popularized many of the adrenaline sports mentioned above. Bungee jumping and base jumping were invented there, and rock climbing and mountaineering are developed to ever higher standards of difficulty on the icy slopes of the Southern Alps. In a one-week period, four young people jumped to their deaths from the tops of waterfalls after a popular soft drink distributor featured the "sport" in its TV ads. New Zealand is a safe place to live, but not entirely—many a proper and sedate New Zealander turns into an animal behind the wheel of a car, ensuring a horrific road toll. It's as if the automobile has become the New Zealander's sacred club because the fearsome accident rate is no more necessary that a shaman's bashing in people's heads.

Although ocean voyaging is not in itself a dangerous undertaking, there's no denying that it offers elements of danger. Many of us have read the books and heard the stories of boats being sunk by whales or caught in typhoons and hurricanes or of crew lost overboard or of boats and crews that vanish without a trace—and that's not even counting the stories of attacks by pirates, desperadoes, loonies, and drug runners.

Such tales are staple fare at any cruiser gathering. In fact, cruising is as dangerous or as safe as we want to make it. The cruising adrenaline freak will find plenty of thrills challenging the weather by sailing in the dangerous zones during cyclone and hurricane seasons or by treks into the roaring forties, the North Atlantic, or the South China Sea. Meanwhile, the rest of us can plod along following the established routes and staying well clear of the major weather systems, but even so we will experience enough thrills and chills, spiced with an occasional moment or two of stark terror, to ensure a ready supply of exciting stories for the folks back home. While I know of no cruiser who will intentionally put the boat in jeopardy, facing danger with impunity, even if it's only perceived danger, is a thrill from which few cruisers are immune—I know I'm not.

Cruising Creates Self-Reliance and Independence

If the absence of fear in the face of danger is stupidity, then courage is the ability to function in the face of fear. Self-reliance is the confidence in your own abilities to make the right decisions under adverse conditions tempered by fear. Millions of dollars each year are spent by corporations to send their executives to confidence building courses where they learn to confront their fears by jumping off cliffs, swinging on ropes across ravines, handling frightening creatures (snakes and spiders and such), and performing other death-defying feats designed to make them better and more effective managers. Likewise, the Outward Bound program has trained thousands of youngsters and young adults to stand tall in the face of adversity simply by building faith in their own abilities and teaching them to handle their fears.

If you quail at the thought of heading out on a two-week passage on a blank piece of ocean where storms rage and there is no refuge outside the strength of your vessel and the determination of the crew, then join the club. Even lifelong cruisers experience a bit of trepidation and personal doubt in the face of a long and difficult passage. Is the boat ready? Did I check the masthead fittings? Are the spreader bolts tight? Do we have enough food? Is our safety gear in order? And the list goes on. There isn't a cruising skipper alive who gets a good night's sleep on the eve of a major departure.

But we go anyway, and when landfall is made and the hook is buried in the mud, cruisers feel much more than a sense of relief that the passage is safely done. They enjoy a sense of accomplishment unlike any that noncruisers will ever experience. Long ocean passages in stormy conditions are challenging, true tests of courage, and genuine builders of self-confidence.

It's Educational

Before we left Marblehead on our world cruise, I probably read about Vava'u at least a dozen times, but nothing I read really registered. I knew it was in Tonga, but I wasn't even sure where Tonga was, and I certainly didn't know how to pronounce Vava'u. Now having been there and spent a few memorable weeks sailing among some of the loveliest islands in the Pacific and having made friends among the inhabitants, I not only know where it is and how to pronounce the name (say it with an adagio tempo as if it were three words like "How are you?") but I also know what the people are like—their religion, their language, their dress, their fears, and their ambitions. I know what they eat and how they live, and I'll never forget any of it.

Both my kids can tie a bowline with one hand, find any place on earth with a sextant and a watch, speak several languages, are accomplished divers, keen observers of the natural world, world-class sailors, and miles ahead of many of their former classmates. But as proud as I am of their accomplishments, I can't brag because they are just average cruising kids. Except for those classes that require special facilities, such as music, physics, and science, cruising kids tend to be scholastically equal to or even ahead of kids ashore.

The educational potential of cruising just can't be denied. Children and adults both benefit by the simplest of actions. Just dropping anchor in a new and strange harbor, rowing ashore in the dinghy, and spending the afternoon in the port captain's office offers an enormous insight into the character and nature of the place you are visiting, and you'll learn whether you want to or not. The popular correspondence schools (Calvert and the University of Nebraska) do a fine job of keeping their students up to speed in the scholastic disciplines (readin' and writin'), and all the other stuff just flows in. World travel offers educational opportunities that aren't available any other way.

Cruising Fosters Togetherness

An ancient bit of cruising wisdom says that if a couple (married or otherwise) can survive life together on a small boat, they can live together anywhere. I suppose it's true. Marital strife certainly isn't unknown in the cruising community—we've met several couples who have quit the cruising life and gone their separate ways. But the vast majority of cruising families that we have met will concede, without reservation, that they are much closer for the experience.

So if you are a fairly typical mom or pop working away at your job 40 or 50 hours a week, spending most of your spare time at the club, talking to your kids between computer games and during the TV commercials, and you think that there must be more to family life, then try family travel on a boat. Cruising, even weekend coastal cruising, is a genuine way of sharing your life with your spouse or children or others who cruise with you.

Cruising Fosters Friendship

We were tied up at the Marinatown Marina in Fort Myers, Florida, waiting for the weather to clear so we could continue our journey to Mexico via Key West, when Susan made one of her typically profound observations: "We've been cruising full-time for only six months, and we've already met more interesting people than in the 10 years we lived in Marblehead." It was

When you live the cruising life, making new friends is as easy as rowing over to the new boat in the anchorage and saying g'day. And when the inevitable potluck happens (they are rarely scheduled), there is never a need for invitations or introductions. Everyone is welcome, and there is always more food than can possibly be eaten in a single go. Impromptu potlucks are a part of the cruising life anywhere two or more boats gather. Usually they happen on shore, but when one of the cruisers is a large Warram catamaran, like Peace, *there is seating for everyone and always room for more.*

true—wonderfully, irrefutably true. Scoundrels and saints, rich and poor, black and white, we had met dozens of fascinating people in those few short months, and the more we cruise, the more people we meet and the more friends we make. And please don't take this to mean that there aren't lots of interesting people in Marblehead. There are, but like most shoreside communities, folks are hard to meet and get to know if they are outside your own social circle. Among cruisers there is only one social circle—the one comprising cruisers.

There exists in the cruising community a delightful camaraderie that attracts interesting and exciting people into a club that is at once exclusive and, at the same time, open to anyone who can follow the rules and pay the dues.

One of the basic concerns parents of young children have when contemplating a world cruise is the fear that their kids won't find enough friends in their age group to allow the normal socialization process that is such an important part of growing up. This was certainly one of our most pressing worries when Susan and I were planning our trip, and we agonized over it. We consulted educators and read everything we could on the subject, and it turned out to be a nonproblem—Sarah and Phillip seldom were in a situation where there weren't plenty of kids around to provide all the companionship they needed. And we made another interesting discovery: in most neighborhoods ashore, kids tend to form cliques and exclusive groups of friends, but this doesn't seem to happen as much among cruising children. Also, age differences are less important at sea than they are ashore. Children raised on boats are often unusually mature and responsible. Phillip learned to start the 25-horsepower outboard on the inflatable at the age of 10, and he could operate it so safely and responsibly by the time he was 12 that we had no compunctions about letting him take it to go exploring or to visit his friends.

Cruisers don't need formalities or introductions to make friends. If there is a potluck supper on the beach, all are welcome; if a boat drags anchor in the night and needs help getting off the mud bank, everyone pitches in to lend a hand; if an emergency arises and help is needed, it's only a very high frequency (VHF) call away. Many of the popular anchorages, especially those in the Caribbean, have daily VHF nets so the entire fleet can stay in touch with each other and stay current on what is happening in the harbor. Newcomers are treated as friends from the day they arrive; by the second or third day, they're almost family. If you are the kind of person who enjoys meeting people and making new friends, then cruising might be the life for you.

The Cruising Life Is a Spiritual Life

No, cruisers don't tend to be more religious than other people. Some individuals are, of course, but when the cruising community is considered as a whole, the religious bell curve is probably skewed away from formal and organized churchly concerns. But when it's your watch at 2 a.m. and the sails are full with a favorable breeze and the stars look like they're close enough to touch and the gurgle of the wake is whispering, "All is well, all is well," it's hard to deny the feeling that there is a power, a benevolent watcher or guardian, if you will, that is making it so.

And when you're hove-to 300 miles from nowhere with the wind screaming through the wires like a hellion on a leash and the waves are crashing on the deck and the crew is huddled on the floor of the cabin because even the strongest lee cloth won't keep them in a bunk, a great many cruisers report a feeling of peace and tranquility that throws logic and reason into the face of dire circumstance.

Not many cruisers will admit to adopting the cruising lifestyle for spiritual reasons, but considering the frenzied life many of us leave ashore, I believe that the cruising life is much closer to the way the forces that created us, be they spiritual or natural, intended for us to live, and that living the way we were intended to live makes us much more sensitive to the presence of those forces. No, ocean voyaging won't do anything to convert the heathen, not this one anyway, but if the heathen is a spiritually aware person, that person will feel closer to the Supreme Navigator while cruising than at any other time or in any other activity.

The Cruising Life Is a Simple Life

When we lived in Marblehead, Susan and I owned a large house in a good neighborhood, two cars, three or four TVs and VCRs, a computer, a garage full of power tools, and a kitchen full of appliances, and our kids' playroom contained enough toys to fill an FAO Schwartz catalog. That we were living the good life, the American dream, was undeniable, but there was a basic problem: we were working so hard to earn the money to buy more stuff (and to pay for the stuff we had bought on credit) that we had little time to enjoy the stuff we already had. We certainly had little time for each other, and the care of our children was entrusted to a full-time nanny.

All that changed when Susan decided we should chuck it all and go cruising. Our transition from being an average shoreside family to a decidedly below-average cruising family took a few years, and we encountered our share of adjustment trauma. We bought *Sultana* and moved aboard. We sold Susan's car and my beloved pickup truck, and we sold most of the rest of our worldly goods, stuff that we thought we couldn't live without, at my sister's yard sale. Treasured family heirlooms and things we couldn't bear to part with, such as my collection of books and Susan's china (she had enough plates to serve a small army at one sitting) went into a storage bin for a few years; then, once we had come to terms with the idea that even heirlooms were an unnecessary burden, we disposed of the lot on eBay. Now our entertainment center consists of a large laptop with a built-in DVD player (which we use to watch educational videos and Netflix movies when an Internet connection is available); we allow ourselves one backpack each into which all our clothing and personal effects must fit; all our tools fit into one locker under the pilothouse seats; and our small-but-efficient galley is a tiny fraction of the huge kitchen we left behind.

We didn't have a lot of money when we decided to buy a sailboat, but we did have some savings, a lot of equity in our house, and a retirement fund that would not be touched while we were cruising and that was adequate to ensure our survival through old age, however long it might be. When we left Marblehead, our primary income was from the rental of our house and a small portfolio of stocks and mutual funds. This left us with an annual income of about $20,000, which was about 25 percent of what we were accustomed to. It wasn't quite enough for us to live on, but we didn't know that until we had been cruising for about six months. We were lucky, however, because in spite of a drastic cutback in our material lives and a shortfall of cash, we were able to muster enough of our resources to get under way in only two years. If you already have a substantial kitty, you may be able to get going more quickly than we did, but more likely you are going to have to start from a smaller base with a five-year plan, as I'll discuss in the rest of this book.

Most people would consider the vast reduction we took in our material goods and living standards to be a huge and unacceptable reduction in our quality of life, but in fact it was just the opposite. Learning to live in a small space with as few material goods as are necessary to live comfortably can reorder your value system on a scale you never thought possible and thereby constitute a significant increase in your real standard of living. There is no question that the cruising life, at its best, is a simple and basic life that appeals to simple and basic people—people like you and me.

The Cruising Life Is an Economical Way to Live

The subject of what it actually costs to live on a boat while cruising is vastly misrepresented by the popular boating press and the online chat rooms, and this can be another prime reason many new cruisers become disillusioned and abandon their cruising plans. I'll have a lot more to say about the economics of world cruising in the following chapters, but for now it's enough to say that the cruising life can still be an economical way to live when compared with life ashore. The economical lifestyle remains one of the big reasons people do it. Just try to be realistic in your estimates of what it will cost to finance the life you really need.

The Cruising Life Is a Clean-Green Life

We live in an era of melting ice caps, desertification of vast areas of our planet, and oceans becoming choked with plastic, all caused by the increasingly profligate lifestyle that a few of us live and a lot of us envy. But fortunately, some of us are becoming increasingly aware of the environmental problems threatening humanity,

Living clean and green by going off the grid has become the mantra to a generation of environmentally aware people concerned with the unsustainable path of the consumer society. But attempts to live up to the mantra are often frustrated by local laws, regulations, and building codes that forbid such earth-friendly devices as rain-catchment systems and composting toilets. The cruising life is automatically off the grid, and if the local bureaucracy objects, there is always a new harbor not far away.

and we are slowly starting to deal with the worst of them. We humans have a long way to go to reach parity with the world on which we live, but cruisers are already there.

No, we aren't necessarily greenies, and our political persuasions are as diverse as our boats. But the cruising life is a practical life, and the most practical way to live is a green life. We eat natural food because it is the easiest and cheapest way to eat; we avoid burning fossil fuels not because we worry about air pollution so much but because we are always trying to save money; we walk instead of drive because our feet are the easiest way to get there, and if we can't walk, we ride a bike or take a bus. We don't carry placards outside power plants or throw ourselves in front of bulldozers building pipelines, and we don't occupy Wall Street or anything else except the most remote of anchorages. No, cruisers aren't greenie activists. We just live green because it is the best way to do it. While others talk the green talk, we float the green boat, and most of us never say a word about it.

The Nays

In spite of all the good reasons for adopting the cruising life, just a few of which are outlined above, we have met far too many people who have chosen the cruising life for the wrong reasons. Most often these cruises end in failure, the crew disillusioned and bitter. I won't spend a lot of time on this subject, but I would be remiss if I didn't mention at least a few of the most common wrong reasons people go cruising.

Cruising Is Not an Escape

Cruising has an understandable appeal to people who are fed up with the lives they are living ashore and who long to escape to the simpler life afloat. I previously said that cruising is an important alternative to the stress and anxiety of modern society. However, it isn't a contradiction to say that cruising is not a way to flee from that life.

If you think that cruising is a way to escape a bad marriage, debts, addictions, the county sheriff, injustice, or a life that isn't going just the way you think it ought to be going, think again. If your life has reached a dead end or you face what seem like insurmountable problems and you are looking to the cruising life for salvation, it is critical that you confront and resolve the conditions that are causing your problems before you depart. These problems, whatever their complexity and nature, won't go away, and they will, in fact, be much more expensive and difficult to handle from a cruising boat than from shore. Often, simply acknowledging your circumstances will carry you more than halfway to a resolution and halfway to the day you can depart on your cruise with a free mind and clear conscience. In addition, by learning to look your problems right in the eye without blinking you will strengthen your already strong character—and strength of character is one of the most important cruiserly attributes.

Cruising Isn't a Way to Find Happiness

This one is easy. If you are miserable and unhappy ashore, it is likely that you will be even more miserable and unhappy afloat. The advice here is the same as above: you must deal with the conditions that are causing your misery before you depart. Whenever I offer this bit of wisdom in a group, someone always asks, "What if I'm just unhappy because I'm not cruising?" My answer is always the same. Contentment (a better word than "happiness") comes from introspection, not from external circumstances. The belief that your lack of happiness stems from the fact that you're not cruising (or not wealthy or not a rock/sports/movie star or not whatever) is a mask for a more profound spiritual need that you must discover before you can ever be at peace with yourself. Find it, and you'll find contentment whatever your external circumstances.

Cruising Is Not a Way to Drop Out of Society

Actually, it is much more common to find disgruntled escapees from industrialized societies among the community of expatriates that inhabit many of the most popular cruising stops, but once in a while you will find one on a cruising boat. The reason for leaving is always the same: "I just got sick to death of greed and corruption and commercialism." So saying, they move to a place like Panama where greed, corruption, and commercialism are so deeply entrenched they make up the very fabric of society. There are many expats who live in foreign countries for the excitement and adventure that it offers, but the malcontents, be they ashore or on a boat, tend to be a sad and bitter lot eaten alive by resentments and anger at demons they can only vaguely identify. If you find yourself with this sort of burden, deal with it first, then reward yourself with a world cruise.

Cruising Isn't a Way to Find Romance

It is surprising how many singlehanders we have met who are looking for a cruising companion. And although there are many wonderful and heartwarming stories of happy couples who met while cruising, the sad fact is that the odds are against its happening. Nothing can describe the joy of cruising with a like-minded companion, but you'll be a lot better off if you can find that companion before you leave home.

Cruising Isn't a Way to Fulfill a Hyperactive Ego

My definition of egotists are people who are motivated by the desire to convince others that they are as wonderful as they think they are. Fortunately, cruising egotists are not too common, but you will run into one from time to time, usually in a waterfront bar regaling the regulars with tales of their derring-do on the high seas, or at the chart table busily writing detailed postings on their Facebook page or on their personal websites. Of course, there's nothing wrong with telling tales in bars—it's an important part of the cruising heritage—and a regular post and photo on the Internet social networks is a good way to keep the folks back home informed of the progress of your trip, but cruising egotists overdo it and are oblivious to the fact that many in their audience have done the same thing, only better, and the rest don't really give a damn.

Count Your Blessings

This one is tough to verbalize, but I'll try. If you have a good job and work that you enjoy, if you have a family and friends to look after and who look after you in return, and if you enjoy good health and the prospects for a long life, yet you find conventional existence slightly boring, don't turn to cruising as a solace to your ennui.

The holding is always better in the next harbor, the water is always cleaner, the palm trees are always shadier, and the beaches are always whiter and sandier, but you must first learn to appreciate the harbor you are in, before moving on to the next one will have any meaning.

Boredom often comes with familiarity; it is synonymous with comfort. We who seek white sand beaches and palm trees swaying in gentle breezes can quickly become immune to the charms of the tropics. After three years of subtropical cruising, I longed for a frosty nose and the zing of my ski edges as they find an icy patch that signals I am about to be flung headlong into the nearest snowdrift.

Before you can cruise with any degree of success, you must develop the habit of appreciating the good things that are yours now and learn to make the best of them. The joys of the cruising life are obvious only to those who can compare them with the joys of shoreside life. If you attempt to compare the pleasures of one lifestyle with the horrors of the other, you will find yourself wallowing in a trough of self-delusion, and you may be shocked when, one day, you realize that the true joys of the cruising life and of the shoreside life are one and the same—they are the joys of life itself, and you don't need a boat to find them.

And the Nay Nays

There are lots of reasons not to go cruising, the very best of which is that you just don't want to. As hard as it is for cruisers and would-be cruisers to understand, a lot of folks don't have any interest in setting off in a sailboat. And except for the fairly frequent (and always unfortunate) situation in which a spouse is coerced into going along by a determined husband or wife, cruising is optional for all of us. However, there are a few good reasons not to go cruising even if you think it is what you really want to do. Here are some of the more important ones.

Cruising Can Be Dangerous

Hold on there! Didn't we just list the aura of risk that's inherent in ocean voyaging as satisfying a perverse human requirement for danger, and didn't we just say it is therefore a reason why some of us adopt the lifestyle? Yes, we did, and we're listing it here as an argument not to go for the same reason. Everyone has personal limits, and although some of us can handle a great deal of uncertainty in our lives—and some of us even thrive on it—others can't handle any at all. Cruising is a safe way to spend your life, but it's not as safe as staying home, and you are bound to encounter extraordinary circumstances that risk your life, health, and property. Unless you can accept the consequences of that risk, you probably shouldn't go cruising.

Cruising Is Expensive

Cruising doesn't require a lot of money, but it does require that you maintain yourself and your boat in presentable condition and that you not depend on the generosity of other cruisers for sustenance. It also requires a reasonable cash reserve for insurance against unforeseen expenses and emergencies. If you are used to a comparatively lavish lifestyle, as were Susan and I, and you intend to reduce what is popularly called your standard of living (as opposed to your standard of life), you must realize before you leave just what you are getting yourself into.

Cruising on a budget can mean many sacrifices in material wealth, comfort, and security. The amount of money you will need for an agreeable cruise depends on your lifestyle and expectations, and I will try to help you determine how much that is in the following chapters. But for now, know that if you don't want to make those necessary sacrifices in creature comforts and material goods, or if you don't have enough money to pay your own way, don't go cruising until you do. The large—and delightful—contingent of ragtag cruisers living from hand to mouth is unfortunately decreasing as the cost and popularity of cruising increases.

Cruising Requires Good Mental and Physical Health

The cruising life is a physical and strenuous life. Unless you enjoy robust good health, don't go. Even more important than your physical condition, though, is your emotional outlook. If you are a gloomy person by nature or if you are prone to neuroses and phobias that you can't control, you probably shouldn't go.

The observation that it's all about attitude is a bit of a cliché, but Tristan Jones famously kept going right to the end even after both legs were amputated. And in 1960, the pertinacious Sir Francis Chichester entered and won the first singlehanded transatlantic yacht race, in spite of being (wrongly as it turned out) diagnosed with terminal lung cancer. Although I never met either of these legendary voyagers, I have personally known as many successful cruisers who carried on in the face of physical, economic, and situational handicaps that would have stopped most of us cold. I have also known just as many would-be cruisers whose plans collapsed because of exaggerated fears or false concerns that most of us would ignore. The difference, as much of a cliché as it might be, is attitude: a good one is as much an asset as a 5-ton kitty, and a bad one is as restrictive as a jail cell.

Cruising Is a Team Effort

There is no way that the cruising life is as important as a sound relationship with your spouse or other life companion. If you are involved in a committed relationship with another person and that person doesn't share your enthusiasm for adventure on the high seas, don't go.

In our travels, Susan and I have met many cruisers who were going along for the ride just to keep their partner (usually, but not always, a husband) happy, with the inevitable result that the cruise isn't satisfactory for either. Recently we met and got to know a dynamic gentleman named Herb who had just purchased a magnificent motoryacht in which to pursue his lifelong ambitions of a retirement cruise. He proudly advised that he would be leaving for the Bahamas as soon as his wife joined him from their home in Cincinnati. I never got the full story, but when the wife finally arrived, she was visibly and vocally displeased (it was really quite embarrassing). After only a week, she and Herb vanished without a parting word, and the fancy yacht was soon sporting a for-sale sign. As sad as this story is, it is far from unusual, and it illustrates a major problem with cruising couples. I don't have any hard data to prove it, but I suspect that this lopsided enthusiasm for

the cruising life is second only to finances as a cause of failed cruises, and it is certainly a major cause in failed marriages among cruisers.

Before you buy a boat or waste a lot of valuable time on planning an ocean voyage, make sure that the ones you expect to accompany you share your enthusiasm. Then together you can plan your cruise as a search for things you both don't have but need. Adventure, independence, broad perspective, understanding, spirituality, compassion, and time shared with each other are a few good ones, but there are lots more. Those who cruise to escape are doomed to fail because troubles follow like shadows that won't be dimmed by the miles.

Sail toward your goal. Never sail away from anything.

4

The Decision to Go

Two Paths Up the Same Mountain

The decision to go cruising is a personal one that everyone approaches in a different way. I have known people who have dreamed of and prepared for the cruising life since they were teenagers. They acquire an encyclopedic knowledge of boats and designers, and they can quote statistic after statistic on gross weight-to-ballast ratios, sail areas, construction specs, and sailing performance. They spend their entire lives preparing to go cruising, and some of them actually make it. With others it is almost an impulse as simple as buying a new pair of shoes or stopping in to see Aunt Betsy because you happen to be in the neighborhood. For Susan, the decision was easy—she just decided that was what she wanted, and that was that. For me, the decision was a little harder. This is how it happened with us.

Mack Jellen and *Hägar the Horrible*

The four of us were sitting around the kitchen table one Sunday after church sharing the funnies from the *Boston Globe* as we ate a late lunch. I was halfway through *Hägar the Horrible* when Susan dropped a small bomb.

"I think we should buy a sailboat and sail around the world," she said without looking up from the gossip column in the magazine supplement.

I choked, and the resulting cough splattered coffee across the table and soaked the funny papers.

"You OK?" asked Susan.

"Yeah . . . choke . . . hack . . . yeah. I just thought I heard you say we should buy a new boat and sail around the world."

"You did. I've been thinking about it for a long time, and I've read a few books on ocean cruising. You know how we enjoy our summer cruises in *Duchess* [the antique 38-foot power-boat we owned at the time]. It would kill me to part with her, but we could trade her in on a sailboat and do some real cruising. I think it would be very educational for the children."

"It would be educational all right. They'd learn how to perish in the ocean."

"I think sailing around the world would be a great idea," said Sarah, who was 10.

"Yeah, me too," said Phillip who was 8. "But it would probably take all summer."

"Didn't you guys see *Jaws*?" I asked trying to inject an element of reason into the conversation. "There are some big creatures out there that just love to take large bites out of small children."

"Your father is just being negative," said Susan. "There is no reason we couldn't sail around the world if we wanted to. Lots of people do it."

"Lots of people don't do it," I countered. "They think about doing it, but most come to their senses and enroll in art classes or take up bridge or something sensible. The few that do it don't have kids in school, and they have tons of money they want to get rid of. You might have noticed that excessive wealth isn't one of our current problems."

"Mack Jellen did it," said Phillip. "We read about him in school, and I bet he had lots of kids."

"That's Magellan," said Susan, "and you're right. He was the first person to sail around the world."

"Yeah, but he got eaten by cannibals. How'd you like to be the main course at some cannibal luau?"

"Sir Francis Drake did it too, and he didn't get eaten," said Sarah. "He got knighted."

"What he got was lucky. They would have eaten him if they had been able to catch him."

"Look," said Susan, "this is a serious discussion. If you don't want to participate, at least don't make fun of what the rest of us have to say."

"Right," I said properly chastised. "There are lots of serious reasons why we can't sail around the world."

"OK, smarty, name one, just one, and don't say we'll get eaten by cannibals."

"I won't name just one. I'll name a bunch, and you can take your pick. For one thing, a cruising boat big enough for the four of us would cost more than this house. For another thing, we couldn't afford it even if we did have a boat. It cost a fortune just to sail around Cape Cod. Think what it would cost to sail around the world.

"And how about the kids' education? You can't snatch Sarah and Phillip out of school just like that." (Here I snapped my fingers in the air for dramatic emphasis while basking in the inner glow of my own glib logic.) "You don't want them to grow up illiterate any more than I do. I know . . . I know . . . you'll say we can educate them on the boat, but we're not teachers, and kids need other kids around. It's called 'socialization,' and without it they'll grow up to be socially deprived, reclusive misanthropes. They won't be able to get jobs, and they'll spend their lives as beachcombers or on welfare. Do you want our kids to be misanthropes?" I paused a moment to let the power of my argument sink in.

"Hurumph," said Susan.

"And what about me? It would take years to sail around the world. I'd be an old man when we got back. I'm too young to be an old man."

"Double hurumph. You're already an old fart."

"Tut . . . tut . . . no personal attacks, remember? This is a serious discussion." I decided to change the focus of my argument from the subjective to the objective. "What about all this stuff we own? We have a responsibility to our possessions, you know. Do you realize we own five TV sets, three VCRs, two cars, a state-of-the-art stereo, hundreds of CDs, two video game machines, two computers, and an electronic coffee pot with a built-in AM/FM radio? Who would take care of all that stuff if we sailed around the world?"

"Yard sale," said Susan without looking up.

"You mean you'd sell my Jimmy Buffett tapes?"

"Not all of them. You can take a few with you if you like."

"Gee, thanks, and what about the cat? I suppose you plan to sell poor Mr. Cat, or are you just going to mosey over to the neighbors and say, 'Would you mind watching poor Mr. Cat while we sail around the world? We'll only be gone about five years.'"

Susan looked up from her magazine, closed one eye and glared at me with the other like a sniper sighting a target. I moved on quickly, spoiling her aim and preserving the spotless luster of my argument.

"And what about our commitments? I promised Bernie Shultz that I'd fix the deck on his new boat by spring. You have your job—you just can't quit after 20 years, ya know—and Sarah has her music lessons. You wouldn't want her to walk out on Beethoven just when she's about to conquer 'The Moonlight Sonata,' would you?

"How many reasons is that? Six or seven? I've lost count, but there is one more biggie: it's irresponsible. Responsible people don't just chuck everything and sail off on a boat." I paused again, leaving Susan speechless in the wake of my verbal juggernaut before returning to *Hägar the Horrible*. I began cleaning the coffee from the last few frames.

After a lengthy and pregnant silence, Susan said, "Just as I thought."

"What's that?"

"Not one good reason."

I knew that further discussion was futile, and I retreated behind the privacy screen of the funny papers. The last frame showed poor *Hägar*, his eyes blackened and teeth missing, standing in the doorway, all shot full of arrows and spears with a large battle ax embedded in his helmet. "It's just been one of those days," he says to Helga.

"I know how ya feel, pal," I muttered. "I know how ya feel."

Dick and the Flying Meatloaf

By that Wednesday the subject of world cruising had largely been forgotten as I drove over to pick up Dick Welsh, a longtime friend with whom I had a standing weekly lunch date. We usually went to Dube's Bar and Grill in Swampscott where the meatloaf-and-mashed-potato special would curl your toes—if any of it ever got past your waistline. We talked of many things at these lunches: the moods of women, the philosophies of men, and the mysteries of life were all popular subjects, but mostly we talked about boats. Dick had been a sailor all his life and possessed an incredible storehouse of nautical know-how, and for years he had been planning to sell everything he owned and become a full-time cruiser when he retired. (Dick sailed into his last sunset two years before the second edition of this book was written but not before he sailed his 32-foot sloop, *Real Gusto*, through the Caribbean, down the east coast of South America, and back.)

Dube's is one of those dark, comfortable neighborhood bars that smell of stale grease, where the TV and air-conditioner are always turned up too high, which the regulars don't seem to change from the 8 a.m. opening to the 1 a.m. closing. Molly, the waitress, was waiting with our coffees as we took our seats at our regular booth in the back corner, and when she spilled a little on the table, it reminded me of the exchange with Susan the previous Sunday.

"Susan wants to sail around the world," I said, just to get the conversation off on a nautical note.

"Great," bellowed Dick slamming the table with the flat of his hand hard enough to make the cutlery jump an inch and slop more coffee into the saucers. "That's terrific news. When do you plan to leave?"

Dick was a large man without any fat anywhere. He was a linebacker for the Holy Cross football team, and he looked like he could still handle the job. He habitually expressed himself with sometimes startling physical gestures. He was also a bit hard of hearing, and it was necessary to speak loudly and clearly for him to understand what you were saying. Like many partially deaf people, he reciprocated by talking very loudly himself. The staff and regulars at Dube's were quite accustomed to being included in our most intimate and personal conversations.

The service at Dube's was amazingly fast, and I paused as Molly placed our orders on the table.

"I don't think Susan is serious, Dick. As soon as she sees how complicated it is, she'll forget full-time cruising. After all, people don't just quit their jobs in the prime of their lives and go sailing off around the world."

Wham! went the hand on the table, up jumped the cutlery—this time accompanied by my meatloaf and mashed potatoes. A quick stab with my fork speared the meatloaf in midair, but the mashed potatoes landed with a plop on top of my green beans.

"Of course they do," he shouted. "They do it all the time." Every head in the bar swiveled in our direction.

"Lemme ask you this," and he lowered his voice to that of a drill sergeant addressing first-day recruits. "Have you ever heard of any guy on his deathbed say, 'I should have worked harder?'"

"No . . . no, I haven't," I admitted.

"And what's the worst thing that could happen to you?"

"Well, my editor cuts out all my best jokes because she thinks they're silly. I really hate that."

"No, worse than that."

"Susan finds out about that crazy brunette over at the yacht club who keeps asking me to crew for her?"

"Nope, worse."

"What could be worse than that?"

"Only one thing."

"Well, I suppose I might get sick and die. That's the only thing worse than Susan finding out about that brunette."

"Right. And what's going to happen to you in the long run anyway?"

"You mean in the really big-time, long-term long run?"

"Right."

"Well, I suppose I'm gonna get sick and die."

"RIGHT." Bam went the hand, up jumped the silverware and my meatloaf. This time the mashed potatoes were a total loss. "So why in hell don't you just go sailing with Susan and the kids?"

"Yeah, man, go for it," said the drunk in front of the TV.

"You know, you really shouldn't let the children miss an opportunity like this," said Molly as she mopped up the remains of my mashed potatoes.

"Ya gotta do it," said Ralph, the bartender.

Traffic Jams and the Voice of Reason

Several months came and went without further mention of world cruising, although the Wednesday lunch with Dick always raised a few questions, and Susan seemed to be spending a lot of time reading boating books, of which the Marblehead Public Library and Dick seemed to have an inexhaustible supply. Then one cold winter day while returning from an errand in Boston, I found myself crawling along in the endless traffic jam that clogs the Callahan Tunnel and the road home. I glanced around at the expressions of rage and frustration on the faces in the cars near me and then let myself slip into a state of reverie and introspection that has for years been my first line of defense against traffic jams. I force my mind to empty itself of any idea of where I am going or when I must be there, let the car creep along with everyone else, and have a little chat with the voice in my head that always seems ready to discuss things profound and obscure. Some would say that I am talking to myself, but it is more than that. The Voice is real and can, at times, be a brilliant conversationalist. Our chats render me oblivious to the erratic meanderings of the cars in front and the mindless honking of the fools behind.

Occasionally I'll pop a Jimmy Buffett CD into the car stereo, and the Voice and I will sing along as best we can. At other times we explore together the higher pastures of thought where our minds can graze on the new grass of fresh ideas. But not this day.

"Today," announced the Voice with that irritating sanctimonious tone it sometimes uses when it wants to lecture me, "we will discuss our future. It seems that you have squandered most of the first 50 years of our life. Let's see if we can save some of the 20 or so that we may, with luck, have left to us." The squandering of years gone by was a favorite topic of the Voice and not one to which I readily conceded.

"Can't we talk about politics?" I pleaded.

"Twenty years is quite a lot of time if we start now," said the Voice, ignoring my attempt to change the subject. "As I see it, we have a choice between continuing to squander the time

allowed us, or we can spend that time in the pursuit of some useful goal. Which will it be?"

"Well, obviously, a useful goal is preferable."

"OK then," continued the Voice. "Let's consider what's available in the way of goals. You must agree that the ultimate goal, as our friend Dick pointed out just the other day, is death, correct?"

"Correct," I said. "However, we are talking about a goal for the remaining productive years of our life, and while death may be the ultimate end, it isn't a goal we should be working for, is it?"

"Of course not. Life, at best, is but a temporary inconvenience that passes quickly enough, and there is nothing to be gained by rushing it. No, our goal for the next 20 years must be life itself, but how best to spend that life? That's what we must deal with here."

This made me pause. The life that Susan and I had forged for ourselves was going as well as could be expected considering the numerous rocky places and two or three major washouts we had encountered in the matrimonial road. We had a comfortable home in a good neighborhood, and the children seemed to be thriving. Marblehead is a major suburb of Boston, but it retains a small-town quality that makes it an excellent place to raise kids.

"One thing's certain," I said. "Whatever goals we come up with must be group goals that include the entire family. In my misspent years, my goals were solitary ones selfishly motivated, and that is very hard on loved ones. So this time, let's make sure everyone is included from the start."

"Excellent," said the Voice. "Then it is resolved that our goals must be group goals. So what will these goals be?

"The goals of youth are nearly always selfish (as you well know) and revolve around an important job, a house in the 'burbs, two cars in the garage, and a TV with a bigger screen than the one on your neighbor's TV. In middle age, the usual goals are to achieve security in old age. The goals of old age are to somehow enjoy the fruits of previous goals realized.

"These are acquisitive, consumption-driven goals, and the problems with them are that, while they are highly stimulating to national and world economies, they can be hollow, superficial, and—once stripped of the mantle of materialism—meaningless. If you want proof that this is true, just look into the faces of your fellow traffic jammers. Their expressions of empty despair, which long ago transcended the quiet desperation of Thoreau, are a direct result of this mindless pursuit of valueless, materialistic goals."

The Voice can get unbearably preachy at times, but I glanced into my rearview mirror, and sure enough, the guy behind me in a snazzy new sedan didn't look any happier than the guy beside me in a battered old pickup.

"Which," continued the Voice, "leads us away from the objective goals of acquiring prestige and property to the subjective goals of acquiring knowledge and ideals. Thus the ultimate goal of life can't be security in old age, which is a ridiculous oxymoron, any more than it can be death. It must be the pursuit of truth and enlightenment. And since humankind is a social animal that cannot be happy alone, the search cannot be a solitary introspection but must be an external group effort of the family rather than the self."

"YES . . . YES," I shouted with excitement at the sudden realization that the Voice was right. "We will cast off the fetters of crass materialism and sally forth into the wilderness of worldliness in pursuit of truth, enlightenment, and the quality of life that has eluded humankind since Adam and Eve blew it in the Garden.

"But now we have the problem of how to best pursue this goal. It's one thing to say we're going off to seek the truth and enlightenment, but it's another thing to actually do it. I can see how we could easily get carried away with the whole Don Quixote, King Arthur-and-the-Holy-Grail routine of tilting at windmills and chasing dragons."

"Must avoid that, by all means," said the Voice. "The first thing we'll need is a compact and mobile environment in which the family group can function during the trip."

"Sounds good," I answered. "First we create a collective environment wherein the group can pursue truth and enlightenment—figuratively speaking, of course."

"Well, actually . . . er, no. Not figuratively speaking at all. Actually . . . oh dear, I don't quite know how to put this."

"You mean we need an actual physical environment?"

"Quite so," said the Voice.

"But that makes no sense. Why would we need to create a physical environment for the merely metaphorical pursuit of truth and enlightenment?"

"Merely metaphorical? You really don't understand do you? A metaphorical pursuit of our goals would never do at all. We must pursue our quarry in the real world like a hound after a hare. We must depart on a great journey of discovery and enlightenment and track that rabbit of reality into its den—if necessary, to the very ends of the earth."

"You're starting to sound as crazy as Susan and Dick. You want me to dislodge my family from our comfortable home and go stumbling around looking for ambiguous qualities like Diogenes looking for an honest man? That's out of the question. I won't do it."

"Very well, then, that brings us back to the first option."

"Which is?"

"Squander what's left as we have squandered that which has gone before. Just be aware that you will rapidly become one of them."

"One of whom?"

"Look around you."

I looked at the drivers in the cars all around me. The expressions of emotionless indifference and chronic boredom would do justice to actors trying out for a part in a George Romero zombie movie. "No," I cried. "You wouldn't let me become one of them, would you? Please, anything but that."

"It may be too late anyway," said the Voice. "Look at yourself sitting there babbling away at the top of your voice to no one at all. You've got that poor guy in the next car scared out of his wits."

"NO . . . NO, it can't be. I'm not one of them—I'm not. You win. I'll do it. I'll do anything. Just don't let me become one of them." As soon as I said it, I felt better, and the old euphoria flowed back over me like an ebbing wave returning to the beach.

"That's more like it," said the Voice.

"We'll need a van," I said, "a minivan big enough for the whole family. Or how about a camper—a Winnebago, maybe?"

"Won't do," said the Voice. "We must cross oceans to far continents and pursue our quarry where there are no roads."

"An airplane, then?"

"Too expensive."

"Camels—donkeys?"

"Too smelly."

"What then, for Pete's sake?"

"How about a boat?" said the Voice.

epiph·a·ny (i-'pif-ə-ne) n., pl. -nies. 3. a. A sudden manifestation of the essence or meaning of something

Thus, Susan and I came to realize that while our life together in Marblehead was a good life, it wasn't particularly fulfilling or exciting for either of us, and we were ready to look for something better. The decision to go cruising was first made by Susan, and for her the decision was an easy one that was made practically on impulse. For me the decision was more painful and required much introspection and uncertainty. My slightly dramatized dialogue with the Voice of reason actually took place, as did many other conversations just like it. It was months before I was comfortable with the idea of full-time cruising. It was a year or more before the combined arguments of the Voice and Susan, with a lot of help from Dick, finally convinced me that, yeah, we could do this thing . . . we could really do it. Then, we were on our way, and nothing was going to stop us. We had seen the light, and we were heading for it with the resolute tenacity of Hillary heading for the Himalayas. We had reached epiphany.

"Epiphany" is the word I use to describe the decision to go cruising wherein you discover that the cruising life is the life for you and you become a cruiser. It is a spiritual crossroads, and it is the point at which you stop merely dreaming about going cruising and start working toward doing it. When you reach epiphany, cruising ceases to be something you would like to do, and it becomes something you must do.

Epiphany can come upon you as slowly as springtime in New England or as suddenly as a well-thrown brick. You must not rush it with hasty and ill-formed decisions, but you must be ready for it when it comes. It is an emotional catharsis, a cleansing and purifying of the soul that will be among the most important turning points of your life. It's crucial that the decision to go cruising be based on a sound analysis of your ability to handle the cruising life and not on daydreams and fantasies. But it is just as crucial that the big decisions be made before the onset of epiphany because, after it arrives, reason and judgment are unalterably changed forever.

You don't have to leave at epiphany if you don't feel ready, and you can keep working if you need to save more money for the kitty, but you must understand that once epiphany arrives, you will become a different person. You will become disdainful of your previous existence, and the beckoning call of the distant horizon will become irresistible.

One-Sided Epiphany

Susan and I are lucky. Although our going cruising was Susan's idea, once I came around to her way of thinking, we were both equally committed to the cause, and our combined efforts and enthusiasm meant that we were able to get our lives in order and get under way in record time. Not all couples are this fortunate. In fact, I believe that a one-sided epiphany is the second most common cause of failed cruises—right behind finances (which we will discuss later).

We meet a lot of cruising couples where one half is a dedicated sailor and determined cruiser and the other half is going along to keep peace with the first half. Sometimes this works, but more often it doesn't, and what starts as mild discord deteriorates into bitter acrimony, which eventually destroys the cruise. Contrary to my preconceptions, in many cases of one-sided epiphanies, the driving force behind the cruise is the woman, and the man has gone along either thinking that he will eventually come to terms with the cruising life or that she will eventually see the light and agree to go home. (I don't know why this surprises me, since Susan was the driving force behind our voyaging life.)

Rarely, however, does a reluctant partner turn into a gung-ho cruiser. In one particularly sad case, a couple with whom we had become close friends canceled their plans to sail around the world, put their lovely traditional ketch on the market, and headed home to Canada when he found he simply couldn't deal with the idea of long ocean passages.

Some couples resolve a one-sided epiphany with compromise. We met Heddy and Steve on *Clearwater II* on the Intracoastal Waterway,

and our paths crossed several times before we made the big jump to Mexico. Steve is an ex-helicopter pilot who, for a good part of his adult life, had dreamed of going cruising when he retired. Heddy, however, loved gardening (a hobby you definitely can't pursue on a boat) and couldn't have cared less about boats and cruising. But they did care about each other, so they agreed that they would buy a boat and cruise for a year or two, after which they would move ashore to a piece of waterfront property they owned. There he could have his boat and she could garden to her heart's content, and they could both live to ripe old age in contentment and harmony. Let's hope so anyway.

In the shipyard in Ipswich, Massachusetts, I got to know another couple who cruised by compromise. They both loved to travel, but his life revolved around cruising sailboats (he owned a lovely Dutch-built steel sloop), while she preferred to travel in a more conventional manner—you know, airplanes and such. Over the years, they had worked out a system: he sailed singlehanded to a new and exotic destination, and she flew to the same destination, checked into the best hotel in town, and was waiting on the dock when he pulled in. They had been doing this for years, and they really couldn't imagine any better way to live.

What should you do if the specter of one-sided epiphany raises its ugly head in your cruising plans? First, remember that epiphany arrives, if it arrives at all, for different reasons and at different times for different people—as it did for Susan and me. Now I can't think of living any other way, and we plan to cruise at least five more years before we hang up our Topsiders and retire to that little cottage in New Zealand. Will something like this happen in your case? Well, to employ a bit of hackneyed phraseology that is always appropriate: Who knows? Only time will tell, so hang in there, and don't give up the ship.

Don't Commit Yourself Until You Have to Commit Yourself

Remember in Chapter 1 when we talked about the large number of would-be cruisers who change their minds and decide not to go? It is critical that you realize early on that you too might be among that majority of people (as high as 99 percent by some estimates) who decide they might be happier if they stayed home. The arrival of epiphany can cause a lot of personal excitement, and you will want to announce your plans to the world. If you do, you will learn the hard way that most of the world doesn't care, and the rest will think you're nuts.

Susan and I were astonished at the yawns we received from boat brokers when we explained that we were looking for a boat in which to take our family on a world cruise. We quickly learned that people involved in the boating and cruising industry (especially boat brokers and salespeople) had encountered so many unfulfilled plans about cruising around the world that most simply didn't believe us. We were unceremoniously relegated to that vast body of tire kickers who drive brokers crazy by looking at boats they have no intention of ever buying, so we simply stopped mentioning our plans. After a while we told everyone who would listen that we were looking for a sturdy vessel capable of extended offshore cruising, and we left it at that—a tactic that greatly extended the attention span of the brokers.

Talking about your plans with friends and casual acquaintances may be a way of gaining the courage to make a major change in your life, but it's the wrong way to do it. The courage to make the change must come from within, not from outside pressures of those who are expecting you to leave. You should not announce your decision to go cruising to any but those who

Fisher 34'

When we stopped telling boat brokers about our plans to sail around the word and just told them we were looking for a sturdy boat big enough for four people and capable of extended offshore passages, they suddenly began to take us seriously. The boat shown is a Fisher 34, a smaller version of Vicarious.

will be involved and your family. If you or your companion decide not to go, you want to make it as easy as possible to back out right up to the last minute. The planning process should be a private celebration of joy to be shared only with those with whom you share your life.

The decision to sail must be a joint decision made by all who are involved. The trick is to understand from the start just what cruising is and to get your personal life sorted out before you commit yourself.

5

Cruising Without a Boat: Meet the Cruising Kitty

Getting Gone

Having been the father of a teenage son who was addicted to the damn things, I am not particularly fond of video games, especially the ultraviolent ones that require no skills to operate and are pointless in their execution—you know, the popular ones. To me video games (and their recent version computer games) are in the same category as jet skis and energy drinks in that they serve no useful purpose other than the enrichment of a bunch of greedy people whom I don't even know and probably wouldn't like very much if I did. There is, however, one exception to my wholesale antipathy for electromagnetic entertainment: the spunky little guy with a mustache in the game called *Super Mario Brothers* (in any of its numerous manifestations). *Super Mario Brothers* is, in fact, the most popular video game ever; it has generated millions of dollars in sales for Nintendo, and it is still selling well more than 25 years after it was first introduced.

I particularly like this game because the hero, Mario, is a cruiser in every sense of the word. He spends his time bouncing happily through life visiting strange and diverse lands looking for adventure and excitement. He isn't out to cause any trouble or to inflict harm on anyone. He just wants to rescue the princess (I suspect he has his reasons), but nonetheless, he encounters the most amazing series of misfortunes. He is knocked down by strange creatures that look like ducks with turtle shells; he is blown up by mean little kids called "goombas"; he falls off cliffs with startling frequency; some ugly green guys throw hammers at him from a balloon passing overhead; he is forced to swim through an underwater labyrinth where he is pursued by sharks, electric eels, and poisonous fish; he is blasted by cannonballs and dumped into lava pits; and he is stomped on by a giant dog named Bowser. In short, saying that Mario is accident-prone is like saying that the Red Sox fade in the home stretch.

You would think that in the face of all this misfortune, Mario would give it up and go home, but no. Mario is a true cruiser; adversity just makes him tougher. He learns to jump over the turtle ducks and to stomp on the mean little kids (they had it coming, folks). He dodges the cannonballs, outswims the sharks, leaps over the lava pits, and what he does to that dog gives new meaning to the word "retribution." But the important thing isn't that Mario learns to handle tribulation, but how he learns it.

Through all his troubles, Mario never once loses his good nature, his cool, or his sense of humor, nor does he complain that life isn't giving him a fair shake—not even once. When he gets kicked off a cliff, he bounces back with a big smile and the determination to avoid that particular cliff in the future; when he gets squashed by giant stone blocks 20 or 30 times in a row, he learns to develop his timing so he can run under them the next time; and when the dog stomps him into a mud hole and kicks him back to the beginning of the game, he runs the entire gauntlet all over again, and then he does it again and again until he finally wears the hostile hound to a nub.

Mario gets by with persistence, determination, and a lot of help from his friends: Yoshi, the dinosaur; Toad, the mushroom; and Luigi, his brother. All are fellow cruisers, and they are there to help out when he needs it the most. He learns by his mistakes, and with everything he learns, he becomes smarter and more powerful. Eventually he triumphs and rescues the princess. Together they go on to develop even bigger and better video games that further enrich the companies that sell them and further deplete the mental resources of the world's youth.

So what can you and I—normal folks who don't have to worry about mischievous goombas and homicidal turtle ducks but who would like to change our lives just enough to go cruising—learn from this hyperactive little Italian overachiever? Lots of things. We can learn that keeping our goal, be it rescuing a princess or buying a sailboat, foremost in our mind at all times will calm the seas and flatten the hills more than any other thing we can do. We can learn that persistence in the face of adversity is critical to success and that failure is as much a part of success as codfish is a part of my Aunt Minnie's chowder.

Failure: The Critical Element

It sounds crazy to say that you have to fail to succeed, but this simple statement is one of life's truisms. If you can get a grip on this one concept more than any other in this book, you've just about got it made. Our hero, Mario, succeeds in rescuing the princess because he prevails over an immeasurable multitude of failures without letting them get him down. He might try a hundred times to make it over that lava pit only to make it across on the 101st try. Lava-pit leaping is something that probably none of us will be much good at on our first few tries, but if we let our initial failures deter us, we might as well let the princess rot in the dungeon and go home and watch *Brady Bunch* reruns. But Mario never gets discouraged. He doesn't say, "Aw shucks, that's 99 times I've been knocked into the fire. I'll never make it across this lava pit." Hell no, he doesn't. With a "Tallyho Geronimo," he flings himself at the pit once again. When he blows it yet again, he says, "Hey, this is great. That's one more failure closer to success," and he has yet another go at it.

And so it is with your quest for the cruising life. Once you decide that you are going to do it, you must consider each obstacle you encounter as an opportunity to advance toward your goal. If you try to stop smoking and don't make it the first time, try again. If you are on the way to paying off your credit card debt and freak out on a new stereo, don't let it get you down. Just keep making those payments, and resolve to never let it happen again. Success and failure are like hot and cold. Both success and cold (called "absolute zero" by scientists) are the immeasurable and mostly unachievable ideals; heat and failure are the tangible and measurable stepping-stones to our goals. When the weather is bad, we talk about how cold it is, but a thermometer measures only heat. In just the same way, we measure the success of people by the failures they have overcome.

You're on Your Way

So now it's settled. You are going to become a cruiser. You have considered all the ramifications of a major change in your life, and you realize that you must proceed with the care of a bomb-disposal squad and the determination of a thoroughbred on the home stretch. You are well aware that the cruising life on a budget is a difficult life fraught with toil, disappointments, and hardships, but you are resolved to face them. You have reordered your priorities so that you can live the cruising life right now, even though you don't have a boat yet. You are living your life based on needs rather than wants—you are living the free-range life of a cruiser.

The Free-Range Life

Have you noticed that free-range chickens and free-range eggs are all the rage these days?

It's interesting how things come around—when I was a kid, that's all we had. We didn't call them "free-range," of course. We just called them "chickens" and "eggs." The idea of buying either in a store would have seemed odd when we had a backyard full of the things. Today the distinction is made between the "new" free-range birds that are presumably allowed some degree of freedom and space to scratch and peck for food, the way chickens have been doing since the dawn of time, and the "normal" chickens that are raised in cages that are only slightly larger than the chickens. The chickens that we had when I was a kid had the freedom to go where they pleased, do what they pleased, and eat what they pleased. If they wanted to fly off into oblivion, as more than a few did, that was fine. If they wanted to go and get eaten by a fox or a bobcat or get themselves run over by the school bus, that was OK too. Most folks in our neighborhood considered losing a few chickens now and then far easier than trying to keep them in a coop.

The majority of the chickens, however, chose to stay in the backyard where they were provided with a first-rate chicken house with nesting boxes and wire on the windows to discourage all but the most persistent raccoons and skunks. In return for hanging around, they were also given a measure of grain every morning and evening, over which each chicken fought with every other chicken in the flock for its share. My first lesson in Darwinian survival came when I realized that the smaller and weaker chickens were the ones that ended up in the stewpot first just because they were the easiest for an eight-year-old boy to catch.

Cruisers are like free-range chickens in a lot of ways. No, we don't have to fight each other over scraps of food, but we have turned our backs on the chicken factory where we were warm and comfortable and fed regularly. We learned to become more confident in our own abilities and to rely on and trust our friends

The cruising life is a free-range, off-the-grid alternative to the stress and pressure of a conventional shoreside life. But you can't live a truly free life without funds supplied by a healthy kitty. Ironically, the health of a kitty depends less on its size than on the demands that you make of it.

and family more than we did before we left on our cruise. If the price we pay for an increase in freedom is a chance encounter with a stoat or a skunk, so be it.

The Cruising Kitty

OK, so now you've got everything you require to go cruising except what? If you are anything like the rest of us, you have everything you need except money—a cruising kitty. Let's take a close look at the care and feeding of this, one of nature's most interesting creatures.

The cruising kitty is a quantity of money that you will have in a handy place (in a bank account, invested in mutual funds, or hidden in the chain locker). You will use it to pay the day-to-day expenses of your cruise. Your kitty is much more than a savings account or an investment program. It is the very essence of your ability to go cruising rather than report to work every day.

Simply stated, the kitty is a tool that you will use while you are cruising—a tool made out of money you have accumulated by working as hard as you can while spending as little as possible. While you are cruising, your kitty will be working; ideally, it will pay all your normal expenses through its interest and dividends earned plus value added through capital growth. In the early nineties, when we departed Marblehead on our world cruise, we were able to invest a rather modest portfolio and get a 10 percent average return on a careful selection of common stocks, enough to get us to New Zealand in style and comfort. The collapse of the dot-com bubble brought that era to a sudden halt, and our portfolio lost half its value almost overnight. Our suddenly emaciated kitty slowly clawed its way back to cruiserly solvency only to be chopped down again when the real estate market collapsed in 2007.

Now in the real world (the *new* real world, not the *old* one) the *Vicarious* kitty is still a little thin in the belly with the ribs still showing, but it is functional, and we are cruising again with only a slightly tighter belt.

Your kitty should actually be a two-part affair (if the allegorical reference to a two-part kitty is anatomically troublesome, think if it as two separate kitties). You need one part of your kitty readily available through cash or through a money machine for your day-to-day expenses, and you need to maintain a large and accessible reserve for emergencies and for nonemergency contingencies and unusual expenses such as canal fees, haulouts, or the bureaucratic requirement that you post a bond equal to the price of a return airline ticket for each member of the crew when you enter French Polynesia.

All cruisers have kitties; you can't cruise without one. But just as no two cruisers are alike, their kitties aren't either. There are, however, enough similarities to permit some broad generalities. In the rest of this chapter I will explain the different types of kitties and how to fatten them up. You don't need to be rich to cruise, but you do need to be in control of your finances. The careful management of your kitty is the way to do it.

Of all the hundreds of things you must do before you can take off on your dream cruise, this one item, building your kitty, can take longer than all the others combined. Your kitty is the second most important factor in the cruising equation—after you and your crew. Without retirement income or a rich uncle who is willing to pay your expenses to get you out of his hair, you will need to spend a major portion of the planning stage for your cruise accumulating and organizing your kitty.

RICHARD AND THE WARM CERVEZAS

Of all the places we stopped to visit on the first leg of our cruise, the tiny Mexican village of Xcalac is one of my favorites. There was no electricity there, when we last visited over 15 years ago, even though there was a huge complex of wind-driven turbines not far away. The only telephone in town hadn't produced a dial tone in more than two months. There were no paved roads for 20 miles in any direction, and there were no windows in the simple board-and-tin houses—only shutters—and very few doors, with just curtains hanging in the entrances. The people were friendly and open, as people are in Mexico, with actions and temperaments that northerners might mistake for laziness until they have been there long enough to learn that

the airless heat of a 90-degree summer day is considered a cold snap. Midday physical activity is unwise in Xcalac.

We had been in Xcalac for several hours, and after completing the check-in conducted by the local military, we were looking for a round of ice-cold drinks to quench our growing thirst. We wandered down the main street, which was also the only street, when I noticed a man and a woman with three children, obviously a family, lounging in the shade of their porch. The man sat in a chair leaning back against the house with his hat pulled down over his eyes, while the woman and the children, two small boys and a pretty teenage girl, sat on the floor. The man never moved, but the woman fanned herself with a palm leaf *(continued next page)*

RICHARD AND THE WARM CERVEZAS *CONTINUED*

while the girl swished her skirt back and forth in a futile attempt to stimulate a breeze.

"*Buscando por una restaurante, por favor,*" I said to the porch, self-conscious of my bad Spanish and trying to roll my *R*s without hesitating between words.

The woman glanced at the man and replied that this was a restaurant and wouldn't we please have a seat. So saying, she shooed the kids into the house and gestured to the floor of the porch.

"*¿Que gustas?*" she asked once we were settled.

"*Queramos dos cervesas y dos cokas muy frías, por favor.*"

She seemed to think the "*muy frías*" part was pretty funny, but she disappeared into the house, and there ensued a rapid conversation with the girl that was way past my ability to understand. Moments later the woman returned, and I noticed the girl running in back of the row of houses toward the only store in town. Five minutes later the girl appeared carrying a tray with two warm cokes and two even warmer beers. We spent a pleasant half hour or so sitting in the shade of the porch, sipping our drinks, and chatting with the woman in our limited Spanish. When it came time to leave, I asked how much we owed. "*Nada, señor,*" she answered. "*Es un regalo*" (a gift). We departed with a very good feeling about Xcalac and life in general. I couldn't help but think that this was what cruising was all about.

We stayed in Xcalac for two or three days. On one occasion we joined Richard, a clean-cut young man from Florida who was singlehanding his small sloop around the Caribbean, for dinner at the only real restaurant in town, a tin shack affair built on poles with a sand floor. When the bill came, after a lovely meal of grilled fish and fresh fruit, we paid for our share with pesos, and Richard paid for his from a large wad of American one-dollar bills. This made the proprietor very happy, and it led us into a discussion of handling money while cruising.

"If you need some pesos, I can sell you some," I offered, trying to be helpful.

"No thanks," he answered. "Never use 'em. Just keep American ones handy, and I never need anything else."

"You mean you never exchange money?" I asked. Money changing and exchange rates are major headaches for cruisers. Exchanging American dollars for a foreign currency is easy, but it can be expensive. In many countries, the best rates are obtained on the street where clip artists and con men are common. Banks often charge a premium, but they are usually honest about it, and you will know where to find them tomorrow. It's frequently impossible to exchange foreign currency for U.S. dollars when you leave a country, and getting stuck with a pile of Honduran limpera or Colombian pesos can be costly.

"Nope, I've never been anywhere that they wouldn't take my ones, so why bother?"

"Wouldn't fives and tens and twenties be more convenient?"

"No way. When you give people a larger bill, they often don't have enough change. When they do, they insist on giving it to you in local currency, and you can get stuck with it. When you use ones, you get just enough change to use for tips and to pay the kids for watching your dinghy."

"Well, how much do you carry at one time?"

"Quite a bit actually. I usually carry enough for a couple of months. Then I get my mom to send me more from my savings account. I keep it hidden in the chain locker where no thief will ever find it."

The Size of the Kitty

The size of your kitty is a personal matter determined by the type of cruise you are planning, your personal needs, and your ability to live an economical life. A fortunate few can live and cruise on just the interest from their kitties, but without a very fat kitty, this is increasingly hard to do in the current uncertain economic climate. Some people don't feel comfortable without a huge bank balance on which to draw, and they stop to replenish the kitty when the balance reaches a level that a lot of us would be happy leaving home with. Many others cruise until the kitty is so emaciated it is practically dead before they stop to revive it. It is all a matter of preference, tolerance, and nature, and you'll have to determine your own style before you go. Regardless of your circumstances, however, I know of no case in which a small kitty is superior to a large kitty.

On *Vicarious* we try to keep our working kitty at around $35,000, which is our budget for one year of cruising. This may sound like a lot, but it must cover all the expenses (food, clothing, education, travel, healthcare, and various favorite frivolities) for two elderly cruisers who live frugally but not with compulsive austerity. This also covers our ever increasing medical expenses and all the operating expenses for a large and rapacious boat. In truth, our kitty is probably only average. Most cruisers we meet who are willing to discuss their finances seem to think that $20,000 to $25,000 per person per year is about right. We've met other cruisers to whom this amount of money is an unimaginable sum, and once their kitty has a few thousand dollars in it, they are off and cruising for as long as it takes for the bank balance to bottom out. One delightful couple cruising with their two children on a homebuilt trimaran were on a three-year cruise with a total budget of $30,000, or $2,500 per person per year. We met them in Samoa where they were eating a lot of peanut butter and banana sandwiches (one of the healthiest meals known to man, as well as one of the cheapest), and they seemed to be getting along just fine.

Of course, the cruising kitty is much more than a quantity of money in a bank account or a wad of bills in the chain locker—it is a system of earning and saving and spending that cruisers approach a little differently than anyone else does.

Three Types of Cruising Kitties

There are two basic types of cruising kitties, plus a third type that combines the first two. They are somewhat analogous to the types of cruisers outlined in Chapter 2, but there are enough differences to warrant going through the list one at a time.

The Ideal Kitty

The ideal cruising kitty is large enough to be self-sustaining. That is, it pays enough through interest and dividends to cover all cruising expenses. It is the nirvana of kitty-land and the type all of us would like to have. Unfortunately, in today's economy, investment income from any kitty smaller than a million dollars is unlikely to earn enough to pay your cruising expenses unless you have an outside source of income (social security, royalties, or retirement income), and the interest on even a million kept in any standard investment isn't going to pay for a lavish cruise.

A kitty of this magnitude is usually possible only for older people who start with substantial savings or, of course, lottery winners and fortune inheritors. The envious rest of us will either have to spend a major part of our lives accumulating such a massive kitty, or we will have to learn to make do with something less. Let's proceed under the assumption that you, like most cruisers, will opt for the latter and leave the former with the folks back in the office.

The Work-as-You-Go Kitty

The work-as-you-go cruising kitty contains enough money to pay the cruising expenses of the crew for a specific period of time, usually one year. Then, the crew goes to work for however long it takes to replenish the kitty. The work-as-you-go approach works best for younger people with skills that are in high demand, and no children, but this isn't always the case. Susan and I have met many working cruisers with children and many others who aren't engineers or computer programmers.

Some cruisers have found that their earning potential while cruising is limited by their lack of skills and by the dearth of well-paying jobs in the most attractive cruising areas. But instead of putting the boat in storage so they can fly home to build up the kitty, as do many commuter cruisers, these hardy folks learn to live within their meager incomes and make do. And some of them make do very well indeed. I've met a lot of cruisers living on low-paying shore jobs, their income being derived from their providing services to other cruisers, or by luck and pluck, or by some combination of all these elements.

Although it's common practice to ignore this advice, the work-as-you-go kitty ought not be depleted below a level that won't cover emergencies and periods when work is hard to find. And because cruising work is nearly always less lucrative than conventional work at home, this is only possible by strictly controlling your expenses.

This approach presents a few problems, however. Working in the countries that are the favorite haunts of the cruising community is becoming more difficult than it once was. Many of these countries are enacting laws or enforcing old laws that are designed to keep jobs for their own citizenry. Most of the countries in the European Union and Australasia have strict laws regarding jobs for foreign nationals, and trying to circumvent them can quickly get you an invitation to leave and even a stiff fine. In other places, the jobs that are available are unattractive and pay poorly. New Zealand and Australia, for example, sometimes wave work permit requirements for foreigners who want to earn some cash picking fruit and other crops, and (at the time this was written) they may look the other way when a cruiser with a visitor's visa finds work as a waiter, cook, or bus person, especially in popular tourist areas where seasonal workers for menial jobs are hard to find.

In other popular cruising grounds, especially in developing countries, it is often possible for a skilled person to stay busy working under the table for other cruisers. Anyone skilled in diesel mechanics, electronics repair, canvas and sail repair, tutoring, and most other services required by cruisers are in demand wherever cruisers congregate. Some of the more oddball services being offered to cruisers by cruisers include haircutting (bound to raise a complaint from the local hairdresser if you're caught), aromatherapy, marriage counseling, dentistry, palmistry and horoscope analysis, and typing and manuscript editing. One enterprising lad in the Rio Dulce promised to cure all of your ills by rubbing the right spots on your feet for a small fee. (Susan tried a session and loved it.)

Unfortunately, this sort of clandestine work is technically illegal in most countries even if the officials sometimes look the other way if the local businesses and residents aren't complaining. You do such work at your own peril, however, because local officials can change their minds very quickly and start to enforce long-ignored laws with harsh penalties.

If you think it's worth taking a chance, be sure to get a feel for the current local conditions and the prevailing attitude of the officials before you hang out your shingle. Don't ever assume that the favorable conditions of a year ago are still valid or that the friendly port captain who let you set up your law practice for a $10 bribe is still in charge. Broadcasting or advertising your business or service on the local cruisers' net is the same as sending a notice to the port captain's office, so it is best to avoid any form of public announcement. The best approach is to ask other cruisers about who is getting away with what and then wait, watch, and draw your own conclusions.

There are several American territories where U.S. citizens can work legally, including American Samoa, the U.S. Virgin Islands, and Puerto Rico. In each of these places, though, the wages for most jobs—even those for highly skilled professionals—are very low. We met several cruisers in Pago Pago working as teaching aides for under $10 an hour and carpenters working in Charlotte Amalie for a mere $8 an hour—much less than half of what these skills would normally fetch back home.

For most cruisers, local work in foreign countries is appropriate for short-term jobs to augment the cruising kitty, but it's seldom enough to revitalize it. Most American cruisers who must periodically work to replenish the kitty either sail to the closest U.S. port or, more often, leave their boats in secure storage and fly home to work.

The Combination Kitty

Many cruisers combine the ideal and the work-as-you-go kitties. They keep the ideal, or self-sustaining kitty, in some type of secure investments where it earns a regular return. These investments might be stocks and bonds, mutual funds, income-producing real estate, or ideally, a diversified portfolio combining several of these vehicles. This kitty is left alone to do its thing and accumulate dividends, and it is called upon only when the cruisers need ready cash to meet some emergency or when a large fixed expense, such as a periodic refit, comes due.

Meanwhile, the work-as-you-go kitty pays for day-to-day expenses and extravagances such as dining out and tourist travel. This kitty is large and fat at the start of the cruise, but it is slowly depleted as the cruise progresses. It is kept in a savings account or in a money market fund where it earns some interest but is readily accessible. The combined kitty is by far the most popular type of cruising kitty because it can be accumulated in a reasonable length of time.

The *Vicarious* kitty is just such a combination kitty. The income from the self-sustaining part goes straight into our working kitty where it is supplemented by other income (a small pension Susan gets from her 20 years of work, royalties, and odd-job income that I pick up doing electrical work and boat repairs for other cruisers), and it is the working kitty that we use to pay all of our normal day-to-day expenses. This system has worked well for us for 20 years, and it is similar to the systems used by many other full-time cruisers we meet.

The Chain-Locker Kitty

Richard, the young cruiser with the one-dollar bills we met in Mexico, had a good system, and although I can't recommend it as an answer for most of us (especially in the Caribbean where thievery is endemic), it worked for him. A lot of cruisers, however, do keep some U.S. dollars secreted about their boats somewhere, usually in some obscure hidey-hole (the chain locker is far too obvious) or, even better, in several hidey-holes. Susan and I regard these dollars as our emergency reserve, and we never admit to its presence or discuss it in any way with anyone

Portland "Pudgy"

The best way to keep your kitty healthy is to minimize your needs. Once you learn the trick of living with a minimum of possessions and luxuries, you will find that even a small kitty can be kept purring with vitality simply because you have reduced your demands on it. If you have a small boat with a shallow draft, you can anchor in shallow water close to shore and the dinghy dock, and you will have no need for a large dinghy with a powerful outboard. Rowing is wonderful exercise, and it is fun, and with this one deviation from the standard model of the cruising life, you can save thousands of dollars. By adopting the simple life, you can be living the cruising life before those who need more can even think of leaving the working life.

who is not a member of our crew. We don't even declare it to the customs inspectors when we enter a country. This is illegal, of course, but hey, so is the extra measure of gin in the bottle in the bilge with the washed-off label.

On *Vicarious* the amount of money in the hidey-hole varies between a couple of hundred dollars to a maximum of a thousand or so, depending on where we are and what we anticipate our needs for cash to be. The amount of gin in the bottle in the bilge with the washed-off label varies with the climate and captain's temperament.

My grandpappy used to tell me, "It ain't whatcha got but whatcha do with it that makes the difference," and nowhere is this more true than in the cruising life. Base the size of your kitty on what you need, not on what others have or what you want.

6

The Cruising Kitty: How to Get One

When we speak of the cruising kitty, we aren't talking about the small hairy carnivore that many cruisers keep aboard for wholly unknown or irrational reasons (*Vicarious* has Nelson, the ship's dog, aboard, which is even more irrational—see "Crewing for Your Pets" in Chapter 11). The cruising kitty doesn't skulk around with an arrogant sneer on its furry face, rip the upholstery to shreds when you aren't looking, or fall overboard in the middle of the night while trying to catch a flying fish. It rests quietly in some obscure corner of some obscure financial institution in some distant place you probably don't even know about. Here it happily gathers assets and grows fat on your efforts and from (we hope) the progress of the world's economy toward prosperity.

The cruising kitty accumulates bulk and grows fat, but it isn't lazy. Indeed, it is one of the hardest working members of your crew and one you can't really do without. It carefully doles out a steady stream of cash for all your daily needs, but more important, it is always ready to spring into action at the first sign of a financial emergency. When a crew member becomes ill, the boat needs critical work, or there is a family emergency back home, it's the cruising kitty to the rescue, the good guys win again, and the world is saved once more from the evil clutches of the anti-cruising villains that plague us all.

The cruising kitty is the most important element of the cruising life. Without one, you can't go cruising, and the size and vitality of your kitty will have a larger impact on the success of your cruise and the extent to which you enjoy your new lifestyle than any other single ingredient. If you are an average aspiring cruiser, at least four-and-a-half years of the five-year period that we have somewhat arbitrarily chosen as a reasonable time for achieving the cruising life will be devoted to fattening and grooming your kitty. In this chapter, we will explore a few of the best ways for you to get your kitty purring with a minimum of effort.

Start Saving Now

If you are serious about cruising, or even if you only think you might be serious about it someday, start feeding your kitty without delay. This is much more important than any other aspect of the planning process, and it is imperative that you do it now. Start by establishing a savings goal as a percentage of your income. Your target should be to allocate at least 25 percent of your take-home pay to your cruising kitty. More is better, much more is much better. If you can't start at this figure, do the best that you can. Putting away 10, or even 5, percent will get you started, but increase it as you're able until you reach 25 percent or better.

How? The most obvious way to fatten your kitty is to work hard and earn a lot of money, but there is another, far more important—and in many ways more difficult—step you must take first. It is critical that you stop spending the money that you are already making, no matter how much money that is, on frivolous and capricious items and services that do nothing to advance you toward your goal. This is the biggest and most important step to the cruising life, and until you take it, you won't be going cruising. Going away in a boat means stopping spending like a shoresider. It means becoming frugal and thrifty like a cruiser.

Minimalism: The Key to the Cruising Life

The term "minimalism" was first used to describe an artistic style of painting that eliminated all the distracting and unnecessary elements while retaining the beauty of the central idea. The early traditional forms of Japanese and Chinese art typify minimalism as do several modern schools. It is a simple and basic style in which the artist uses just enough paint and the minimum number of brushstrokes to convey his or her vision without denigrating or compromising the final image. Our simple and basic approach to the cruising lifestyle is the perfect analogy to minimalism, wherein one acquires and uses only what one needs to live in reasonable comfort. There is no need to wait until you are ready to leave on a cruise to adopt minimalism; you can start living that lifestyle now.

The minimalist life is an economical life so there will be extra money for your kitty. It's a rewarding life, but it requires some practice. In the following few paragraphs I'll discuss how you can achieve minimalism—and even if you decide not to go cruising, you will find it to be a fulfilling way to live.

Dropping Out of the Consumer Society

Most of us have become used to life in a society where we are judged by the kind of car we drive, the neighborhood we live in, the degrees our kids are accumulating, and the thickness of our pay envelope.

Consumerism has a few dramatically negative aspects, of course, and any society dedicated solely to the consumption of its resources will, like a band of overly enthusiastic cannibals, eventually consume itself, but in spite of two major worldwide financial disasters in the last 15 years, it is still working. From tiny family-run businesses in the jungles of Brazil to huge factories in China, the world is focusing on cranking out enormous quantities of products that feed the voracious appetite of the consumer. The jobs thus generated are elevating the living standards of millions of previously poor workers around the world, and their prosperity is further fueling the demand for products. It is an upward spiraling whirlwind of ever-increasing demand, production, and consumption, and its end is not in sight. It's a wonderful system, indeed, but it isn't for us. We're going to drop out of the consumer society.

Dropping out doesn't mean we can't enjoy the fruits of consumerism. In fact, by taking advantage of the benefits that accrue to us by our inevitable proximity to shopping malls and car dealerships while refusing to participate in the actual process of commercialism, we can garner huge rewards that can elevate our lifestyle to a lofty altitude far above that of a typical high-flying consumer. We need to develop the will to live at a subsistence level in an environment where we are surrounded by abundance and luxury. We need to ignore the temptations of an overindulgent society, to do without things that don't directly affect our welfare and our survival. We need to do this for one reason only: to save the money we need to fatten our kitty just enough so we can buy a boat and go cruising.

Every year, the citizens of developed countries buy billions of dollars' worth of goods and services that they don't need, mostly on credit. As people fight to move up the socio-economic ladder by acquiring better stuff, they are delighted to sell the old stuff, particularly ego possessions like cars and boats, for a fraction of their original cost. I know several racing skippers who buy a new set of sails every year because the old ones get "stretched." True, these sails aren't any good for cruising (most racing sails are now Kevlar or other fabrics that don't

stand up well to the demands of cruising), but when they are sold, it starts a chain reaction that results in a bargain somewhere down the line on sails suitable for cruising.

The same principle applies to cars. We don't want to be the second owner of a luxury car—still too expensive—but the sale of that car will cause a chain reaction, and sooner or later we will be able to pick up a 10-year-old Toyota or Subaru in great shape for a few thousand dollars. And when we are ready to sell it, we will recoup most of what we spent on it.

For we who would be cruisers, the path is clear. As we decline to participate in consumerism while practicing minimalism and maintaining our income until we are actually ready to leave, we will be able to amass a substantial excess in the bank account that we can use to reduce debt and fatten the cruising kitty.

Consumerism, Conformity, and the Wealthy Cruiser

If you are a wealthy person, fear not. You don't have to forsake consumerism to go cruising, for consumerism—and materialism—is alive and well in the cruising community. Cruisers are, after all, human beings, and just like everyone else, we lust for the bigger and better. The problem develops when this natural desire for improvement overrides our judgment on practicality and available resources. There are literally thousands of products on which the cruising sailor can spend money (my hard drive is home to nearly a gigabyte of digital marine catalogs), so any of us predisposed to profligacy will find ample opportunity to exercise it in the cruising world.

Among cruisers who can afford to do it (and a lot who can't), there is a distinct trend to move up to bigger and fancier boats. Even beginning cruisers are showing up in 50- or 60-footers when a few years ago 35 feet was about average. But in boats, as in many things, bigger isn't necessarily better. Big boats can mean big problems and big expenses. And the third biggest cause of failed cruises, right behind people problems and money problems, is having too much boat. Cruisers with trade-up fever often graduate to a bigger boat than they can handle both physically and financially, and they end up tied to a marina, or they just sell the boat and go home.

As a quick example of the initial cost of a bigger boat, take the very popular Catalina 36 versus the Catalina 40. At this writing, the *YachtWorld* website (www.yachtworld.com) lists 42 Catalina 36s with an average price of less than $50,000. There are a dozen or more of the newer Mark IIs available for less than $100,000. When we move up to the Catalina 40 (which is, despite the howls of protest from Catalina owners, a longer version of the same boat), we have 30 boats listed with an average price of nearly $124,000 for an older boat (built before 2000) and the better part of $200,000 for a newer one. That 4 extra feet doubles the cost, and this formula holds true for most other production boats. Yes, I realize that these are asking prices and that the actual selling prices will be about 15 percent lower, but you get the point: small and simple gets you sailing toward the horizon much faster than big and flashy.

It is always tragic to see cruising dreams shattered, but when they are shattered by something as easily avoided as overindulgence in large boats and fancy equipment, it is particularly sad.

This trend toward more boat is good news for us little guys. The big boats can't get into the small anchorages that are most often the best and least crowded, and when rich folks buy their big new boat, they are often willing to sell us their little old boat at a bargain price. When the first edition of this book was written, *Sultana* was moored about 200 meters from Eric and Susan Hiscock's penultimate cruiser,

Wanderer IV. The Hiscocks admitted that this boat was a mistake; she was way too big for two people to handle without a lot of trouble, and when they built their last boat, *Wanderer V*, she was a full 10 feet shorter on deck. Even then, the Hiscocks often missed the convenience of their little 30-footer, *Wanderer III*.

Meet Your New Minimalist Lifestyle

Your new minimalist life will affect all aspects of the way you live. Minimalism is the art of learning to spend just enough money to stay alive while maintaining your health and dignity at a level that will allow you to maximize your income. You can't live in the woods eating lichens and bugs and expect any potential employer, or anyone else, to take you seriously, but you can reorder your life so that you spend money on just those things that you need to maintain yourself at an essential level of civilization and decency while forgoing unnecessary luxuries and indulgences. The necessary changes in your routine are not as difficult as you might think, but the changes will require concentration and effort. First you have to learn the rules; then you must learn to apply them one at a time.

First, Get Rid of Your Smartphone

This first step will be a real test of your determination as it is one of the hardest. This ubiquitous electronic marvel that you carry everywhere you go (a recent survey determined that more than 25 percent of us sleep with the things) is one of the most amazing manifestations of the electronic revolution to come along since the Apple II. Once you get used to the tiny screen and develop the knack for typing on keys that average a square millimeter in size, the current versions of the most popular smartphones will do nearly everything that a laptop would do just a year or so ago—but that's not why you have it.

Smartphones are the single most successful consumer products to come along since potato chips (Apple's 2014 revenues from the iPhone alone are projected to exceed $15 billion) partly because they are amazing devices but mostly because of a brilliant marketing campaign.

Smartphones aren't sold as convenient ways to make phone calls or even to text nonsense to friends. Smartphone are sold as an experience, as the mechanization of cool, and as a signal to everyone around us that we are up-to-date and with it—never mind that no one is likely to care that we are up-to-date and cool.

Unless you really need to carry your entire photo collection and all your music around in your pocket, get rid of your smartphone and cancel your contract. Then buy a $15 pay-as-you-go flip phone from the drugstore. It will do everything you need it to do (mostly make calls and send text messages), and it won't ruin your day when you accidentally drop it overboard. My last smartphone was an LG Optimus that cost $750. When I dropped it overboard, it didn't ruin my day; it ruined my whole month. The Optimus was replaced by a $15 Go Phone from Walmart, which stayed with me until we sailed away from U.S. waters. Now I have no phone at all, and as uncool as that is, I don't miss it a bit.

Now Consider Your Living Quarters

Getting rid of your smartphone was tough, wasn't it? Traumatic even. But if you were able to do that, the rest will be as easy as a walk on a beach in the Bahamas. Once we have your communications sorted out, we can turn to your house. Start to think of the place where you now live as temporary—a transitional abode where you will live before casting off for the cruising life.

If you are paying rent for your home or apartment and you won't be leaving on your cruise for two or more years, consider buying a tiny house in a good neighborhood. Your rent is coming right out of your cruising kitty. Buy a house, and make the equity part of your kitty, but don't make the mistake that many home buyers make: don't buy the biggest and most expensive house you can afford. Remember, you are living your new free-range life based on your needs, not your wants. Find a good neighborhood, and buy the smallest and least expensive house you can be comfortable in that is reasonably close to your work and the other services you will need—because the minimalist life also means minimum driving. Minimum effort for maximum gain in all things is the watchword.

You need to get used to living in small spaces anyway, and a small, cheap house means small, cheap expenses—heat, insurance, and the like. If you buy wisely, the appreciation of the house will cover a portion, if not all, of the rent you would have paid plus the sales expense. It may even contribute to the kitty when you sell it. You might even consider the possibility of renting your house when you leave, but be cautious. Make sure that the laws where you live are favorable to the landlord (some areas have laws so skewed to the needs of the renters that small-time renting isn't tenable) and that there is a reliable property manager willing to take it.

If you live in a metropolitan area, a small, inexpensive condo might be the answer to your housing question, but be extra careful of condos. In many suburban markets, a condominium won't be as good an investment as a single-family home, but in the city a condo may be the only affordable option. This isn't always true in either case, so do some homework on your own neighborhood before you decide what to buy. It is important to proceed with extreme caution when buying any kind of real estate because the wrong move could easily end your cruising plans. If you have never bought a house before or if you are otherwise unfamiliar with the real estate market, you should consult a trusted professional, one who has no financial interest in your purchase of a specific property.

Fix It If You Can

If you are handy with tools and know what you are doing, buying a rundown house in a good neighborhood and spiffing it up for resale while you are living in it is an excellent way to reduce living expenses and build the kitty. In fact, if the circumstances are just right, it can be the closest thing to a surefire ticket to the cruising life that there is.

If you aren't handy with tools and plan to become a budget cruiser, now is the time to become proficient at fixing things yourself, and the best way to do that is to become our own repairperson. When the showerhead starts to leak, reach for your tool bag rather than Googling "local plumbers" on your laptop. And if the tile in the shower is getting shabby, heigh yourself off to the nearest big-box home repair megastore and check out the tile section. Often the employees of these stores are quite knowledgeable and eager to help with detailed instructions. Plus many of these megastores offer free seminars on esoteric skills like tile laying and showerhead fixing.

True, you aren't likely to need tile-laying skills too often in the cruising life, and budget cruising boats seldom have a real showerhead, but any technical skills you can pick up will build your mechanical self-confidence, and many translate very well to other more needed skills. Knowing how to tile a wall will help a lot when you need to replace the insulation and soundproofing on your engine room, and knowing how to repair a leaking showerhead will come in handy when your lift pump starts sucking air 300 miles away from anyone who even looks like a mechanic.

Fixing broken things yourself is one of the best ways to relieve stress on your kitty. And acquiring the skills to do simple (or even complex) home repairs before you leave will help the kitty grow fat faster and will make your transition from the shoreside to the cruising life that much easier. Fixing up a run-down house for resale is a proven way to quickly build a kitty, but you must proceed with caution as small mistakes can cause big problems. Large mistakes can be catastrophic.

If you are going to make a profit in the real estate market, the following must apply. (The first three items pertain to any house or condominium; the last two are specific to fix-it-uppers.)

- You must buy the house at a good price under favorable terms.
- The house must be in a good neighborhood.
- The real estate market in your area must be expanding; stagnant or down-trending markets won't do.
- The project must be realistic and within your capabilities to do it in the time you have available.
- Many run-down old houses, like run-down old boats, are too far gone to be fixed up for reasonable money. You must be able to distinguish between the cosmetically ugly and the structurally hopeless when buying either.
- Most areas will allow you to work on your own house, but you must be familiar with and comply with all building codes and licensing requirements.

If You Already Own a House

If you already own your own home and it is of reasonable size with a reasonable mortgage, terrific. You are halfway to the cruising life. However, if you own a large home with a large mortgage, and your departure is more than two or three years away, consider selling it and buying a smaller house for all the above reasons. If you think you can save some money by trading down to a smaller house, be careful to compute all of the costs involved in the transaction before you make up your mind. Make sure you factor in the legal fees, bank fees and points, commissions, moving expenses, and all the other little odds and ends that cost money. Know for sure what the true cost will be before you sign on the line.

Renting

I have been a landlord on three separate occasions, and in all three cases it has been a most unsatisfactory experience. I am now convinced that the stereotype of the landlord as a greedy, conniving tightwad with a black hat and twisted mustache is spot-on accurate. If you don't fit this stereotype, you're going to get your butt slam-dunked through the hoop of reality by the moral equivalent of the best of Michael Jordan and the worst of Attila the Hun.

I seem to have a genetic defect that manifests itself in a desire for people to like me, and I was born without a defense mechanism for dealing with hatred. And let's face it, people hate landlords. The tenants hate 'em, the local governments hate 'em, the courts hate 'em, and, hey, I'm no different than anyone else—I hate 'em too.

Don't rent your home to tenants without thinking about all the ramifications. The tax, liability, and insurance problems of renting a private home are more than most cruisers want to deal with. Even if you are the personification of Simon Legree, finding and dealing with tenants can be time-consuming and expensive, all of which detract from the cruising experience.

There is one other caveat I will offer on the subject of repairing and renting a house as a kitty-fattening tactic. I know one young couple who dreamed of a world cruise and decided to finance it by renting their house and moving in with her parents. This worked so well that they soon bought a second rental unit and then a third and a fourth. At the end of two years, they had a dozen units rented, and they were making so much money that the cruising life was relegated to the retirement years. They both admitted that the stress and workload was greater than either of them liked, but they couldn't walk away from all that money. As unlikely as it seems at first, unexpected prosperity can kill cruising plans just as dead as poverty can.

Consider Next Your Automobile

Several years ago, when we lived in New Zealand, I was returning to the United States on a business trip, and I requested the travel agent to have a rental car waiting for me at Logan Airport in Boston. Being a frugal sort and a true minimalist, I ordered the smallest and least expensive car they had available, a Chevrolet Geo. After a long flight that was delayed by weather, I finally landed a little after midnight on a Friday night. I collected my bags and took the shuttle to the rental yard—the very empty rental yard. There wasn't a Geo in sight. In fact, the only car they had left was a huge white Oldsmobile loaded with every goody in the book and less than 200 miles on the odometer. Since I had a confirmed reservation, I got the white monster at the Geo rate, and I drove away a happy man.

The Geo would have gotten me where I was going just fine, but that big Olds got me there with panache. As soon as I slid behind the wheel I ceased being a lonesome and bone-weary wanderer and became a man of importance and substance. I sat on the polished leather seats and felt the power and prestige of a flashy new car flow from the wheel through my hands. As I drove, I observed with bemused disdain the envious glances of the common people in their Fords and Chevy Geos. I was once again a cool dude with a new set of wheels, and I loved it.

The automobile is the single most expensive item most of us own. (Your house might cost more, but it's usually less expensive than a car because you get most of your money back from a house when you sell it.) Western culture is a culture of automobiles, and most of us could not live the way we do without a car sitting in the driveway for every adult member of the family. Furthermore, our automobile defines who we are. It is the first important item many of us buy, and our place in society is broadcast for all to see by the type of car we drive. This is why many of us buy the most expensive car we can afford and will happily spend a year's earnings supported by a 62-month loan on a car. The monthly car payment is as much a part of the average worker's life as the daily commute; few of us even consider living without one.

Massive amounts of money are spent on advertising to capitalize on our tendency to derive our image from the car we drive. And if the advertisers can't convince at least 30 million Americans each year that the new models are the greatest thing to happen to humanity since cultivated wheat, the entire U.S. economy suffers. We are told our new car makes us sexy, young, exciting, vibrant, smart, and irresistible to the opposite sex, and we lap it up like kittens at a milk saucer. There is nothing inherently wrong with the lopsided importance of automobiles in our society—the car culture accounts for between 20 and 30 percent of the U.S. gross domestic product, depending on whose statistics you use—and it is one of the most important things that makes life as we know it possible. However, if you plan to go cruising, turning your back on the car culture is one of the first things you must do, and it is an important first step in learning to lead a minimalist life.

Would-be cruisers have to stop looking at cars as status symbols and start looking at them as convenient ways to get around town. Most cruisers and all minimalists think of cars as mechanical devices for getting from one place to another in reasonable safety and comfort,

nothing more. They don't care a fig about what the car looks like. This is a very dangerous attitude—if everyone thought this way, it would lead to the collapse of the automobile industry, the closing of factories around the world, massive layoffs, and worldwide unemployment. But don't worry, the economies of the world are safe. The idea that the automobile is the source of all our well-being is so deeply ingrained that none but you and I and a few other cruising minimalists are ever going to believe otherwise.

If you own a car on which you still owe money, get rid of it and resolve never to buy a car or anything else except a house with borrowed money. If you can't sell the car for enough to cover the balance on your note, you're faced with a dilemma. Car dealers play a little game with people who are in this unenviable position—it's called "trade in." They offer you an inflated trade-in value for your old car, then add the difference to the price of the new one. (Most dealers are candid about having separate trade-in and cash prices for the cars they sell.) Quite an effective ploy to inflate your monthly payment, isn't it? Usually the best you can do in this situation is sell the car at a loss, then pay off the balance as best you can. If you buy a good old car, a minimalist car, the savings realized in the first year should be enough to cover your loss and get you back on track.

Aged but Able

Some great things have been happening in the used-car market since the first edition of this book was published, most of which have been a benefit to us basic and budget-minded cruisers. In general, cars are actually better than they were 20 years ago: they are more reliable; they last longer; and with the universal adaptation of electronic ignition and computer controlled systems, they require far less maintenance. The good old days of adjusting our own spark plugs are long gone, and only a few dedicated auto enthusiasts and perhaps the occasional masochistic flagellate bothers to change his or her own oil.

Buying a used car from the bottom end of the market is, hands down, the best way available to save money for the kitty. When we were shoresiders, we selected our automobiles for status and self-esteem. The actual practicality of our purchasing decisions was always a distant third among our considerations. Conversely, when shoresiders sell a car, it is very seldom because it is no longer reliable or running well. They sell it just because any vehicle that has seen a lot of asphalt pass under its belly has lost all of its sex appeal and is thus ready for the scrap heap no matter how well it is running. Statistics tell us that the average 5-year-old automobile has lost all but 35 percent of its original purchase price, and a 10-year-old vehicle in good running condition can be had for less than 10 percent of its original price.

While we are building our kitty, it is critical that we take advantage of this situation and get the most practical car we can find—sex appeal and status be damned. I have it on very good authority from Tom, a mechanic friend who is an expert on the used-car market, that the best values in the past 10 years are small foreign cars, particularly Hondas, Toyotas, Subarus, and Hyundais. Tom also believes that American cars being made today are just as good as the small foreign cars, but that wasn't true just a few years ago.

I won't recommend any specific car here, but look for a basic model that is in great condition, 6 to 10 years old, with a low-tech radio and a minimum of accessories. Restrict your search to small cars with four-cylinder engines, and look for a four-door body style in a popular model, one you see a lot of on the road. Make sure that it has good tires and that the AC and heater both work, if you think you need these luxuries. For the most part, a car is in good condition if it looks like it is in good condition, but have a trusted mechanic check it out for you.

If you don't know a trusted mechanic (they can be scarce), I have had excellent results with the AAA prepurchase inspections services.

Basic models of small cars without frills are much more likely to be cheap and reliable because they don't have as much stuff to break, and seeing a lot of a specific model on the road is testimony to reliability and sound construction. If the car is a weird color and has a few dents, so much the better—bargain city here we come—but shun rust like a kid shuns boiled cabbage.

Don't even think of financing your purchase. Decide how much you want to spend; then withdraw the cash and have it readily available.

Spend an hour or so on the Internet checking eBay, craigslist, Autotrader.com, Cars.com, and any local or regional advertising services you can find. Don't neglect the local newspapers (if you still have one) or any free car-trader magazines. This will give you a good feel for what cars are available and how much you can afford to spend.

Concentrate your search on private sellers. Most dealers aren't interested in selling the "junkers" we are looking for. The few dealers who do sell bottom-of-the-market cars will get a premium for them, and they are always sold as is, so you have no recourse anyway. Private sellers are usually more flexible in price and will often accept a low offer just to get the thing out of the driveway.

Make everyone you know, and anybody you don't know who will listen, aware that you are actively looking for an old beater that has a good probability of lasting two or three more years. Chances are that someone knows someone else who knows someone who has just what you want.

Cars with a few dents or ones with faded paint are OK (cosmetic defects are actually a big plus as they will keep the price low), but avoid cars that have been obviously mistreated.

It is most likely that an owner who doesn't bother to keep up the exterior of a car won't pay much attention to the important maintenance items either.

When you do find the right car, get the Carfax (www.carfax.com) report, and check the maintenance record. Reject any cars that have been in major crashes, and don't consider any salvage cars (these have been written off by insurance companies and have been resurrected, often by unscrupulous dealers and con artists).

If you buy a perfectly good old car, you will save much more than the interest on the loan. A good old car will have most or even all of the depreciation wrung out of it, so when it's time to leave on your cruise, you can often sell it for about what you paid for it. In most states you will save a fortune by purchasing only the minimum insurance required by law plus, perhaps,

a little extra liability. Car theft has reached epidemic proportions in many places, but few thieves are interested in our good old car.

When Susan and I were looking for a boat, we bought a 20-year-old Mazda Miata sports car from a dealer in Salt Lake City, Utah, for $2,500 sight unseen. Even after fixing everything that needed to be fixed, we had less than $5,000 invested in a car we drove from Alaska to Maine to Florida to Texas and back again over two years. When we finally found *Vicarious*, we had driven that car, loaded with all our camping gear, for many thousands of miles (just how many thousands is unknown because the odometer was broken and we were too che . . . I mean frugal, to fix it), and we could have easily sold it for about what we paid for it. (Instead, we gave it to my brother-in-law for a pittance because he is a good guy.)

Driving an old car doesn't have to mean driving a junker. When we were looking for a boat, we bought this 20-year-old sports car for $2,500. We spent that much again fixing it up; then we spent two years and many miles looking at boats from Alaska to Texas to Florida to Maine. We slept in a tent and cooked over a camp stove, so the kitty suffered hardly at all.

Like most of our minimalist principles, these basic rules of good-old-car ownership hold true no matter what your lifestyle. By turning your back on the contrived status and symbolism of the new-car cult and driving a good old car, you can effect a huge increase in your real standard of living.

Of course, when you finally leave on your cruise, you won't have a car at all, so now is the time to get used to a bicycle.

Good Cruisers Eat Good Food

Now is the time for would-be cruisers (and any others who want to improve their lives) to learn to eat simple and basic foods in balanced portions and reject as much prepared food as possible. "Eat when you are hungry and stop before you are full" is a cliché that I plagiarized from somewhere, but it should become the first rule of the cruising diet. Planned meals at specific times are terrific social occasions and a mainstay of family life, but it is much better to snack and nibble your way through the day than to stuff yourself full at the dinner table.

The practical answer is compromise. On *Vicarious*, when conditions permit, dinner is a time to gather around the pilothouse table where we discuss the events of the day and the plans for tomorrow, where we tell jokes and reveal fears and foibles. The meals are balanced and tasty (especially when Susan cooks) with a variety that reflects local habits and available supplies, but the portions are small. Anyone who is hungry can munch on peanut butter, veggies, fruits, and bread and crackers at any time between meals.

Few foods are improved by processing. Fresh peas, for example, are a wonderful source

When we were in Mexico a typical meal was a bit of local goat cheese (queso de cabra), parma ham, fresh avocado, sweet red peppers, Susan's amazing salsa verde, sliced prickly pear cactus palms (nopales) with lime juice, and lots of crusty bread. Quick, easy, delicious, and incredibly healthy. (OK, so the ham has a dab of carcinogenic nitrates in it. A measure of evil can be overlooked in the face of near culinary perfection.)

of fiber and vitamins, but canned peas have very little nutritional value—it says so right on the can. All right, so they have a little fiber—so does pine bark. Eat fresh raw fruits and vegetables when you can. To cook fresh vegetables, simply drop them gently into boiling water for a few minutes—just long enough to bring out the colors and flavors and subdue a bit of the texture.

Ditch the junk food, shun anything with added sugar, eat everything else in moderation and in balanced portions, and you will never need any fad diet.

Learn to Cook

Simple and basic cooking is fun and can be learned by any simple, basic person who is willing to work at it a bit. If you don't already know the fundamentals of cooking, many junior and community colleges have adult evening programs that are almost sure to include a cooking class, or you can get a friend to teach you, or you can just get a good cookbook and keep experimenting until you get it right. It sometimes takes a while, but cooking is one of those skills in which the learning progress is obvious and continual—which is one reason why cooking is satisfying and rewarding. Once most people get started, they develop their own momentum and don't ever want to stop learning.

Concentrate on learning how to prepare dishes that require only a simple and basic galley. A few of every cruiser's favorites include one-pot meals (which are the basis for many meals afloat and come in handy for potlucks); easy and tasty soups, stews, and extra-spicy goulash; and quick breads such as pancakes, waffles, biscuits, and muffins. As a bonus, these are healthy foods too. (See Chapter 13 for more information about galley layout and design, and for a few of my previously top-secret recipes—the one for Captain Garlic's World-Famous Spaghetti Sauce is worth the price of this book alone.)

One of the best training manuals for onboard cooking is *The Boat Galley Cookbook* by Carolyn Shearlock and Jan Irons. This is more than just a great cookbook with tons of basic from-scratch recipes; it is also a detailed primer on how to cook on a boat with a minimum of fuss and frustration. We'll talk more about cookbooks in Chapter 13, but get the Kindle edition of *The Boat Galley Cookbook* now and start practicing cooking for the cruising life right in your home kitchen.

Don't worry too much about your cholesterol or your blood pressure unless your doctor tells you that you have a problem. Most basic foods are naturally low in salt and cholesterol anyway, and if you do have a health problem that requires a special diet, the minimalist cruising life is the best way to deal with it because it's the healthiest way to live there is.

Consider Your Health

Cancel your health club membership, and sell all your exercise machines (except, perhaps, a simple weight set). These things are bad for your health. If you're like about 80 percent of us, you paid for your club dues and your Schwinn 520 Reclining Multi-Tortional AbBuster with a credit card. All that money for principal and interest needs to go into your kitty.

And if you're like about 90 percent of Americans, you're not using these things anyway. Every time you plan to go to the club for a workout, something comes up and you put off going until later, and the Schwinn 520 is collecting dust in the basement. (Come on, admit it. It's true, isn't it?)

Learn exercise techniques that don't cost anything. Buy a good pair of stout shoes (not special walking shoes, just simple crepe-soled shoes with sturdy uppers are fine), wear heavy socks, and walk everywhere you can, every time you can. Walk with panache and enthusiasm; head up, chest out, arms swinging. Hum a little tune if you like, and think what it's going to be like walking along the beach in Bora Bora.

Get your heart beating and your lungs working. If there are some hills or a long flight of stairs nearby, walk up and down them as often as you can. As you become more fit, start walking with a small backpack filled with the Sunday newspaper (if you still have one). Every week add a newspaper until you are carrying 30 to 40 pounds. Leave room for a bottle of water and a snack, but keep walking.

If you're a runner, great. Now it's time to quit. It's too easy to get injured while running. Tendons get torn, backs get injured, ankles and knees get twisted—none of which are compatible with cruising, and running isn't necessary anyway. A brisk walk gives you all the aerobic and muscular exercise you will ever need. So stop running, and walk, walk, walk. (But keep your running shoes to walk in.)

If it's too far to walk, ride your bicycle. Biking is as good a cardiovascular exercise as walking, and it's faster. If you don't have a bike, buy a cheap used one that's hard to pedal (an old three-speed is ideal)—you'll save money and get more exercise.

As you gradually move away from being a consumer toward becoming a minimalist, you will be amazed at how little you need to live a comfortable and rewarding life, and you will be able to put excess funds into the kitty—your passport to freedom. Don't delay for a minute. The trick is to adopt the minimalist's lifestyle now to prepare for the cruising life.

Get Rid of Useless Possessions

Start now to sell all your excess possessions, stuff that you won't be needing once you start cruising, and put the money straight into the kitty. Extra cars, sporting equipment, stereo gear, computers, those exercise machines, kitchen gadgets, televisions, and large power tools are a few things you won't need while cruising. If you

won't need these things cruising, you probably don't need them now, and you will be better off without them. One of the hardest decisions for most beginning cruisers to make is what not to take with them. As a general rule, it's always better to take too little than too much, and the more you can do without, the better off you'll be.

Store the Rest

During the past recession, when businesses around the world were shutting down or cutting back, one emerging industry continued to grow without even a hint of a letup: the self-storage industry (now at $22.5 billion annually in the United States and still growing). Western societies have become insatiable black holes of consumption, and even during a recession, we were buying so much stuff that we filled our oversized houses with their three-car garages to the bursting point and needed external storage units to house the excess.

This proliferation of storage facilities is a symptom of the excesses of consumerism, but the existence of so many storage facilities is a good thing for us, and I know of few full-time cruisers who don't have a small unit someplace close to home base.

Let's face it, not many of us can get all our worldly possessions on a boat, no matter how big it is. When we first departed Marblehead, Susan had a lot of family heirlooms, and I had a lot of books (tons of books) that we couldn't bear to part with. We ended up with a storage unit larger than most apartments. After a few years and the gradual acceptance that the cruising life for us was going to be longer than a three-year interlude, the burden of paying rent on the storage unit became onerous, especially after we realized that all that stuff we had in storage wasn't missed even a little. In fact, we were hard pressed to even remember just what it was we had squirreled away for the future. Thus, on one extended trip back to the United

States from New Zealand, I opened an eBay account and over the course of about six weeks, I sold the lot for enough cash to finance a year-long sojourn to Fiji, New Caledonia, and the Great Barrier Reef of Australia.

Cancel All Your Memberships Except to the SSCA

Cancel or don't renew your memberships in expensive clubs and organizations—that's right, even the yacht club—and put that money into the kitty. Keep your membership in the Seven Seas Cruising Association (SSCA) for the valuable back issues of their cruising bulletin, each of which contains firsthand reports from cruiserly destinations around the world. This vast collection of personal experiences goes back for years and includes personal accounts of visits to all of the popular destinations and a growing number of just recently explored new possibilities. And the best part about it is that the database is searchable so you can retrieve firsthand information with the click of your mouse.

You may want to subscribe to a few sailing magazines in order to feed the dream while you feed the kitty, but it is best to resist the temptation. A lot of the same information is free via the Internet, and there is still the reading room at your public library. That subscription money is better used as kitty food.

Credit: The Most Frivolous of All Frivolities

Several years ago, my good friend Jerry, who is a little eccentric, decided he had had enough of renting a place to live, and he approached a bank for a loan to buy a house. He was a hard working guy who made a decent living in a small one-man business that taught scuba diving on an academic level to budding marine scientists at several area universities. He had learned early on

that when you have a sporadic cash flow from a seasonal business, it is wise to keep all your bills current and to deal on a cash basis with as many suppliers as possible. He was quite surprised when the first bank he approached refused his application for a mortgage on the grounds that he had never borrowed money and therefore had no credit history on which they could base their loan. He tried another and got the same story. He finally gave up after several more banks told him the same thing. Several years and a few credit cards later, he did finally buy a tidy little condo in a Boston suburb.

This isn't an unusual story, and most of us can recite similar ones. It is ironic that you can't borrow money if you don't owe money, but it's true, and it's a vivid illustration of the value our society places on debt and credit ratings. I know several people who have credit card balances that exceed their annual before-tax earnings, and they are happily paying exorbitant interest rates and annual fees using one credit card for cash to pay off others while charging nearly everything they buy. Many people seem not to realize that when you use a credit card, you are borrowing money. It is amazing how many people actually believe that someday they will pay off all those cards and be free of debt.

The credit system isn't all bad, of course, and easy credit at reasonable rates for the masses is one of the secrets behind the phenomenal growth in the Western economies since the end of World War II. Just read the newspapers around Christmas, and you can get a clear picture of the importance of consumer spending on the overall economy. A slow shopping season can shake the very foundations of society with profound effects on unemployment, interest rates, the stock market, and that undefined but critical element called "consumer confidence."

Banks, other lending institutions, and social planners all have elaborate formulas that compare debt, age, income, history, where you live, and the kind of work you do. These mathematical factors are used to determine how much debt an economically healthy family or individual can carry without getting into financial trouble. They work just fine for shoreside dwellers, but it's a different story if you want to go cruising. Unless you can be happy with a short cruise, you simply aren't a candidate for the cruising life if you owe a lot of money. With this in mind, let's take a look at the dark side of debt and consider how to get rid of it.

Consumer Debt and the Cruiser

Consumer debt is the lock on the gate to freedom. Monthly payments are like fenceposts that surround us and keep us hammering away at jobs we don't like in situations we'd rather not be in, and the interest on those payments is the barbed wire that connects the posts and ensures that we don't do anything foolish like buy a boat and sail away. Before you can become serious about adopting the cruising life, it is critical that you start now to open that gate by getting out of debt.

Consumer debt is money that you borrowed to buy anything except your house. Credit cards are the most common form of consumer debt, followed by auto loans, layaway plans, and equity loans on your house that you use for vacations or refrigerators. Consumer debt is a massive burden to many families, and for many it is the single most stressful element of modern life.

Debt and the Cruising Kitty

How do the foregoing comments on debt relate to those we made on the cruising kitty in Chapter 5? Wouldn't it make a lot of sense to use all of our resources to pay off all our debt before we start building our kitty? In a purely economic sense, yes, it would because the interest you are paying on your debt is most likely to be much higher than the interest you will receive on the budding savings account that is the early stage of your kitty. But on a practical and emotional level, it doesn't make any sense at all. It is important that you get your kitty started before you do anything else because that kitty will quickly come to symbolize your commitment to the cruising life. It is a positive element in your life that you can view with pride as you watch it grow. Your debt, on the other hand, is a psychological millstone that represents nothing.

A Payment Schedule

Once you have your kitty growing, you must next add up all your debt exclusive of your home mortgage and calculate a payment schedule that will get you debt free within five years. Make sure that you allow a comfortable margin to live on while you reduce your monthly payments and that you continue to build your cruising kitty. This usually means that you won't be able to allocate any more than 20 percent of your income to debt reduction, which may not be enough to satisfy some of your creditors.

Unhappy creditors can be a problem, and dealing with them will require some negotiating skills on your part, but if you are making an honest attempt to pay off an honest debt, most companies will go along with a reasonable payment schedule. Your first responsibility is to your family and the cruising kitty, not to the banks and credit card companies, but you must remember that your bills are legally and morally binding commitments that you entered into on your own with a free will. You need a clear conscience when you go cruising so don't turn your back on your debts. Many communities now offer consumer credit counseling services free to the public. Counselors offer help in setting up a payment schedule, and their involvement will sometimes get creditors to accept different terms than they would otherwise.

Kill All the Credit Cards

The most difficult part of your debt-reduction scheme won't be making your monthly payments—you have probably been doing that all along. It will be in developing the willpower and discipline to stop yourself from accumulating more debt. Doing so could be the hardest thing you do to get moving toward the cruising life since you gave up your smartphone. In some chronic cases, people simply can't stop charging stuff, and these folks need stronger medicine than they'll find in this book. The rest of us will find it hard enough, but if you really want to go cruising, you can do it, and as a first step you should cancel all your credit cards but one (or possibly two if you want to have one stashed for emergencies). Then get a debit card and keep that loaded with enough cash for your daily expenses.

Many cruisers use credit cards for cash advances from ATM machines and banks, for renting cars, and for identification. In most of the first world countries you will be visiting, you will hardly be out of sight of the ubiquitous money machines. Nearly all banks in developing countries are happy to deliver a bundle of local currency against your credit card. But a cash advance against a credit card usually carries the highest interest rate allowed by law, and unlike charges, for which interest isn't assessed for 30 days, the banks start charging for cash advances the moment the machine or the bank teller hands you the money. Therefore, cash advances are the most expensive way there is to borrow money short of resorting to a loan shark. The answer is to use your debit card for all your ATM withdrawals and pay no interest at all.

Credit card use throughout the world is so pervasive that having one with you at all times is practically a necessity, and you should not try to go cruising without one. Many people will accept them as identification, and some countries, like New Zealand, will accept a credit card as proof of solvency, which is a requirement for a visitor's visa. Although there are exceptions, you can just about forget renting a car if you don't have that little plastic slab. The trick is to use your credit card only when you must and to pay for everything else with your debit card. Then make sure that any purchases you do make on your credit card are paid off promptly.

When we were returning from our shake-down cruise to Canada, we pulled into Boothbay Harbor, Maine, and we decided to rent a car to visit some friends who lived inland. Finding a phone booth by the public landing (this was in 1992 when the smallest cell phone would barely fit into carry-on luggage), we called the only local number in the Yellow Pages under "auto rentals."

"Yup?," asked the voice that answered the phone.

"Do you rent cars?" I asked.

"Yup."

"Do you have one available?"

"Yup."

"How much is it?"

"It's $15 a day."

"Do you charge for mileage?"

"Can't, speedometer's broke."

"We'll take it. Do you take credit cards?"

"Nope."

"What do you take?"

"Whatcha got?"

We finally settled on cash. The car, a surprisingly tidy late-model Chevrolet, was delivered to the dock with a full tank of gas. When we were finished with it two days later, I called the number and asked where we should deliver the car. "Just put the money in the glove box and leave her on the dock," said the voice.

Things like this happen all the time while you are cruising, but they seem to happen more in Maine than anywhere else. Thus, coastal Maine is one of our favorite places on earth in or out of a sailboat.

Hesitate, Don't Consolidate

One other thing before we leave the vulgar topic of credit cards and move on to something a bit more nautical: in struggling to find a path through your financial labyrinth, don't fall for the "consolidation loan" scam. These tempting offers, which are familiar to anyone who has a credit card, involve borrowing money from one lender to pay off credit card debt—ostensibly to give you the convenience of writing one check each month and saving you the nuisance of writing a separate check for each credit card. What they really do is clear your balances on your credit cards to encourage you to charge more stuff. It's sort of like trying to save bullets by putting all your snakes into one box then shooting the box. It doesn't work. You still have to shoot the snakes. Unless the new interest rate and fees (don't forget the fees) for the consolidation loan will save you a lot of money (unlikely) and you have the willpower to never use credit cards again, don't even consider this type of loan.

Work to Live

If you are lucky enough to be earning a lot of money working at a good job, you have a tremendous advantage in your quest to fatten your kitty and complete all the dozens of other tasks that are necessary before you can shove off. But remember, once you begin cruising, that income is going to stop, and there will be long periods when you won't want to work or won't be able to. That job you left is going to look awfully good from the vantage point of a small boat in a faraway place, so make sure you are making the most of it while you've got it. You need to take advantage of the planning period to accumulate as much cash in the kitty as you can.

Change Your Working Attitude

Many people who are working at jobs they aren't thrilled with find an eight-hour day at the office or at the plant to be exhausting. They collapse in front of the TV with a drink or two and hardly move except to eat dinner and go to bed. This was my routine for many years, and I never had a hint as to why I didn't have any energy. Finally, in desperation, I went to the doc. He gave me several thousands of dollars' worth of tests and decided that I was suffering from chronic fatigue syndrome. "Get plenty of rest, and drink lots of liquids," he advised. "And don't worry about it—it's probably genetic."

The hackneyed expression "we are what we eat" is, like most hackneyed expressions, true. But it is also true that we are what we do. Most of us consider our job as our life's work—our career—and we identify ourselves with our employment. Thus, in our shoreside lives most of us focus on our jobs. We live so we can work, and if our work is dull, lifeless, and uninteresting, then we too are dull, lifeless, and uninteresting. In the cruising life, you will turn the tables on the system. You will begin to work so you can live, and this small change in attitude makes a mighty difference.

You will become animated and exciting because your life is animated and exciting even though your work remains dull and commonplace. What were once insurmountable obstacles are now mere bumps and minor potholes on the road to the cruising life.

An interesting transformation will take place once you decide to go cruising. You will likely become so obsessed with accumulating enough cash in your kitty to make cruising possible that your work might take on new meaning.

When your job focus becomes accumulating money for your kitty, you suddenly have new reasons for getting out of bed in the morning. This will change your attitude about work. And you will have reached another important turning point in your life; by making your job secondary to your kitty, your job becomes a means to an end—the freedom of the cruising life.

Don't Fear Losing Your Job

Thinking of your job as just a job instead of a career and knowing that you will be leaving soon unshackles you from the fear of losing that job; therefore, you become free to take chances and risks that would have been unthinkable when you lived for your work. It is very possible that your new freedom will manifest a measurable increase in the quality of your work, a renewed interest in what were once boring projects, and a new respect for your job, the people you work with, and the company you work for.

It is also possible that you will be fired.

Many upper and middle managers fear nothing so much as a motivated worker. This is especially true in government jobs and older industries with entrenched management, but it can happen anywhere.

If you have trouble coming to grips with the prospect of losing your job and having to look for another, perhaps this simple mind game will help. First, consider your job and all its advantages—write them down on a slip of paper if it will help. Your list might include security, healthcare, regular income, high income, fascinating work, promotion possibilities, and anything else that you might like about your employment. Next, we're not going to list the disadvantages; in fact, we'll pretend that there aren't any. Remember in Chapter 1 when we found that cruisers (the good ones anyway) never ran away from anything? Well, we wouldn't leave a perfectly good job just because of a few trivialities, so if there are a few negatives in your job, just forget about them.

Next, we want to contemplate humanity. That's right, all of it. You don't have to write it down. Just think about all the people in the world in all their billions and in all their multitudes. Now consider the fact that the majority of those people don't work for the company that you do, and they are quite happy with that. Many don't do as well as you do, of course, but many do better, a few do a lot better, and all of them seem to be getting by. Does that make you feel more comfortable? Good, but we aren't done yet.

You probably know at least one person who was fired or laid off at some time. (It is important that it not be recent because it takes most of us a while to sort things out when we change jobs.) How is that person doing now? Chances are, that person is doing just fine. If you think about this fact a bit, you should get some comfort from the realization that you don't really need to fear the loss of your job; if other people can deal with it, so can you. No, you don't want to chuck away a perfectly good job at this point, but it really wouldn't be a total disaster if you did have to find another way to grow your kitty.

Maximize Your Income While You Can

With your new found enthusiasm for your job, you will find you are invigorated by your work, giving you boundless energy for additional work, but don't worry about becoming a workaholic. Workaholics are people who are driven to work at obsessive levels to compensate for something that is missing in their lives. We all know one or two of these unfortunate folks who hammer their lives away at compulsive levels to accumulate the wealth that they tragically mistake for happiness. With each success, they gather more wealth, but when it doesn't bring the contentment that we all seek, they think this means that they haven't worked hard enough and they redouble their efforts. Trying to satisfy greed with money is like trying to put out a fire with gasoline. The most we can hope for these folks is that when they die, the kids will have the sense to spend the money on something useful, like a cruising sailboat.

Recently in Beaufort, North Carolina, I met the owner of a huge sport fisherman ("She's got twin turbos and 800 ponies; gets me to the stream in less than an hour") who also was also the owner of a major car dealership in Raleigh. During our short conversation, he mentioned that he also owned a condo in Aruba, three top-end snowmobiles, and a 40-foot camper. Twice he was compelled to mention that even though he was a high school dropout, he made more money than the president of Duke University, where he had season's tickets for all the basketball games and never missed a one—not even the away games. The interesting thing about this person was how important it was to him that I have all this personal information, all delivered in a conversation that lasted less than half an hour.

Because would-be cruisers are accumulating money to satisfy the urge to change their lives rather than to satisfy the urge to accumulate money and things, the toil and hard work makes more sense and doesn't use us up so remorselessly. We work our butts off not to garner wealth but to go cruising, and that makes all the difference. We aren't workaholics, we're cruisaholics, and that's better.

How to Become a Cruiseaholic

Cruiseaholics are people who are driven to work at obsessive levels so they can save enough money to go cruising and thus change their lives. It's easy to become one, but you have to work at it a bit. Once you get your regular job in order and adjust your attitude so that it becomes the best damn job in the world, and once you achieve the mental stamina that makes you show up for work half an hour early, eager to jump into the old harness and pull that damn wagon the way it's never been pulled before, you're ready to branch out. Work overtime if you can, but get paid for it—remember, you don't care about brownie points anymore. Work two or three jobs if you can find them; wait on tables, grease cars, mow lawns, sweep floors,

paint your neighbor's house, do whatever you can that is legal and moral to make more money. Often, working at something you enjoy for less money than you would make working at something you hate can pay more in the long run.

In addition to your regular job, try to get part-time work that will teach you skills you can use for yourself and other cruisers while cruising. Diesel mechanics, sewing, electronics, carpentry, teaching, welding, outboard-engine repair, bartending, and cooking are a few good ones. Take a job with a business that caters to the growing Latin American community as a way of brushing up on your Spanish while you earn the big bucks. Remember that once you leave on your cruise, most temporary jobs that will be available to you won't pay near what you think you are worth, so get what you can now, while you can.

Put Your Money to Work

A major mistake made by a great many would-be cruisers is to never start their kitty or to delay starting it until it is too late because "I don't have enough money for a serious investment program." If you don't have the minimum for a brokerage account, don't worry about it. Few of us do when we start. Keep your kitty in a passbook savings account or in a money market fund at the bank until you accumulate enough for a more sophisticated option. If you are employed at a regular job (as opposed to being self-employed), have your paycheck deposited directly into your account with as much as possible going into the savings. Start your kitty now no matter how much or how little you can put into it. A few hundred bucks will get you on your way to the cruising life. Remember, a cruising kitty grows like an onion with successive layers built upon a tiny core. Without that tiny core, you and your kitty aren't going anywhere.

7

The Cruising Kitty: How to Feed It After You've Got It

A feast is made for laughter, and wine maketh merry: but money answereth all things.

—**Ecclesiastes 10:19**

A Humble Supplication

I am not nor will I ever become, under any circumstances, a qualified investment counselor. The following advice on investing your kitty is based on my own experience mucking about with *Vicarious*'s kitty and on observations I have made in 40 years of investment experience. I am relating a system that has worked for us, not one that I think will work for you. Investment counseling is far too complicated, and the variables too vast, for me to presume to advise you in any way on how your kitty should be invested. So please take the following as only a guide to the process of setting up an investment plan rather than a plan to be adopted blindly. For a cheerful, insightful, right-on-target overview of the fundamentals of saving and investing, read the current version of *Personal Finance for Dummies* by Eric Tyson. Tyson explains it better than I can and in far more detail, and his book isn't just for dummies. In fact, I think Tyson must be a cruiser.

If you do choose to take any of what follows as advice and in so doing you should lose some money, don't blame your humble but sympathetic author. And if in the even more unlikely event that you should be wiped out in the process, please don't sue. For one thing, it would make me feel terrible, and for another, it would be unlikely that you would ever collect anything because, as one who has developed the wretched habit of following his own advice, it is quite probable that I would have been wiped out too.

Grooming Your Kitty

Once you have accumulated a fairly substantial hunk of cash, say, $5,000 more or less (it'll happen faster than you think), in your money market fund or savings account, you will want to start thinking about more sophisticated investments. This is when you want to learn all you can about risk management and investing in mutual funds and the stock market. You don't need to become a financial wizard, but you do want to make informed decisions about investing your cruising kitty. The best source of information on investing is free from your all-service brokerage, from the Internet, and from your local library. Here's a brief primer on risk and investment to get you started.

Risk Management

Risk management is a fascinating subject and one that is fast becoming a major focus of study in academic institutions. It is also appropriate to the cruising life because cruisers practice risk management every day in the normal routine on the high seas. Every time we are about to depart on a passage, we carefully consider all the relevant conditions and weigh the risks involved in going against those of staying in port.

Let's say you are at anchor in Apia, Western Samoa, waiting for the weather to clear so you can make the jump on a passage to Suva in Fiji. This isn't a long passage, it only takes four or five days, but it is a dangerous one that demands clear weather and careful navigation to avoid intervening atolls and reefs. There is a strong cold front approaching, and you are trying to decide whether to go now or wait for the front to pass. Cold fronts, of course, are nearly always followed by clear weather, but they are

also followed by flat seas and light winds. If you wait until tomorrow, will you be able to catch the backside of the front and ride it into the forecast high and thereby reduce your exposure to the predictable light winds? What if you leave now? Will you be clobbered by gale-force winds when the front arrives, or will the winds moderate as they approach land and give you the boost to get most of the way through the high before it develops and the winds die? You must consider as much of the available information as is pertinent, but ultimately you must go with the feeling in your gut.

From the hypothetical to the real . . . We were in Nuku'alofa Harbor waiting with about a dozen other boats for a clear weather window to start the trip to New Zealand when the catamaran *Sudden Laughter* pulled in after an extended cruise to Mururoa to protest the French nuclear testing that was going on at the time (thankfully, the last as it turned out). After a day or so of replenishing supplies and undertaking a few minor repairs, the ship was making ready to leave in spite of a huge weather system developing in the Tasman Sea.

"Haven't you heard the weather report?" I asked one of the crew.

"Never listen to the bloody things, mate," he answered. "All they do is scare ya."

"Hey, you're going to get the shit kicked out of ya on any trip to Kiwiland, so you might as well get it over with early on," added another member of the crew.

When we caught up with *Sudden Laughter* in Nelson Harbor several months later, I found that they had indeed gotten clobbered about two days after they left, but after the front passed they had an easy sail to Nelson. We, on the other hand, had taken a more cautious approach and had waited another week or so for the weather to clear before we left. After suffering through light and variable winds for a week, we got hit by a southerly gale that had us hove-to for two days, blew our main to shreds, and continued to howl for more than a week. Like the guy at the carnival roulette wheel says, "Ya pays yer money and ya takes yer chances."

The same approach to risk that we apply to our cruising decisions is appropriate for selecting among the dozens of ways you can invest

A destroyed mainsail was the least of our problems when we got hit by a southern gale on the way to New Zealand. The bowsprit was cracked when the bobstay let go, and the entire rig was loosened to the point that we feared losing the main mast. We sailed the last 400 miles with the mizzen and baby jib. More adventuresome boats that took a chance and left ahead of a cold front a few days earlier than we did had a brief spell of rough weather, then clear sailing for the rest of the 1,200-mile trip.

your kitty, and the goal of investing is also analogous to the destination of a passage. We want the trip from where we start (at investment) to be quick and safe to our destination (our investment goal). We also want a smooth trip with no storms and rocky seas that make the boat bounce up and down, making the captain and crew fret and worry about the whole thing sinking out of sight forever. But storms are a reality of the cruising life, just as falling markets are a reality of investment. While we will do anything to avoid trouble, we must be ready for it when it invariably arrives. Thus we have life rafts and EPIRBs and signal flares and radios and all manner of safety gadgets to ensure our survival should that sinking sensation suddenly set in. So too do we have safety nets for our kitty.

Of course, risk is the easiest thing in the world to avoid. All you need to do is stay in harbor and never make the passage. You'll have plenty of company because we've never seen a harbor yet that wasn't full of shiny yachts that will never see an open ocean. Either they weren't fit for ocean travel, or their owners didn't have the confidence to go offshore. The owner of one of the nicest cruising boats in Marblehead Harbor has his boat professionally delivered to Penobscot Bay in Maine every year (an easy passage of about 135 nautical miles). At the end of a two-week cruise, the delivery skipper takes the boat back to Massachusetts. Lots of boat-owners (and investors) do the same thing even though it's expensive. And although it's safe and comforting to pay someone else to take the risks, you will also miss out on most of the fun.

But you can't eliminate all the risk of cruising by simply not going. A few years ago I read the tragic story of a man from Tennessee who, in the prime of his life, was relaxing in the cockpit of his sailboat with (we can presume) a nice tall drink, a cigar, and a good book. The boat was tied safely to a marina dock, and the guy was living a life that was about as risk free as you can get. But his luck was running out. A plane flying high overhead lost a large bolt from the landing gear, and . . . you know the rest of the story, don't you? That's right, the bolt fell 25,000 feet, crashed right through the awning of the boat, and smashed that drink all to hell.

The Relationship Between Risk and Return

To get people to accept higher risk, investments have to pay a higher average return over some time period, otherwise we'd all have our money in savings accounts or ultrasafe government bonds. But that higher risk translates into periods of gains and losses that we hope will average out to a higher return (the classic upward-trending sinusoidal line of stock market returns). In investing and in cruising, we can choose to stay in harbor for a risk-free (but boring) existence, or we can choose to risk heading off to sea and be rewarded with the highs and the lows of the cruising life (which for most of us who try it adds up to something better than the shoreside life we left behind).

The Relationship Between Risk and Time

To get that higher average return, the investment needs to remain in place through the cycle of highs and lows. For the stock market, most investment counselors say, this means at least 5 years and 10 is a lot better. Larger returns might be made by moving quickly in and out of the market, but so might larger losses.

The process of buying and selling securities on the very short term (usually less than 24 hours) is called "day-trading," and it is classed as among the most stressful of occupations. Sometimes stocks are held for only a few hours, and fortunes can be made and lost in a single large transaction. Day-trading also has a famously high suicide rate, and it probably isn't a great way to get to the cruising life.

Without excellent information (read, inside information), the average investor is more likely to get trounced than to make a fortune buying and selling stocks over short time horizons. And don't forget, every time you buy and sell a security, your broker will want to be paid for the service, and these fees will often negate any returns. So lacking inside information (an accurate weather forecast), your experiences during a two-day passage are likely to be more extreme than over a three-week passage. In two days you'll probably either have great weather or get trashed; during a three-week trip, you'll see a bit of everything and come out closer to what the pilot charts call average weather for that passage in that season.

Diversification

Diversification is an integral part of risk management. It reduces the dependence of the overall return on a single investment by spreading portfolio risk across companies, industries, sectors, and even countries. But there are two kinds of risk involved: *systematic risks* that are inherent in the system and reflected by the underlying (once national, now global) business cycles, and *nonsystematic risks* like the consequences of the recent blowup in the Middle East (notably Syria) and the near destruction of the economy of Japan by natural disasters. While diversification will eliminate or reduce the effect of nonsystematic risks on your portfolio, you cannot diversify away systematic risks.

If a company like Facebook does something stupid, like using customers' photos in advertisements without authorization, as it did not too long ago, or if the government rules against a major airline merger, as it did with the aborted conspiracy between American Airlines and U.S. Airways, the reduced prices of these stocks will not overly affect your average return because other stocks in your kitty will be going up enough over the long haul to offset these losses. However, the risks from global disasters such as a total collapse of the Chinese banking system or a nuclear war between Pakistan and India would affect all markets and cannot be diversified away.

The first and most important thing to learn about investing is that there is no gain without risk and that a risk can result in a loss; substantial risks can result in substantial losses as well as gains. There's no room for crybabies; if you can't take the loss, don't take the risk—it's that simple.

Investment Vehicles

The following is a list, in order of increasing risk and increasing average returns, of a few of the investment options open to you once your kitty has a few thousand dollars available to get you started on a serious investment program.

Bank (or passbook) **savings accounts** are, of course, the most common and the easiest ways to save money. Savings accounts are available anywhere, they are as safe as investments get, you don't have to worry about fluctuations in the financial markets, and you might even score a new toaster when you open one. The only creditable risk is that the interest you earn will barely keep abreast of inflation. A savings account will preserve your money, but it won't put the money to work, and when the interest rate on passbook savings falls below the inflation rate, as is the current situation, keeping your money in the bank can actually cost you.

Certificates of deposit (CDs) are a way of investing money for a specific length of time for a known dividend that you will collect at the end of the investment period. They carry low risk, pay a modest return, and are available from any bank and most lending institutions. The disadvantages of CDs are that your money is not accessible for the life of the CD without substantial penalty, and the return is low compared to other options (though higher than a savings account). As long-term investments, CDs are appropriate for timid investors and those who don't care to take the time to learn about other avenues. They can also be useful as places to "park" money you're likely to need at a specified time in the near future, such as when you know you will need a new engine or a 10-year refit. A ***CD ladder*** is a basket of CDs with staggered maturity dates (6 months, 12 months, 18 months, and so on) that can make sense in this instance because you know the money will be there no matter what happens to the stock market. But at today's interest rates, you can't expect your CDs to increase in value.

High-grade government bonds pay a fixed interest rate, and they have a value that fluctuates with prevailing interest rates and their maturity date. They deserve a prominent place in your cruising kitty, but they need to be selected with care. High-grade bond funds are mutual funds that specialize in various types of bonds, preferred stocks, and a variety of government issues. There are a lot of these funds, and selecting just the right ones can be daunting for a neophyte investor. It is worth a bit of study, though, because bond funds should be an important part of your kitty. Like everything else, they must be selected with care, so consult a professional if you don't feel 100 percent comfortable with them.

Preferred stocks are much like bonds. They pay a fixed return, but they have no maturity date. In the past, investors would offset the risk associated with common stocks by buying bonds or preferred stocks, but the notion that bonds and preferred stocks can be used to hedge common stocks has taken a beating recently, with the stock and bond markets moving together rather than in opposite directions.

Common stock funds are mutual funds with full-time managers who spend their days and nights buying and selling profitable stocks for you, the investor. The value of a common stock fund (called the *net asset value*, or NAV) is determined by the average market value of all the securities in the portfolio (and this is often in the billions of dollars) divided by the number of fund shares outstanding. The manager does all the work of buying and selling while the diversification of the portfolio helps to smooth out the lumps and bumps of the market fluctuations. They are just the ticket for a large part of our cruising kitty. The good ones pay a healthy total return (growth in market value plus dividends), and they are easier to select and carry less risk than individual stocks. International stock funds are also available. These are riskier than domestic funds because they are affected by currency exchange rates as well as the fluctuations of the component stocks, but they represent a useful way to move some of your eggs into another basket.

Cruisers who don't want to take the time to get any more involved in the complexities of investing can stop right here by putting a big part of their kitty in a diversified portfolio of CDs, common stock funds, bond funds, and perhaps some ready cash in a money market account. The following vehicles are a lot more tricky to use, they require more time for maintenance, and the risk is proportionately higher than with the vehicles listed above. Therefore, most cruisers should probably avoid them simply because they require too much attention. We have better things to do with our time than fret over the machinations of a fickle stock market. However, the aggressive investor or the cruiser who is truly interested in following market swings will need to at least consider the next five vehicles.

Individual common stocks, on average, have paid the highest returns for the lowest risk of any investment vehicle in the past 50 years. The key word here is "average" because even in a rapidly rising market, there are always a few losers, and in any kind of market it is just as easy to pick a loser as a winner. Selecting the right common stocks requires much study and more than a little luck. Mistakes can be costly. The value of a common stock is determined by the price someone else is willing to pay for it and little else. Thus the price of a good stock can fall quickly if it falls out of favor with investors, and a bad stock can skyrocket if it becomes trendy with the in-crowd of investors. Professional investors are very much like lemmings and tend to follow the person in front of them even if that person runs off a cliff into the sea. Even the most adventurous cruisers should never let the amount of money invested in individual stocks (as opposed to common stock mutual funds) exceed 25 percent of the total kitty.

American depository receipts (ADRs) provide a means of investing in overseas companies through the U.S. stock exchanges. ADRs trade through the various markets just the way stocks do. They tend to be more speculative than stocks, but they can still be excellent investments. Only a small part (no more than 10 percent) of your cruising kitty should ever go into select ADRs, but that small part can return large gains (and, of course, losses). I like ADRs, but most investors would prefer to invest in global or foreign stock funds and let the fund managers do the choosing.

Closed-end mutual funds are traded on the exchanges just like ADRs, and they should also be approached with caution, but they also deserve consideration for the aggressive kitty. Just like common stocks, closed-end funds are worth what somebody else is willing to pay for them. Typically, they trade at a discount to the net asset value (NAV) of the stocks they own. Among these funds are some that specialize in stocks of one country; these represent a convenient vehicle for targeted foreign investments. Cruisers and cruisers-in-training should be long-term investors—but if you feel compelled to trade, you're less likely to lose your shirt trading closed-end funds than individual stocks.

Low-grade bonds, sometimes called *junk bonds*, are speculative, and you should only invest money in them that you never expect to see again. Don't discount them entirely though—Xerox, McDonald's, IBM, Intel, and a lot of others got started by issuing junk bonds. If you buy junks, don't buy a lot of them.

A **junk bond fund** can be a hedge against a falling market because when investors (we're talking about the big boys and girls here) decide to get out of stocks, they often go into junk bond funds because, while they tend to be more speculative than high-grade funds, in a down market they tend to return what these heavy hitters are used to getting from their stock funds. Don't even think about buying junk bonds unless you know exactly what you are doing because in most cases, the risks are far greater than the rewards.

There are a great many other vehicles with which you can make and lose money. Real estate investment trusts (REITs), the commodities (pork bellies and such) market, and short selling are just a few. These are sophisticated investments, however, best left alone by cruisers and anyone who is not a full-time professional investor.

In the early 1980s, being the clever investor that I was, I jumped at the chance to buy a small safe deposit box full of South African krugerrands and Canadian maple leaf coins (1-ounce gold coins) at a mere $450 dollars each because "everyone" knew that gold was headed for $500 an ounce and was sure to go higher. When we departed on our world cruise in the early nineties, those coins had gained negative value (I love spin terminology) and were worth a robust $285 each. Having learned yet another lesson in investment strategy and become even more clever, I sold the coins and bought stock through ADRs in a Vietnamese bicycle company (really, I couldn't make this up). As I write this, gold is selling at well above $1,300 an ounce having recently plunged from a high of nearly $1,900 an ounce as the economy recovers. Now, having become more clever than ever, I realize how easy it is for a misguided amateur investor to turn a large amount of money into a small one with hardly any effort at all.

As for the Vietnamese bicycle company? Well, Susan and I agree on a lot of things, and one thing we agree on most of all is that I will never again even mention Vietnamese bicycle companies.

Dividend Reinvestment Options

Automatic reinvestment plans will use the dividends you earn from a security to buy additional shares of that security, usually without any fees or commissions. If your broker offers this, be sure to sign up. Your cash dividends will go into your securities account rather than your cash account, where they won't earn as much (in the long term).

Your broker will ask if you are interested in growth stocks or income stocks. Tell him or her that all you want is more money at the end of the month than you had at the beginning of the month and whether they call it growth, income, or seaweed soup doesn't matter a bit. (There are some differences in the tax consequences of growth and income stocks that you don't need to worry about until you build a large kitty or unless you want to really get into investing.)

Worry-Free Kitties

Investing your kitty is a lot easier than most professional money managers want you to believe. It is about 25 percent science and 75 percent gut feelings borne of familiarity, which means it is highly instinctive, which is why so many cruisers are good at it.

Read a few online issues of *Barron's* and *Forbes* magazines (just ignore the multitude of advertisements that extoll the super-rich lifestyle) or any other financial periodical, and a few books from the library (*Against the Gods* by Peter L. Bernstein is a classic on risk management that is also a fun book to read) to learn the mechanics of investing. Then stay current by reading an occasional online version of the international edition of *Bloomberg Businessweek*.

Don't Cry, Diversify

I've covered this once already, but I'll say it again because it is the most important part of your investment program. Diversification is the key to investing for the cruising life and the single best way to protect your investment in any situation. If your entire kitty were invested in one moderately risky investment, say, common shares of a high-flying software company, it would be difficult to sleep at night. However, if your kitty were divided among 10 moderately risky common stocks in three or four unrelated industries in three or four countries, what happens to any one stock doesn't matter that much, so you don't have to worry about it as much. Also, by diversifying your kitty, you won't have a lot invested in any one area so that the consequences of your mistakes won't be as dire. Thus you will be training yourself not to make mistakes at the same time you are learning not to worry about the ones you do make.

How Not to Buy Stocks

Don't ever invest in "tips" from your dentist or some guy you met in the boatyard, and ignore anything you might read on the Internet until you confirm it with your broker. Be especially leery of anything that you read in cruising books written by grouchy old guys in classic boats.

A huge resource of investor information and assistance is available online, but there is an even larger body of nonsense and more than a few world-class scams. Until you are comfortable with investing your kitty and convinced that secure and conservative investments are necessary, you must stay away from this stuff, or at least learn to take everything you hear and read that doesn't come from a trusted professional with a large grain of salt. Even articles in national magazines can contain bad advice about bad investments, so you need to be skeptical about the most reputable sources of investment advice.

Especially beware of life insurance salespeople. At our modest level of investing, many websites that claim to offer financial advice will try to sell you life insurance. As soon as you hear the term "life insurance," walk away. There is nothing wrong with life insurance, but life insurance is life insurance, not an investment.

Ignore trendy investments (as opposed to trends, which is another thing) and fads. You can't keep up with them from a cruising sailboat anyway. The media gurus and personalities who so love to predict what is going to happen to the market or to favorite stocks and funds are a great source of information on the current state of affairs and are whizzes at analyzing historical data that can help you make up your mind which investments you want in your kitty. These folks are professionals in a difficult and complicated field, and you should listen to what they say, but when they are trying to predict what is going to happen in the future, they get it wrong as often as they get it right.

The important thing to remember is that if you've done it correctly with conservative long-term investments, you can sleep soundly with no need to worry about what happens in the market.

Planning for What Comes Next

Let's face it: you aren't going to cruise forever. The charm of distant anchorages in strange places may eventually wear thin. You might tire of the gypsy life and begin to yearn for some permanent dirt under your feet and a vegetable garden out in the backyard, or you may want to do other things you can't do on a boat. More likely, you'll just grow too old to keep up with the vigorous life of the active cruiser. Whatever the reasons you give up the cruising life, when you do it, you're going to need some resources.

The most common mistake cruisers who are returning to shore make is to count on the resale of their boat for retirement funds. Of course you can sell your boat when you give up cruising, but I guarantee that you're not going to get nearly as much as you think you'll get for it—but we have said that before.

The point is that cruisers are notoriously bad at planning for the day when they must hang up their Topsiders. As you design the financial strategy for your cruise, you must take these needs into consideration and plan for them accordingly. Beyond this caveat, I can't say much because individual circumstances, needs, and ages vary enough to make any specific advice useless.

Acting as your own investment counselor can be expensive and time-consuming even if you have the knowledge and skills to follow and interpret the machinations of a fluctuating market. If you don't have the skills, doing it yourself can be deadly. And why bother when there are legions of qualified professionals who are willing to do it for you for a minimal fee or even just for the privilege of doing it.

Our Personal Investment Journey

When Susan and I first started cruising full-time, over 20 years ago, we were planning to do it for 3 years, then return the kids to school, try to get our jobs back, and resume a normal life. But after the first year, it became obvious that the 3-year plan wasn't going to fly and cruising was fast becoming a lifestyle. We had very little money in those early days—just a monthly check from tenants who were renting our house and a bit of income from an investment account with Charles Schwab, where we had deposited our kitty when we departed. It was a hand-to-mouth existence for us at first, but we managed nicely by living cheap and spending only what we had to spend.

But then, when we reached New Zealand, circumstances changed dramatically. I flew back to the United States and spent several months selling our house and liquidating all our possessions. And, to make a long and complicated story short and simple, we ended up with a larger pile of cash than we had ever seen in one place in our lives.

Selling our house and all our stuff didn't make us wealthy by any stretch, but we were able to complete a refit of *Sultana* with enough left over to fatten the kitty to the point that hand-to-mouth living was no longer an issue. We could suddenly indulge in previously frivolous activities like eating out on occasion and renting a car now and then without being consumed by guilt. And that gut-wrenching feeling you get when the ATM machine refuses to cough up because your debit card is dry ceased to be a common concern.

Up to this point, I had been buying and selling stock and mutual funds with the meager funds in our original kitty, and I was actually

89

doing surprisingly well with it. But as many readers of the first edition of this book have kindly pointed out, this was during a booming economy when a blind monkey with a dart board would have done well in the stock market.

The Easy Way Out

When *Sultana*'s refit was complete, we headed north into the South Pacific with no definite idea of where we were going or how long we would be gone. Anticipating communications difficulties that would complicate a self-managed stock portfolio, we turned the entire kitty over to our previously ignored financial advisor, and we haven't looked back.

Our advisor at the time was a gregarious lad named Tim, and when we visited him in his office in Manchester, New Hampshire, we essentially said, "Here, you do it." That proved to be one of the best decisions we have made in our history of cruising. Gone were the debilitating and time-consuming concerns with the daily machinations of the Nikki, the DAX, the Hand Sing, and the FTSE 100. When Tim retired, our account was turned over to a succession of advisors, and they have continued to look after our interests with diligence and patience, and the *Vicarious* account has prospered by their efforts.

Naturally our portfolio fluctuates along with market swings, and no financial platform can be immune to the traumas that wiped out the kitties of legions of cruisers in 2008. But the aggressively conservative program set up by our advisors has allowed us to ride through all the financial machinations of the last decade with hardly a concern for the welfare of our now plump and pampered kitty.

There are a lot of brokerages and investment programs available on the Internet, but Charles Schwab is the only one I have had personal experience with. In the past 20 years we have used this firm, and we have been satisfied with all their services, especially their high level of customer service, which is critical when you move around a lot.

My best advice for choosing a brokerage is to do a lot of research; be very careful of what you read on the Internet because it is a minefield of scams and cons; favor a firm with a long history over a new startup; and read carefully the advice in Eric Tyson's book *Personal Finance for Dummies* that I mentioned earlier in this chapter.

Most mutual funds and brokerage houses have minimum amounts for opening an account that range from $500 to more than $25,000 (a few go into the millions), depending on the type of account and a lot of other factors. The minimum for a regular investor-line account at Schwab is $5,000 as this is written, but check for yourself because the number is bound to change. If you don't have enough money to satisfy the minimum, let your cash accumulate in a savings account at a bank until you do.

With investing, as in all things, when you are smart and earn money, people will say you were lucky. When you are stupid and lose money, people will say you were stupid.

8

Planning for Departure

*Plans are useless, but
planning is essential.
Always be ready to
change the plan, but
never change the goal.*

—**ANCIENT CRUISING
WISDOM**

Uncle Freddy and the Pompadour Kid

My earliest sailing experiences were aboard my Uncle Freddy's
29-foot Herreshoff sloop *Mazuka*. She was a fine old boat built
somewhere in New England sometime in the 1920s. If she
looked a bit run down and shabby, she suited our purpose just
fine, thanks, and when I learned to sail on her, she still sported
hemp lines and cotton sails. Like most Herreshoff designs, she
also sported an enormous sinusoidal keel and a draft of over
6 feet. In the shallow waters of the Chesapeake Bay, this meant
that a good part of our sailing time was spent waiting for the tide
to come in and float us off whatever sandbar the keel had decided
we would colonize that day. That pleased me to no end because it
provided opportunity to cavort in the warm bay waters with my
two cousins, chase tasty blue crabs through the shallows with the
ship's long-handled crab net, dive for oysters, and pursue other
activities more interesting to a 14-year-old than mere sailing.

Let's back up a bit. When I say "learning to sail," that may
not be quite accurate. Uncle Freddy was the undisputed captain
of *Mazuka*, and as such, he did all the sailing. I spent most of the
time while under way on the foredeck practicing my sullen look
and working on my pompadour. This was the early 1950s, and
my teenage world was firmly under the influence of the recently
departed James Dean, and the sullen sneer, defiant squint, and
Lucky Strike dangling from pouting lips (when my mom wasn't
looking, of course) were critical to post-adolescent survival. It
was a jungle out there, and if your pompadour didn't stand up
just right and your sneer didn't intimidate properly, you were

doomed to a life of ignominy and disgrace. I never did master the sneer, but I had a terrific sullen scowl, and my pompadour and ducktail rivaled those of the upstart Elvis himself.

Anyway, I didn't learn to sail on my uncle's boat, but I did learn something about what makes a sailboat go and why it does the things it does. I also learned a lot about what you can't expect a boat to do, like carry a 6-foot draft through 4 feet of water, or get you home in a hurry when you really need to get home in a hurry. I learned that sailboats are fun, that my life wasn't in danger when the thing heeled to a stiff breeze, and that if I kept in the lee of the main by the mast, I could avoid the wind enough to preserve my pompadour. In a word, I learned to like boats and to respect them, and that changed my life.

Learning to Sail

We've assumed all along that you know how to sail. If you don't, don't worry. The basics are pretty easy to pick up, and you'll learn quickly once under way. It's quite amazing how many people who have no previous sailing experience become successful cruisers. It isn't at all uncommon to meet folks from places like Iowa and Nebraska and Arizona who had never so much as been aboard a sailboat when epiphany struck and they decided to become cruisers. In Belize we met a couple from Ontario who had spent 10 years building a 50-foot ferro-cement ketch and who had never seen a body of water larger than an inland lake until they launched in Lake Superior.

Of course, some of these people never do become adept sailors—in fact, some of the best cruisers we have met are klutzy sailors even after years of experience. In the Cook Islands we met a family on a salty old gaff-rigged schooner who looked like the epitome of stereotypical mariners—striped jerseys and sailor

hats and everything but the parrot. I spent several happy evenings talking traditional boats and how sailing used to be with the skipper of this fine anachronism. I gathered he knew just about everything there was to know about boats and how to make them travel—until I watched him and his family try to leave the harbor. When they cast off, it was obvious they were having trouble controlling the boat under power, and they finally had to hire a local boat to escort them out the narrow channel. Then, like a couple of blinking amateurs, they stumbled off over the horizon with the main blanketing the foresail and the jib flapping useless in the breeze. I was astonished at their ineptitude but not really surprised when I heard through the coconut telegraph (one of the most efficient communication systems on earth) that they had reached Australia before most of the fleet after an uneventful and presumably enjoyable cruise—proving once again my contention that judgment on when and where to sail, navigation skills, and strength of character are far more important to the cruising life than sophisticated sailing skills.

Another group of cruisers lies on the opposite end of the cruising spectrum. These are folks who might become disenchanted with the cruising life because they know how to sail, but can't. Many people who develop sophisticated sailing skills on high-tech boats are not happy with the low-tech, outdated boats that are so common among budget cruisers. It must be frustrating indeed to possess the skills to make a lightweight class boat fly around the buoys at the head of the fleet and then be stuck with an overloaded, under-rigged, slow-moving cruising tub. We've met a few of these folks, and they constantly like to talk about what they would do to the old girl if they had the money for new sails and rigging. This is fine, of course, and we all like to blue sky about ways we would improve our boats if we had thc cash, but I'm convinced that some of these former racers who can't afford a high-tech boat would be happier staying home until the kitty was big enough to allow them to sail the way they want to sail.

Sailing Schools

We have met lots of active cruisers who got their start by learning the basics of sailing from a commercial sailing school, and most agree that it was a satisfactory experience. In spite of this, I remain a bit skeptical. It is important to get as much sailing experience as you can before you buy a boat, but it is even more important not to spend a lot of money getting that experience. The sailing schools that have flourished in recent years are terrific and usually good value for consumers. But we're no longer consumers, are we? We need that money in our kitty. Besides, most of these schools use old Solings or newer J/80s or some other class of boats that is a dream to sail. It's great fun and a great way to develop respect for sailboats and to meet a wonderful bunch of fun and interesting people, but it doesn't teach you that much about cruising sailing.

One thing that a sailing school will do, however, is to get someone new to sailing through the innate mistrust of sailboats that comes from our highly evolved determination to remain vertical (unless sleeping or propagating, neither of which is normally associated with sailing schools). A few lessons with a good instructor may help get a timid person past the fear of tipping over and instill the confidence that we all need to sheet her in hard and head off toward distant destinations (where perhaps to indulge in a bit of propagating and a nap).

Bareboat Charters

Bareboat chartering is a popular way for wannabe cruisers to sample the cruising life, but it isn't really a great way to go about it. Chartering may offer good value to consumers looking for

an exciting vacation, and they are an entrée into cruising for a lot of folks with deep pockets, but they're too expensive for those of us struggling to build a kitty, and they don't teach much about cruising anyway. The boats in the bareboat fleet are usually lightweight production models with cut-down rigs that would be inappropriate or even dangerous for offshore cruising. Many times most of the work of provisioning, navigating, and maintenance is done for you by the charter staff, and many charter companies even provide cooks. You are also restricted as to where and when you can sail and where you can anchor. To add insult to injury, many charter companies actively discourage any contact with the cruising community, a fact that has always puzzled me and deserves a slight deviation from our stated topic.

I first became aware of a curious segregation between cruising sailors and bareboat charterers in the Virgin Islands when I noticed that boats sharing the same harbors would clump up like flocks of sheep and goats—all the sheep were at one end of the harbor, the goats at the other. It quickly became apparent that these two groups were looking for different things from their cruises. The cruisers were looking for peace and quiet; the charterers were looking for fun—and fun to charterers often means crowding a dozen or more people onto a 40-foot catamaran, getting drunk, and making noise until 2 a.m. This helped explain why there was a lack of dialogue between the two groups, but it still didn't explain the obvious antipathy with which the two groups viewed each other, nor did it explain why the charter operators told their customers to avoid cruisers.

It wasn't until we got to Vava'u in Tonga that I discovered the real reason. Neiafu Harbor is home to a large charter fleet run by the Moorings Company. The manager at the time was an energetic young man named Bill Bailey (no "Won't-you-come-home?" jokes, please—it's no wonder the poor guy lived in Tonga), and I wasted no time asking him about this phenomenon. He wouldn't talk, but I struck up a conversation with one of his crew who made it all clear.

"Hey," he said defensively. "Most of our customers come all the way from the United States or from Europe and pay thousands of dollars for a few weeks sailing in one of our boats. They think it's a bargain, and it is when you consider the cost of running an operation like this. But then they see the damn cruisers in their junky old boats and find out that some of these guys sail around these islands for a whole year and don't spend any more money in a year than what they are paying for a few weeks, and it causes trouble. Suddenly they think we are trying to rip them off, and they want to know how we justify charging so much." He paused for a moment to get his emotions under control, but it didn't work. "We even had a couple from Seattle who had been coming here for years get friendly with a cruising couple. Now they come and stay on their friends' boat for nothing—can you beat that?"

Crewing at Yacht Clubs

If we can't spend money and we don't have a boat yet, how are we going to learn to sail? Well, if a yacht club is nearby, there's your answer. Posting a notice that you would like to crew often brings a flood of calls, but be careful whom you crew with, and don't just hop into the first boat that comes along. Be particularly cautious if you are asked to crew on a racing boat.

Many racing skippers possess intense personalities and emotions that are hard for others to understand and tolerate. Many races deteriorate into screaming matches that often carry over to the protest committee and even to the courts. This is fine because it keeps a lot of self-important and potentially dangerous people off the streets and in the committee

rooms where they can't do any real harm. The problem is that the screaming and profanity are most frequently directed at the crew instead of the opposition. Punching your skipper in the nose for calling you a lame-brained idiot (the usual epithet is much worse than that) when you got the traveler car a quarter-inch out of position on the last tack teaches you nothing about sailing or cruising. (However, I imagine that it is a most satisfactory experience.)

If you agree to become a member of a racing crew, the skipper usually assigns you to one line to pull or one winch to crank when you are yelled at. It's possible to crew for years under skippers like this without having a clue as to what's going on, and the only thing you become good at is pulling one line and hating the skipper.

Community Sailing Programs

By far one of the very best ways to learn the basics of sailing is to participate in one of the many community sailing programs across the country, especially if you are new to sailing and need to start from the beginning. These programs vary from place to place, but they all focus on getting novice yachts people on the water as efficiently as possible. Most community sailing operations charge a small fee for joining, then start new members with a course of classroom instruction on sailing theory and practice before getting on the real water with a real boat. New students are usually taught on the small class racing dinghies such as the Rhodes 19, Star Class, then move up to crew boats like the 470 or Soling. It has been said that if you can sail a Soling well, you can sail anything well.

The program I am personally familiar with is the Boston Community Sailing Program that has been teaching kids and adults to sail since just after World War II. My kids learned the basics there as have thousands of others, many who went on to become world-class sailors.

The best source of information on programs that might be in or near your neighborhood is the Internet. Just Google "community boating" and you will get dozens of responses.

Crewing for Friends

If you have a friend who owns a sailboat, no matter the size, hint around that you'd like to serve as crew; chances are good that you'll find a willing teacher. It is much better to learn to sail on a small simple boat with a crew of two or three than on a large boat with a large crew. Small boats are harder to sail well than large boats, but you will learn more quickly. The owner of a small boat will be much more likely to let you participate in all aspects of sailing than will the skipper of a large boat.

There is a limit to the small-boat theory, however, and I would suggest not trying to learn sailing techniques on sailing dinghies less than 14 feet long. These little boats are great for kids (Phillip learned on an Optimist, and Sarah graduated to a Laser), but they aren't for adults, and the more adult you are, the more they aren't for you. Small-dinghy sailing requires the agility of an Olympic athlete and the humility of a saint. You must squat on the floorboard of the boat like a frog looking for a bug and be prepared to fling your weight about in a reckless fashion to prevent the whole thing from flipping over on top of you. When you don't move quickly enough, you capsize, and if you are anywhere near as proficient a dinghy sailor as your aqua-phobic author, most of your dinghy sailing time will be spent in the drink trying to right the damn thing so you can carry on into the next gust of wind and start the whole process over again.

Cruisers like me are noted for our great agility of mind and spirit and less so for agility of body. My advice is to leave the small dinghies to the small people and those few adults who are predisposed to strenuous physical activity and other forms of self-torture. Try to find a spot on a bigger boat, like a Soling or a 470.

Crewing for Delivery Skippers and Singlehanders

One raw and rainy October night, I was working late getting our old powerboat ready to haul for the season when I heard a timid knock on the hull and a thin voice request permission to come aboard. When I assented, a woman in her early twenties climbed into the cabin and asked if I was preparing the boat to move south. She was visibly disappointed when I told her the boat was being hauled out for winter storage in the morning. Being reluctant to send her back out into the cold, I fixed her a cup of coffee and invited her to sit for a while.

Her name was Lisa, and she had spent the past three years hitchhiking around the eastern United States and Caribbean on cruising yachts. She had, however, waited a bit too long and had missed the major southern exodus of New England boats. When I commented that hitchhiking about on boats seemed like a rather dangerous way to travel for a young person, she laughed heartily and said that there were advantages to being rather homely—not to mention her third-degree black belt in *feng shui* (or maybe it was *kung chopsui*). She had experienced only one or two unpleasant moments in her travels, and nothing she couldn't handle. She also said that whenever she was ready to move on, she almost always had her choice of several boats from which to choose and that her present situation was unusual.

Lisa finished her coffee and went off into the night looking for adventure and a ride south, and since she never reappeared, I assume she found both. Since then, I have met several people doing just what Lisa was, and it seems to me that it's an excellent way for a single person or even a couple to learn about the cruising life without buying a boat or otherwise making a major commitment.

In any major harbor frequented by cruising sailors, there are usually several boats looking for crew to help on a voyage. Often, the boats are large, fancy yachts, and their regular crew doesn't feel confident or comfortable moving these yachts by themselves. A crew's berth on a large yacht with a reasonable skipper can be a very pleasant way to travel while learning the ropes—but don't become spoiled! Although it is always great to see how the other folks live, we don't want the good life of electric winches, flat-screen TVs in every cabin, multiple heads, and state-of-the-art hardware to seduce us away from our stated goal: to become simple and basic cruisers.

Another possibility for a berth is to seek out singlehanders about to embark on a passage. Insurance companies quite rightly frown on singlehanded passage making, and they often insist that the boatowner find crew. Many singlehanders, even those who carry no insurance, will welcome an extra hand to stand watch and provide conversation.

One of the best ways to get experience cruising and boat handling anywhere is by crewing for a delivery skipper. Hundreds of newly sold boats are delivered all over the globe by professional delivery crews, and if you can secure a berth on one of these yachts, you will be learning from a professional sailor whom you can usually count on as being one of the best. If you've made even a short passage or two as crew on a cruising yacht and can provide solid references, there's a chance that a delivery skipper will offer you a free berth; cooking skills give you extra leverage. If you're good enough, you might even get a return airplane ticket out of the deal, and if you are really good you might even get a small paycheck. Many people who purchase boats do their own delivery and might just welcome you aboard as cook or an unpaid deckhand.

Bear in mind, if you are thinking about seeking a crew slot on any boat sailing into foreign waters, that international maritime law makes the skipper responsible for the welfare of the crew, and crew can demand that they be returned to their homeport by the quickest means possible. Thus in addition to a valid passport and any necessary visas, you will also need a return airplane ticket from the country you are visiting. A ticket isn't likely to be provided by the skipper as part of the deal for your first few trips while you are learning the ropes, so he or she may insist that you hand over a ticket or a sum of money equal to the price of the return fare on departure. Naturally, this requirement has led to some dicey moments between captain and crew, so make sure everyone understands the situation before you commit yourself to a crew slot. The other major requirement is that you be flexible enough to drop everything and take off for a week or more to take advantage of opportunities as they arise.

Boat brokers are the best sources of information on current deliveries. One tactic for finding appropriate brokers is to do a search on the *YachtWorld* website for boats that are for sale in your area, then ring the listing broker and explain that you are looking for a delivery berth. Unless you are lucky, you will have to call several brokers before you get someone willing to help you, so be persistent, but even if a specific broker can't help directly, he or she will probably have a feel for the current situation in your area and will offer advice accordingly.

In recent years, the Internet has become a primary source for skippers looking for temporary crew and for crew looking for skippers. Most online forums, such as *CruisersForum* and *Cruising Anarchy* have a "crew needed" section with opportunities all over the world, and most have a provision whereby crew looking for a berth can advertise. These ads are sometimes free and should bring quick results, especially if you offer to share expenses—but you may want to avoid the ones requesting a photo.

As unpaid crew, you will often be asked to kick in for the fuel and provide your own food, but make sure everyone understands who pays for what before you agree to go. Be aware that when a skipper accepts expense money from a crew member, even for little things like a case of beer, the boat could be considered an unlicensed charter boat. In certain areas like the Virgin Islands and the Galapagos, where the licensed charter operators guard their turf like pit bulls guard their backyards, this can mean a world of grief for the skipper. In the worst scenario, the skipper and crew can be jailed and the boat confiscated—not something you ever want to be part of in any country.

Yet another approach to finding a crew berth is the one used by Lisa and most other maritime vagabonds. Simply hang out around any big marina where there are a lot of yachts, and let everyone know you are looking for a crew berth. Check first with the harbormaster or other authority person extant (APE), and let him or her know what you are up to. APEs like to know what is going on in their territories, and a pleasant one (quite rare, unfortunately) will even give you a few pointers. If the APE objects to your approaching boats directly, ask if you can post a notice on the bulletin board instead. Prospective crew have even been known to have flyers printed that they hand out in yacht club and marina parking lots.

One last point before we chuck the subject of crew berths into the wake and leave it behind forever. The foregoing advice is good and sound, but most of the cruisers I know who need crew seem to find them hanging around waterfront bars. I would not and could not in good conscience ever recommend that a person looking for a crew position take to hanging around in bars, but it does seem to work, and hey, who am I to argue with tradition?

USCGA and U.S. Power Squadron Courses

So sailing off with some person you don't know to somewhere you've never been is a little too heavy in the adventure department? Well then, what else is there? One of the ways to learn the basics, and even more about sailing and boat handling, is to enroll in local evening classes. Both the U.S. Coast Guard Auxiliary (USCGA) and the U.S. Power Squadron offer a series of excellent courses covering all aspects of boat handling, seamanship, and navigation (traditional and electronic). Most are free or carry a small charge for materials, and in my experience the quality of instruction has been excellent. The teachers are experienced sailors with a firm knowledge of their subjects. However, they are not necessarily experienced teachers, and only a few will have had extensive cruising experience, but I have never found this to be a problem. The classes are usually small after the first few nights (there are usually a lot of dropouts for some reason), and a camaraderie quickly develops among the students and staff that makes the learning friendly and easy.

It is very easy to make friends while taking these courses, and very often you will meet fellow students who have just purchased a boat and need crew. You wouldn't usually be learning from an expert under these conditions, but it could still be valuable experience in the water.

Learning About Cruising

You should, by now, have a pretty good idea of what you are getting yourself into, and you have probably decided, "Yep, this is it. I'm really going to do it." That's great, but don't quit your day job just yet. We still have a lot to do.

Cruising Seminars

Be very cautious before you spend money on commercial cruising seminars. They can be entertaining and informative for noncruisers, but they can be expensive, and most of the people giving the seminars are no longer cruising. The speakers are often so busy giving seminars that they don't have time for cruising anymore. Worse, many of them are opinionated, a trait shared by many cruisers. (Thank God your knowledgeable but unbiased author has escaped such a fate.) Susan attended one, for example, where the lecturer insisted autopilots and wind vanes were useless.

Boat show seminars can be good sources of information, and they are often free (or admission is included in the entrance fee for the show). Furthermore, they are often presented by world-class cruising couples such as Lin and Larry Pardey or Beth Leonard and Evans Starzinger.

No matter who is giving the seminar, be skeptical about anything you are told about cruising destinations until you read everything you can find on each one. As stated above, cruisers tend to be a bit opinionated, and they base their opinions on their own experiences. A good experience for one can often be a nightmare for another.

Fellow cruisers have often advised us to avoid a place where they have had a bad experience; we've gone there anyway and found a wonderful place to visit—for us. Other times we've been told that such and such a place was a paradise for cruisers only to find a place we were indifferent about. We rarely find a place we don't really like; when we do, it's usually close to a city, but this reflects our prejudice and preference for quiet rural areas. Other cruisers prefer the hustle and bustle of busy harbors, and we've even met some (quite a few really) who actually like Pago Pago.

Would you like to know where you can find a free cruising seminar almost every evening of the week? Head for the aforementioned waterfront bar. (Just watch out for the ones that have a gold-painted sculpture of a pineapple or a rooster instead of a name—they tend to be pricey and populated by yuppies.) Seek any group of cruisers therein, strike up a conversation, and offer to buy a round of beers. A single round should get you about three hours of uninterrupted cruising lectures, plus you will glean untold bits of useful information such as the IQ, dietary habits, and sexual preferences of the harbormaster, who snuck off with whom to do what, and which grocery stores offer the best discounts on case lots of Spam and Dinty Moore beef stew.

You're Almost Ready

We have pushed the fast-forward button, and it's several years, perhaps five years, later. You're almost ready to go. You're living in a tiny house in a good neighborhood, wearing old (but neat and tidy) clothes; eating simple, basic, and nutritious meals; exercising regularly so you're a paragon of physical fitness; and you're out of debt. Your kitty has grown fat and healthy, and you've developed a harmonious relationship with your mate, your kids, and anyone else who plans to go cruising with you. What next? By now you have probably formed a pretty firm plan about where you want to do your cruising. If not, it's time to start thinking about it.

Susan and the Wonder Cruise

Many folks don't believe me when I tell them that Susan is the driving force behind our adopting the cruising life, but it is true. No, I wasn't exactly dragged into it screaming and kicking against my will, but I was at first skeptical of the basic philosophy of world cruising (it seemed a little decadent and a lot impractical), and I was a little reluctant to leave behind a lifestyle that could only be described as a good thing. But leave we did, and in spite of a few difficult times and a lot of amateurish foibles, neither of us has ever looked back or regret-ted for a moment our decision. Although we thought we had made very careful preparations and paid a great deal of attention to the specif-ics of what we were going to do with our cruise and where we were going to do it, the trip that transpired only vaguely resembled the trip we planned.

The first cruising scheme that Susan came up with was for us to take off as soon as the chil-dren were safely away at college, and this suited me just fine. At the time our youngest was 8, and I figured that the ensuing 10 years or so would be plenty of time for Susan to forget the whole thing and come up with something practical for us to do when the chicks had flown and the nest was empty. If my "Yes, dear . . . of course, dear" approval of the idea rang a little hollow, it was at least approval, and that's all Susan needed. As subsequent revisions of Susan's scheme brought our departure date closer and closer, every hint of reluctance I voiced brought forth a "But you said you liked the idea."

It wasn't long before Susan decided that 10 years was too long to wait and that she didn't want to go cruising with some grumpy old guy as her only company, so she resolved to leave earlier and take the kids with us. "Great idea," I answered. "We'll leave in 9 years instead." But then Susan decided that if we were going to go cruising with the kids at all, we had to do it now or the kids wouldn't be kids anymore. My comforting 10-year lead time had been reduced to a frantic 2.

Once we had decided to leave while the children were too small to mount any seri-ous opposition to our plans and I had decided that any further resistance to Susan's cruising strategy was futile, we settled on the idea of a three-year circumnavigation that would get us back to Marblehead in time for Sarah to grad-uate from high school. We would buy a boat, sail to Bermuda, then to Panama via the Virgin Islands, transit the Panama Canal, and cross the Pacific to Australia in the first year. In the second year we would pay a brief visit to Singapore and Sri Lanka, then blast through the Red Sea and spend the winter touring Europe by train. Our third year would see us across the Atlantic to the Caribbean then up the East Coast to home in time to get the kids back to school by September and for me to pick up the shambles of a normal life.

Even now I marvel at this lovely prac-tical plan. In our naiveté, we didn't know any better—and we certainly didn't know that the size of our bank balance—which could only be described as small—would have such a large effect on our ultimate cruising "plan."

When we began looking at cruising boats, we were shocked at how expensive they were. The first few brokers we talked to snickered when we told them how much we had to spend, and we quickly learned not to say that we planned a circumnavigation if we expected any response other than bemused indifference. The consensus among brokers seemed to be that we would need to spend at least $250,000 if we were going to get a safe and reliable boat that four people could live on for three years. This was rather disappointing because that figure was almost twice our budget for the entire trip. If we had found a boat for half that amount, we still wouldn't have had any money left for the trip, and if we had set aside enough money for the trip, we wouldn't have had enough for a boat. "Ah well," I said. "It was a great idea, but it obviously won't work, so I guess we'll just have to go back to spending the rest of our lives like normal people."

But neither Susan nor Sarah (who had become a staunch supporter of the cruising guru) would have any of this. Susan had gotten hold of Annie Hill's *Voyaging on a Small Income*, and Sarah had read about the adventures Herb and Doris Smith in their book *Sailing Three*

Oceans: Building and Sailing Schooner Appledore so every time I started to backslide, one or the other of them would whack me back on track with a quote from one of these books. I came to dread the sentence "If they can do it, so can we."

Both of these books are about people who went cruising after building their own boats, and while I have worked with boats most of my life and would have felt comfortable enough building one for us, the minimum two or three years the project would have added to our get-away plans wasn't good enough for the girls. So we compromised again, and with the compromise came more changes in our plans. We would buy an old boat in reasonable condition and fix it up for our trip, which would, I figured, add only about a year to our departure time. That still wasn't good enough. Once we were resolved to leave, the whole crew wanted to go now. And even I, the reluctant captain (no one else wanted the job) of our expedition, didn't want to wait any longer than necessary.

Our first plan evolved into our buying an old boat, getting it into seaworthy condition with as little fuss and expense as possible, then sailing it as far as we could before stopping in some faraway and exotic land to fix it up enough to continue the voyage. Thus we rescued *Sultana* from under a pile of pigeon guano in a barn in Maine, got her hull repaired and her sails patched enough so that we could leave, and sailed off without the slightest idea of how far we could get before the need for major repairs would stop us cold.

When we left Marblehead, I figured that we would be lucky to make it to Florida before the old girl gave it up, but from Florida we made it to Mexico, and so it went from one stop to another until we found ourselves safely ensconced on the hard on the South Island of New Zealand. If it hadn't been for a major gale that destroyed the last of our sails and broke our bobstay, we would have easily made it to Australia.

When we found Sultana *in a barn in Maine, she was in far from sail-away condition, but we didn't have the time or money to fix her up properly. After doing just enough work to make her safe and seaworthy, we sailed south hoping to make it as far as Florida. Three years later we sailed into Nelson Harbor in New Zealand having made it halfway around the world with no major problems.*

Our old boat, for which we had paid $25,000, just 10 percent of what the brokers told us would get us a minimum cruising boat, had made it nearly halfway around the world, and she had done it without a hitch. We experienced far fewer problems than many cruisers had on the same trip in brand-new boats. Does this prove that old boats are better than new ones? You bet it does, and that's a major part of what this book is about.

This chapter, however, is not about the relative superiority of old boats over new ones; it's about plans and how they change. Each time we met a hurdle to Susan's initial cruising plan, we found a way to jump over it, but each jump meant a change in plans that often raised a new hurdle. The need to stop and effect major repairs to the boat shot the three-year plan all to hell, and the trip that evolved from the initial plan bore no resemblance to it whatsoever, but it was a great trip nevertheless. Since then our current plan is to have no plan at all, but this hasn't worked either; every time we talk to the folks back home, they inevitably ask, "What's your plan?"

Destinations: The Long-Range Plan

Make all the plans you want, but don't make schedules. Plans tend to remain flexible and tentative right up to the last minute and as such are easier to change or back away from than schedules, which tend to become rigid and dictatorial. Schedules don't work in the cruising environment, and they can actually be dangerous because they lead people to sail into bad weather when they otherwise would stay in harbor. On several occasions we met cruisers who just had to get someplace so badly that they were compelled to leave in the face of an approaching frontal system, or with the boat in less-than-perfect condition, or shorthanded, or with some other condition that made staying much more sensible than going. The usual reason for such hasty impropriety is to meet family or to pick up new crew or to get an existing crew member to an airport in time to make a flight. It's called the I-got-to-get-to-Cartagena-by-Christmas syndrome, and it happens only with schedules, never with plans.

I've mentioned earlier that it's best not to announce your plans until just before or after you depart. Naturally, as the time for departure draws close, it would be cruel and inconsiderate not to tell family members and your most trusted friends that you are planning to leave and that you will be gone for quite a long time, but everyone you tell should be made to understand that cruising isn't like a trip to Disneyland. You can't have a daily itinerary, and you can't know just where you will be at any one time. Small changes in conditions or small events can require major changes in cruising plans, and you must remain flexible to take advantage of unexpected opportunities and to respond to emergencies and adverse conditions as they arise. After fighting gale-force headwinds for several days on our trip from the Tuamotus to Papeete, we simply decided we didn't want to go there anyway, changed course, and had a great sail to Raieatea. We never did get to Papeete, even though we had told everyone that it would be one of our major stops.

Tell Mom and Dad and the grown-up-and-moved-out kids what's up, but always bear in mind that unannounced plans are easier to change or back away from than announced ones. We've changed *Vicarious*'s plans so many times that anyone trying to follow them would think she—and we!—were schizophrenic.

Reading Your Way Around the World

One of the most important things you can start doing once you make up your mind to go cruising is read every cruising book you can get your hands on. By now you should be best pals with Slocum and Chichester and Hiscock and Tristan Jones, on speaking terms with the Pardeys, the Smith family, Robin Lee Graham, and Tania Aebi, and looking forward to meeting all the rest. Nigel Calder and Charles "Chappy" Chapman should be your trusted technical advisors; while Steve and Linda Dashew will keep you posted on how to cruise the good life once you finally hit the big one in the state lottery.

Don't neglect Melville, Conrad, Robert Louis Stevenson, Jack London, or John Masefield either. They may not have a lot of practical information to offer, but they sure get the old sailor's blood boiling. They make you yearn for the salt spray on a heaving deck, a tarred queue, hardtack, and dead whales. *(OK, OK, forget the dead whales. Make that "friendly whales.")*

While we are at it, let's not neglect old Nathaniel Bowditch (even though we have no intention of reading the book named after him—I'm convinced that nobody has actually ever read *The American Practical Navigator*). But you should by now be familiar with the principles of navigation he refined. By the way, if you are ever sailing in Marblehead Harbor on a local boat, you will undoubtedly be shown Bowditch Ledge where the story goes that old Nathaniel, after navigating for several years around the globe without mishap, ran hard aground on his return. The story is a complete fabrication, and all Marbleheaders know that, but it is too good a story not to pass on—proving once again that while truth might be stranger than fiction, fiction is often more fun.

Deciding Where to Go

One of the popular misconceptions that shore-siders have of cruisers is that we enjoy the freedom of going anywhere we want to go as long as there is navigable water nearby. Although that may be true in a philosophical sense, in practical terms nothing could be further from the truth. Cruisers are not only at the mercy of the winds, weather, and world currents; they must also be constantly aware of the political situation in any area they plan to visit. Most cruises progress from east to west because of the prevailing wind directions; hurricanes, typhoons, and cyclones dictate when it's safe to visit certain locales;

crime and health problems may influence some cruising plans; and an uneasy political climate can make for an uneasy cruise.

All this means that we can't just up anchor and head off for anyplace we want to go. We must know where we are going, what we expect to find there, how long we can stay, and what is the best time of year for the voyage. Therefore, we must study and plan—and starting to do so about a year before departure isn't too early.

The beginning cruise planner will want to have four sources of information on hand. The first is a good computer with a Kindle reader and a big hard drive. The second is a copy of Jimmy Cornell's book, *World Cruising Routes*. The third is a complete collection of the back issues of the *Seven Seas Cruising Association* bulletins (SSCA, remember, we introduced them in Chapter 6). The fourth is a copy of Beth Leonard's book *The Voyager's Handbook*.

The practicality of any passage is often determined by the direction and strength of prevailing winds and tides, and many times a passage that looks like an easy run is, in fact, quite difficult. The trip from Bonaire to Cartagena, for example, is an easy albeit rough two-day downwind sail, but to sail from Cartagena to Bonaire by the direct route is a practically impossible bash to windward. Although the format is confusing until you get used to it, Jimmy Cornell's book is invaluable for his observations on problems such as this one and for computing distances, routes, and the times required for any given passage.

Each issue of the *SSCA Bulletin* is a collection of letters that active cruisers write, giving advice and information on specific areas they have visited. These letters are similar in tone and content to posts on the online cruising forums in that they tend to be wordy, the writer's point is often obscure, and they are sometimes used as a soapbox by cruisers who have an ax to grind with a business or supplier.

Even so, the *SSCA Bulletin* is an invaluable resource for trip planning. As you read through back issues, you will get to know a lot of cruisers before you meet them, and you will get a good feeling for the flavor and atmosphere of a country or a specific harbor—all of which will help you decide whether you want to visit that place. All the popular cruising areas and routes are well represented, and most issues include three or four in-depth letters by different correspondents. It is important to read them all to form a consensus based on the viewpoints of different contributors. All the back issues for the past 10 years are available to members online and can be downloaded and searched.

Beth Leonard has an amazing ability to gather and analyze data, and her book is full of rock-solid advice on every aspect of cruising from buying fuel and food to how many comic books you should have in the head. She wrote *The Voyager's Handbook* during a three-year circumnavigation wherein she kept track of every item in meticulous detail. Since then, she and her partner, Evans Starzinger, have logged thousands of additional miles at sea, and the second edition of this book reflects that increased experience. (Beth doesn't really write about comic books in the head—that's just something I made up. So who's perfect?)

Charts: Paper and Otherwise

The electronics revolution has changed every aspect of the cruising life (as we discuss in Chapter 14), but one of the most profound transformations is in the way we get from the beginning of a passage to our destination and the aids we use to do it. You will repeatedly hear the admonition (in this book and most others that purport to know something about the subject) to never rely on electronics as a primary source of charts. This is common sense, but an increasing number of cruisers are ignoring it and relying digital charts alone.

The situation is a lot like it was with GPS when it first became available. All of us parroted the same advice: "GPS is great, but you would be a fool to get rid of your sextant." Now, with the universal acceptance of satellite positioning, redundant GPS systems are all but ubiquitous among cruisers, and sextants are getting increasingly scarce. *Vicarious* still has a sextant aboard along with the tables to make it work, but with about a 10-year lapse between sights, the skipper might just find it embarrassing if he were called upon to use it.

The point is that, whereas satellite positioning technology has stabilized with a high degree of reliability and little likelihood of dramatic changes in the near future, the same can't be said for electronic charting. Digital charting and navigation technology are still under intense development, and the systems aboard *Vicarious* offer a perfect example.

Our primary navigation system, after our paper charts, is a large multifunction display that incorporates data input from a chartplotter, radar, automatic identification system (AIS), compass, autopilot, depth sounder, and GPS all on one screen. This amazing apparatus was installed at great expense about five years ago by the previous owner. Of course it became outdated once it was two years old, and it would now cost several thousand dollars to get it current. Just the out-of-date charts for the East Coast of the United States and Canada would cost more than $300 to update.

Is this system reliable? Well, yes, it is, usually. But one day recently off the coast of Maine, we were sailing happily along giving some friends a demonstration ride in *Vicarious* when we were suddenly engulfed in the thick fog that is characteristic of this part of the ocean. Having sailed a lot in Maine, we have no fear of fog; the radar was lighting up any other boats in the area, and the chartplotter was happily displaying our exact position. Everything was dandy when the plotter gave a loud click and the screen went blank. After I stared at the vacant display for a half a minute or so (the feeling, I suspect, is akin to that of a skydiver whose chute fails to open), it gave another click and came back to life; then just after my sigh of relief, it gave a final click and went blank forever (forever being until I got back to our mooring and found the loose connection in the power supply).

Fortunately we had our paper charts open to the correct area, and we could have easily reverted to the buoy-to-buoy dead reckoning that worked so well in years gone by, but even this wasn't necessary. We simply whipped out the handy tablet computer (in this case an iPad), and we turned on the Garmin Blue Charts that we had loaded as a backup and sailed happily on. Our guests didn't have a clue to what had happened.

The point of mentioning this rather common incident is a comparison between the "old" Raster Navigational Charts (RNC) technology in the five-year-old chartplotter and the newer and more accurate electronic navigational charts (ENC) systems available over the Internet. The app for the Garmin Blue Charts was free to download, and the charts for the East Coast of the United States and eastern Canada cost less than $50. To be fair, we need to include the cost of the tablet computer of, say, $600, even though most cruisers will have one anyway. Compared to the $650 cost of the tablet system, the chartplotter itself cost about $2,000 when originally installed, and the update for the charts cost just over $300. With professional installation and a reasonable set of charts, the chartplotter could have cost the better part of $6,000. With all the interfaces, the total cost of a new equivalent system could exceed $10,000.

The Blue Charts seem to do everything that the chartplotter charts can do; they are updated automatically and for free anytime

we connect to the Internet; they have virtual worldwide coverage including the Northwest Passage, which isn't available on the chartplotter; and they interface with *ActiveCaptain* (about which more later), also not available on the chartplotter. This raises the question: who would willingly pay over three times more for a product that doesn't do as much as the cheaper alternative?

Of course, this is the sort of thing that makes books go outdated as soon as they are printed, but I hereby predict (and remember, you heard it here first, folks) that the traditional digital chartplotter is the next cruising dinosaur taking its place next to your Loran C receiver. There is nothing that the expensive multifunction chartplotter can do that can't be done with a comparatively cheap tablet or laptop computer, including interfacing with your radar, GPS, and depth sounder. And with continuing developments in Bluetooth and other wireless technology, that interface is bound to become ever cheaper and easier to install and use.

But (major Aretha Franklin–sized but here) how advisable is it to have all that information on one display to begin with? Our recent incident in the Maine fog, where we lost all our electronic input just because of a single ground fault, might indicate that it isn't wise at all. But (smaller Lindsay Lohan–sized but) my call on it is that a consolidated display is fine and is very useful provided that there is both complete redundancy in individual electronic displays plus an old-fashioned set of paper charts reinforced with a captain who can actually read them.

Someday (and it could be soon) digital navigation will relegate paper charts to the same ignominious fate that the GPS foisted onto the sextant. But that day isn't here yet. A lightning strike or a complete battery failure can still render all your electronics and all your communications useless. This may not be anything but mildly terrifying if it happens near shore where other boats can be counted on for assistance, but if it happens offshore, it could be serious indeed.

Every modern cruising sailboat should be equipped with the best electronic navigation system the skipper can afford, but as of this writing, it shouldn't be considered a replacement for your paper charts.

Having paper charts on board is only half the battle because they are useless unless you know how to read them. Dead reckoning skills, especially offshore, come with practice. So every so often, turn the electronics off and see how you do with just a chart and compass. Most old timers, like your elderly but amazingly spry author, won't have much trouble sailing with the basics because this is the way most of us learned to do it. But it is surprising how many

newcomers to cruising not only don't carry paper charts aboard but are also totally perplexed when confronted with one. We met one couple with ambitions to circumnavigate who went so far as to remove the compass from the helm station because their course over ground (COG) with magnetic and true headings was always displayed on their chartplotter. When I asked what they would do in an emergency, they blithely explained, as if I were a complete moron, that they would simply read the display on the autopilot. Ah well, better a complete moron than a partial one.

Guidebooks

Traditional printed guidebooks are another area that is changing almost daily with the relentless intrusion of electronics into our cruising lives.

As electronic navigation becomes ever more reliable and economical, paper charts are becoming more expensive, less reliable, and harder to find. Eventually electronics will replace the paper charts altogether, but not yet. The dangers of getting caught mid-ocean with no electronics or battery power is a real one, and the only defense is a backup paper chart and the skills to use them.

Not too long ago, every cruising boat had a library full of these essential tools, and the ones we no longer needed were among our most valuable trading materials. Now, with the increased importance of the Internet comes a drastically decreased importance of printed guidebooks and a corresponding increase in the importance of having a reliable access to the Internet—not all the time, of course, but periodically.

Many guidebooks from traditional publishers are now available for your Kindle reader, and the Internet is full of self-published guidebooks written by knowledgeable cruisers. While many of these self-published works are, let us say, less than Shakespearean, others are very well written indeed and can be very useful. The advantage of this vast assortment of guides is that when we are about to enter a new anchorage or cruising area, we now have a reliable selection of up-to-date viewpoints from a diverse body of authorities. True, often these viewpoints are conflictive and contentious, but they are useful nonetheless. In the past, there were only one or two guides available for any given cruising area written by someone who might or might not have spent time there, and that was several years ago. Now, with access to the Internet, we can download a cornucopia of information with just a few clicks of a mouse or the swipe of a finger.

ActiveCaptain

ActiveCaptain is a website started in 2007 to provide updated information to cruising sailors. It is global in scope and self-perpetuating in that the majority of the information that it contains is contributed by cruisers. From its modest beginnings with less than a thousand subscribers, *ActiveCaptain* has grown into the most important and convenient source of relevant data for just about every cruising destination in the world. It is as if someone has written a comprehensive cruising guidebook for the entire planet.

The information in *ActiveCaptain* is as up-to-date as the last entry and as accurate as the veracity of the contributor. This one website will provide advice on the best entry procedures, anchorages, facilities or lack thereof, the price of fuel, the names and telephone numbers of local services, the name of the kid at the fuel dock, and any other tidbits that the contributor thinks you will find useful. And it interfaces with a growing number of electronic charting programs so that all the information pertinent to your immediate destination is available without leaving the main screen of your computer or chartplotter.

As I write this, *Vicarious* is anchored in the Great Salt Pond on Block Island waiting for a nasty occluded front to go away so we can proceed south to the Caribbean. *ActiveCaptain*, with over 20 separate listings for this popular spot, tells me everything I need to know about the place. The listing for the outer anchorage alone contains over 40 reviews, and the most current was posted only three days ago. Within a day's sail of here, there is detailed information on hundreds of other anchorages, marinas, launch ramps, and every other conceivable marine service, all instantly available and up-to-date.

What else can I say here? If you have a computer with Internet access or a tablet computer with 4G capability, subscribe to *ActiveCaptain* (it's free), and add your review to every place you stop. If you don't have a computer, get one if you can possibly afford it. This one program is well worth the coast.

Popular Areas to Cruise

As your cruising plans evolve, remember that the most popular areas for cruisers are popular for good reasons. They are either easy to reach with good harbors and facilities, or they present attractions that make cruising there worthwhile. Other stops may be popular simply because they are on the way, convenient places for rest- ing, or with easily accessible markets where you can replenish the larder. Popular spots also have the advantage of a local population that is used to dealing with folks on boats and who under- stand that we have needs and requirements different from those of *normal* tourists. The people who run the hotels at a few of the major tourist stops tend to resent cruisers because we don't show up with several thousand dollars to blow on a week's fun in the sun, but the local people around most popular anchorages have come to value cruisers for the solid and predict- able contribution they make to the local economy. Generally, the more touristy a spot becomes, the less appeal it has for cruisers anyway.

Of course, this doesn't mean that you shouldn't strike out on your own and sail into areas that aren't among the most popular— after all, that's what cruising is about—but if you rein in your adventurous zeal to explore until after your first year of cruising the beaten path, you will be better off. You will gain a wealth of information from hanging around experienced cruisers. It's an education through association that you can't get from any other source, and when you need assistance or advice, the old-timers are always there when you need them. So for the first year at least, stick to the most popular areas, and save the more adven- turesome stops for when you have accumulated a few barnacles on your bottom.

As you plan your cruise, keep in mind that you don't have to sail around the world if you don't want to. In fact, most cruisers don't. Many who set out on a planned circumnaviga- tion never make it, not because they give up or run out of money (although that certainly does happen often enough) but because they reach an area that fits their concept of paradise, and they decide to stay right there. Many boats in the South Pacific sailed here 10 years ago on a circumnavigation and are still here, and the

same is true of the Mediterranean. The most popular cruising area, by far, is the Caribbean where thousands of cruisers spend their entire cruising careers moving from island to island, and between Central and South America, and they wouldn't think of going anywhere else.

These cruisers don't stay in the Caribbean because the sailing is easier there—in fact, some mighty tough conditions prevail between Cuba and Venezuela. But many Caribbean cruisers like the fact that they can get any- where they want to go in three or four days, don't like the expense and changeable weather of the Mediterranean, and don't care to make the one- or two-week-long passages required in the Pacific. More and more island governments and emerging countries in the Caribbean are becoming cruiser friendly, and their growing economies are providing services and supplies where they weren't available just a few years ago. Although problems with crime, pollution, and poverty plague many of these countries, overall the Caribbean is a wonderful place to cruise, and many cruisers consciously make the decision to go no farther.

Brown-Water Cruising

Not only do you not have to sail around the world if you aren't so inclined but you also don't even have to go offshore if you don't want to or if your boat isn't up to bluewater work. Many cruisers never leave the Intracoastal Waterway (ICW), the southern rivers, or the Great Lakes, and several thousand boats cruise between the Bahamas and Florida every year with never a thought of going anywhere else. One of the most interesting cruisers we ever met has sailed for more than 10 years, and he claims he's never gotten out of sight of land. Another chap we met in Florida sticks to the rivers; he claims that if one shore is good, then two are twice as good. "It shore does simplify navigation." (That's his joke, not mine.)

Preliminary Plans

At this early stage you'll want to make only the preliminary plans about where you might like to visit, and there are two good reasons for this. One, the political climate for many cruising destinations is constantly changing. Right now the worldwide trend is toward slowly improving conditions for cruisers in the Caribbean with Venezuela's showing an improving attitude but worsening crime, and Cuba's becoming ever more receptive to cruising boats.

Conditions in the Pacific are typically stable, but Australia and New Zealand are no longer bargain destinations due to the high values of their respective currencies. The Indian Ocean remains terrorized by piracy, but Madagascar, which was showing great potential as a major cruising destination just a few years ago and then descended into a cesspool of crime and corruption after an all-too-familiar political upheaval, has recently recognized the benefit of catering to yachts heading south around the Cape of Good Hope, so conditions are once again slowly improving there.

All of the above is, of course, information of the moment and, as such, can change as it is being written. So how do we ensure that the data on which we are basing our plans is trustworthy? Once again the Internet comes to the rescue. The best all-round resource for determining the current political climate and security situation in any given area or country is the website *Noonsite* (www.noonsite.com).

This popular site is very much like *Active Captain,* but concentrates more on politics. It also contains the most comprehensive Internet list of worldwide piracy attacks. Be careful reading these reports because they can scare the snot out of an oyster. Just keep in mind that there are a lot of cruisers out there and not that many serious attacks. That doesn't mean that you should blithely sail into an area with a high concentration of crime. Just be aware that reading the *Noonsite* worldwide list of incidents can leave you with a distorted impression of the actual dangers involved.

The second reason for making preliminary plans is that, no matter how much reading you do and how much time you spend on the Internet and no matter how much sailing and coastal cruising you have done before you leave on your cruise, the environment you meet will never quite match your expectations. The conditions you find won't necessarily be better or worse than what you expected, but they will most certainly be different. That's because we all have a different response to a given situation, and paradise to one is hell to another. We were told by one seasoned cruiser, for example, that Belize was a boring place to visit because there was nothing to do. What he meant was that there were no nightclubs and casinos there, an enormous plus for simple cruisers like the crew of *Vicarious.*

The First-Year Plan

I know, I know. We haven't bought a boat yet. We'll get to that, I promise. But for now, let's concentrate on putting together a plan for your first year of real-live cruising. I have no intention of trying to tell you where you should go, but I will make some suggestions about how you should proceed for your first year, regardless of your circumstances.

The first 12 months are a make-it-or-break-it period for many new cruisers. It is during this time that you learn what you have gotten yourself into, and you will make more mistakes than in any other period of your cruising life. You will find out more about yourself and your companions than you ever thought possible, and you'll face both gloomy disappointments and cheerful surprises as never before. I'll never forget the first time we ran

Sultana hard aground on a sandbar and had to be pulled off by our fellow cruisers. We were embarrassed and humiliated beyond measure to think that we could have let such an amateurish thing happen to our wonderful new-old boat. Now, after having been aground dozens of times in all sorts of conditions, we realize that it is just part of the cruising life—and the more adventuresome you are, the more your bottom paint suffers. We even run aground intentionally from time to time to anchor for a few moments on a rising tide or to careen the boat. To compensate, we have become highly skilled at getting ourselves off anything we get ourselves on to and only rarely require any assistance.

Full-time cruising is different from any other type of sailing you've ever done, regardless of your experience, and you should work hard at making it as easy and uncomplicated as possible. The first year should be a year of learning what you and your boat can do. A week-long passage in rough seas is easy enough to read about in books, but many who try it for the first time without a few easier passages under their belts find that they never want to do it again. It's much easier on everyone if you make your first few overnight passages one-nighters. Then when you develop the confidence to handle a 24-hour passage, do a few two-nighters and so on until you can stand on the foredeck and look a week of rough water

The first time we ran aground in Sultana, *we were mortified. But we soon learned that running aground is a common occurrence, especially in such places as the Caloosahatchee River (where this patient cruiser is awaiting the returning tide), the Bahamas, and many popular anchorages with imperfect anchor-holding properties. The more adventuresome your cruising, the more practice you will have in getting free of sandbars and mud flats. You will also learn (probably the hard way) to stay well clear of rocks, coral, and lee shores in any form.*

right in the eye without blinking. It won't take long, I promise you, so resist the natural tendency to fling yourself straight into the blue-water environment with a cruise to Hawaii or Bermuda. Go instead to Santa Catalina or Block Island, and when you get there, spend a few days enjoying the sights and sounds of a new harbor. After all, cruising isn't about passages. It's about places and the people you meet in them—and one of the first people you will meet is yourself.

Start with Coastal Cruising

Even if you have had a lot of offshore experience, you need to build confidence in your cruising life skills, and the best way to do this is by coastal cruising. Make the first six months to a year a series of short easy passages with long stops between them. Short day sails in an interesting area will let you get accustomed to life on a small boat. You'll have fun while you're learning, and if you do get into trouble and need help, it is readily available.

DON'T DO HEAVY WEATHER UNTIL YOU ARE READY FOR HEAVY WEATHER

We know one young Australian couple quite well who bought a boat in which to tour the world on retirement. For five years, Bob and Alice looked forward to departing as soon as he got his 20 years in with the large IT company he worked for. Bob is a macho kind of guy who likes to do things his way (hey, it worked for Frank Sinatra) while Alice is the more timid and conservative member of the team. About a year before they were planning to go, they bought a heavy-displacement traditional cruising boat and set about learning how to make the thing go.

Being a dedicated do-it-yourself type who finds it difficult to take advice from anyone, Bob taught himself to sail and could soon make the boat go pretty much where he wanted it to go. Never mind that his sail-trimming techniques provided considerable amusement at the local yacht club and waterfront pub.

After becoming satisfied that he had mastered the basics, Bob announced that it was time to get some heavy-weather exposure, so he and his bride sailed blithely offshore into a building gale. They returned the next day with the predictable horror stories of 50-foot waves and hurricane-force winds

slamming them about like a boxer on a speed bag. The fact that the predicted gale never materialized and the conditions never exceeded moderate with 25-knot winds and 10-foot seas didn't matter; they showed all their friends photos of the interior of their boat with food and every other loose item piled onto the cabin floor.

That would have been enough for Alice, but not Bob. As soon as the next storm hove into view, they were off getting even more exposure to the rough conditions that Bob predicted they would meet on their upcoming journey around the world. Having once again proved Einstein's observation that doing the same thing brings the same results, they waited a few more weeks, and against Alice's vociferous objections, they did it again. This time, when they returned, Bob had a severely sprained shoulder, and Alice had an egg-sized bruise on her forehead.

At this point, a lesser person might have admitted that while the fling-yourself-off-the-end-of-the-dock method might do for learning how to swim, it wasn't an effective way to master boat handling in difficult weather, but

(continued next page)

DON'T DO HEAVY WEATHER UNTIL YOU ARE READY FOR HEAVY WEATHER *CONTINUED*

not Bob. He announced to his increasingly attentive group of friends that all this proved was that he and Alice needed more practice playing with big waves and high winds

This is when Alice, having overcome her natural temerity, announced that if Bob wanted more experience sailing in hurricanes, he was welcome to it. Not only was she never going to set foot on a boat again but if Bob persisted in his plans for a cruising career, she was checking herself into a nunnery, if she could find one, as far away from the ocean as she could get.

Bob was forced to capitulate, and they compromised by trading the boat for a Surfer's Paradise condo that has a view of the ocean. Here Bob can enjoy all the heavy weather he wants by sitting on the balcony during storms while Alice does her shell art in the small studio she set up in a spare bedroom.

This somewhat-embellished-but-otherwise-true anecdote illustrates my point very nicely: don't rush into difficult sailing situations. Let your cruising skills develop naturally and gradually by learning to handle advanced conditions as you encounter them. Don't feel you must cross the creek with a running broad jump when there is a perfectly good log on which to cross step-by-step.

The Inside Passage of British Columbia and the Sea of Cortez are good destinations for beginning West Coast cruisers. Cruisers who start from the East Coast are a little better off because the Atlantic offers several attractive options for neophyte cruisers. The Intracoastal Waterway, the Canadian Maritimes, and the Bahamas are topnotch cruising areas that offer protracted coastal cruising. It's possible to visit dozens of new and fascinating places in these areas with only an occasional overnight passage.

Leaving Home

It is important to get out of your immediate home waters as quickly as possible, but it is a good idea to stay in a familiar geographical area. Does this sound contradictory? Well, it's not really. Getting out of your familiar surroundings quickly makes you feel like a cruiser right away and gives your ego and confidence terrific boosts. However, staying in the same geographical area will keep the cultural and environmental shock of drastic change to a minimum. Staying in touch with friends and family for at least the first few months with an inexpensive call or text message from your cell phone is often comforting for all members of the crew. Furthermore, it will ease the fears of the folks at home, and if you have children aboard, it is particularly helpful if they can chat with a friend at home from time to time.

Most of the anxiety and stress of the cruising life comes from the passages we must make to participate in it, but most of our time is spent at anchor, not on the high seas, and most of our happiest moments are while we are in harbor. The skills we will need to live on a boat at anchor are more difficult to learn and much more important than sailing skills. This isn't to say that sailing skills aren't important. They are, of course. But it's your living skills that will determine how satisfying you find your new lifestyle. All cruisers learn to sail, but many never learn how to live on a boat. Thus you should devote most of that first year to learning all the intricacies of life on a small boat and save the easy stuff, like learning to like long passages, for later.

Sultana's first cruise after we left Marblehead was up the coast of Maine into the Canadian Maritimes. Then we cruised down the Intracoastal Waterway and spent several months sailing among the Florida Keys. In our first six months of full-time cruising, we made only two overnight passages. By the time we were ready to head across the Gulf of Mexico to Isla Mujeres, we had been cruising for nearly a year, and we were just beginning to feel like competent sailors. We were ready for what was to be our first real bluewater experience.

Don't Become a Liveaboard

Many "experts" advise living on your boat for at least a year before you depart on a major cruise, and while I hate to risk the derision of my fellow cruisers (especially them that's experts), I believe that this is very bad advice. There are profound and fundamental differences between cruising sailors and people who live on boats while maintaining shoreside lifestyles—those we call "liveaboards."

People often confuse the two, but they aren't the same thing at all. "Liveaboard" is a collective term that describes people who live on boats instead of in houses and who remain in one place or in one area for long periods. Some live on boats for economic reasons, some like the romantic image that living on a boat imparts, and others just love boats. Most liveaboards lead normal lives with regular jobs, kids in school, nice autos in the marina parking lot, and a plugged-in TV and computer. The only difference between them and shoresiders is that they live on a boat in the water instead of in a house on land, which means that most of them require all the comforts that all other shoresiders require. Liveaboard boats become so encumbered with power cables, water and sewer pipes, cable TV hookups,

air-conditioners, and telephone lines that they frequently become permanently moored to a pier or wharf and few ever do any sailing.

Cruisers, on the other hand, are people who live on boats so they can travel from place to place. They seldom have regular jobs, their children are often home-schooled, and they hardly ever own automobiles. Where liveaboards tend to congregate at docks in marinas, cruisers tend to anchor out and shun the amenities of shore hookups.

There is nothing wrong with liveaboards, of course, but in some areas, particularly in the southern United States, the liveaboard fleet has gotten very large, and their propensity to pollute harbors and their reluctance to pay property taxes has caused some communities to retaliate by enforcing strict anchoring laws, which directly affect cruisers.

Because the two lifestyles are so different I strongly advise people who are interested in trying one to not get involved with the other. It's nearly impossible to maintain a normal job and other shoreside frills and responsibilities while living like a cruiser, and if you try it, you will likely become so frustrated and disenchanted that you will quit the cruising life even before you start. The gulf between liveaboards and cruisers is just as wide as that between your shoreside life and your cruising life. And the leap from the shoreside life to the liveaboard life is just as upsetting as the leap from the liveaboard life to the cruising life. Who needs two traumatic changes in two years? So please, don't try to live on your boat for an extended period before you take off on your cruise.

The transition from the shoreside to the cruising life can be difficult and traumatic, and when approached improperly it can end your cruise before the first dock line is cast off. The trick is to make the first year afloat, your transition year, a success by making it as simple and basic as you can.

9

Living Aboard and Acquiring Skills

Why do you go away? So that you can come back. So that you can see the place you came from with new eyes and extra colors. And the people there see you differently, too. Coming back to where you started is not the same as never leaving.

—TERRY PRATCHETT, *A HAT FULL OF SKY*

An Incident at Aitutaki

Have you ever noticed that when you make an exceptionally seaman-like maneuver in a boat, there is hardly ever anyone around to appreciate it, but when you do something that is extraordinarily stupid, half the population of China will be on hand to watch the disaster unfold? I am convinced that inscribed in some cosmic rule book is an otherwise-unwritten law stating that foibles must be witnessed by vast multitudes of bystanders while triumphs go unnoticed. Perhaps this is as it should be because it helps to slow the natural progression toward arrogance among those fortunate few who enjoy more than their fair share of spectacular achievements. But for us klutzes who enjoy only an occasional minor triumph, it is manifestly unfair.

A long time ago, when Susan and I bought our second sailboat, a sleek 23-foot production boat that had popped fully formed from a mold in some factory in Florida, we set off from the Ipswich Bay Yacht Club on our first real cruise up the coast of Maine, without knowing too much about what we were doing. We were, in fact, as green as new lettuce, but our enthusiasm more than compensated for our dearth of sailing skills, and we had a wonderful time cruising among the inlets and islands of Casco Bay and Boothbay Harbor. When it was time to return home, however, disaster struck. As I pulled the starter cord on our brand-new Chrysler long-shaft outboard, it rumbled to life with a throaty purr, then coughed a few times, made a few clanking noises like there was an elf in there with a hammer trying to get out, expelled a single puff of black oily smoke, and died, never again to function as anything more dynamic than a very large and expensive paperweight.

We were a little panicky and despaired of ever getting our new boat back to our homeport when a local lobsterman rowed over in his dinghy to see what the fuss was all about.

"Dang outboards," he began after we explained our plight. "Never trusted 'em myself. Good thing ya got yer sail up there and don't need no outboard. Never had no use fer tha dang things anyway." He then rowed away, leaving us staring at each other and thinking, "Why didn't we think of that?"

We sailed off the mooring with just the main, then got the jib up and had a delightful sail into the large harbor that was our day's destination, and dropped the anchor for the night. The next morning we were off at the crack of dawn, and after a few hours of being becalmed among a sprightly pod of pilot whales, we had another day of perfect sailing conditions.

When we reached the mouth of the Ipswich River, a difficult entrance under the best of conditions, a strong southeasterly was blowing a semigale with a flooding tide. We blasted over the bar with both wind and tide in our favor, going about as fast as our little boat had gone since she was dropped off the delivery truck. We practically flew up the river skipping across the tops of the waves, but as we approached the club floats to which we wanted to tie up, we were faced with a slight problem. We were traveling far too fast to stop. If we had tried to round into the wind, the current would have carried us past the floats as soon as we dropped the sail, and we would simply have continued traveling upriver backward. We only had one chance, and if we had missed it, it would have been hours before the wind and tide changed enough to allow us to get back to the floats.

With only a few seconds to decide what to do, Susan moved to the bow and lowered our big Danforth over the bow roller until the flukes were just barely in the water. Then, 200 feet from the floats, I rounded smartly into the wind, Susan let go of the anchor, and I hopped onto the cabintop and dropped the main with a clatter onto the deck. The boat hesitated for a moment, the jib luffed frantically, and then we began to drift backward. When we were opposite the floats Susan snubbed the anchor rode on the deck cleat, the anchor grabbed the sandy bottom, the boat stopped cold, and the current swung us ever so gently up to the floats. As our gunwales bumped lightly against the fenders, I stepped off the boat with the spring line and made it fast.

A master stroke of nautical genius. We had executed with perfection what was undoubtedly one of the greatest maritime maneuvers ever pulled off by two greenies with a new sailboat. After a moment my hands stopped shaking, and I looked around, ready to bask humbly in the admiring glances of the gang of hangarounders who were always hanging around the floats on Sunday evening. Much to my horror the dock leading to the floats was empty, the clubhouse was shuttered, and the only car in the parking lot was ours. Our shining hour had gone unwitnessed, unheralded, and unremarked. And Susan didn't care. She was a little miffed at the jib for flapping at her the way it did as she tried to deal with the anchor line, and all she could think about was home and a hot bath.

If witnesses for our few triumphs are scarce, then those for our many foibles are correspondingly plentiful. We had been anchored in the tiny harbor at Aitutaki, New Zealand, for several weeks, enjoying the beaches, making new friends, and exploring the outlying islands in our inflatable, but now it was time to haul anchor and move on. Bright and early on the day of departure a large group of well-wishers and onlookers gathered on the harbor quay to see us off. The channel that led through the forest of coral heads and out through the surrounding reef was narrow and shallow, but we had come in with no trouble, and I didn't anticipate any trouble getting out. *Sultana* had poor visibility from the helm, so our normal procedure for negotiating a narrow channel was for me to take a position on the bowsprit, for Phillip and Sarah to stand by the port and starboard shrouds, while Susan took over at the wheel. I signaled minor changes in course to keep us in the channel or to get us around encroaching coral heads, and Sarah and Phillip relayed the signals to Susan. We had done this many times, and we had developed a set of hand signals, so there should have been no need for verbal communication. As we headed out of the anchorage, I gave the power-up signal, indicating I wanted Susan to give *Sultana* some juice. With all those people watching, I wanted our departure to be smart and seamanlike.

All was going well as we motored along with a good turn of speed. The channel at Aitutaki makes a sharp zigzag as you leave the anchorage and enter the main channel. You must zig sharply to starboard and head directly toward the quay; then, just as collision with the rocks is imminent, you must zag to port. I should have realized that Susan, or any thinking person for that matter, would be reluctant to point the bow straight into a pile of rocks, but I was familiar with the channel and assumed that she was too. When we approached the zig, I signaled that Susan should slow and turn to starboard, but since she could see nothing to starboard except the rock pile, upon which stood lots of happy waving people, and to port she saw nothing but open water, she naturally turned to port away from the perceived danger. Her maneuver elicited a frantic response from the kids and me. The three of us took to hopping up and down like a bunch of bungee-jumping

monkeys while gesturing violently to starboard. I even succumbed to my racing-skipper friends' nasty habits and began screaming in a piercing shriek.

"Starboard . . . STARBOARRRRD . . . STARRRRRBOARRRRRRRD . . ."

We struck the reef halfway through the last "starboard." We all heard a sickening grinding sound, the deck heaved, I flung arms and legs around the furled jib to avoid being hurled to my doom, the bowsprit rose to point heavenward, and we stopped. Susan shut the engine down, and I just sat. I plopped my butt down on the top of the deckhouse and stared in stunned silence at the people on the quay, all of whom were staring in stunned silence back at us. Finally one of our friends, a Maori lad from New Zealand named Mike, dove off the quay and swam to *Sultana*'s rail.

"Looks like you might be stuck, Mate," he said in a tentative voice.

I continued sitting and staring in dazed disbelief while wondering why all those people on the quay couldn't find something better to do than stare at us. After a while I decided I had better do something useful, like maybe crying, but then I thought better of it and sat and stared some more.

It was Mike who got things going again. He recruited a local fishing boat to pull us off, but even with her twin engines and *Sultana*'s diesel in full reverse, we didn't budge. Finally, Mike swam back to the quay, dragging our two spare 100-meter nylon anchor lines tied together and secured the bitter end to the trailer hitch of an onlooker's car, and with that extra boost we managed to slide *Sultana* back into deep water.

Fortunately, and in profound testimony to the advantages of a full keel and a strong hull, there was no damage—not to the boat, anyway. The skipper's ego was smashed to a fare-thee-well, however, and as I continued to sit on the cabintop in a state of mute introspection, Mike and Susan took *Sultana* out through the channel without further incident. When we cleared the fringing reef and were safely on our way, Mike gave a cheerful salute, did a backflip off the bow and set out to swim the quarter mile or so back to the island. We never saw him again, but he is high up there on the list of the hundreds of wonderful people we have met while cruising, and we will never forget him.

Some months later the incident at Aitutaki was almost forgotten, the splints and dressings had been removed from the skipper's pride, and except for some massive residual scar tissue, it looked like a full recovery was imminent. I was sitting in one of the many waterfront bars that line the harbor front at Nuku'alofa in Tonga sharing a beer with a new acquaintance who had just arrived from Fiji. We were discussing all things nautical and naughty that strangers talk about in waterfront bars all over the world when the conversation stalled for a moment.

"Say," said my new friend. "Did you hear about the jerk who ran his boat up on the reef in the Cooks?"

I lowered my head and hunched my shoulders so he couldn't see my face, formed my arms into a protective circle around my glass, then slurped some of the head off my beer without lifting it off the bar. He couldn't see my half-crazed expression or my teeth bared in a vicious snarl. "No, no, I haven't heard that one yet," I lied.

"Well, ha, ha, ha, not much to it really. This guy has his whole family on board so he, chuckle, chuckle, puts his wife at the wheel then, snicker, snicker, orders her to run the boat full steam right up on the reef, ho, ho, ho. Stupid jerk probably didn't know where the channel was, yuk, yuk, yuk, not that it's not marked or anything like that—whole damn town was there to see it too—guy in Suva told me about it. Amazing some of the people out here in boats these days, ain't it?"

"Hey," I answered, further hunching my shoulders. "There was probably some logical explanation, like maybe the throttle stuck or the rudder broke or somethin' like that."

"No way, the boat was in perfect condition. Sometimes I think they should give an IQ test to everybody who wants to buy a boat. Dumb ass, could'a drowned his whole family pullin' a stunt like that."

"Slurp, slurp . . . I bet the sun was in his eyes."

"Naw, the guy was just a jerk."

"Slurrrrrp, slurp, slurp . . . I bet the throttle stuck and the rudder broke and the sun was in his eyes all at once—yeah, that's probably what happened. Poor guy couldn't help it, really."

"You know the best part?" my gleeful friend continued. "The boat is so far up on the reef that they can't get it off with a towboat so they run a line ashore, and you know those junky Russian cars called Ladas? Well, they tie the line to a Lada, and he gets them off. Can you imagine the humiliation of running aground like that in the first place, and then having to get towed off by a Lada?"

Cruising Skills

I've said several times that life skills are more important to the cruising sailor than are sailing skills, and there are several reasons why this is true. When many of us decide to go cruising, it's only natural that we study everything we can get our hands on about boats. But we gloss over the dramatic changes in lifestyle that moving from a large immobile house to a tiny boat entails, or we assume that living in the confines of a boat is something that we will just have to get used to. But it doesn't happen like that. To become proficient cruisers requires developing two separate sets of skills: *cruising skills* will enable us to get the boat from one place to another safely and to maintain it in good repair;

noncruising skills enable us to live a happy and rewarding life while residing on the boat.

I realize that this book treats critical skills such as sail handling and anchoring in a rather cavalier manner, but there are already a zillion or so books out there, really good books, that discuss these things ad nauseam, and I am loathe to add to the pile. Earl Hinz wrote an excellent book that covers every aspect of anchors and anchoring, and there are dozens of books listed on the Amazon.com website about sails and sail handling. Anyway, we're going to learn these things whether we want to or not. The first time our anchor pulls out in a rain squall at 3 a.m., we'll become experts at setting anchors, and the first time we nearly take a knockdown because we thought the cold front sneaking up from the south didn't have any wind in it, we'll become converts to the principle of reducing sail before the sail reduces us.

Navigating

It's amazing how rapidly technology can come upon us and change our lives. If it doesn't change our lives, technology at the very least affects the way we live significant parts of our lives. Some of us grouchy old codgers often have trouble accepting such dramatic changes. When we departed Marblehead for our world cruise, I laid on a music library of a hundred or so cassettes and was just starting to realize that perhaps these newfangled compact disc players did indeed have some small advantage over magnetic tapes, especially after having to plop most of *Sultana*'s music into a dumpster because the tapes had been eaten alive by a voracious fungus.

Then some years later, we converted all our thousand or so CDs to digital and stored them on an iPod backed up "in the cloud." We now have so much music that it would take a month to listen to it all. Jimmy Buffett alone would take over a week of 24-hour listening, and we

are constantly finding songs that we don't have a clue as to where they came from. Our huge box of CDs that formerly took up an entire large locker has been reduced to the size of a small Hershey bar.

Back when Loran first became available, I thought it was exceedingly clever, but that it would never catch on because you could never beat the good old chart and compass. Then came GPS with advantages that were obvious even to traditionalists like me. In fact, the universal adoption of GPS has been one of the most significant technological developments since the magnetic compass, and it has revolutionized cruising and cruising navigation.

Prior to GPS, the lack of navigation skills and their perceived complexity kept many would-be cruisers safely in sight of the local lighthouse. Traditional navigation with watch and sextant isn't really that difficult (probably on par with high school algebra in complexity), but many people, when confronted with gadgets bearing scales and wheels, and books with columns of numbers and formulas, were convinced that such awesome apparatus required a graduate engineering degree to master and stayed home.

There is no way to know for sure, but I suspect that a lot of people who wanted to go cruising in the past didn't because of the perceived complexity of traditional navigation. Now anyone who can afford a $200 gadget and has minimal reading skills can become a world-class navigator with about 15 minutes of study, and he or she can navigate from here to anywhere with a mind-boggling accuracy that was unimagined just a few decades ago. As discussed in Chapter 8, with a relatively simple chartplotter interfaced with GPS, radar, and a dependable autopilot, we can now navigate at night, in the fog and rain, with our eyes closed, from our bunk in the forepeak, or even while comfortably ensconced in the head. The cook can do it, the kids can do it, and with a little training, the ship's cat could probably do it too. Instead of accuracy to within a few miles that we got with traditional means, we can now navigate to within a few inches of anywhere we want to go.

Don't Forsake the Sextant

All this electronic wonderfulness has a downside, though, especially to us hoary curmudgeons who enjoy the challenge of doing difficult tasks with style and dash and actually liked things the way they used to be. With every new technological advance, a thin layer of the mystique of life is stripped away, and I firmly believe that our short stay here on earth is diminished by that. When I was in school, a slide rule peeking out from a shirt pocket symbolized an active intellect—and even though I kept mine out of sight so it wouldn't interfere with my carefully cultivated James Dean image, I was proud of my ability to use one. Then along came electronic calculators, and they shot the mystique of the slide rule all to hell. Now anyone with one finger and the hand-eye coordination to hit a quarter-inch square with it can perform complex mathematics.

Is this sour grapes coming from a grouchy old-fart reactionary as Susan claims? Not a bit. I wouldn't even consider for a moment trading my fourth-generation Apple iPad for anything—especially not for a slide rule. That sucker has nearly 100 apps already loaded and plenty of room for more. I even have an app for developing my own apps. If the instructions for it were printed, it would be longer than the Manhattan phone book. After a month of intensive study, I've finally discovered how to download the damn thing, and if I can ever figure out which function to start with, I'll soon be able to figure out what it actually does. Hot damn . . . maybe there's hope for humanity after all.

GPS is another example of how rapidly emerging technology can affect our entire lifestyle. Global positioning became a necessity for every offshore sailor as soon as it hit the market. Its universal acceptance was instantaneous, and it has led to the nearly complete abandonment of the sextant. This is unfortunate even though complete reliance on the GPS system has become accepted by many of us. This tendency to forsake the sextant is perhaps not as reckless as it once was, but the sailor with the skills to safely navigate across long distances without electronic assistance retains a standing advantage over those who can't. Traditional navigation methods are not as difficult to learn and use as you might think, and they're fun besides.

SARAH

As we sailed Sultana *across the Pacific Ocean, navigating with a sextant was a part of Sarah's and Phillip's homeschooling program—to the extent we had one. Today a working familiarity with celestial navigation is becoming increasingly rare, but it is still a useful skill to acquire.*

The ability to find a speck in the ocean like the Galapagos Islands with our sextant, watch, and *Nautical Almanac* is much more than just an emergency backup to the GPS. It is one of the few useful links with tradition that dates back to the Middle Ages. Indeed, skill with a sextant has long been a symbol of the cruising life. Just look on your bookshelf, and notice how many covers of your cruising books are adorned with a photo of the author hanging from the shrouds while taking a shot with the sextant. If there isn't one on the cover, there'll be a photo of a sextant inside for sure. Can you imagine a cruising book whose cover shows some befuddled clown with a quizzical expression punching buttons on a box? Probably not.

Knowing how to use a sextant gives an enormous boost to self-confidence, sets you apart from the hoards of newcomers who consider navigation skills in the same category as the sounding lead (amazing how many boats don't carry lead lines any more) and the cat-o'-nine tails. (What? You don't have a cat-o'-nine aboard?) Besides, a basic knowledge of the principles behind traditional navigation gives you an understanding of what's going on when your GPS tells you what to do to get somewhere.

The Columbus Method

A more basic means of navigation has also become a lost art—the Columbus method, also known as the sail-in-the-general-direction-of-where-you-want-to-go-until-you-see-something-then-try-to-figure out what-the-hell-it-is method. This is the method by which I first learned to sail, and it has always served me well when all else has failed.

Once while crossing Massachusetts Bay on a foggy pitch-black night in the late 1960s with my cousin Steve, we motored all night through an oily black sea, using only a Boy Scout compass and a map on the placemat from the restaurant where we had enjoyed our dinner. At about 3 a.m., we spotted a lighthouse. After consulting our placemat, we determined that it had to be either Halifax, Nova Scotia; Gloucester (our destination); or Marblehead. After eliminating Halifax as being out of range, we resolved to sail toward the light until we spotted a boat. If the boat were a grungy fishing boat covered with rust, we would be in Gloucester; if it were a palatial yacht with a uniformed flunky on the bow prepared to fend off any idiots in sailboats who might emerge from the fog, we would definitely be in Marblehead. As it turned out the first boat we came across was neither a fishing boat nor a yacht but a Coast Guard cutter looking for pot smugglers. "Close enough," said Steve. "This has to be Gloucester. Marblehead would never tolerate pot smugglers—Cabernet Sauvignon smugglers maybe, but never pot smugglers."

Watchstanding

Much nonsense has been written about watches and the necessity of keeping them, most of which might have come right out of Captain Bligh's handbook. Rigid watch schedules are a major pain in the butt on most small cruising boats, and crews who try to initiate them often have morale problems. It is much better to maintain a flexible watch schedule that simply ensures someone is on deck anytime the boat is under way. Obviously, much more diligence is required in places like the Yucatan Channel (where an average of three or four freighters are in sight at any one time) than in the middle of the Pacific Ocean where you can sail for weeks without seeing a sign of another boat.

Many cruisers don't stand regular watches, and singlehanders, by definition, can't. On *Sultana* we developed a standardized schedule based on preferences. During daylight, someone must be on deck at all times—and that person never left the deck while the other three were below without asking to be relieved.

On *Vicarious*, things are only slightly less formal. We realized early on that one of the most critical parts of any passage is a well-rested crew, so during the day, one of us is either resting, reading, or trying to get some sleep while the other remains alert. Then after dark, Susan takes the first watch while I try to get more rest or sleep. She stays at it until she gets sleepy, which is usually around midnight; I take over and go to about 0300, then Susan takes over until 0600. If she wakes up, that is.

Susan does all the cooking on our passages, so if she doesn't wake up and if I'm not about to fall asleep at my post, I'll keep the watch until she does wake up. It really isn't self-sacrifice and consideration for my mate that keeps me at the helm. It's hunger. A sleepy cook is a worthless cook, and by letting Susan sleep through her watch, I ensure myself a sumptuous breakfast and, with a little luck, lasagna on Friday.

In high-traffic areas, things get a little more formal of necessity. We usually alternate in two-hour shifts, and Susan wakes me anytime we have three or more AIS targets within 3 miles or when we have one within a mile that represents a clear danger.

Noncruising Cruising Skills

Earlier, I mentioned a few skills that cruisers find useful either as a means to achieving self-sufficiency or as services to sell to other cruisers as a means of prolonging the life of the cruising kitty. These are skills that don't have anything to do with sailing or boats, but they will make your life afloat more enjoyable and maybe even profitable.

Cooking: The Most Important Skill Aboard

This isn't an exaggeration. A crew that eats well is well, and a continual supply of nutritious food is a critical element of a successful cruise. It is so important that all of Chapter 13 is devoted to food and the galley.

Mechanics

Early in my youth I was classified as a hoodlum. I was, of course, thrilled with this designation, but tragically, inasmuch as I had never done anything really wrong other than wearing my Levis too low, snarffing a few Luckies in the boy's room, and wearing my hair too long, I was never a candidate for reform school—an exalted institution to which all of us James Dean wannabes aspired. As a compromise, I was sent off to what is now called "vocational arts" but was then known as a "trade school." Simply stated, trade school was a reform school where they let you go home at night.

After gaining admission to the hallowed halls of Bladensburg Trade School (BTS), I was given a battery of tests that revealed my previously unknown aptitude for automobile mechanics. (The fact that automobile mechanics was the only class that had space at the time was pure coincidence, I'm sure.)

The courses I took at BTS turned out to be some of the most valuable that I have ever taken in that they proved beyond question that I didn't possess even a hint of mechanical aptitude. After my graduation, my dad let me do a valve job on his nearly new 1953 Chevrolet station wagon. When I got the lifters in upside down, thereby necessitating the replacement of the entire engine, he was quite calm about it really. In fact, he never even once spoke of it again. That was my last foray into the field of auto mechanics. After finishing college (which I attended solely to avoid ever having to work on cars for a living), I took a desk job with the telephone company and actively avoided any contact with automobiles other than with door handles and steering wheels.

My phobia of things mechanical carried over to the cruising world. When we began our cruise, I felt qualified to fix just about everything on the boat except the engine. However, after being billed the equivalent of $200 in today's money for a basic oil change at a marina run by a guy with the amazingly appropriate name of Captain Rob, I resolved that a renewed interest in things mechanical was in order.

I spent the next few months reading and studying everything I could get my hands on about diesel engines. I even went as far as to climb down into the cramped and dark engine room and check out our old Ford four-banger. I sat on the transmission and read the entire section on diesel engines in Nigel Calder's *Boatowner's Mechanical and Electrical Manual*, and when I climbed out, I felt competent to fix just about anything that ever showed the poor judgment to break. In fact, way down deep inside, I may have secretly hoped that the engine would blow up just so I could have a go at rebuilding it.

Unfortunately for my ego, diesel engines are among the most reliable mechanical contraptions ever invented, and *Sultana*'s old clunker was among the best. It wasn't until we were off the east coast of Mexico that I got a chance to try out my newfound mechanical skills. We were a mile or so off a lee shore in a 25-knot breeze with about a 4-foot sea on the beam when things got dicey enough for me to resort to artificial power. *Sultana* motorsailed like a dream, and we could often gain about 10 points on the wind just by starting her engine. In this instance, I felt we could clear an approaching headland without tacking if I used a few rpm's of the prop for a boost.

Needless to say, this was a dumb thing to do. Just as we were clearing the headland, no more than a hundred yards from the reef, and right after I said to Susan, "Boy, are we in trouble if the engine quits," the engine stopped dead. Naturally the first thing we did was panic, and in so doing we lost enough way so that we couldn't tack. This forced us to wear ship, which brought us within a few heart-stopping feet of the reef, but it did get us going back the way we had come and away from those threatening fangs of coral and rock.

Once we were clear of the reef, I plunged into the engine compartment, tool kit in one hand, Nigel Calder's book in the other, and attacked the enemy. Four hours later, battered and bruised from being flung about in the engine compartment and soaked in diesel fuel, I located a fuel line that had been blocked by sediment kicked up by the rough seas. I got the engine running again. Today, after spending what seems like half a lifetime in a succession of engine compartments and thumbing my copy of Calder's book to a tattered rag, I believe that it would take me all of 10 minutes to clear the same obstruction and get old Betsy back online. In fact, I could do it in my pajamas with one hand tied behind my back while wearing a blindfold.

My purpose here isn't to brag about my accumulated mechanical skills but to illustrate my point that, no matter how much of a mechanical klutz you might be, you will need to learn to fix diesel engines if you are to survive as a budget cruiser. It's much better that you do it now in night school or in home study than wait until you are on a lee shore off the coast of Mexico with 4-footers bouncing you around like an olive in a martini shaker.

Electronics

When I started sailing all those many years ago, a knowledge of electronics would have been superfluous because the electronics inventory on Uncle Freddy's *Mazuka* stopped at the running lights—and they never worked because the battery was always dead. Today, however, *Vicarious* needs hundreds of amp hours of battery power just to find her way out of the harbor, and her main circuit breaker panel has

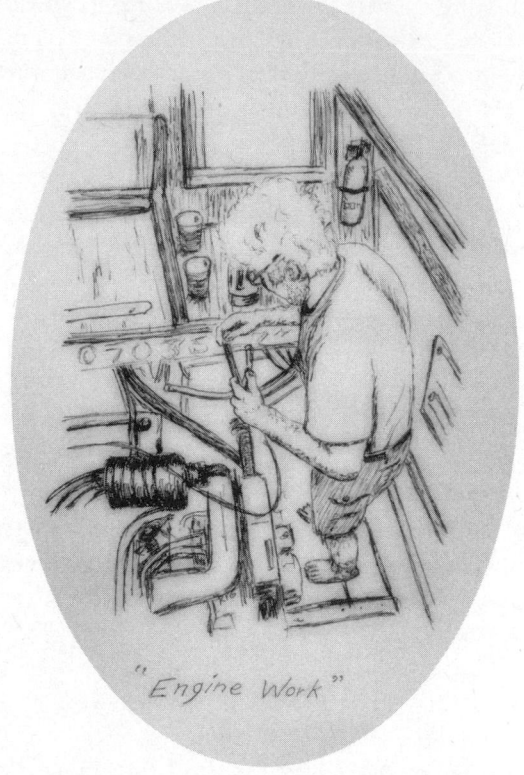

"Engine Work"

A familiarity with diesel engines is one of the first skills you should acquire as you move toward the cruising life. Not only will mechanical proficiency save wear and tear on your beleaguered kitty but it will also make you popular with other cruisers who aren't as well prepared as you are.

more toggle switches than an airliner's cockpit. We have radios, depthfinders, radar, navigation devices, chartplotters, electronic strobes, autopilots, and even a curious little round thingy under the floorboards that promises to beep cheerfully just before we are to be blown to bits by propane leaking into the bilge. And that's just the "necessary" stuff. If I started in on the iPads, iPods, laptop computers, backup hard drives, and all the other paraphernalia that we might be able to suffer through life without, I'd need the rest of this chapter just for the list.

Cruising yachts today rely on their electronics just as much as they rely on their diesel engines—but diesel engines are rather primitive and simple contrivances that most of us can come to terms with after a little study. Understanding electronics, however, requires nothing less than a pact with the devil. Only a select few will ever comprehend what goes on inside all those boxes when you push those buttons. In short, unless you have made said pact with Lucifer in the form of extensive electronics training, you can forget about fixing your own electronics. To make things worse, a single drop of saltwater, or even humid tropical air can convert thousands of dollars of electronic apparatus into worthless pieces of junk in seconds. A lightning strike can turn every transistor and resistor on your boat into a miniature firecracker leaving you with nothing but yet another woeful tale with which to entertain the troops at every cruiser gathering you attend for the rest of your life.

Electronics are at once essential and sensitive to breakage and impossible for those without special tools and training to repair. The best we can do is carry a spare of the essential ones (a VHF radio and a GPS) and train ourselves to carry on without the others when necessary. After all, Magellan didn't need electronics, and neither did Drake, Columbus, Slocum, or my Uncle Freddy.

Electrical Equipment

Although you can't fix your own electronics, unless you are a certified electronics person, every cruiser should have an intimate knowledge of electrical circuitry and Ohm's law. You should know how circuit breakers and fuses work, be able to find short circuits and track down the sources of stray voltage, be proficient at chasing circuits from the battery to the device and back to ground, and be familiar with the mysterious workings of your digital electrical multimeter and your test light. You must know how your generators, alternators, and inverters work. You should understand that your batteries are reservoirs of power, the very life blood of your electronics, and that they must be replenished or they will dry up and become useless. You must understand that the green powder that collects on your electrical terminals is your enemy whose goal is to deprive you of your most valuable equipment—and the enemy pursues that equipment with the fervor of an evangelist chasing sinners. You must understand the guiding philosophy of galvanic action—how it can destroy a boat and what you can do to prevent it. And you must know all about bonding circuits.

While you can usually find a competent diesel mechanic in most popular cruiser destinations, finding a good electrician is often impossible. And if you do find one, once you get the bill, you will usually wish you hadn't. Recently, I spent a solid week rewiring the helm station on *Vicarious* to get the gauges and switches just the way I wanted them. I was able to use almost all of the existing materials so the entire job ended up costing less than $50. If I had hired a professional to do the same work, the cost would have been in the thousands.

Unfortunately, this book is nowhere near long enough to go into the details of the electrical troubleshooting skills that you will need to become an effective cruiser, and I'm not really qualified to write about it anyway. But if you already have a basic knowledge of electrical theory, you don't have to go any further than your copy of Nigel Calder's book, wherein you will find several hundred pages of clear and concise information on the subject. If you don't have even basic knowledge of electrical circuitry, you could do a lot worse than taking a course on electronics at a community college or night school.

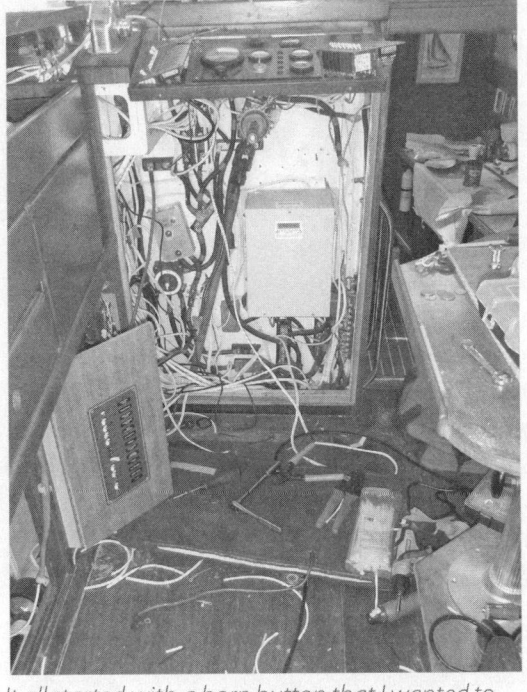

It all started with a horn button that I wanted to move because it was often bumped accidentally. The existing wire was too short, so rather than replace it, I decided to move the breaker panel, which was also poorly located. The primary fuse panel was in the way of where I wanted the breaker panel so I moved that to a separate compartment where it would be more accessible. After a week of electrical work, the entire helm station had been rewired, and the horn worked just fine.

Carpentry

One of the things I like to do best is work with wood. I swoon to the sound of a jack plane zinging off heaps of golden curls from the surface of a pine board or the seductive rhythm of the bow saw as it rips a mahogany plank into something useful or beautiful or both. Wood is my thing, and if I do say so myself, I am good at making it into stuff we need. While you don't need to develop this degree of religious fervor about woodwork, a few basic carpentry skills will be worth the effort on any boat, and if you happen to be among the fortunate few who are blessed with a wooden boat, they will be essential.

Again, a few hundred bucks dropped on the cashier's desk at a community college is an excellent place to start, but if you do take this path to woodworking proficiency, make sure that you take classes that emphasize the use of hand tools. Skills with a thickness planer and an 8-inch jointer are going to be marginal on a boat, but the ability to sharpen and use a chisel, plane, and handsaw will be invaluable. Once you get the basics, pick up a copy of Fred Bingham's book, *Boat Joinery and Cabinetmaking Simplified*, read it cover to cover, practice with a few basic projects using nothing but hand tools, and then make it a permanent part of your cruising library.

Once you develop basic carpentry skills, there are a few power tools you should have. These are made possible by the emergence in recent years of efficient and reliable 120-volt and 240-volt inverters. A rechargeable drill is practically a requirement for mast work, and a small jigsaw that takes the same batteries will be a help in many situations.

Housekeeping

Everyone knows that when two or more people live together in the confines of a tiny boat, everything must be picked up and put away when it isn't in use. "Everything in its place, and a place for everything" is a necessary creed to live by. On *Vicarious* every item on the boat has a designated storage spot that belongs to that item alone, and there is not a single item that doesn't have its place. When a new item comes aboard, the first thing we do is assign it a storage spot; then we make sure the entire crew knows exactly where that spot is. Each of us scrupulously returns each item to that designated spot the moment it is no longer being used. Everything on the boat is neat and tidy, and the hideous specter of unsightly clutter never raises its ugly head. Not on our boat. Nosiree, Bob . . . I wish.

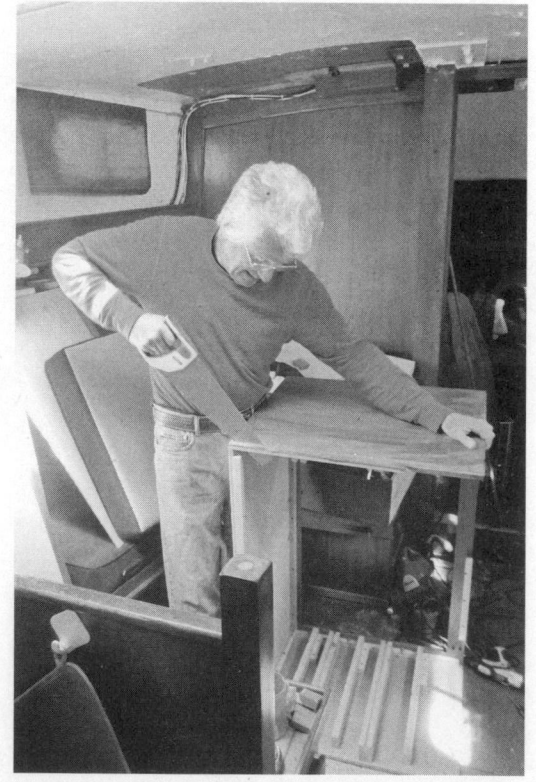

Carpentry skills aren't as critical as mechanical and electrical skills, but a friendly relationship with basic hand tools will stand in good stead when it is time to remodel the interior of your boat.

The only reason that I mention housekeeping as an acquired skill (it's confession time here) is that the crew of *Vicarious* are so wondrously bad at it. Susan and I are both a couple of unrepentant slobs with gear and clutter everywhere, and if anyone were ever to just once put something back in the place it came from, Susan would be right there with the ship's thermometer from the first-aid kit. But that's not the worst part. While on our world cruise in *Sultana*, those rare instances (only slightly more frequent than the appearance of Halley's comet) when we got so fed up with all the junk lying around and actually cleaned the place up, we would go for weeks and months without being able to find anything.

"Where's the can of corned beef I was keeping here in my underwear locker?" Susan would ask the day after a major cleanup, or "What happened to the dead squid I was dissecting for my science project?" asked Phillip. Once, on San Andres Island off the coast of Colombia, I used my nifty little low-angle block plane and my whizbang ratcheting screwdriver to fix a loose fixture in the cockpit; then I put both tools away in a special place where they wouldn't get lost. Two years later, as I was tearing out a storage locker to refinish it, I came across rusted remains of the block plane—but I never did find the dang screwdriver.

On *Vicarous*, Susan and I do try to be neat and tidy, and we will continue to fight the good fight for order and organization, but I have noticed a curious phenomenon on some other people's boats. You may not believe this (it came as quite a shock to me), but there are some boats out there that have achieved the high degree of tidiness to which we aspire. Their decks are meticulously laid out with all the gear properly stowed and secured, and their interiors are orderly to a fault. But there is a curious problem here. Those skippers and crew who have mastered the art of neatness seem to have also mastered the art of being consummate twits, and their neat and tidy boats have all the warmth and charm of freshly cleaned goldfish bowls. Meanwhile, those boats that maintain a certain degree of clutter or have that lived-in and homey look (and my friend Mauri's aptly named ketch, *Goatlocker*, comes to mind here) are warm and comfortable. So the lesson is clear: be neat and tidy and keep everything as shipshape as you can, but don't forget that people are *living on the boat*, and with people comes a degree of disorder and confusion. Learn to love it—it's life.

While a degree of clutter and disorder down below is a normal part of living on a boat, it's a different world on deck, especially during a passage. Here, clutter is more than an unsightly nuisance. It's dangerous and can even be lethal. Loose lines can fall overboard to foul the prop and rudder; unsecured gear and equipment can be lost overboard in rough seas or can shift violently, causing damage to people; and items secured on the deck walkways can trip crew who are trying to tend sails. Even at anchor, a little thing like an unsecured halyard can drive you crazy with its slapping on the mast when the wind comes up at 2 a.m.

On *Sultana* we learned the hard way to keep the decks clear and the gear tied down. On our first major passage, we lost the staysail when it was blown overboard in a gale because the sail bag wasn't tied to the deck, and two jerry cans went by the boards for the same reason. Don't learn the hard way. Keep the deck clear and everything thereon secured. If you have equipment stored on deck that you won't need on a passage, such as boat hooks and boarding ladders, the traditional place for it is in the forepeak with all the other loose jun . . . I mean gear.

Personal Hygiene

While we are on the neat and tidy subject, a few words about personal hygiene while cruising: Its importance is highly overrated. While talking to groups about cruising, someone will always come up to me and say, "Oooooh, how can you stand to go that long without a bath?" To which I usually answer, "It's tough, but you get used to it." But this is a cop-out. The real answer is that there is no problem keeping clean on a boat. A liter of hot water in a bowl with a lot of soap and a washcloth is more than enough to keep the most finicky cruiser clean. Except on the longest passages where water conservation is important, I like to shave every other day or so. I know it doesn't fit the scruffy world-class cruiser image I should be cultivating, but it makes me feel good, so I do it.

Skills You'll Need Ashore

Sultana's first stop at a foreign port was at the lovely Mexican island of Isla Mujeres in the Yucatan Channel where the Caribbean meets the Gulf of Mexico. There we had our first encounter with the terror of third-world bureaucracy, the port captain, and learned firsthand the importance of diplomacy.

Diplomacy

In its simplest form, diplomacy is the art of getting people to do something you want them to do; in its most complicated form, diplomacy is the art of getting people who hate your guts to do something you want them to do. Diplomacy goes hand in hand with tact and common sense, and the importance of these three skills in dealing with officials of foreign governments, especially governments in developing countries, cannot be underestimated. And in my observation, the cruising community is unequivocally bad at all three.

When we reached Isla Mujeres off the Caribbean coast of Mexico, the port captain's office was in a plain cement building—somewhat like a concrete bunker—with no glass in the windows and no proper door at the entrance. When the four of us from *Sultana* entered the bare waiting room, around which were scattered a few rickety folding metal chairs, another American cruiser was there ahead of us. We could see the port captain in an adjacent room, which was also bare of any adornment, sitting at a metal desk reading a newspaper. The American skipper sat fidgeting

in his chair for a while, then jumped up to glare first at his watch, then at the captain. Finally, he stuck his head into the captain's office and asked in a loud voice, "Excuse me, but could we puulleeeze get some help out here?"

"Minuto, minuto . . . asiento," said the captain in an angry voice gesturing the skipper back to his chair.

Perhaps 15 minutes later, the captain emerged from his office, took one brief look at the skipper's papers and told him, in florid Spanish, that he needed to go to the police station first and hustled him out the door. The American obviously couldn't understand a word of what was said, and he stumbled off down the street muttering under his breath.

On hearing this, I got up to leave since we hadn't yet been to the police station either, but the captain caught my eye, and I felt I should say something.

"Buenos dias, señor Capitán. Necetamos voy a el policia tambien."

"Oh, I think we can handle that for you right here, amigo," said the captain in broken but perfectly legitimate English. "Have a seat."

Ten minutes later we were back on the street with our passports stamped and ready to enjoy what was a very enjoyable port indeed. The good captain even took the trouble of correcting my deplorable Spanish. (It's *Él Capitana* in Mexico, never *Capitán.)*

We have witnessed this same scene unfold in port offices halfway around the world. It is amazing how many cruisers have chips on their shoulders as they enter into negotiations with port officials and try to bully or intimidate officials. It never works. What does work is a polite, even obsequious, smile, patience, and a head nodding in assent to everything the official says. You need to keep in mind your objective—to get the appropriate stamps in your passport and a *zarpe* in your pocket, not to make a statement for human dignity and fairness, nor to indulge in macho posturing or a contest of wills. Swallow your pride and bob your head, and if you are kept sitting in a drafty office for half a day, sit with a happy smile on your face. Nod your head every now and then as if agreeing with what the official is thinking. It's tough, but it works. Only once in all our stops have we ever lost our cool—that once cost us a hundred bucks.

A Gift for the Port Captain

A word here about bribes. Graft and bribery are a major part of the culture in many parts of the world. In Spanish America, giving small gifts to officials is a normal part of daily life. Public officials in most developing countries are woefully underpaid, and it is unlikely that our friend the port captain in Isla Mujeres made enough from his yearly salary to pay for the wristwatch at which the American skipper was glaring. If port captains are to support their families, they must make up the shortfall of income from graft. Usually this graft is built into the fee schedules, and the officials skim their take off the top, but in a few countries, especially those not visited by a lot of yachts, the graft is on top of the normal fees.

That being said, we have found the best policy is to never mention a bribe unless you are specifically asked for one, act surprised and confused by the request when it does come, then offer no more than half the amount requested. Many progressive governments recognize entrenched graft and greedy and corrupt officials as being a major hindrance to healthy economic growth, and they are trying to stamp out these practices. When you approach officials for the first time, you have no way of knowing if they are good guys or bad. If you boldly offer a bribe to a good guy, you could find yourself in an embarrassing situation or even, in an extreme case, in front of a magistrate. By pretending naive ignorance of any requirement for a bribe, you can often avoid the matter entirely. If you are braced for a bribe and can't avoid it, just pay it and get on with your life. Don't insist on a receipt, and don't take a digital photo of the offending official (a suggestion I read only recently). Just smile and hand over the money. We have been forced to shell out extra cash only in Cuba, Belize, and Panama, so if you handle it right, bribes will not be not a problem.

By the way, don't ever offer an official in French Polynesia, Australia, or New Zealand a bribe or "gift." These three countries particularly enjoy an officialdom that is virtually free of graft and corruption (not totally but nearly so). The officials you meet will be by-the-book, straight-laced, goody-goody-two-shoes types who take their jobs and integrity very seriously. Sometimes they can be a bit officious, but even then they are usually friendly about it.

Language

It is amazing to me how many cruisers there are in the Caribbean who never make an attempt to learn Spanish. We have met people who have cruised there for years who can't count to 10 in the native tongue, which is not only disgraceful, it's stupid. Most people I have met who aren't interested in learning even the basics of Spanish say that it's not necessary because there is always someone nearby who speaks English, and it's true, there usually is. But try switching roles for a moment, and pretend you are the proprietor of a store in downtown Halifax, Nova Scotia, and a Spanish-speaking person comes in demanding that you provide an interpreter. Would you do it? Probably, if there were enough money at risk. Would you resent it? You bet. Would you charge a little extra for the trouble? Hell no, you wouldn't. You'd charge a lot extra for the trouble, and that is just what will happen to you if you venture forth into the Spanish-speaking world without making an effort to learn a little Spanish.

Remember our experience at the port captain's office in Isla Mujeres? The ability to use just a few basic Spanish phrases changes your entire relationship with many public officials. Just a simple "Good morning" ("Buenos dias, señor") and a brief apology for not speaking proper Spanish ("Lo siento. No hablo español muy bien. ¿Habla inglés?") will likely change an indifferent or even hostile official into a friendly one. Likewise, knowing how to count and how to ask the price of an item in a shop ("¿Quanto es esto? Por favor.") will go miles toward getting you the best price, and maybe even making a new friend.

Of course, if you are headed on an extensive cruise, Spanish isn't the only language that you should become familiar with. The French particularly respond well to attempts to communicate in their language, and on Bora Bora I had one official refuse to respond in English until I made an effort to break the ice in exceedingly bad French. If you intend to visit any French-speaking countries, a basic knowledge of the language is well advised.

Skills to Sell to Other Cruisers

I am not enthralled with the idea of cruisers' selling services to other cruisers for several reasons, some of which I have mentioned earlier in this book: it seems a bit mercenary, and it detracts from the idea that we are all in the same boat, helping each other out as our abilities and needs dictate; commercial activity by visitors to foreign countries is often illegal and must be conducted on the sly; the quality of work by itinerant cruisers fluctuates from the acceptable to far below substandard; and finally, most trades and professions today require a substantial investment in specialized equipment, and few sailboats have the space to use this equipment even if they do have it aboard. We have met several cruising sailmakers, for example,

who do acceptable work with an onboard sewing machine, but a sailmaker without a loft is at a serious disadvantage. Likewise, a diesel mechanic without a machine shop or a dentist without a proper chair and drill is going to be handicapped in providing excellent service.

Because it is difficult to judge the degree to which itinerant craftspeople are qualified to do a job, people are often reluctant to hire them. We hired a guy in the Rio Dulce who called himself a marine engineer and claimed to be a qualified rigger to help install a new roller furler. He got the forestay about 4 inches too long, and instead of recutting it, he compensated by taking up on the bobstay and backstay. This threw the whole rig out of balance and eventually led to the failure of the bobstay. I have probably wasted more colorful language on that particular self-styled engineer than on any other person we have met. I thought of him all the way across the Pacific every time we tried to get the main to set properly.

That being said, cruisers with skills that are in high demand will find a ready market in harbors and ports frequented by other cruisers around the world, and doing such work is a popular means of kitty renewal. Here is a rundown of a few of the favorites.

Mechanics

If you are a qualified diesel mechanic and wish to sell your services to fellow cruisers, you will find no scarcity of work in most of the popular harbors around the world. The question of the legality of pursuing your trade is a matter between you and the local officials because most large harbors have a ready supply of mechanics who could become vociferous if they discover you are competing with them.

While in the Rio Dulce, we had some engine work done by an enterprising young man named Frank who was cruising with his wife and small daughter aboard their meticulously reconstructed Chinese junk, *Concubine*. He billed himself as Doctor Diesel, and he was quite aggressive in soliciting work. From all outward appearances, he was operating a successful business and seemed to have as much work as he could handle, and the work he did for us was first rate.

Sewing and Sailmaking

The ability to repair sails is always in demand, of course, but there is also a steady market for dodgers and cockpit shelters, sail covers, and all manner of canvas stuff. If you can make the ubiquitous canvas tote bag with loop handles, you'll find buyers. If they are monogrammed with the ship's name and hailing port, they'll sell like hot dogs at the ballpark. The absence of a sail loft makes major sail repairs on a boat somewhat difficult, and making new sails for anything larger than the dinghy is out of the question, but it is surprising how well some ship-bound sailmakers learn to handle small repairs on large sails in the confines of a cockpit.

Fiberglass Repair

Repairing gelcoat and fiberglass damage to fiberglass boats is a natural trade to sell to other cruisers, but it isn't as easy as it might seem. Many cruisers don't get too concerned about cosmetic damage to the topsides, and they let the dings and dents that are a normal part of cruising accumulate until it is time for a major refit. Of course, any major damage such as structural failure or holes in the hull means the boat will have to be hauled. Any yard equipped to haul a cruising yacht is also most likely equipped to make major repairs, and it isn't going to take kindly to outsiders scooping off their work.

In U.S. and Canadian ports, as well as in other countries where it is legal, however, a skilled fiberglass worker can usually find hourly work at local boatyards and with boatbuilders.

Skills in making invisible gelcoat repairs (more an art than a skill) are particularly desirable where there are a lot of expensive yachts.

Carpentry

Because most serious cruisers are passable carpenters themselves, there isn't a big demand among the sailing community for woodworkers. However, if you have house building skills, you can make a lot of money quickly if you find yourself in the right place at the right time. When we were in Charleston, South Carolina (one of our favorite stops on the East Coast), the downtown was still recovering from a major storm the year before, and skilled finish carpenters who could help restore the grand old Victorian mansions were in high demand and pulling down top wages. Likewise, there was a building boom in Fort Lauderdale where experienced framing carpenters found all the work they wanted.

Varnishing and Painting

Like carpentry, most cruisers can handle whatever painting and varnishing chores that come along. Again, however, if you find yourself in a U.S. or Canadian port where there are a lot of local yachts, passing around a simple flyer or posting a notice on a yacht club or marina's bulletin board might bring some responses.

Teaching and Tutoring

Enterprising people with teaching skills might find themselves with a steady, if not large, income. Most cruisers who have children use homeschooling or correspondence schools for educating the little darlings, and if you possess knowledge in subjects that parents often find difficult—language, math, science, or music—you will often find work for an hour or two a day. The pay won't be great, but it's rewarding work, it's a great way to meet people, and you'll seldom find any problem with the local officials.

Arts and Crafts

When we first got to Tonga, we were approached by a distinguished-looking gentleman with a short white beard and the patina of a long-time cruiser who asked if we were interested in buying any of his authentic Maori jewelry. He had several display cases full of stylized fishhook pendants, broaches, and rings and bracelets carved from whalebone, tortoise shell, exotic rainforest woods, and all manner of politically incorrect materials.

We declined to buy anything, but we did have a chat. It turned out the guy was from Marblehead, and until about 10 years earlier, he had lived about six blocks from where we did. The irony of traveling halfway around the world to buy authentic native jewelry from a guy who was practically a neighbor was too much to take. Collecting native handcrafts from around the world (molas from the San Bias Islands, carved masks from Guatemala, tapas cloth from Fiji and Tonga) is a major pastime of cruisers, but I prefer to buy mine from natives, not from guys from Marblehead.

However, if you happen to possess artsy-craftsy skills and are visiting any port where large cruise ships dock, you can make a lot of money in a short time just by setting up a simple stand somewhere in the path of the disembarking hordes. Usually there will be an area where artisans gather, and often you can just set up and join in. At other times, in more organized areas, you will need to get clearance and perhaps pay a small fee to the designated authority person (DAP) to secure table space. In some places, because you are a foreigner, your participation will be restricted (or even illegal), in which case you can count on paying a large fee to the DAP.

We have met several cruisers who supplement their incomes with handcrafts, and there are one or two who do so well at it that they don't have to do anything else.

Skills to Sell Ashore

In many places, particularly in developing countries where the wages for skilled workers is are measured in a few dollars a week, trying to find a job in the local economy isn't worthwhile, but there are a few exceptions. Most of the skills listed above as appropriate to sell to other cruisers may also be sold ashore, but some are appropriate only for the shoreside domain.

Food-Service Skills

Any experience you might have had in restaurants, cafeterias, bars, or other divisions of the food-service industry will stand you in good stead in the cruising life. In fact, waiting on tables, bussing them, or washing dishes is practically a tradition among budget cruisers. The work at these menial jobs is often hard, and the hours are long, and the pay is low, but the jobs are available nearly everywhere. These kinds of skills are particularly valuable in resort areas such as Key West and Honolulu, and a job in those places can be yours for the asking. The big hotels are likely to be controlled by unions, but there are plenty of smaller places that are always looking for help.

In New Zealand and Australia, there is such a shortage of dedicated help in many of the tourist areas like the Bay of Islands and Cairns that even though it is technically illegal for foreigners to work in these countries without hard-to-get work permits, the officials may look the other way, at least during the busy tourist season when the demand is highest. This same situation exists on many islands in the Caribbean and may be the case in Europe. I don't know, I'll let you know when we get there.

Food-service jobs are easy to get in the United States too. If you are planning to work on your cruise and will be depending on shoreside employment for income, you are well advised to take a part-time job in a local restaurant or bar and learn all you can about waiting tables, food preparation, kitchen management, and bartending. The work is there whenever you need it.

Engineering

I'm not sure what engineers do, but they have been defined as folks who try to figure out how to do with two bolts what most of us can do with one. I'm not sure what that means either, but I suspect it isn't very complimentary. We seem to meet all sorts of engineers on boats. I've met a civil engineer in Belize who was working on a water project of some sort or other, a computer engineer in Guatemala doing reprogramming of some hospital's computer system, a mechanical engineer teaching local technicians how to use sophisticated welding equipment in Honduras, and a self-styled marine engineer in Guatemala who made a career of destroying other peoples' boats for money.

As I said, I don't know just what it is that engineers do, but apparently whatever it is, they do it all over the world and seem to turn a pretty good buck doing it. If you are one—an engineer, that is—there is a good probability that you will find ample opportunities to exercise your skills.

Crop Harvesting

With muscle and a little effort, you can make a few bucks while visiting Australia or New Zealand during the crop-harvesting season. I'm not sure what it is about picking apples or berries or kiwi fruit or tomatoes that turns folks off, but it is gosh-awful hard to find people willing to do it. Perhaps it is the endless hours in the hot sun lugging a heavy apple bag, or mastering the back-breaking duck walk of the tomato picker, or enduring the painful spines of the kiwi plant, or the fact that most people who live in these countries can make more money by going on the very generous dole and staying home to watch the soaps on the telly than by working in the fields.

Whatever it is, picking fruit can be a terrific way to spend a few productive months ashore. If you are good at it, crop picking can be quite lucrative. Our friend, Randy, on *Mariah*, works both the Australian and New Zealand seasons and makes enough money to spend the rest of the year cruising in luxury. I have heard of many other people doing the same.

The work is hard and the pay is low, but expenses are nonexistent, there is more work than you can ever handle (in season), it's outdoors and healthy beyond measure, and you are bound to meet some terrific folks. And isn't that what cruising is supposed to be all about? Isn't that what life is supposed to be all about?

Web Page Design

If you are a geeky sort of cruiser and understand PHP, HTML, XHTML, JavaScript, CSS, jQuery, Wordpress, and perhaps a half dozen other popular scripting languages, the ones that make web pages do all the things that web pages do, you should be able to turn a buck by practicing your craft on a boat. Web page design takes very little in the way of physical equipment and relies on the designer's experience, training, and mental acuity. All you really need is a good computer, a selection of specialized software, a powerful Internet connection, dedication, technical skills, and a lot of time. Oh yeah, and a few customers willing to pay for all the foregoing.

I haven't actually met anyone on a boat that is doing this, but there must be some. Having dabbled in the art myself over the years, I can't see why it wouldn't work. If done properly, it could work quite well. Many successful web designers operate solely on the Internet, so actual physical location is often incidental. You would also be free of the regulations and the interference of regional officials that make working from a boat difficult for many occupations. The downside would be the time it takes to do computer scripting. The technology changes so rapidly that much of a designer's time is taken up by just staying current.

As an alternate plan, brochure-type web pages (static pages that have no interactive features and provide information only) are quick and easy to do on Wordpress. If you possess Wordpress skills (which are considerably easier to learn than full scripting skills), you should find eager customers among the community of small businesses in any population center.

One more possibility before we leave the world of geekdom behind: personal web pages and blogs are hugely popular with the cruising community. A good one is a brilliant way to share information and keep in touch with the folks back home. Most of these are self-generated through dedicated websites such as Blogspot (www.Blogspot.com) and Google's Blogger (www.blogger.com), but there are a significant number of technically challenged cruisers who would like a blog but don't have the skills or the desire to set up a blog themselves. Would these folks pay money to have one professionally done for them? Who knows. It might be worth an ask. They can only say no. Or maybe they would beat you up and throw you overboard. But what the heck, that happens to me every time Susan finds a pair of dirty underwear that I forgot to put in the hamper.

Once you are cruising, you will be called on to solve an ever-changing array of problems that will challenge every skill you can muster. You can't call a plumber when you are 500 miles from the nearest land, and there is no hospital emergency room to which you can rush the victim of a medical crisis. You need to be able to handle these things yourself, and the more skills you have in your bag of tricks, the better and safer your cruising experience will be. The trick is to acquire as many of these skills as you can before you shove off and to keep acquiring them once you are under way.

10

OK, Let's Buy a Boat

We must sail sometimes with the wind and sometimes against it— but we must sail, and not drift, nor lie at anchor.

—OLIVER WENDELL HOLMES, JR.

Delphus and the Doofus

After Susan decided she was going cruising and I decided that if I didn't want to live the rest of my life in hopeless desperation and lonely despair I had better go along too, the next logical thing for us to do was to buy a boat in which to pursue our insanity . . . er, fantasy. At the time we owned a large antique powerboat that we dearly loved, so after I convinced Susan that there was no way such a boat could make it around Cape Cod much less around the world, we began looking for a replacement.

The criteria for our ideal craft were simple enough: we needed a commodious boat that was livable and comfortable for four people, two of whom were growing at a frightening rate and who found a three-story, 14-room "post-Victorian" house with a three-car garage and a workshop to be barely adequate. It must be inexpensive to buy in boat terms (we figured we could spend up to a maximum of $125,000, and I will never be able to consider that much money to be inexpensive for anything, no matter what it is). It needed to be in good enough condition so that we could leave within a year of purchase. It needed to be seaworthy and safe for offshore cruising with a crew who didn't know a lot about offshore cruising. It needed to be inexpensive to maintain because after spending that much money for a boat, we weren't going to have a lot left over for upkeep. And it needed to be as warm and homey and welcoming as our old boat.

This didn't seem like a lot to ask at the time, but we quickly discovered that our list of needs, no matter how reasonable, eliminated about 99.99 percent of all the boats on the market that brokers touted as cruising boats (a brokerage term that means anything that isn't a high-tech racing boat). Our search took us from the tip of northern Maine, where we had to chip ice off the winter covers of several boats, to the Virgin Islands where I suffered from severe sunburn. We looked at trimarans and catamarans and monohulls of every size and description, and we had several notable close encounters of the disaster kind.

In one case, in a fit of blind passion, I became determined to buy a floating monstrosity named *Delphus*, a huge Chinese-built ketch that had been used in the Caribbean charter trade. The problem was that I fell in love with the boat that was pictured in the listing that the broker provided. She was 54 feet on deck and of a style that might be called Asian Gothic, with teak taffrail and hand-carved trail-boards on the bowsprit. She had an ornate, solid teak spiral stairway leading below decks to a paneled main cabin big enough for the next Democratic National Convention, and she sported enough bunks to sleep half the after-work crowd at Marblehead's Rip Tide Lounge.

This hulking heap of Chinese hostelry had been repossessed by the bank from the previous owner who had neglected to tender the agreed-upon sum to said bank at the end of each month, and the poor boat had sat at anchor in the hot tropical sun for more than a year. The bank had originally wanted $300,000, which was the assessed value of this treasure, but as the relentless Caribbean rays worked their mischief and the boat steadily deteriorated, the bank had steadily reduced its objective. The word was out that the bank was now prepared to accept any offer short of a giveaway that wasn't so ludicrous as to attract the attention of the bank examiners.

Delphus was a mess. Inside she was dirty and moldy. Outside, the sun had eaten away every bit of varnish from the vast expanses of woodwork; the marten-gale boom had rotted away, thereby loosening the rig to the extent that it looked dangerous; much of the metal work was corroded; and the wooden spars showed signs of substantial internal rot. It should have been obvious that the boat needed a major refit and that to bring her back to a serviceable condition would cost about what the boat would be worth in a restored state. In other words, *Delphus* wouldn't have been any great bargain even if she had been given to us for nothing.

But I was in love. I was blinded by the fact that the base price for a new model of this particular make of boat was $750,000—so blinded that I couldn't see the tragedy that was right in front of my eyes. In a hypnotic trance of rapture, I made an offer of $85,000—the amount that the broker thought was the minimum the bank would accept. I figured that would leave us $35,000 to get the boat back into condition. I know, I know, I should have known better, but don't forget, I was in love, and a man in love is not responsible for his actions.

On the way back to my hotel room, I thought of all the wonderful things I would do to make that boat a showpiece and all the terrific places we would go in it. I couldn't wait to call Susan and tell her the great news. But it was not to be. When I returned to the hotel, I received a message with an urgent plea to call the broker. "Great," I thought, "the bank didn't waste any time in snapping up my offer." But when I returned the call, the broker wasted no time in breaking my little bubble of self-delusion. It seemed some other guy had made an identical offer to the bank just a few hours ahead of me, and in a fit of hasty disregard for the prospect of additional offers, the bank had accepted.

I was desolate and staggered to the bar to drown my wretchedness in a couple of pints of draft lager. The Marriott bar in Charlotte

Amalie looks out over the harbor, and I had a clear view of *Delphus* riding at anchor. From a mile and a half away, she sure looked fine. I was working on my third pint when a young man with the air of the sea about him sat down in the next chair, and I wasted not a moment in unloading my tale of woe.

"What!" he exclaimed. "The *Delphus*? You weren't thinking of buying that @#$% pig, were you?"

"Who? Me?" I was somewhat taken aback by the intensity of his vitriol. "Well, actually . . . you see . . . I thought that . . . maybe somebody could . . . er, fix her up or somethin' like that . . . maybe?"

"Fix *her* up?! They ought to fix her up into an artificial reef or somethin' like that." He was really on a roll. "Or maybe you could fix her up into a bonfire or somethin' useful like that. Ho, ho, ho. Anything to get that floating piece of @#$% out of the harbor."

As it turned out, the guy was a paid skipper on one of *Delphus*'s several sister ships that were part of the crewed-charter fleet that used Charlotte Amalie as their homeport. I bought him a beer, and he gave me his opinion of these fine boats. They couldn't sail worth beans (he didn't say beans), they were top-heavy and under-rigged, and in three years of trying, he had only once been able to tack the sister ship without turning on the engine—and that had been in a howling gale when every inch of sail she carried was flying in an attempt to "scare the beans" (he didn't say beans) out of some particularly obnoxious charter customers. "We almost got her rail under and were making about 6 knots, which would have been great except we were going sideways. Damn boat always sailed sideways better than forward. I think that the only reason we were able to tack that once was because the wind shifted."

Later that night I called Susan. She knew I was looking at our dream boat and was waiting for my call.

When looking for a boat, it is critical that you learn to resist superficial exterior appearance and keep focused on your goal of buying the best boat for the job at the lowest price. When I first saw this CT-54 moored in Charlotte Amalie Harbor, it was love at first sight. Its classic Robert Perry lines and commodious accommodations disguised a worn-out boat in critical need of a major refit. From a distance she was lovely, but up close she was a disaster of rot, peeling varnish, rust, and despair. If my generous bid had been successful, buying her would have ended our cruising career before it ever got started.

"Did you buy it?" she asked.

"Naw," I answered. "I didn't like the way she looked, and I think she was top-heavy and under-rigged."

"No kidding. I thought you really liked that boat."

"Well, I did at first, but if you know anything about boats, you can spot these things close up. She didn't look like she would sail worth beans to me. In fact, she looks like she would sail better sideways than straight ahead."

Looking at Boats

Assuming that you have groomed and nurtured your kitty to maturity, have made all the necessary changes in your attitude and outlook so that in searching for a boat you aren't seeking a measure of status or a symbol of prestige, and that you have otherwise gotten your head square on your shoulders and ordered your day-to-day existence so that the cruising life looms large on the near horizon, let's go look at some boats.

It would be a great advantage if I could simply provide you with a list of which boats in each price range you should be looking at, but of course, I can't. I have no way of knowing what your minimum requirements are, your toleration for discomfort, or your personal resolve and resourcefulness, and all these factors determine what kind of boat will work for you. Even so, I can offer a few guidelines that will get you started in the right direction.

When Susan and I were looking for our ideal boat, we spent more than a year in the process and ended up buying one of the first boats we looked at. During that year we looked at big boats and little boats, fat boats and skinny boats, beautiful boats by famous designers, and ugly monstrosities "designed" up by someone with only a vague idea of what constitutes a proper yacht. It could be argued that since we ended up with a boat we saw and liked early in our search, looking further was a waste of time. That was not the case. The year we spent groveling through boatyards up and down the East Coast was an education, and although *Sultana* was the third or fourth boat of several hundred that we looked at, it took us a full year of hard work, heartache, hysterics, and heroics to learn that she was just the boat for us.

We learned a great deal about cruising boats in that year, but we learned even more about ourselves and what we wanted out of our cruising life. We learned some things about others too, things that we would have just as soon left alone. We learned that among a few friends and associates, and even family members, the active pursuit of a dream can engender anger in those who may not approve of the decision to live what can only be called an alternative lifestyle. Even worse was the envy and resentment from those who had developed a keen desire to do something meaningful with their lives but lacked the resolve to act on their desires. One close friend in Boston, for example, refused to acknowledge any of our cards or letters for more than two years because he thought that taking the children out of school to go sailing was egregiously irresponsible and would doom Sarah and Phillip to a life of illiteracy and sloth. Fortunately, we are now friends again, but there are others with whom we aren't.

These lessons came hard, but it was the accumulated experience and knowledge that gave us the confidence to finally make our choice and buy our boat. You'll learn too, and although there is no shortcut to this learning process, you may graduate from the school of hard knocks more quickly than did Susan and I.

Sneaking a Peek

In spite of my remonstrances against worrying about the boat until you are ready to leave, you have been sneaking off looking at them anyway, haven't you? Not only that, you already have a pretty firm idea of your ideal cruiser, and it's most likely a Stinkley Blue Water Maximum Magnum with Jacuzzis in the heads and Voxy Blaster stereo throughout. That's just fine. I kind of like that one myself even if it does remind me of *Delphus*, but even if we combined our kitties, we couldn't make the down payment on the starboard winch handle. And remember, we are resolved to pay cash for our boat.

No Room for Error

We have already discovered that the importance of the boat in our cruising plans is often overrated and that any well-built and seaworthy craft can be made to do the job. However, this bit of philosophy does not hold true for the buying of the boat, which in itself is the most important element of your preparation for the cruising life. A serious mistake in the purchase of the boat in which you are going to cruise can, as it has for many others, end your dream forever.

I will be eternally grateful to my unknown savior who beat me to the bank with his bid for *Delphus* because if we had bought that boat, as I was determined to do, we would never have gone cruising. We would have been stuck with a white elephant that would have drained away our meager resources like a ditch drains a swamp—just getting her home would have consumed a major part of our $35,000 reserve. Today, Susan and I would both be working trying to accumulate the cash required to repair her spars and rigging enough to just get her going again.

Let's Make a Few Resolutions

Before you venture out into the field and begin looking at real-live boats, let's make a few resolutions that will help avoid expensive and disappointing pitfalls. Divine Providence is a wonderful lady when she is on your side, but she is a fickle lover, and to depend on her to keep you out of trouble would be foolish and irresponsible. The boat-buying jungle is rife with the alligators and boa constrictors of poor judgment that are lying in wait to eat you alive, and they are packed with the quicksand of overindulgence that's waiting to suck you down.

The best lessons are those we learn from the mistakes of those who have preceded us, so let's start with a list of problem areas encountered by others who were a tad less cautious than you will be.

Shun the Hairy-Headed Hyperbole

Unlike the docile bole, the hyperbole (pronounced hyper-bole) is a dangerous creature with a curious method of attack. It looks innocent enough at first, even cute, as it greets you like a long-lost friend. Then, as it gains your confidence, it morphs into a fanged beast with a fiery hypnotic gaze and claws especially evolved for snatching its favorite prey, kitties, which it devours with a sadistic glee.

Once indigenous to the Madison Avenue section of New York, the hyperbole has extended its range over the entire world. It is a tiny creature for its size and lurks innocently between the pages of popular magazines, printed brochures, and on countless web pages. Its favorite haunt, however, is in the cavernous reaches of boat shows where it resides among the displays of the most popular sailing yachts and behind the toothy smiles of its minions, the specially trained salespeople whose brains it has colonized and forced to do its bidding.

The bigger, fancier, and more expensive the boat, the more hyperboles you will find skulking in the shadows always alert and ready to pounce from behind, deprive you of your dreams, and feast on fresh kitty.

Like a cobra stalking a rabbit, the hyperbole attacks by hypnotizing its victim. Once you are in its power, it will force you to offer up your kitty for the slaughter and to sign a stack of papers ensuring that your cruising plans are over. Typically, victims of a hyperbole attack gradually awaken from their trance facing new monthly payments for a mortgage, insurance, boatyard bills, and yacht club dues; a large invoice for a wardrobe of the latest designer yachting togs; a floating condominium with a sail that probably will be used only three or four weekends a year; and fond memories of the fat and healthy kitty that used to be.

Beware of Buying Too Early

Many would-be cruisers buy a boat too early in the formative stages of their preparations because they misjudge the importance of the boat in their plans, and that's understandable. A lot of people planning to adopt the cruising life are lifelong sailors whose love for boats is the prime attraction to the cruising life, and it is very difficult to explain to these folks that their plans would be much better served if they did not own a boat until they were almost ready for departure. These people have likely owned a boat for years, and to be without one is unthinkable. But it is time to rethink the unthinkable, and if you own a boat and want to go cruising, consider getting rid of the boat now. Buying another when you are ready to leave will, in most cases, greatly expedite your departure. Boats are sinkholes for cash and time, and by selling your boat now, you will free up all the money you would be spending on it, plus you will have a lot more time for more important things like kitty building.

I have mentioned this problem before, and perhaps it is starting to sound a little stale, but I'll repeat it one last time (I promise). Owning a boat during the planning process can double your time until departure and can even preclude your ever going cruising. Owning a boat large enough for successful and comfortable cruising is hopelessly expensive. I know of no instance when owning one during the planning stages is preferable to not owning one and putting the considerable money saved in your kitty and letting it go to work for you. It is easy to delude yourself into thinking that you are saving your rent or your mortgage payment by living on the boat and to believe that there is an advantage to working on the boat to get her ready to go.

But if you add up the real cost of such a venture versus the cost of living in a tiny apartment near your work, there is usually no contest. Don't forget to consider the money you will be adding to the kitty by bagging groceries part-time at the local grocery store instead of paying big money to the boatyard for the privilege of spending that time doing boat work.

The only way you can really determine what cruising boat is right for you is by cruising. It is better to add amenities to your boat as the need arises while you are going somewhere than to try to anticipate your needs years in advance of departure. The best example here is (once again) watermakers. They are hopelessly expensive and time-consuming to buy, install, and operate, yet if you pay attention to the online forums, the magazines articles, and the legions of hairy-headed hyperboles, you would think that anyone leaving the dock without one was a fool of the first order. The truth is that almost all watermakers go unused most of the time, and a great many are never used at all. The exception is lightweight performance boats that must have watermakers because they don't have tankage adequate to get them between ports.

One more argument for not being a boat-owner before you are ready to depart, then we will leave the subject forever (well, probably not, but I'll try). When you start installing expensive gear and upgrades in your boat with a five-year departure plan (or even two years for electronics), you can guarantee that stuff is going to be outdated by new technology long before you leave. Then you are stuck with antiquated gear that you paid new price for while older boats with more patient owners sail away with new stuff right out of the box. When AIS was first introduced, it was a must-have improvement in safety and convenience, but it instantly relegated every radar and chartplotter that couldn't be retrofitted (nearly all of them) to the back shelves of the Good-Used-Boat-Stuff-Cheap shop.

The trap is an insidious one, and owning a boat in which you plan to cruise exposes you to the risk of becoming an addicted planner and wasting all your resources on your boat when you should be concentrating on your kitty. We all know people who really want to go cruising, but they can't, and the terrible irony is that they can't go cruising because they own a boat and must work night and day just to pay for it.

Avoid Buying Too Big

There are a bunch of reasons for buying a big boat: big boats are more comfortable than small boats at sea and at the dock or on anchor; big boats are usually faster than small boats; they are more prestigious to own; and there is the perception that big boats are somehow safer than small ones. In spite of all the advantages of larger boats, the budget-minded cruiser can keep more money in the kitty by buying a small boat than by any other method of economy.

The big reason for a small boat for a budget-minded, basic cruiser is the cost. Once again I refer to the comparison between the ubiquitous Catalina 36 (not a great coastal cruising boat but, by consensus, not horrible either) that was mentioned earlier, as compared to her 40-foot big sister. The extra 4 feet increases the comfort, speed, and seakindliness of the bigger boat while doubling the purchase price and, depending on the tastes and cruising style of the owners, vastly increasing the cost of ownership. As a general rule, 3 or 4 feet on the waterline doubles the price and operating expenses of otherwise similar boats, and examples of this phenomenon are everywhere.

We crossed the Pacific with a couple from England sailing happily in a nearly new Crealock 34 from Pacific Seacraft, which to me is a perfect cruising boat for two people. When they got to New Zealand, they decided, as we did, that the cruising life was not going to be the temporary interlude as first planned; instead, it was going to be a lifestyle. But rather than planning a life at sea on their little Crealock, they decided that they needed a larger boat. The British pound was trading favorably against the kiwi dollar at the time, so

This Cooper 37 motorsailer, Gypsy Lady, was for sale on Victoria Island in British Columbia for a reasonable price. We fell in love with its spacious layout, clean lines, and fine sailing qualities. Alas, at only 11,000 pounds displacement, it was far too light for extended offshore cruising, so we had to keep looking.

they contracted with a Whangarei builder for a 40-foot aluminum hull, then spent four years fitting out the interior and rigging, doing most of the work themselves.

As they worked, the pound steadily lost ground against the kiwi with a corresponding increase in the projected cost of the new boat. But four years later, they launched and set sail to rejoin their life of adventure and romance. We lost touch with them at this point (it happens a lot in the cruising life), but several years later, we heard through the coconut telegraph that they were back in London working to accumulate another kitty to resume cruising. That was 15 years ago, and we haven't heard from them since, but a dull sensation deep down in my gut (where such feelings reside) speculates they are still working to pay for that boat. I can't help but think that if they had stuck with their lovely little Crealock, we would be looking forward to bumping into them in some obscure anchorage where even the thought of big-city drudgery is forever banished.

The mistaken idea that big boats are somehow safer or more seaworthy than small boats is a myth popular with new cruisers, as is the idea that there have been major advances in technology that make new boats better than old boats. Today's cruiser who knows how to sail well would be much safer at sea in a 40-year-old 29-foot Pearson Triton than most inexperienced cruisers would be in many of the new 40-footers being popped from molds in modern boat factories around the world.

People who buy big cruising boats find that they are as hard to sail as they are to pay for; that their access to ports is limited by a deep draft; that they need extra crew for difficult passages; and that, once in a comfortable harbor, they tend to stay there because getting them going again is so much work.

Small boats cost much less to maintain than big boats do. Dock and haulage fees, fuel, sails, storage, paint, and materials are all cheaper for a small boat. Boats that can be careened on the beach are assets where the tide allows careening. They can fit into small harbors, and there are many more free anchorages available to small boats than to big ones. Owners of large boats seem to prefer marinas where they can connect to shorepower, cable TV, and WiFi and where they can get rid of some of that extra cash they all seem to have. Repairs on small boats are easier and quicker to make, and you will be better able to manage them yourself. But the strongest virtue of a small boat is the very fact that it is small and as such epitomizes the concepts of freedom and flexibility that are the essence of the simple cruising life that is your destiny. With a smaller boat, you have smaller worries and smaller problems, and that has to be a better way to live whether you are cruising in a small basic boat in the Med or living in a small basic condo in Manhattan.

But How Small Is Too Small?

Of course, the concepts of too big and too small are relative. Some time ago, I met a woman in the Caribbean who had been raised on a 32-foot sloop with four other children. I come from a family of seven also, but my early years were spent in a large farmhouse in the country, and even there things were a bit cramped. But this woman (her name was Gertrude) claimed to have lived a happy childhood and can't remember conditions being crowded at all—which shows that small to one person is large to other. The important thing is to select a boat in which *you* can be comfortable. However, it is even more important to buy a boat that is no bigger than the smallest one in which you will be content.

If this sounds tricky, it's because it is tricky. We have met many cruisers whose plans ended prematurely because their boat was too big, and several who gave up because their boat wasn't tough enough to stand up to cruising conditions, but I can't recall meeting even one who gave up because his or her boat was too small. If you must err, it is critical that you err on the side of too small rather than too big. You can live with "too small" for a while or correct it for a price that won't kill the kitty, but too big is often deadly.

Abstain from Buying Prestige

We all like to own good stuff, and we are justifiably proud of the good stuff we own; the old saw that "you get what you pay for" is nowhere more true than in the cruising life. This desire for quality, however, has been corrupted by the hairy-headed hyperboles of consumerism that drive so many of us to buy expensive things not so much to get quality, but to earn what we perceive to be the admiration of our fellows. We have already discussed how ownership of material things equates to self-esteem in our society and that none of us is immune from the desire to impress others. But you must fight this desire for the admiration of your friends with all your resources lest you spend the time you could be cruising in a reasonable boat working your life away trying to support a very expensive mistress.

Most people who matter in this life will be much more impressed by your ability to get by and live a happy and productive life while practicing a low-impact minimalist existence than they will impressed by your ownership of a flashy yacht.

A Liability, Not an Asset

Many cruisers think of their boat as an asset (an asset in accounting terms is something that will make you money), and this is a dangerous delusion because it serves to seduce us into spending more on the boat than we should. Try to think of the boat you are about to buy as a financial liability (something that is going to

cost you money), and don't ever justify the purchase of an expensive boat with the argument that you will be able to recoup the money you spend by selling the boat after the cruise is over.

In the late 1970s the U.S. tax laws were changed at the behest of pleasure-boating interests to allow boats that were large enough to be lived on to be treated as real estate. These laws were important to the boat lobby because the industry was then in a deep recession, and the changes allowed buyers to apply for 20-year mortgages on boats, deduct the interest as a second home, and depreciate the capital if the boat was chartered. The most important change, however, was psychological in that it encouraged people considering purchasing a large expensive boat to view it as an investment in the same category as a house or other real estate, an amazing bit of economic voodoo that worked wonders for new-boat sales. Many buyers were led to believe that their new purchase would even appreciate in value, a phenomenon we haven't seen outside of a few go-go years in the early 1970s and which collapsed completely with the recession of 2008.

Some cruisers buy boats expecting to sell them for the purchase price when they get home. I know of a Marblehead cruiser who left on a three-year circumnavigation on a popular and expensive yacht only to find that when he returned, the market for used sailboats had slumped and his boat, now pretty beat up from the rigors of the trip, was worth about a quarter of what he paid for it. I've also heard of a wealthy southern accountant and her husband who sold their family mansion and sunk all their money into a new 55-foot cruising palace. The boat was way too big for two people to handle, and their dream turned into a nightmare. The cruise ended after about 18 months, during which time she estimated the boat lost over $100,000 in value.

And finally, in an almost unbelievable instance of self-delusion, a man from Portland,

Maine, convinced his wife that if they sold their house and sailed around the world, he would write a book about their adventures, the boat would become famous (presumably along with him), and they could thus sell the boat for a tidy profit. The voyage progressed as planned, but the last I heard, the book remained unpublished, the boat remained unsold, and the wife hadn't been seen for a while.

Your Boat as a Durable Good

Even though the tax laws may let you treat a boat like real estate, it is much smarter to consider your boat "durable goods," as the economists call it. As such, your boat is in the same category as a car or refrigerator, and its value will steadily decrease until it becomes worthless and you have to pay someone to haul it away. Considered this way, your boat is something you are going to use up over the life of your cruise, and anything you get for it when the cruise is done is extra.

A surprising number of people who are considering becoming cruisers are also considering becoming subsistence farmers. The 20-acre spread in Idaho or Kentucky where you can grow a crop of organic alfalfa and free-range chickens while you enjoy the good life living off the land has a similar attraction as the cruising ketch with a crop of free-range barnacles on the hull. Thus, the farming fantasy is much the same as the cruising fantasy, and the appeal of returning to a simple life is identical. My advice to anyone who would ask is always the same: if you need to get your money out of your investment, go for the farm every time.

Pay Cash

Here's a quick exercise for determining if you have enough money in your kitty to go cruising. Take the total amount in your kitty, deduct the maximum you think you must pay for a suitable boat (and again "suitable" means different

things to different folks), and deduct another 50 percent of the price of the boat for upgrades, repairs, and for any changes you need to make. If one-half the remaining kitty is enough for you to live on for about two years, you have enough to go. The remaining half is for emergencies and contingencies, one of which will surely be that you underestimated the amount you will need to live on for two years. (Don't fret about this last item. It's a fact of life, and it happens to everybody. Plan for it now, and it won't be a problem.) No matter how much money you have, however, it would be financially inadvisable to have any more than 15 percent of your total net worth wrapped up in the purchase price of a cruising sailboat; 10 percent would be even better.

Do not ever under any circumstances borrow money to buy a cruising boat. (Am I starting to repeat myself? Good, this is one message that needs repeating.) If you do, you'll spend the rest of your life or a substantial portion thereof paying off the loan and not cruising. If you really want to go cruising, you can work hard and save the money in one quarter of the time that it will take you to pay off a loan.

Lenders and salespeople have learned to make borrowing money easy and painless, which is why millions of credit card users are happy to pay up to 25 percent on consumer debt. The hairy-headed-hyperboles even try to make a boat mortgage sound like the smart thing to do by letting us believe that we are getting such a good bargain that it justifies buying now and paying the interest.

Never forget that the "mort-" in "mortgage" means dead, which is what your cruising plans will be if you borrow money to buy your boat. If you can't pay cash for the boat you want, you aren't ready to go cruising. Either lower your sights and buy a less expensive boat, or go back to work and earn some more money.

Insurance

Insurance for old boats is hard to find, and when you do find it, it's so expensive you may wish you hadn't. Insurers will dictate where you can sail without losing your coverage, and they may insist that you hire a professional delivery skipper or extra crew for what they consider difficult passages. Not too long ago, it wasn't at all unheard of for insurance companies to deny coverage to boats less than 40 feet that were headed offshore with fewer than three people as crew. (And it's not unusual for requirements to get tighter after major storms result in increased claims.) Singlehanders can almost never get insurance without hiring crew or lying to the insurer.

A lot of people believe (and your adventure-some-but-never-reckless author is right there among them) that going without insurance makes for a better and safer sailor. Susan and I have owned two boats that each experienced hurricanes, and the difference in our attitude in each case is representative of my point. In the first case we owned a new Hunter that was insured to the hilt (it had to be because we borrowed money to buy it, and the finance company insisted we carry full coverage). When a major hurricane was predicted to hit the north shore of Massachusetts, I took off the sails, doubled the anchor lines, went home, and slept well, secure in the knowledge that if disaster struck, we would be getting a new boat. If it hadn't been for my basically intact personal integrity, I may have even been a bit disappointed when the storm shifted south and cleaned out Rhode Island instead.

In the second case we were cruising the coast of Maine in *Duchess*, our old wooden powerboat, a craft no insurer in his or her right mind would even think of covering, when Hurricane Bob blew in from the Caribbean. I wasn't about to try to ride it out with my family aboard, but I put out all three anchors with every bit of rope we carried, and I spent most of a day securing everything I could. Then we were hustled off by the National Guard to a makeshift shelter in a local high school gymnasium while the storm howled through. In the morning we walked to a bluff that overlooks the bay where *Duchess* was anchored. I'll never forget the sense of relief we felt when we found her safe and sound several hundred yards from where we left her.

I don't have any hard data to support these assumptions, but when we talk to cruisers who have decided to spend the cyclone season in Tonga or Fiji, both of which get slammed by major tropical storms every few years, rather than make the run to Australia or New Zealand, the majority seem to have hull insurance. Those who do take the more prudent route and clear out, don't.

I think you will find the same situation in the Caribbean. Boats that are left there to be turned into kindling by hurricanes are nearly all insured, while many boats that seek the havens in Europe, South America, or New England are uninsured. If this is the case, and I believe it is, the cruising community and boatowners in general can direct their thanks for the problems of getting and paying for hull insurance right at those who insist on leaving their boats in the northern Caribbean and mid-Pacific, then wrack up enormous claims when storms blow through these cyclone- and hurricane-prone areas.

A Few Things to Look for in Your Cruising Boat

I have already said that I can't give you much guidance about what specific boat might be best for you, any more than I can tell you how much you should spend on it (outside of a few standard guidelines for quality construction and seaworthiness). However, there are a few features that every cruising boat should have. Here are the ones I think are the most important.

Heavy-Duty Construction

When considering a cruising boat you plan to take offshore, don't fall for the line that lightweight boats are faster than heavy boats. They *are* faster, and they do indeed go to windward better, but the added performance in no way compensates for their drawbacks, which are many. Very few light boats can be comfortably hove-to and must be driven through the nastiest weather, which can be exhausting to the crew, and dangerous. To sail well, a light boat must be kept light, which means inadequate tankage and inability to carry a decent supply of stores and equipment. The math is simple: if you have a 10,000-pound boat and carry 2,000 pounds of stores, you have increased the weight of your boat by 20 percent, and she'll be a pig to sail. If you have a 30,000-pound boat and you bring on 2,000 pounds of stores, you've increased the weight less than 10 percent, and since she is probably less than a sprightly sailer anyway, she won't even notice the extra weight. A lightweight production boat is going to have a higher initial purchase price than a suitable heavy-displacement boat, and the lightweight gear in it is going to be more fragile and will break more often than the heavy-duty gear found on most traditional designs.

In any group of active cruisers, you will find plenty of arguments in favor of large, lightweight, and fast cruising boats, almost always from owners of this type of boat who have never sailed in a traditional heavy-displacement boat. On all the cruising forums, you will get an even more vociferous set of opinions, mostly from posters who plan to go cruising someday but haven't actually been offshore yet, and from catamaran owners. While considering these arguments, keep this in mind: in the 25-plus years since the first edition of this book, I have been paying very close attention to why cruising plans don't work out. And the majority of cruisers who give up the cruising life soon after they try it are sailing in large, lightweight, and expensive production boats. New cruisers who start out in a traditional boat are much more likely to continue cruising, and fewer than a third of them give it up sooner than planned. Multihull cruisers are a separate category—their success rate is higher than cruisers in lightweight monohulls, but still not as high as the success rate of cruisers who start out in smaller and heavier traditional hulls.

A heavy boat is much more comfortable and easy to handle in a seaway than a light one, and it is considerably safer in most cases. In any price and size range, go for the heavy boat over the light boat every time.

Solid Construction

Akin to heavy construction is solid construction—but the two criteria aren't the same thing. Many quality boats were built with cored hulls as a means of thickening the hull and correcting some of the obnoxious qualities of fiberglass boats, notably noise and internal condensation. Also, many decks were strengthened by laminating plywood or balsa cores into the fiberglass. This is not a sign of inferior construction, just the opposite in fact, but cored and laminated hulls are prone to delimitation and water saturation that can ruin a perfectly good boat. When water infiltrates a laminated deck or a cored hull, the repair costs are often more than the boat is worth, so if you are considering one of these boats, make extra sure it passes survey without reservation.

Solid polyester boats from southern waters can also have saturated hulls, and the fix can also be expensive although the consequences aren't as dire. It is an excellent idea to ask your surveyor to specifically state on the written survey report that the hull has been checked with a moisture meter and has been found to be free of water saturation. If he or she can't give you this assurance, you should probably pass on the boat.

A Known Design

Some wonderful boats are out there cruising that were built and designed by the cruisers who are sailing them, but yacht design is a complicated technical field that is part science, part experience, and part innate artistic ability. The beautiful creations of L. Francis Herreshoff, John Alden, WEB Crealock, and many others sport lines that are identifiable from across the bay (but unfortunately, so do most self-designed boats). Other designers such as Bruce Roberts and Phil Bolger specialize in practical designs that are less lovely to some eyes but are nonetheless excellent and seaworthy boats.

Unless you are a trained and experienced boat designer, you have no way of judging how good or bad a particular design might be except by the designer's reputation and work. Quality of construction is fairly easy to spot after a little experience, but quality of design is best left to the experts—and even many of them get it wrong. Go for a quality-built boat from the board of a known designer, and leave the home-designed or heavily modified boats alone. Bear in mind too that a respected design holds resale value better than an unknown one.

A Full Keel

Here's one that is good for an argument from any high-tech yacht owner, but I am convinced of the superiority of a well-designed full keel with a cut out port for the prop over any other design. Bolt-on fin keels particularly are an abomination in the cruising environment. Many designs leave the prop exposed and the rudder unprotected, and they have no bilge so any water that gets aboard sloshes around like swill in a slops bucket. I have already related how

we ran *Sultana* onto a reef in the Cook Islands with no more damage than a few scratches on the bottom paint. If we had tried that particular trick with a boat that had any kind of bolt-on keel, we would still be there. Modified full keels with a cutaway forefoot and a skeg-hung rudder are OK too, even though they sacrifice some control under power because the prop is usually too far away from the rudder, and the prop is slightly more vulnerable to damage. The most important thing to look for is a boat with an integral keel. If the ballast is bolted onto the keel, that's fine, but the keel should be built right into the boat.

Keel-Stepped Mast Versus Deck-Stepped Mast

There are two basic methods of stepping a mast on the boats you will be looking at. The most popular with boats built in the past 20 years or so is to step the mast directly on the keel through an opening in the hull to allow access. The other is to step the mast on the cabintop with a strong compression post in the cabin to transfer the load to the keel. The keel-stepped masts may be marginally stronger, but they are prone to leaking through the mast opening. The deck-stepped mast may be a bit safer in that if the rig goes by the boards in a storm, there won't be a gaping hole in the cabintop. Either way, the important factors are the quality of the construction and the condition of the boat.

With deck-stepped masts, be careful of the condition of the deck under the mast and above the compression post. Some boats (notably Nauticats, strongly built motorsailers from Finland) don't have adequate support between the layers of the deck laminates and are prone to compression. This may look like a fairly innocent problem, but it is an expensive and difficult repair. Any sign of water pooling on deck under the mast on any deck-stepped boat may well be reason to keep looking.

New Boats Versus Old Boats

Often my brilliant arguments that old boats are better than new boats are brushed aside and discarded as the incoherent ramblings of a disgruntled old cruiser who sails in a disgruntled old boat because he can't afford a shiny new boat. OK, there just might be a modicum of truth there, but just a modicum. Some beautiful boats are being built by first-class yards today, better than anything that has ever been built before, and I am the first to admit it. Companies like Hinckley, Shannon, Pacific Seacraft, Morris, and many others build cruising boats that are stronger and safer than any of those built in the years past. And new wooden cruising boats are being built by several yards on both coasts of the United States that specialize in high-quality, all-natural-ingredients, ultra-expensive craft. The problem, of course, is that the stripped-down economy version of these new glass or wood boats costs the better part of a million bucks before the hull gets wet, and even a good used one goes for much more than we budget-minded basic cruisers would ever spend on a boat.

Some of us would like a new boat, but even the lowest-priced production boat that is even close to offshore capable is way over our budget, and that's before the considerable fit-out expense. The fact is, you are way ahead of the cruising game in an old Pearson Alberg 35 (there are currently eight listed on *YachtWorld* for under $30,000), Allied Seabreeze (currently five are listed for less than $35,000), or any similar old-fashioned boat than in any of the new boats being produced in the "affordable" category.

In all fairness to modern production boatbuilders, most of the economies dressed up as improvements that are touted by the hairy-headed hyperboles are necessary in today's world of astronomical production costs for any product, and boatbuilding is a tough racket to be in. Just look at the list of builders who tried to build quality boats who aren't with us any more—Pearson, Allied, Bristol—while others, who spent more money on advertising gimmicks than on lay-up schedules, are still around. Some of these boats make adequate coastal cruisers, but as the inventory of good old boats is depleted, more and more budget cruisers are turning to these lightweight production boats for offshore cruising.

This is a dangerous trend—not so much because of the inherent lack of seaworthiness but because cruisers who try ambitious passages in many of these boats find they can be uncomfortable in a seaway, and their much-touted windward abilities are exhausting because they can't heave-to well. Bashing to windward at 7 knots in heavy weather can be exhilarating for a few hours, but it wears thin after a few days. Sailing lightweight boats in extreme conditions isn't much fun for most of us, and if offshore cruising isn't fun, why do it?

Let the Search Begin

As you look for your cruising boat, always bear in mind that you are looking for a bargain. You aren't trying to cheat anyone, but you must find a good boat at a reasonable price if your cruising plans are going to work out. The better the boat and the more reasonable the price, the better your cruise will be.

It is the universal nature of those who sell their boats to overestimate the value of their craft. Most boats you look at that haven't been on the market for at least a year are going to be overpriced. It takes at least a year for many sellers to become pragmatic about what they are going to get for their boats.

In today's post-recession market, good cruising boats are going for a fraction of what they were selling for just a few years ago, and this can be a bitter pill for many who have lavished care and affection on their treasured craft. When Susan and I made the difficult decision to sell *Sultana*, we put what we thought was a reasonable price on her considering the recent complete refit and her pristine condition. Two years later, we reluctantly accepted an offer that was less than half what we had expected to get for her. When we bought *Vicarious*, her owner was in exactly the same position as we had been, so for us it turned out to be a financial wash, but the experience was traumatic anyway.

Look at Lots of Boats

As you begin searching for your ideal boat, it is important that you look at as many boats as possible, but always pay especially close attention to those that have been on the market long enough for the owner's expectations to become a little more realistic.

Try to resist the natural tendency to focus on a specific type or style of boat. As a budget cruiser, the more flexibility you can retain in what you are looking for, the greater the chance you have of finding your bargain boat. It's amazing how hard this basic truism is for people to understand. All the boat brokers I know confirm that it's always the people who have little or no money who show up with a long list of requirements that specify the builder, style, sail plan, hull material, galley configuration, and even the color of the hull. Thus, this type of "client" is classified as a bottom feeder, and it is the primary reason why many brokers often show a lack of enthusiasm when one shows up. Likewise, prospective buyers who announce at the top of their lungs that they are looking for a boat in which to sail around the world are greeted with a yawn and inched firmly but politely toward the door.

You can easily avoid the bottom feeder label (it is more a matter of attitude than the amount of money you have). Sit down with a good broker and tell that broker that you only have so much money to spend, that you are looking for a sturdy bluewater-capable boat, that you don't care what shape it's in as long as it's a good value and repairable, and that you are looking for a bargain (leave out the part about sailing around the world), and you'll find brokers who are interested and helpful. Good brokers can be your best allies because they know what is available and where, and they can greatly reduce the time you waste looking at boats that aren't suitable or that are substantially out of your price range.

Don't forget to poke around boatyards for south-end boats. They're the ones you'll find at the south end of a north-facing boatyard back along the fence where the owners have put them to get them out of the way after trying to sell them for a year or so. They are old and dirty and moldy and forlorn and just what you're looking for. A few of these south-enders could become great cruising boats once a few layers of crud and neglect are stripped away, and they will be available for a good price. But with the number of good boats on the market for more than fair prices, it could be an expensive mistake to burden yourself with a boat that needs major repairs or updates. Sadly, many of the south-end boats that were restorable just a few years ago are destined for the landfill simply because it usually costs less and is a lot less trouble to just buy one that is ready to go.

The same is true of building your own boat, a popular option just a few years ago. Today with the astronomical cost of materials, building your own boat will cost a lot more than buying a serviceable equivalent on the used market, even if you do every bit of the work yourself.

A Simple and Basic Boat

As you look at boats and become familiar with what is on the market and at what price, remember that as a simple and basic cruiser, you are going to want a simple and basic boat. This means a boat that is easy to sail and comfortable to live on, a full keel or a modified full keel with a cutaway forefoot, and a deck that is free of spinnakers or complicated sail inventory. In fact, a good cruising boat should be able to carry the entire inventory except for the storm jib and trysail on the spars where they belong. Any extra sails will just eat up valuable storage room. Avoid complicated and fancy sail rigs, especially spinnakers.

The trick is to find a boat whose owner doesn't want it around anymore. In fact, the more the owner is anxious for the boat to go away, the better off you're going to be and the better your chance of finding a real bargain.

Also remember to look for the smallest boat you think you and your crew can be comfortable in, but don't overdo it. Make sure you have enough boat so that your crew doesn't become so cramped that all they can think of is going home. Look at as many boats as you can. The perfect boat for you is out there somewhere, waiting. But you have to go find it because it isn't going to come to you.

Necessary Travel

Unless you are lucky, finding the right boat will involve some travel (and therefore expenses) because the number of good cruising boats in a specific price range is small, and they will be widely scattered. Fortunately, many places where you will be most likely to find boats are also fun places to visit: Panama, the Rio Dulce, the Virgin Islands, and the islands in the southeastern Caribbean are a few prime examples. Treat travel to these areas like a working vacation and enjoy yourself.

A few places are famous for being where bad cruises tend to come to an end—resulting in a concentration of bargain boats. Charlotte Amalie Harbor in the U.S. Virgin Islands and the Caribbean entrance to the Panama Canal are two. Calling or emailing brokers in any area that you plan to visit beforehand is a good way to save time and ensure that the broker has listings that you might be interested in before you spend a lot of money on airfare. If you do need to travel to find a boat, don't be frivolous about it. Keep the health and welfare of your kitty foremost in mind, and avoid any unnecessary expense.

Fix-It-Up Boats Versus Project Boats

A fix-it-up boat is one that is basically sound but requires upgrades and a minimum investment in time and money for repairs and new gear to get you on your way. A project boat, on the other hand, is one that is basically sound but requires a large investment in time and money and will most likely preclude your ever getting on your way. It is often difficult for the novice or even many experienced amateurs to tell the difference between a reasonable fix-it-up and a cruise-killing project boat. Many older boats that look like they are nearly ready to go, aren't, and if you catch the fix-it-up fever with an inappropriate boat, the disease can be terminal to your cruising plans.

A fix-it-up boat is a great way to get on the water without spending a lot of money, but watch out. Make sure you know what you are getting into, especially if you have never tried it. Boat work is a lot more difficult than it appears. Inexperienced buyers tend to underestimate the cost of repairs, even minor repairs, by a factor of at least 4. Even the most experienced professional boatwrights find estimating the extent of repairs to be the most difficult part of any job.

One of the dangers in fixing up an old boat is that the repair project can become an end in itself, and the potential cruiser becomes so involved in getting the boat ready that the actual cruise never happens. Another more insidious danger is that the potential cruiser will get involved in an overambitious restoration and suddenly the kitty is empty and the boat is still not ready for the water.

Badly conceived and poorly executed restoration projects, like boatbuilding projects, can stretch out for years beyond the original estimates and are probably responsible for killing countless kitties. I've seen this happen more times than I care to think about, and any drive through the country within a hundred miles or so of any coast will reveal the rotting hulks of someone's cruising dream sitting in a field surrounded by weeds and wildflowers.

Even with a fix-it-up project that is more realistic, it is easy to spend more time and money repairing an old boat than you would have spent on a better boat in the first place. It is possible to start with a junky $10,000 boat, spend $50,000 on repairs and upgrades, and end up with a very nice $20,000 boat. You will see many boats on the market that look good on the outside but have, in fact, come to the ends of their useful lives and are worthless. One of these can easily empty even a large kitty before it is close to being ready to go in the water. It is critical that you not be suckered into buying a derelict boat because if you do, your cruising plans are over.

Ignore the Extras

As you appraise the value of an old boat, concentrate on the boat itself, and ignore the extras—at least in the beginning. It is easy to become blinded to the obvious faults of a bad boat by a plethora of fancy gear that is included in the deal. That long list of stuff is great to have, but don't pay much for it unless it is still in the box it came in. Any electronics (radios, radar, GPS, depthsounder, and so on) that are more than a few years old are guaranteed to be outdated and worthless, and many that have remained installed on a boat that has been in storage for a few years will have deteriorated beyond repair. Much electronic apparatus that has been abused in this manner will work for a short time, then need replacing, so even if a piece of gear like an SSB or radar seems to check out OK, don't add anything to the price you pay for the boat because of it. Sails and running rigging may be strong enough to start you off, but they too will probably need to be replaced within a year or so.

The Hull

For all practical purposes, the budget-minded cruiser is going to be looking for a fiberglass boat. That's not to say there aren't a lot of beautiful boats on the market made from wood, steel, aluminum, and even cement, but, excepting the last, boats built from all these materials in good enough condition to fit into our plans are going to kill the kitty. Perhaps the initial cost will look OK, but the ancillary costs of steel and aluminum, things like insurance, greatly increased survey fees, and the cost of necessary upgrades and repairs makes anything but fiberglass untenable in most cases.

True, you might get lucky and find a Dutch-built steel boat or an excellent example of the aluminum-welder's art at a reasonable price somewhere, but don't count on it. Besides, there are so many great deals available in our price range in fiberglass boats, it doesn't make much sense to consider other materials.

Readers of my other books and the first edition of this one know me as a big (some say irrational) fan of wooden boats, and I remain so. I've owned and renovated two wood 40-footers and loved both of them. But the sad fact is that where there were dozens of great old wooden boats available 20 years ago, today there are just a few, and fixing up these few into serviceable cruising boats is made untenable by the high (no, make that astronomical) cost of materials.

The Sail Plan

Cruisers, like all sailors, love to argue the merits of the various sail plans, but it really doesn't matter that much when you are looking for a serviceable cruising boat. Be open to any sail plan and any hull material as long as the boat meets your needs and is available for a reasonable price. The sloop, ketch, schooner, junk, and cutter rigs all have their advocates, individual characteristics, disadvantages, and advantages. But much more important than the type of rig is that it be balanced, appropriate to the boat, and easily handled in all conditions. The modern yawl rig, by the way, is an interesting anomaly that owes its existence to an antique Cruising Club of America (CCA) rule, but if you would happen across an old Bermuda 40 that suits your needs, by all means, grab it.

Like a lot of things, the sail plan is a matter of personal choice. *Vicarious* and *Sultana* are both ketch rigs for two reasons: because that is the rig both boats carried when we bought them and we were stuck with them whether we liked it or not, and because of the flexibility and balance of the split sail plan. But all traditional sail plans are good as long as they match the boat.

The Engine

The specific hull material and the design of the rig aren't that important, but the engine is another matter. You need a good diesel engine of adequate horsepower to drive the boat into headwinds and through large seas and to move the boat for long distances when there is no wind. Many cruising boats, especially older

and less expensive ones, are underpowered for safe and effective cruising. You should figure at least 2 horsepower per ton of displacement; 3 is better, and 4 is a lot better.

There aren't many serviceable boats around anymore that haven't been converted to diesel, but if the boat you are looking at has a gasoline engine, especially an Atomic 4, or if it has an older diesel without enough power, this doesn't mean you shouldn't buy the boat. Changing engines is a common and fairly easy thing to do, although not easy enough for you to try it yourself unless you have done it a couple of times on other people's boats. Several manufacturers make replacement diesels for the ubiquitous Atomic 4 (by far the most popular gasoline engine of the prediesel era) that bolt right in, and in many cases you can use the existing exhaust and transmission. However, engine changes are expensive. A new one usually runs between $15,000 and $25,000 depending on the size and complexity of the installation. If you are lucky, you might find a used or reconditioned engine for less than half the cost of a new one.

An Exhausting Task

Speaking of exhaust, I would caution you to be extra careful here. Offshore cruising boats need a high-lift wet exhaust system with a good siphon break to guarantee against water incursion from a heavy following sea. As a large sea overtakes a boat, the stern squats and submerges the exhaust, sometimes to a depth of several feet. This forces seawater down the exhaust, and in the case of an inadequate installation, through the manifold and into those cylinders that stopped on the exhaust stroke when the engine was shut down and thus have valves open. When you try to start the engine, a slight amount of cranking closes the valves and creates a rigid hydraulic lock. If the seawater isn't cleared from the cylinders quickly, the engine will be ruined. This is a common cause of diesel engine failure in cruising sailboats.

Don't assume that just because a boat has lived 25 or 30 years without any evidence of exhaust problems that you won't have them either. The vast majority of large sailboats, even those used in the charter fleet, go for many decades without ever being subjected to heavy weather. Most coastal cruisers and charter boats head for shelter when the seas get much over 3 feet, but cruisers don't have that luxury.

When the 20- or 30-footers come rolling in from the Southern Ocean, you'll just have to hunker down and enjoy them while you can, but you must make sure you still have an engine when things calm down. If you aren't familiar with terms like "water lift" and "siphon break," get out a good manual and read the section on exhaust several times before you look at any more boats. If your boat needs a replacement exhaust, you can figure on spending up to about $5,000 on it, so this is not an area to be taken lightly.

TANK VENTILATION LESSON LEARNED THE HARD WAY

Proper fuel tank ventilation is an easy-to-overlook item that should be on every potential cruiser's prepurchase checklist, a fact that was brought home on a recent passage from Morehead City, North Carolina, to the Abacos in the Bahamas. This is popular run with the snowbirds as it is a straight shot of about 500 nautical miles due south from the Beaufort Inlet offshore buoy.

We were a day late taking advantage of what looked like a perfect weather window, but just as we entered the Gulf Stream, we encountered the most extreme sea conditions that we had experienced in years. It was only our third offshore excursion in *Vicarious*, and we were very pleased with the way she handled huge waves with winds gusting to 40 knots or so. When the winds abated and swung to the south, we continued by motorsailing into the still heavy seas. Everything was going well until the engine, which had performed flawlessly for 200 hours since we bought the boat, suddenly died. Investigation revealed that both fuel tanks and the day tank were full of seawater. The engine was obviously done for the rest of the trip.

At this point, we noticed that we had also lost our VHF, the primary bilge pump, and our weather fax.

With the boat sailing well, we would have no trouble reaching our destination, but the thought of entering a strange harbor under sail coupled with the apprehension of engine repairs in a notoriously expensive environment made us rethink our plans, and we changed course for the Florida coast, 250 miles to the west.

As we entered the Gulf Stream for the second time, we ran straight into a strong norther that eventually lead to extreme sea conditions and an "assist" (it wasn't a rescue as, except for exhaustion, we were in no real danger) by the U.S. Coast Guard that involved two 45-foot RB-M launches, a 90-foot cutter, a Seahawk helicopter, and a dozen or more military personnel in an operation that took over 12 hours.

All this because the previous owner had installed replacement tank vents facing forward into the waves instead of aft facing away from them, and I had failed to notice it.

Cruising Without an Engine

Don't be tempted to try to go cruising without an engine in your boat. A boat that can't get out of the way is a big hazard to navigation in parts of the world where there is a lot of traffic. It is quite possible for a large vessel to run down a cruising yacht without ever being aware of it, and several such tragedies have happened recently. A cruising boat anchored in the Mississippi was run down by a barge at night, and another cruising yacht was struck and sunk by a log carrier off the coast of New Zealand. In neither case were the crew of the larger vessel even aware of the collision.

In many parts of the world and anywhere on the open sea, any yacht interfering with a fishing boat is fair game, and some skippers will try to push a smaller boat out of the way rather than interrupt a trawl. Our friends Ruddy and Don aboard the 27-foot *Chamois* reported being rammed at night off the coast of Ecuador by three men in a powerboat. Naturally, they were terrified and thought they were being attacked by pirates, but I think it is much more likely that they had accidentally sailed into an area where nets had been set by people who were protecting their turf in a hostile and inappropriate manner.

Would you be in the right if you found yourself in any of the above situations? You bet you would—technically—but the bottom of the sea is littered with the bones of many technically-in-the-right boats, and you don't want to be one of them. When you find yourself in the path of any large commercial vessel with any possibility of collision, the first thing to do is get on the VHF and confirm that the captain of the oncoming vessel sees and can avoid you. If you can't make contact, you must get clear of the danger zone immediately without the slightest regard of who has the right of way, and that often requires an engine. One of the truly useful innovations since the first publication of this book is the automatic identification system (AIS) that is required of all large commercial vessels. An AIS signal is usually visible long before you see the actual ship, giving you that much added time to take evasive action.

As a cruiser, you must be self-reliant and independent. This means you must have the ability to move your boat against the wind, and when there is no wind, if for no other reason than to keep out of trouble. In many parts of the world popular with cruisers, particularly the Caribbean, Asia, the East Coast of the United States, and the Mediterranean, yacht rescue is a growing industry. In the United States, Sea Tow charges $300 and up for a basic tow off a sandbar. In other parts of the world, cruisers have been gouged thousands of dollars for simple tows, and in extreme cases, rescuers have claimed salvage rights to the vessel. It is critical that when you get yourself into trouble you be able to get yourself out of it, and having a big reliable engine is one of the best insurance policies you can buy.

After saying all this against the idea of going cruising without an engine in the boat, I have just finished reading *My Old Man and the Sea* by David and Daniel Hays, the firsthand adventures of a father and son who sailed around Cape Horn in their engineless 25-footer, *Sparrow*, and all I can say is well done, lads, really well done.

What's Your Price Range?

How much you end up spending on your boat is a personal decision that must be made by you in consultation with your kitty, and no one else can really help you much. Acceptable cruising boats are available in all price ranges, and you might even see one listed in the "Free Boats" section in the classified pages in the back of *WoodenBoat* magazine. Here are a few of my personal thoughts about what you can realistically expect in each price range.

In recent years the predominant vehicle for advertising used boats for sale (along with most everything else) is the Internet. There are dozens of websites that list yachts on the market, but the dominant one at this writing is yachtworld.com. With just a few keystrokes or taps on a screen, you can have a comprehensive worldwide listing of every boat in your sphere of interest with a complete description, photos, price, and availability. You can narrow your search to dozens of categories (price, fuel type, make and model, and geographical area are just a few). This flexibility allows you to compare features and prices with every other similar boat on the market anywhere in the world.

When Susan and I were looking for a replacement for *Sultana*, we finally settled on a Fisher 37 as the boat for us. There were 20 listed on *YachtWorld* at prices between $50,000 and $500,000. The most expensive was a beautiful boat lying in Croatia, which we ruled out for several obvious reasons. The least expensive was a semiderelict on the hard in Texas, which we also ruled out. There were seven in North America listed for $125,000 or less. So, as we were on an extended camping tour of the continent anyway, we spent the summer of 2012 driving from Alaska to Quebec to Florida and Texas looking at boats. We finally, in November, found *Vicarious* in North Carolina, bought her for a bit more than we had planned to spend, and moved aboard immediately.

Every broker I know or have met recently lists on *YachtWorld*, even those with their own sites or who use other mass listing sites, so this easy-to-use website is a logical first step in your search.

A broker friend in Florida summed the change in used-boat marketing strategy brought on by the Internet and websites like *YachtWorld*, very nicely:

"In the past, I would take a few 35-mm photos of a new listing, wait several days to get the slides developed with several sets of duplicates, send them along with the ad copy to the magazine or other media I was using; then, for national media, I'd wait a minimum of 30 days for the ad to appear in print. Usually, it took 60 days and often more. Now, I take a bunch of digital shots, the more the better, with my smartphone, plug them into an app I have for *YachtWorld*, type in the copy, and the ad is on the Internet before I leave the dock. In the past, changes in price or details were impossible; now I can change anything with a few taps on my iPhone."

After spending an hour or so on *YachtWorld*, here are a few of the boats in each category that I (superficially) decided might be of interest to potential world and coastal cruisers.

Free

A much-quoted bit of wisdom in the cruising world states that there is nothing more expensive than a free boat, and this is, indeed, a truism. If you care (dare) to look for them, free boats are easy to find. There is a monthly listing in *WoodenBoat* magazine, and there is also a dedicated website (boneyardboats.com) that lists boats available for no cash payment. An inquiry around any boatyard that looks like it has an oversupply of derelicts along the back wall will usually result in a response of, "Take it away and good riddance."

But don't do it. Free boats are free because no one wants them, almost always because the owner realizes that it is going to cost much more in time and money to get them into usable condition than the finished boat will be worth. Be particularly leery of any free boat on which the owner has foolishly lavished extensive or expensive repairs and upgrades.

The Carl Alberg–designed Pearson Triton was one of the early traditional boats that helped make the cruising life possible. And this one, lying abandoned in a swamp in South Carolina, was free for anyone who wanted to tow it away. Tragically, with the price of materials today, this classic is probably too far gone to save, even if you did all the work yourself. Free boats are usually the most expensive boats you can buy.

Nothing I know of can blow through a cruising kitty quicker than a free boat that needs "a few little things to get her going." So I repeat: don't do it.

Under $10,000

If you only have a small amount of money to spend on a boat and don't (for whatever reason) have any prospects for earning more, or perhaps you feel that you just have to get on with it right away (such as how Susan and I decided we had to get under way before our children grew up), you may take heart from the fact that there are a lot of cruisers out there in boats that were purchased from the very bottom of the cost spectrum. Lack of money shouldn't keep you from the cruising life if you want to go badly enough and can endure the hardships of living in a tiny boat with little income.

We have met many boaters over the years who are cruising in the lower reaches of the socioeconomic spectrum, and many of them do just fine, thank you, in spite of having little cash and few assets. If you are determined to join them, you should, perhaps, look for an older outboard-powered production boat 23 to 27 feet long that is in good enough condition to preclude heavy repair bills. Then restrict your cruising to sheltered coastal areas such as the ICW or the protected rivers. To be more ambitious would invite disaster either from wasting valuable resources trying to resurrect a worn-out larger boat that has deteriorated beyond the point of practical renewal or from succumbing to the temptation of asking your craft to deliver more than it can and attempt passages that it can't safely handle.

A superficial perusal of *Yacht World* as this is written reveals 326 boats for sale in this our lowest category, but none of the ones I looked at were of interest. I'm sure that there are a few in there, but wading through a list of derelicts can be depressing, so I gave it up after a short time. Good boats in this bottom category are probably much more likely to be listed locally or on craigslist than on the international listing sites, as many brokers won't handle them.

Very small and very light boats tend to be very uncomfortable boats, and living on them can be more like camping out than cruising. Living on a tiny boat full-time can turn into an endurance contest, and then the danger is that the experience will quickly exhaust your kitty and sour you toward the cruising life forever. Therefore, the best advice for anyone with such a limited amount of money is to bite the bullet and go back to work for a few years and earn some more. Better yet, sell the bullet, and put the money into your kitty. The patient and persistent approach is certain to work out better in the long run, and you will actually end up saving time.

$10,000 to $25,000

A lot of good boats are available for $25,000 and less, and a few of them may turn out to be good offshore cruising boats. If you are limited by this sum, you should look for an old-but-sound fiberglass hull about 30 to 38 feet long with a serviceable engine and a healthy list of recent upgrades. Yet another alternative is to look for a larger and cleaner production boat that is too light for offshore work and then restrict your cruising to coastal and sheltered waters.

A quick inspection of *YachtWorld* listings reveals 832 boats in this category in the United States and Canada. Of particular interest is a 37-foot Alberg yawl listed for $20,000 with basic inventory, some new sails, a serviceable engine, and not much else. Also of interest is a 38-foot Seafarer ketch offered for $18,000 with a recent Perkins diesel, a nice interior, and basic electronics. Both these boats would be worth a look, but there are probably a hundred or more in this category that would be appropriate to get a budget cruise under way with a minimum of fuss.

Most large boatyards will have a back section full of boats with owners who have been unsuccessfully trying to sell them. The common scenario is that the boat was overpriced to start with, then it sat in the weather for a year or two and deteriorated to the extent that it lost much of its value. A terrible looking boat is nearly impossible to sell so the owners gave up, and the boat sat for a few more years and deteriorated even further. Sometimes these ugly old boats can be bought for a bargain price, but be very careful. Give yourself some time to think, exercise good judgment, and retain the services of a competent surveyor.

When Susan and I were looking for our dream boat, we had a total budget (boat plus repairs and upgrades) of about $100,000. We eventually found *Sultana* in a barn in Maine and bought her for $24,000. Even after having substantial hull and engine work done on her, we still had a lot less than $40,000 invested. This was largely luck because we were prepared to spend much more, but the fact that we did not have to empty our kitty to buy our boat was one of the big reasons why our three-year cruise to New Zealand with our children was such a resounding success.

$25,000 to $50,000

If you can hold out long enough to accumulate $50,000 to spend, you will find yourself with enough money to buy a decent, if not posh or grand, cruising boat. There are nearly 1,500 boats listed in the United States and Canada in this category with perhaps hundreds of bargains. Of particular interest (to me, of course, you will find others) are a 42-foot Irwin, fully sound and ready to sail away for $49,900; and a 45-foot Alden schooner that needs an engine, sails, and nearly everything else, listed for only $39,000. (OK, OK . . . without at least $200,000 in the kitty for repairs, you would be insane to buy this boat. But, hey, I like old schooners, and we can all dream a bit now and then.)

$50,000 to $75,000

If you are looking for a large boat with a lot of room (in spite of my remonstrations to keep it small) and you have about 70 grand to spend, you could do a lot worse than looking at some of the better (but older) examples of the William Garden– or Bill Crealock–designed Taiwan-built boats. These boats have well-deserved reputations for heavy construction, sloppy workmanship, and inferior hardware, and there are thousands of horror stories about them.

I have seen chainplates pull out of hulls, turnbuckles snap while being routinely tightened, and whole sections of teak trim simply fall off because they were glued on with no mechanical fasteners. However, if you look for one that has been used as a bluewater cruiser for 20 years or so, most of the problems will have been discovered and corrected by the previous owners.

Many of the older Taiwan-built boats have laminated plywood and fiberglass or cored decks under teak, and when fresh water gets in there (often through fastener holes), the boat is quickly rendered into junk because it will cost more to fix the decks than the boat is worth, even if you do the work yourself. Any sign of sponginess in a laminated deck should be a sign for instant rejection of any fiberglass boat.

A friend in New Zealand recently bought a beautifully maintained Garden-designed center-cockpit ketch, then had to shell out major cash for new water and fuel tanks because the original iron ones had rusted through, a job that involved removing most of the cockpit and much of the deck. If you consider one of these great boats, be sure that you get an exhaustive survey before you condemn your kitty to a premature execution for a crime it did not commit.

Your options open up when you have $75,000 to spend. Besides a generous listing of the teak lovers' dreamboats mentioned above, there are a number of fiberglass workhorses listed. A clean Allied Seawind ketch that appears to be in sail-away condition with a new Beta Marine engine is listed for $85,000 and would be worth a look. Perhaps an offer of $75,000 would put her on your mooring. There is an older Cape Dory 36 in Maine listed for $79,500 whose owner would surely listen to a reasonable lower offer. There are several decent Alberg Pearsons listed for under our $75,000 limit and a particularly nice Sparkman-and-Stephens–designed Tartan 37 for $74,000 that sounds too good to be true. (If it sounds too good to be true, it probably is, but what the heck, take a look anyway.)

$75,000 to $100,000

If you are able to come up with more than a hundred grand or so for your cruising boat, consider yourself lucky, but you are about to leave the price range to which this book is dedicated. That's OK, the rest of us less fortunate folks wish you well, but we will also entreat you to reconsider your decision to spend this much money on something as ephemeral as a boat. Thousands of adequate cruising boats are available for less than $100,000, and if you work hard and find one with which you can be happy and put the balance of that money back into the kitty or use it to fix up your less expensive boat to get it just the way you want it, you will be buying peace of mind and contentment on a level unavailable to those who sail in pricey boats. You will also come to know the real joy of living well with less—a joy that is becoming so difficult to find in our consumption-obsessed world.

Once you break the $75,000 barrier, you will find a lot of fine cruising boats on the market. You might even get lucky and find a well-built steel or aluminum boat whose owner is willing to entertain offers in this price range, and a well-worn, older Bermuda 40, a fine cruising boat by Hinckley, sometimes going for under $100,000. Many of the large Taiwan-built boats are in this category, some of which will be offered with extensive inventories of spares and gear.

Of particular interest in this, our top-dollar, category in an amazing Alden 44 aft-cockpit cutter lying in Annapolis, Maryland. If, in spite of my admonitions to avoid such nonsense, you insist on a prestigious boat with sex appeal, this might be the one for you. Not only do you get a fancy boat that looks like it cost several times the $99,000 ("price reduced

by an anxious seller who wants it gone") asking price but you also get a fully found seaworthy cruiser that will take you anywhere.

Except for rare exceptions to the rule, like those mentioned above (which unfortunately will be long gone by the time you read this), the one thing that $100,000 will not buy, unless you are very lucky, is a large cruising boat in pristine, sail-away condition. Most boats in any category (even new ones) will need a little cosmetic work, perhaps a new sail or two, and a thorough stem-to-stern, windex-to-wormshoe check of every component in the boat—and that's after your surveyor gets done with it. It's reasonable to suppose you may spend 50 to 100 percent of the purchase price on your first-year refit to put the boat into safe, comfortable, sail-away condition. I'll discuss how to go about doing this economically in the next chapter, but first let's take a look at a few of your humble but keenly observant author's favorite boats.

A Few Favorite Boats

Keep foremost in your mind that any full-size (40 feet or so) cruising boat you find under $100,000 will have had a lot of water under its keel and be nearing the time for a major refit. However, there are plenty of these boats that will have a few years of carefree cruising left in them before this happens, and this is just what you need to get you on the water and exposed to the cruising life. If you buy right and exercise care in your choice of a boat, when the time does come for the refit, you will know just what you want, and you will have enough money left in your kitty to get it done without strain or worry.

As you review the endless parade of boats that are offered for sale, you will quickly develop a fondness for certain types, designers, and builders. In our year of looking at everything that came on the market that was even close to our price range, we learned as much about what we didn't need and what we could get along without as we learned about what we just had to have to get by. Here are a few specific makes and models that we liked or at least came to respect. They may not be the type of boat for you, and several of them aren't my kind of boat either, but they do represent the sort of value in quality boats that will do the job. That's what you should be looking for.

Old Wooden Boats

If Susan and I should ever become wealthy in material terms (we are already wealthy beyond measure in immaterial terms), which is about as likely as our cruising to the moon, I can see us finishing out our cruising days in that big John Alden schooner mentioned above. Naturally, we would have it done over first, in Maine by craftspeople of our own choosing, and I can easily envision the bill for this do-over exceeding the million-dollar mark. (It would be the binnacled snooker table in the main saloon that puts it over the top.) But short of this idealistic and highly improbable occurrence, we will keep plugging away on *Vicarious*, which, once the current repairs and upgrades are complete, will be ready for another 35 years of world cruising.

Old wooden boats have a peculiar attraction for certain folks like your peculiar old wooden author, and Susan and I have owned and renovated two of them. The first was *Duchess*, a 40-foot power launch built by Hinckley in 1938, and the second was a plywood ketch, also 40-feet long, built in Newport, California, in 1957. We cruised in and loved both these boats for many years, and we would be in a wood boat now if it weren't for the expense and the fact that I am grown too old and wise to do what is necessary to resurrect another one.

Unfortunately, the stock of old wooden boats that fall within our criteria has steadily decreased over the years, either because they

have deteriorated to the point that bringing them back to standards would be too costly or because they have been restored and are now overpriced for our purposes. A timely review of the wood boat listings on the *YachtWorld* website revealed 77 wood boats with asking prices under $100,000 that might make good cruising boats. All but two of these were immediately rejected because of their deteriorated condition or because of the high cost of getting them ready to cruise. The last two—another schooner, this one designed by Howard I. Chapelle and with a $65,000 asking price, and a George Buehler–designed, home-built cutter 36 feet long apparently in superb condition for a bargain price of $35,000—would probably make excellent cruisers for anyone with some basic woodworking skills and a positive attitude.

Fiberglass Boats

Of all the nonwood boats built, here are a few of my favorites. Not all of these are boats that I would choose for myself, and these certainly aren't recommendations for you (you will have to determine what is the right boat for you all by yourself, perhaps by using the following as general guidelines rather than preconditions), but they are indicative of boats that are popular with the serious cruising fraternity and are available in our price range.

Fisher 37

The Fisher 37 is included here and listed first because it is the boat we are living in and cruising on as this is written. As a heavy-displacement motorsailer with amazing seakeeping abilities, *Vicarious* suits perfectly the needs of an elderly cruising couple more interested in safety and comfort than speed. This is the style of boat that draws epithets such as "oyster crusher" and "sardine carrier," both of which are descriptive of the type and not, to my mind, at all derogatory.

At the moment, there are nine Fisher 37s listed on *YachtWorld*. The one with highest asking price, at $215,000, is well out of our reach. Three of the others are boats that Susan and I looked at more than a year before this was written and rejected because of the deteriorated condition (decisions reinforced by their continued availability). Of the five remaining, the one with the highest asking price, at $109,000, looks like a dandy if the seller is just a bit flexible in price and you don't mind going to Spain to pick it up. The lowest asking price of $64,500 is for a fine looking boat located in Croatia. Of the boats we haven't looked at, there are only two located in North America: one in Virginia listed for $98,500 and another in Marina Del Rey, California, listed for $89,000. That's a long way to travel, but sometimes that's what you have to do.

Westsail 32

Any discussion of cruising boats has to include the Westsail 32 as, more than any other craft, it is the boat that started it all. In the early 1970s, cruising as a lifestyle was virtually unknown to all but a few oddball hippies with more stars in their eyes than brains in their heads, and one or two egregiously impractical Englishmen (Sir Francis Chichester is still a personal hero). Then came an article in the June 1973 issue of *Time* magazine that changed everything. The Westsail 32, a boat that had been built on the West Coast since 1971 with very good sales, was featured in a four-page spread titled "The Cruising Life," and sales rocketed upward. Before the company was knocked out of business by the fuel crises 20 years later, over 800 boats had been built, and dreamers around the world had a new focus for their reveries.

This classic boat has an amazing number of detractors. Most anyone will be happy to tell you the Westsail 32s are hopelessly slow (their nickname is "wet snails"), and they don't really make good cruising boats, but very few of these detractors have ever been aboard one, and I bet none has actually ever sailed one. What they mean is that Westsails look slow and cumbersome because they look like a turned-over turtle.

In truth, the number of these little boats that have successfully circumnavigated is in the hundreds. They have survived pitchpoles and knockdowns and come up smiling with the rig intact, and they can keep sailing in the most incredibly bad conditions—long past the point where larger but lesser boats are hove-to or lying ahull. With their heavy displacement, tiny but secure cockpit, and simple sail plan, they are one of the safest boats afloat, and their extreme beam makes them more comfortable than many boats with 5 or 6 more feet on the waterline.

A lot of Westsail 32s were sold as kit boats with the interior finished by the owner, many of which were beautifully done with exotic hardwoods, and the quality of finish far exceeds anything a factory could have produced. However, even more were poorly done with a superficial plywood interior that would be very easy for a handy person to remove and redo, and if you can find one, you may have found a real bargain. Poorly finished kit boats that are in otherwise top condition often sell for less than $25,000. Westsail 32s in sail-away condition can be had for $50,000 to $75,000.

In the later years of production, Westsail brought out several larger boats up to 44 feet that were also built like a steel ball, but there were far fewer of them built, and good ones usually go for well over $100,000.

The current *YachtWorld* website lists 20 Westsail 32s on the market for between $88,000 for a pristine one in Mexico to $19,000 for a hopeless derelict badly damaged in Hurricane Sandy. All but the last would appear to be suitable to our purpose and would be worth a look.

Morgan 41

I don't like Morgan Out Islands much. They are ungainly, almost ugly to my eyes, and they are miserable creatures to get to sail well. Not only that, they have carpeting on the floor, and I would never sail in a boat that has carpeting on the floor—that's where a proper wooden cabin sole should be. In fact, I wouldn't even mention the Morgan Out Island in this book if it weren't for the fact that there are a lot of them available, and the people who are cruising in them seem to love them. They will defend the lousy sailing qualities to the death, and some even claim to like that stupid carpeting.

I do have to admit, however, the old Morgans seem to be better sea boats than they ought to be, and once you are in harbor, they are very comfortable with lots of interior space and a commodious center cockpit big enough for the entire fleet to enjoy a major potluck feast. And their shoal draft opens up an entire world of shallow bays and rivers where a deep-draft boat will never be able to venture.

A pretty much worn-out Morgan Out Island can be found for about $25,000, but a real good one will still be under $80,000, and yes, if I had to, I could learn to love one, after I ripped out that stupid rug and installed proper flooring, that is.

At this writing, there are only three Out Island 41s listed for sale on the *YachtWorld* website, an unusually low number for this popular boat. The cheapest has an asking price of $37,500, and the most expensive is listed at $69,900. All three look like they would be suitable for cruising with varying degrees of upgrades.

CSY 44

For about a decade from the mid-1970s to the mid-1980s, the CSY Company (originally Caribbean Sailing Yachts) dominated the bareboat charter industry with major operations in all the most popular cruising grounds. To ensure a steady supply of rugged and safe yachts to man its fleets, and operating under the adage that if you want something done right, you have to do it yourself, CSY designed and built its own boats. The resulting CSY 44 is one of the most sturdy cruising craft ever constructed from fiberglass on a production basis.

Most of the CSY boats were sold as leasebacks to investors who had a lot more money than they needed but who needed a tax dodge to keep from giving any of it to the government. (The change in tax law that partly closed this loophole is one reason why CSY went out of business.) Quite a few CSYs, though, were sold as private yachts.

Most of the boats sold to investors for charter were built with an abbreviated rig and a reduced sail area to keep the customers, most of whom think they are Philippe Jeantot, out of trouble. These boats with the abbreviated rigging are only marginal sailers, but they are adequate for cruising, and the full-rig versions sail very well for a boat that weighs in at well over 30,000 pounds.

The old CSY charter boats that you find on the market, the ones that were retired because they were worn-out and required more to get them going again than they were worth, have nearly all been redone by dedicated owners, so there are a few of the older walkover type (newer ones are called "walk-throughs" because the forward and aft cabins are connected) that have been refurbished that might succumb to an offer of $60,000 or $70,000 once the owner has had the boat on the market for a year or so at half again that amount. Clean, never-chartered CSY 44s with the full rig and deep keel usually go for over $100,000.

You might see a few CSY 37s on the market, but I really don't know too much about them except that they embody the same heavy construction as their big sisters, they are one of the ugliest boats ever built, and quite a few of them are in the cruising fleet whose owners are very pleased with them. You will also see a CSY 50 once in a while, and it's a huge bathtub of a boat with a skimpy rig. These boats, which were built by Gulfstar in Florida, are CSYs in name only, and they bear no resemblance to the other two.

At the moment there are a dozen CSY 44s listed on *YachtWorld*. Two of these are asking $149,000 so they are safely out of our price range. Three others are just over our maximum (one at $115,000 and two at $114,900), but they might succumb to a lesser offer. Of those remaining, the lowest asking price is $59,000 for an older but very clean walkover model. There are no derelicts here, which would indicate how the owners of these fine boats tend to value them and look after them.

Valiant 40

Like the CSY 44 reviewed above, the Valiant 40 is toward the top of our price range. In the past, this proven Bob Perry design was one of the best deals around for a classic cruising boat. The older Valiant 40s with hull numbers 101 to 259 were built by the Uniflite Company using a defective fire-retardant resin. This resin, which was used by the builder in a noble attempt to combat the tendency of fiberglass boats to burn like blast furnaces when they get going, proved to be particularly prone to blistering, and not just below the waterline. The gelcoat of the old Valiants bubbles up everywhere. Some have more blisters than a toad has warts, and the blisters go deep, often involving several layers of cloth. At this point, the majority of the old Valiant hulls have been stripped and barrier-coated with epoxy, a marginally effective fix that doesn't preclude future blistering.

Even so, an older blistered Valiant sells for about half of what a newer unblemished one sells for, and much less than the $500,000 or

so that you would pay for a current version. A few years ago, you could buy a blistered Valiant in sailable condition for about $40,000. Today, the word has gotten out, and most of these super bargains have been scooped up, but you still might find one for around $60,000 if you persist and aren't shy about making offers. That $30,000 or $40,000 difference between a blistered boat and a clean one is a lot of money to save for a little bit of ugly and a lot of class.

There are presently 19 Valiant 40s listed on *YachtWorld*, of which 13 of these are close enough to our $100,000 maximum to warrant a look. The lowest asking price is $50,000 for a 1975 boat lying in the Azores. The details don't mention blistering, but don't be surprised if you find it.

Tartan 37

This boat has been around since 1967, and it has proven to be a capable and comfortable cruising yacht able to get you anywhere you want to go. It's not my kind of boat (it's too plastic, and I hate that ski-slope stern that wastes deck area), but if I found myself with a choice between this boat at a bargain price and the boat of my dreams (whatever that is) for a lot of money, I could learn to be very happy in a Tartan. Because the design has been around so long, there have been a lot built (nearly 500 were built before the design was modified into the Tartan 372 in 1988), and there are usually quite a few on the market. The older ones can be excellent values.

With a little luck and a lot of looking, you might find a usable version of the Tartan 37 for under $50,000, and even an up-to-date version with modern electronics can be had for well under $100,000.

Outside of the foolish CCA "racer-cruiser" styling from the 1960s and 1970s (which I admit doesn't seem to bother most people), the biggest problem is that Tartans are considered small by today's standards (which can actually be a big plus), and the centerboard models, like most centerboards on cruising boats, can be noisy as the keel slats back and forth in a cross sea. Also, the centerboard trunk tends to get clogged with mussels and barnacles and other sea creatures. I have seen several Tartans whose frustrated owners have glassed over the centerboards, choosing to sacrifice a bit of windward performance for the peace of mind that comes from not having a centerboard to worry about. There are other keel options available (a deep-draft version and a Scheel Keel version were both offered), but most of the boats that I have seen are the centerboard models.

YachtWorld currently lists 20 Tartan 37s for sale. The most expensive is a beautiful 1979 model in Annapolis asking $80,000. The lowest asking price is $44,500 for an equally lovely boat in San Diego.

Making an Offer

When you finally find the boat you want, the first thing you must do is to go away and think about it for a while. How long is "a while"? That depends on you, but it should be long enough for you to make sure you are proceeding in a rational rather than an emotional manner. Don't forget that a good sales effort can pluck your heartstrings like Jimmy Buffett plucks his guitar, so go somewhere quiet and spend an hour or a day or a week asking yourself the questions we've discussed above: "Is the boat too big? … too small? … too expensive?" "Can we get her in the water with a minimum of effort … time … expense?" "Will she be seaworthy … safe? … easy to sail? … easy to maintain?"

Don't worry if it isn't the perfect boat for you. There's no such thing as a perfect boat anyway. Just make sure she will do the job you want her to do without strangling your poor little kitty. Don't worry about the asking price.

Make your offer based on what you think you can pay, even if it's only a fraction of what the seller expects to get. Don't worry about the actual value of the boat either, as long as you know your offer is lower. The only thing that should concern you at this point is how much you can pay and what the seller will accept.

There is often a psychological advantage in offering about 10 percent less in your first offer than you can pay in the end. Doing so allows the seller the face-saving option of rejecting your first offer while imparting a feel-good attitude about talking you up to a higher price. You'll get the boat at a price you can afford, and everyone will feel better about it.

Don't be astonished if your offer is rejected, and don't be intimidated into offering even a little more than you want to pay. If the seller is indignant or offended by your offer, be polite, and make sure that everyone understands that you've offered as much as you can and that your offer will stand for a while. If your first offer isn't refused, you've probably offered too much anyway.

Getting a Survey

The importance of getting a survey on any boat you are considering can't be overemphasized. Even the simplest craft is a complex creation of many diverse disciplines. Literally thousands of things can be amiss that even knowledgeable boat people can overlook. True, the majority of these potential problems are minor, and no boat is free of all of them, but others can be both hard to detect and fatal. A bad deck-to-hull seam on a fiberglass boat, for example, is invisible in dry weather, but it can cause leaks that make life aboard a misery at best. At worst the seam can fail in heavy seas and sink the boat. Intergranular and crevice corrosion in an aluminum or steel hull and in major hardware components is likewise invisible and hard to detect, as is rot in a wooden boat. All of these problems and many more can mean the end of a boat that looks just dandy on the outside. Hundreds of other items such as poor engine mounting, water saturation, stray electrical current, or inadequate wiring are common and repairable, but the repairs can be expensive, and you want to know about those expenses before you buy the boat.

When you find a boat you are interested in, first agree on a price with the seller, but make the price contingent on the results of a good survey. If you are using a broker, the broker will undoubtedly recommend one or several surveyors, but you are better off getting one yourself based on recommendations of other boatowners in the area who are not involved in the boat-selling industry. The convention is that the broker is working for the seller (in some states, brokers are required to tell the buyer this) and the surveyor is working for you, the buyer. In reality, the broker is working for the broker who is trying to sell boats, and the surveyor is working for the surveyor who is doing surveys, and you are left to look after yourself. Even the most honest surveyor may be reluctant to kill the sale of a broker who sends in a lot of business.

Because the buyer pays full price for the survey, you can order just what you want. Some surveyors specialize in certain kinds of boats (steel, wood, luxury yachts, commercial vessels, and so on) so try to find a surveyor who specializes in the type of boat you are looking at, and spend a little extra on a full survey. That means the boat is checked in the water and out, with a full engine run-up and a test sail thrown in for good measure. Whatever you do, don't trust a survey that was done last month on the same boat for some other potential buyer even if the seller or the broker offers it for free. Such an offer is unethical at best, and in many areas it may even be illegal.

Once the results of the survey are available, you can decide not to buy the boat if catastrophic difficulties are discovered, or you can renegotiate the price to get it into line with what the repairs would cost. As a third option, you can request the seller make the repairs before you buy the boat, but make sure your purchase is contingent on a new survey if the repairs are major—or at least contingent on the approval of the original surveyor if the repairs are minor.

Surveys and the surveyors who do them are negative by nature and tend to reveal the bad things about a boat and ignore the good things. The final price should always be renegotiated based on the worst items discovered in the survey and what it will cost to repair them. When we bought *Sultana*, the surveyor came up with a list of 52 items that he deemed critical enough to require immediate attention, and that list knocked a full third off what we ended up paying for the boat.

Building Your Own Boat

Although I have never built a cruising boat, I know lots of people who have. There was the man in Ipswich who spent the better part of 10 years building a lovely Tahiti ketch on the banks of the Ipswich River, only to discover that his wife was terrified of tipping over when the boat heeled in a breeze. And then there was the young man on the south shore of Boston who started building a 40-foot Bruce Roberts ketch in his backyard when he was 17 years old. We met him when he was 29, and the boat was still nowhere near complete.

Many backyard and part-time builders of cruising boats I have known over the years never finish the boats they are building even after 10 or 15 years of work, and of those few who have, most have never gone cruising. There seems to be some fundamental difference between the type of people who are good at building boats and those who are good at sailing and cruising in them—it is rare to meet someone who is good at both. Of course there are exceptions to this statement, and those exceptions shine like diamonds in a fist full of pebbles.

The most successful boatbuilders are those who cruise long enough to know exactly what they want in a cruising boat, then go to work full-time building just the boat they want. On Hunga Atoll in Vava'u, we met the crew of a steel ketch who had cruised in their first boat for many years, then gone ashore in England. Keith, the skipper, spent two years designing and building *Sammy Ley*, one of the loveliest and most comfortable cruising boats I have ever been aboard.

What can would-be cruisers learn from these somewhat casual observations of the building machinations of our fellows? Well, perhaps not to undertake a boatbuilding project unless you have a very long time between now and your expected departure, and then only if you have already built several boats and know exactly what you are doing. Even in that ideal situation it is wiser to cruise for a few years on a small and inexpensive boat so that you will know just what you need when you do go ashore to build your dream boat. For most of us

it makes much more sense to go to work and sedulously save our shillings for the kitty, then let the kitty build our boat.

The reality of today's used-boat market is that not as many of us are building our own cruising boats as there were a decade or so ago. With so many quality boats available for such reasonable prices, it doesn't make a lot of sense to spend the considerable time and money that new construction demands, unless of course, you are a hopeless perfectionist or have big piles of cash lying around and just prefer to make your own stuff.

Ours is a free-range life in an artificial world, and to be successful at simple and basic cruising, we need first to shake off the standards of behavior that society uses to keep us tethered safely to the dock. We need a good old boat that doesn't cost a lot of money to buy, outfit, and maintain. The trick is to find just the right one by looking for price and condition rather than for style and features, then get it on the water as quickly as possible. Do the fix-it-up once you are on your way, and only look back to wave good-bye to conventionalism, conformity, conflict, consternation, commercialism, corruption, and conspicuous consumption. (OK, OK . . . so maybe not corruption.)

11

Dinghies and Dogs: A Few Things You Thought You Needed but Don't

*We are happy in
proportion to the things
we can do without.*

—HENRY DAVID THOREAU

An amazing assortment of consumer products is available to those of us fortunate enough to live in the consumer society, and these products are designed to help us get the most from our sports, lifestyles, and vocations. No matter how esoteric a nautical undertaking we pursue, from Olympic one-design racing to ship-in-a-bottle model building, there will be hundreds of companies offering thousands of products that promise to make our efforts more enjoyable, safer, and easier than they would be without them. Most of these companies claim that you can't fully appreciate your activity without their product, and many are quick to proclaim you a fool for even trying to get by without one.

Of course, no matter how loudly the public relations statements and advertisements extol the virtues of their products and their commitment to us, their esteemed customers, the cynical old coots among us realize that their primary purpose, indeed, their only motive for offering their products no matter how wonderful, is to extract more green from our wallets and thereby improve their profit margins at the expense of our beleaguered kitty.

Profit margin is a euphemism for "greed." And greed is the second most powerful motivator there is, right behind the inexplicable yearnings of Adam as he watched Eve sharing a mango with a lascivious singlehander on an atoll in the Cook Islands.

Saturn Kaboat
w/ Nelson

There are a lot of things that you don't need on a cruising boat. And as a rule, when you must have something, the bigger that thing is, the more trouble and expense it will be. This is particularly true with dinghy things and dog things. A small lightweight dinghy will do 90 percent of the tasks that a big heavy one will do, and it will be a lot easier to handle. A small lightweight dog will produce only a fraction of doggy byproduct that a big dog produces and at a fraction of the cost. The twice-daily trips ashore are required no matter what size the dog, but a small dog is easier to carry in a small dinghy than is a big dog. In the cruising life, small and simple things are nearly always better than big and complicated things.

(I'm certain it was a mango in the Cooks. The apple/mango misunderstanding is probably the result of translation difficulties. *Apple* in ancient Aramaic sounds something like *mango* in French—I think. My theory is reinforced by the observation that lascivious singlehanders are sometimes associated with leg less reptiles, especially when caught sharing a mango on the beach with a clueless young lady wearing nothing but a fig leaf.)

OK, we are getting off topic here. This book isn't an economic treatise, nor does it have anything to do with Old Testament history, so let's just make the point that the combination of the free market, competition, and the profit motive has resulted in an astounding quantity of gadgets and doohickeys that we can buy for our cruising boats. The profit motive ensures that most of these products are useful; competition ensures that most are constantly improving and are reasonably priced; and the free market ensures that most will be promoted with a deluge of exaggerated claims in magazine articles and targeted advertisements that make us dread opening our laptops.

The companies that want to sell us their products know just how to push all our hot buttons. Through celebrity endorsements, advertisements, peer pressure, and product reviews in magazines, we are bombarded with information and misinformation cajoling us to purchase every manner of device for our boats. Most of these products are useful on some level, as useless products have proven hard to sell no matter how much money is spent on promoting them.

Our job here is to sort through all these products to determine, first, which products are indeed essential to our ambitions as budget world cruisers. Then, in the unlikely event that our kitty hasn't become so emaciated as to need emergency care, to select from the ones that aren't essential but might be useful enough to justify further expenditure.

So how do we determine what to buy and what to leave on the shelf? It's hard to know with absolute certainty, but here are a few steps you can take that will help. Every time you consider adding a product to your cruising inventory, you should ask yourself the following questions.

Why do you want this thing? Is it because everybody else has one? Or is it because Betty Bebop used one when she circumnavigated Antarctica while standing on her head and really liked it a lot? Or could it be because the guy at the boat show said it represented the cutting edge of technology and it was a big improvement over last year's model? Or perhaps you want one because it is super cool and having one is sure to make you a super cool guy. Maybe you want it because you really need it, but probably not.

These few questions may sound silly, but they aren't. All but the last one, actual need, are among the top motivators for our purchasing decisions. Peer pressure, celebrity endorsements, model changes dressed up as technological advances, and a false sense of self-esteem are all among the top 10 reasons we buy stuff. (The number one purchase motivator is fear: "What will everyone think when we show up at the round-the-world rally with a 30-foot boat? Mike and Jane have a 40-foot boat now, and they will make us look *soooo* insignificant and shabby.")

Actual need as a purchasing motivator is way down on the list simply because, in our affluent consumerist society, if there is anything we really need, we probably already have one. That is why, since the late fifties, advertising expenditures for consumer products and services have been in inverse proportion to people's actual requirements for the products. We may really need a few quarts of milk, a pound of butter, and lots of fresh vegetables every week, but none of us needs a trip to McBurgerLand for a double-cheese-and-bacon MegaBurger with free (this week only) up-sized fries and a soft drink.

Marketers and retailers know all this of course, and they know full well that 90 percent of your buying decision is subconscious. Most of us have no idea why we buy stuff. When we want a thing, we just want it, and that is all we need or want to know about it. This is what makes this first question—why do you want this thing?—so important. Until we learn to answer this question honestly, we will continue to waste money on stuff we could do without, while our cruising plans and our poor kitty suffer the consequences.

Is this thing cost-effective? In other words, will the benefit received from the addition of this thing justify squeezing the kitty just one more time to buy it? Is the additional comfort, safety, or convenience gained in spending $5,000 for a weather-tight cockpit enclosure that will probably need replacement in five years worth the $1,000 per year average cost?

What are the detrimental effects of buying this thing? Is installing a generator in the engine compartment going to restrict access to the engine and make it harder to change the oil and filters? What is that cockpit enclosure going to do to the classic lines of your boat? How about the handling qualities and windage? If you upgrade the dinghy to a rigid inflatable boat (RIB) with a 15-horse motor, will you be able to get it on deck? Where will you stow the extra gasoline cans?

How much maintenance will this thing need? Most of us don't go cruising so we can spend time changing the oil in the generator or pickling the watermaker every time we enter port. Maintenance is an important part of the cruising life, and all of us spend a lot of time in the engine compartment trying to figure out why the freshwater pump stopped pumping, or we're up the mast trying to get the windicator to indicate the wind. We already have more drudge work than we can handle, so adding to the workload with unnecessary high-maintenance gadgets is foolish. Fixing a broken chain on bicycle, cleaning the accumulated grease from the bottom of a gas grill, chasing down an electrical fault in an inoperable bow thruster, or spending hours on a computer trying to locate a replacement turnbuckle for your furling mainsail are all pastimes we could do without.

The answer is easy. The fewer optional items on your boat, the less time you will spend maintaining them.

Where are you going to put it? Ideally everything on a boat should have a specific storage place, no matter how small or large it is, so never buy anything until you know just where you are going to stow it. Susan and I have had a kettle type of charcoal or gas grill on every boat we have owned, but we put off buying one for *Vicarious* for a year while we agonized over the amount of space it would occupy in the lazarette.

Be especially careful if the answer to this question is to store the item on deck. Everywhere we go, but especially in the Caribbean, we see cruising boats loaded with wind surfers, bicycles, kayaks, gas generators, and on two occasions, motor scooters. We went through this phase ourselves on *Sultana*. In our first year we accumulated all of the above, except the motor scooters, but by our second year we had disposed of everything on deck but the life raft. It seems that the joy of sailing offshore with an uncluttered deck is a lesson that can be learned only by experience. I suspect that this is why all that stuff we see on the decks of boats in the Caribbean is gone on many of the boats we see in the South Pacific.

Are you really going to use it? Bicycles, sewing machines, kayaks, esoteric tools, single-use kitchen gadgets (like waffle irons or bread machines), scuba gear, fishing rods, and gas grills are all items purchased by many new cruisers who end up never using them or using them so seldom that they are a waste of money and space. As I said, we have a small gas grill on board *Vicarious* but only because past experience tells us that we will use it a lot. For us a gas grill works, but we encounter many cruisers who have them and they are practically new after many years of travel.

There are many products available that conjure up an image of fun or usefulness that often never materializes after we buy the thing. Kayaks and bicycles are good examples. It is easy to imagine gliding soundlessly along the shore of some remote bay in the Abacos or peddling happily through the Bora Bora countryside to refresh your supply of taro in some distant village. But both kayaks and bicycles are expensive, large, and cumbersome, even the fold-up ones. You need one of each for every member of the crew, and there is often paraphernalia that goes along with them—helmets, paddles, and such—that also costs money and takes up space. In our experience, anything that requires assembly prior to use or is awkward to get into service often remains disassembled and stored away to be used only on occasion.

Opinions on Stuff

Here are a few opinions based on personal experience and observation on a few of the most common products that we are often told we must have but that really are optional. Some are actually quite useful while others are frivolous.

The Dinghy

It may seem odd to be including in a chapter about things that you don't need a discussion of your dinghy, something that you definitely do need. It is hard to even imagine trying to go cruising without a suitable tender for the main ship. Indeed, a durable and utilitarian dinghy is as essential to the life afloat as the family car was back when you lived in the suburbs. The ship's tender is the only way to get ashore in any remote anchorage that doesn't provide launch service; provisioning is next to impossible in many cruiser destinations where you can't tie up to a dock; and a dinghy with a reliable outboard motor opens up possibilities for adventure and exploration that wouldn't exist without one.

That analogy to the family car is an apt one. Of course you needed an automobile when you lived shoreside, but you did not need a huge gas-hog of an SUV with four-wheel drive and a turbocharged eight-cylinder engine to get the groceries home from the megamart or to get the kids to hockey practice. Likewise, you don't need a large dinghy with a big motor to accomplish the basic provisioning and transportation jobs that a dinghy needs to do.

But there are other less practical but fun functions that a small dinghy can't do well: exploring attractions far from the anchorage, scuba diving with all the appropriate gear, transporting huge mountains of provisions back to the mothership, and zooming through a crowded anchorage at top speed just to see how many enraged skippers you can get to throw their handheld radios at you, to name just a few. And if you are cruising with your children, teens or preteens, getting by without a practical dinghy is practically impossible.

So, as with most everything about the cruising life, when selecting a dinghy, we are once again faced with a conflicting spectrum of equally attractive features. If we choose a small, slow, practical dinghy, we can't have a big, fast, fun one, so let's look at the choices we must make to get just the right dinghy for us without taking the fun out of the function.

First, Some Dinghy History

Susan and I began our search for the perfect dinghy many years ago when we bought our first: a tidy little Avon Redstart "soft-tail" that was just large enough to be useful yet small enough to roll up and stuff into the lazarette of our tiny first sailboat. That little Avon lasted nearly 10 years and three progressively larger boats until Sarah and Phillip came along. The 8-foot donut became progressively more cramped as they became progressively larger.

The kids were still small when we decided to trade in the old Avon for something that would accommodate a family of four. Thinking ahead to the looming teenage years, we invested in a 14-foot Zodiac with a plywood floor and

a 25-horse Mercury outboard on the transom. This became the tender to *Duchess*, an antique 40-foot Hinckley powerboat in which we explored the world, or at least that part of the world that lay between Cuttyhunk Island and Saint Andrews, Nova Scotia.

Those five summers that we dragged the huge Zodiac up and down the coast of New England were formative ones for Sarah and Phillip, but they also saw a progressive transformation in the psyche of their harried parents. Without ever talking about it or even noticing the effect it was having on our lives, Susan and I became closer as a married couple during those trips, and the four of us were functioning better as a family than we ever did ashore. Gradually, as our lives of shopping malls, dull jobs, and traffic jams became more tedious and meaningless, the call of the sea became irresistible. As dreamy emotions slowly prevailed, we dispensed with reason and common sense, sold all our stuff, quit our jobs, and sailed away. When we finally traded the *Duchess* for *Sultana* and headed south, the trusty Zodiac trailed along in our wake or was bundled and tied to the foredeck when we ventured offshore.

It was in the steamy heat of the Florida Everglades that we first noticed that our trusty Zodiac was suffering from a terminal disease common to old Hypalon boats in the tropics: the seams were leaking air in a dozen places, a condition that would become progressively worse until eventually the old boat wouldn't hold any air at all.

We knew that once the seams start to go on a Hypalon boat, she is done for because it won't stop and there is no way to fix it. So we donated her to a missionary dentist who was headed to South America. He painted a big white cross on the bow and shot the tubes full of urethane foam house insulation, thereby resurrecting the old boat for a new life saving heathen souls and fixing their teeth.

Although we no longer had an inflatable, *Sultana*'s inventory, when we bought her, included a fiberglass Dyer sailing dinghy that was slung from the stern on a sturdy set of davits. While the kids honed their small-boat sailing skills up and down the Florida Keys, I rediscovered the joy of rowing, and I vowed never again to be without a hard dinghy.

The Dyer was a lovely boat that easily carried two adults or even two adults and one preteenager, but when we loaded the entire crew of four aboard, a dry arrival (or any arrival for that matter) at our destination became a study in probability theory for the kids' home-schooling lessons. Another problem was that, while the Dyer rowed like a dream, the idea of trying to mount our 25-horse Mercury on her transom was a joke that quickly became stale. Thus, when we departed Key West for Mexico, the section of deck previously occupied by the Zodiac contained a new 12-foot bright-red Achilles inflatable.

The combination of the Dyer rowing-and-sailing dink with the powerful inflatable served us well all through the western Caribbean and across the Pacific. But then on the atoll of Aitutaki in the Cook Islands archipelago, disaster struck. While we were anchored in the small harbor inside the reef, someone (we never determined who, but speculation rages on 20 years later) forgot to tie the painter of the dinghy to *Sultana*'s stern cleat, and when we woke in the morning, our beloved Dyer had drifted away in the night and was gone forever.

When we got to New Zealand, we replaced the lost Dyer with a similar, locally made fiberglass dinghy, and we traded in the old Mercury outboard for a smaller 15-horsepower Mariner. After a three-year stint rebuilding *Sultana*, we did a year-long circuit of the South Pacific, this time without our daughter, Sarah, who had jumped ship for college in California.

After we returned to New Zealand, Phillip soon followed Sarah in his own search for the meaning of life, and Susan and I were left with what seemed like a cavernous empty boat and an overlarge inflatable dinghy.

Years later, after selling *Sultana* and abandoning the cruising life forever (we thought), we found ourselves aboard *Vicarious*, our new (for us) 1975 Fisher ketch moored to a marina dock in North Carolina. Although she was in more-or-less cruise-away condition when we bought her, *Vicarious* did not come with a tender, so we embarked on a dedicated search for a dinghy suitable for an elderly-but-fit cruising couple of modest means, a determination to keep going until we couldn't, and a dream of the cruising life that refused to die no matter how many times we whacked it on the head with the war club of reason.

The Perfect Dinghy

Susan and I have owned a lot of dinghies, from small ones that were way too small to be practical to big ones that were way too big to be practical and a plethora of medium ones in between. The only type of dinghy we haven't owned is the one that most other cruisers are using: a medium-sized RIB with a 10- to 15-horsepower motor on the back. Susan claims that this is because I am a contrarian old fart who refuses to do what everybody else is doing.

Perhaps there is a modicum of truth here, but just a modicum. I have tried these popular boats many times, and I agree that they have several attractive features: they can carry a phenomenal load (I have seen as many as six adults and a dog heaped into a 10-footer—not safely but not sinkingly either), and in spite of their size and modest horsepower, they are fast when lightly loaded. But they have a few problems that, to me, outweigh their positive features: they are expensive, wet, impossible to row efficiently, and a magnet for thieves. Plus the

PVC boats prevalent today will last an average five years if you are lucky, and for me, that isn't long enough for a $3,000 to $5,000 investment (including a motor).

Thus, from long experience, we have determined that the perfect dinghy for us is two dinghies. Perhaps that seems a bit excessive for a minimalist-preaching reprobate old hippy, but read me out before judging. The advantages of two dinghies are many. First is the redundancy. Most cruisers head out with a ton of spares in the hold: engine parts, fuel and water pumps, filters by the dozen, gallons of oil and transmission fluid, two or three spare Jimmy Buffett CDs, and a few of everything else that is deemed to be critical. Well, dinghies are critical too, so a spare just makes sense.

Next is security. Losing a dinghy in a remote spot with no other boats around from which to summon help can be a serious situation. Several times in our cruising career, we have lost a dinghy, as related above in Aitutaki, almost always through carelessness. In all but that one case, the errant dinghy was retrieved simply by launching the second dinghy and going after the escapee. Also, leaving one dinghy secured to the mothership while traveling ashore with the second makes the mothership appear to be occupied, which can be a major deterrent to thieves.

But the most important advantage of two dinghies is utility. *Vicarious* has a small narrow inflatable called a KaBoat made by Saturn and mounted with a 2.5-horsepower propane-powered outboard made by Lher (http://golehr.com/lehr-marine/) Outboards. This boat is a full 10 feet long with standard-diameter tubes, but it is only a bit over 3 feet wide. The narrow beam has a small effect on stability while the 13-inch tubes allow for impressive load-carrying ability. The KaBoat will easily carry Susan and me and a month's worth of groceries with room left over

Choosing a dinghy always creates a conflict between opposing philosophies. We partly solve the dilemma by having a hard dingy for rowing and an inflatable for utility. The Portland Pudgy (here being trialed by cousin Roger) is fun to row and doubles as a certified life raft. The Saturn KaBoat is a light-but-utilitarian inflatable that is easily propelled by the 2.5-horsepower Lher propane engine.

for Nelson the dog, a bag of kibble snacks, and an extra six pack of the skipper's favorite inspirational liquids. It also has four small fin keels on the bottom, making it the only inflatable that I know of that rows quite well.

The Boatyak is no speed demon, but the little propane outboard is plenty of power to drive the thing through all but the roughest conditions. We have made many exploration trips of 10 miles or so, and except for once when we got lost in the Florida marshes (which can't be blamed on the boat, no matter how hard I try), without issues or problems.

The second of *Vicarious*'s two tenders is, of course, a hard (noninflatable) rowing dinghy. It's called a Portland Pudgy, and it is made in, of all places, Portland, Maine. This little beauty rides on the davits in all conditions, rows very well, has a larger load capacity than many inflatables, and is unsinkable. It is also, because of the unsinkable feature and its excellent design, the only dinghy that is certified by the U.S. Coast Guard as a four-person life raft—a fact that we will visit again in the next section.

So, after 40 years of looking, Susan and I have arrived at dinghy nirvana. The combination of the inflatable KaBoat and the hard Portland Pudgy is perfect for us. But of course, that doesn't mean that they would be perfect for you. Even more than your personal automobile was back in your previous consumerism-consumed life, your dinghy (or dinghies) is an extension of yourself, and the selection an appropriate one can be as easy as just buying the same one everyone else has. Or, like cruising itself, it can be an adventure of experimentation and discovery that leads to your own version of dinghy nirvana. This could also find you in the exact same dinghy as everyone else, of course, but I think not. And if it does, so what. The next time you are landing at some crowded dinghy dock, you can proclaim to the multitudes that they were right after all, and that skinny old

coot who thinks he is a smart ass just because his narrow inflatable fit perfectly into the last space available is wrong again.

Commence Surviving

I have no way of knowing just how many of the life rafts carried by cruisers ever get used in an emergency, but I do know the number is very small, no more than one in a thousand, and it is probably much lower than that. I also know that in the past 25 years of talking to every cruiser who I can corner in conversation, I have yet to meet anyone who has ever had to abandon ship in a situation calling for a life raft. I know it happens, I've read the life raft sagas just like everybody else, but it doesn't happen often.

The decision to take a life raft cruising with you is one you must make on your own given your individual needs for security, the size of your boat, and your finances. A life raft costs a lot of money (between $3,000 and $5,000 is about average depending on the model and features), it will take up a huge amount of space on deck or down below, it will be a nuisance to maintain, and worst of all, it will be useful in only a small portion of cruising accidents.

Life rafts can and do deteriorate over time even when stored properly and not used. Thus, it is imperative that if you have one, you get it inspected at least once every three years—and once a year is not too often. The older the raft, the more frequent the inspections should be. Never attempt to do your own inspection. If you do, I can guarantee you will not be able to get the raft back into the container, plus you will void your certification certificate. Most manufacturers have a list of repair stations authorized to perform inspections, but it can be very costly and a terrible nuisance if you are cruising in the remote areas. Most cruisers who have a life raft have it inspected whenever they can get it done for a reasonable price, which usually means when in or near a big city, regardless of the schedule. Inspections cost about $300 in the United States and can be much higher or lower in other areas. I suspect that Europe is the most expensive and Southeast Asia is the cheapest place to get this work done.

Two general types of life rafts are available to the cruising sailboat: coastal and offshore. The coastal rafts are light-duty, lightly constructed models that usually have a single flotation tube with two chambers, a noninflating floor, and a manually erected canopy. They are designed for use where there is a high probability of a quick rescue, say, within 24 hours. Since the advent of 406 EPIRBs, this is a much larger area than it once was, and the cruising boat on a budget can consider the combination of a coastal life raft and a 406 EPIRB to be adequate in most areas of the world.

Offshore life rafts are more robustly made from heavier fabrics. They usually have at least two flotation tubes, an inflatable floor, and an automatic canopy. Naturally, they cost more, but they are heavier and much more durable than the coastal models.

Life rafts are stored either in a canister that is attached to the deck or in a valise that is kept belowdeck. The deck-stored models are usually the better choice because the valise models are too large and heavy to be easily deployed from belowdeck. Before you buy a valise life raft, make sure you realize just how big and cumbersome they are. If you are going to go to the trouble and expense of buying one, you will want one that can be deployed almost instantly—15 seconds max.

In many situations, deploying and entering a life raft is more dangerous than staying on the boat. Storms at sea can be terrifying, and there is a natural tendency to draw a false sense of security from the presence of a life raft—but even a moderate storm can render a life raft unusable. High winds and steep waves can easily make successful deployment and boarding

highly problematical. People have been lost as they attempted to enter a life raft, only to have the boat recovered later intact and still seaworthy. If you do decide to take a life raft cruising with you, resolve right now to never attempt to use it unless you must. The raft must be reserved as a last resort, and it must be used only when the boat is on fire or actually sinking. "Always step up into the life raft" is a tried-and-true rule.

Dinghy Life Rafts

There have been several attempts in the last 50 years or so to develop a practical dinghy that would serve for a life raft, or perhaps a life raft that would serve as a dinghy. The only one that I have had any personal experience with (and that was third-hand with a friend's boat in the Caribbean) is the venerable Tinker Traveler. This was a delightful dinghy to sail when rigged with the optional kit, and it could be set up with a canopy for use as a make-do life raft, albeit an uncertified one.

Alas, Tinker was one of the many victims of the recent recession, and it is no longer in production. The ensuing gap is being filled nicely by David Hulbert in his Portland, Maine, dinghy factory. David designed and is building the aptly named Portland Pudgy, a roto-molded polyethylene dingy that rows and sails well, and as I have mentioned previously, it is the only U.S. Coast Guard certified four-person hard-bottom life raft in existence.

The advantages of a hard (noninflatable) life raft are many. The periodic ritual of getting the thing recertified every other year or so is no longer necessary; there is no heavy, bulky, and very expensive canister that will in all probability never be needed or used taking up valuable deck space; there is no $3,000 to $5,000 hole in your poor kitty where money used to be; the hollow sides have access ports to a large storage area with room for all sorts of supplies and a secure stowage for your abandon-ship bag; and you (and your loved ones) have the peace of mind from knowing that should disaster strike, you are fully equipped with a top-quality certified life raft and are ready to commence survival.

One particular advantage of the Portland Pudgy that we enjoy on *Vicarious* is the way David designed it to be carried on davits, which is normally a bad practice when traveling offshore. The danger of the dingy's being swamped by a large following sea and ripping off the davits is a very real one. Most offshore voyagers lash their hard dingy to the deck forward of the mast where it blocks forward visibility and impedes the flow of water when heavy waves wash over the deck. The Pudgy, however, has a sturdy sling that suspends the boat on its side with the bottom facing aft making it impossible to fill with water, and where it acts as a buffer to following winds and seas.

The only drawback to this system is that it precludes windvane steering, which I would dearly like to have on *Vicarious*. We do find that with the ketch rig, we can balance the sails to self-steer most of the time anyway so we have struggled along without a windvane—so far.

Water, Water, Everywhere

Many cruising books provide a heap of information on water management. Unfortunately, nearly all the information is wrong and focuses on the need for an onboard electromechanical watermaker. The fact is that there is a lot of stuff you don't need on your boat in order to go cruising, and one of the things you don't need the most is a watermaker.

If this is true, you might ask, why is there an almost unyielding pressure on boaters in general, but cruisers especially, to buy these functionally tiresome and very expensive devices? We have all read the articles and product reviews online that treat watermakers, radar, and chartplotters as essential gear, and the worst of these give the impression that if we don't have these items on board, we are not only uncool and not with it, but quite possibly stupid as well.

The reasons for this incredible hype lie not with the companies that make these devices, nor with the media that tout them, but with the society we live in. We thrive on consumption. If consumption stops or even slows perceptibly, our society will collapse, and our people will starve, so in a real sense consumption isn't just essential to our society. It is our society.

I won't bore you with a lot of supporting data on this statement because I have already filleted that particular mackerel, and I think you know where I stand on the subject. However, I will repeat for emphasis that if you want to go cruising, you must learn to turn your back on consumerism in general and on such things as watermakers specifically.

So what's wrong with watermakers? Although I don't have enough room to do the subject justice, here are a few failings:

- They are expensive to buy. A good one will cost more than your chartplotter and your 406 EPIRB combined.
- They are expensive to maintain. The monthly bill for prefilters and biocide can easily equate to a good meal ashore in a first-class restaurant for the whole crew. Plus they will use more electricity than your refrigeration and your radar combined.
- They are complicated and delicate. Most cruisers I know have a lot better things to do than work on watermakers. The pickling and maintenance schedule must be followed to the letter or very expensive repairs will result.
- They can't be used in harbors that have less than pristine waters because the filters will clog; thus they are useless about 90 percent of the time.

I won't even mention such things as the space they take up and their lack of reliability, but let's give it a rest after this one last thing. Watermakers aren't necessary. *Sultana* made it almost halfway around the world with four people on board, and we never ran short of water. On *Vicarious* we catch 90 percent of our water on deck when it rains, and the rest we get ashore. We add a bit of bleach to get rid of the germs; then we run our drinking water through a Seagull IV filter to get rid of the bleach. We carry 200 liters per person on a long passage. That's a lot, but we use it freely, and our total cost for water in over 40 years of cruising won't pay for a single prefilter. We have, however, encountered several other cruising boats that have run short of water on many occasions. They were all boats that relied on watermakers for their main supply.

There are certain areas of the world that are popular with cruisers (the Bahamas and Sea of Cortez, for example) where freshwater isn't readily available and rainfall is unreliable for much of the year. Watermakers are nearly universal in these areas, but the affluence of the cruising community is also quite high, and I am convinced that most cruisers in these areas have them because everyone else has one. But when analyzed through the microscope of reason and practicality, the need for a watermaker evaporates into mythological mist even in these dry areas.

In any harbor in any evolving economy that doesn't have a ready supply of freshwater, the local equivalent of a twenty-dollar bill will get you enough quality water delivered to your boat to sink it. The watermaker on *Vicarious* (yes, we do have one, so I can speak from authority here, but only because it came with the boat) makes 7 gallons an hour, and it cost over $7,000 to install. That means if my estimate of $20 per load is correct, I can have my tanks filled 350 times for the same money. When you add $1 per gallon cost for the water from a watermaker (a conservative composite estimate made up of depreciation, cost of filters and maintenance, electricity, and a minimum of 10 hours of labor per year), you can triple that number.

One fellow cruiser, defending his total reliance on his watermaker in the face of the above argument, stated that it was the only way he could guarantee the quality of his water supply, right after regaling the entire pub with his sad tale of having to empty and flush his brine-contaminated tanks when a membrane failed. He is also the sort of cruiser who won't eat in local restaurants because "you can never be sure what you are getting in those places."

Drinking water purity is easily assured by using a reliable water filter (as mentioned, *Vicarious* has a Seagull IV from General Ecology, http://generalecology.com, but there are many others), which most boats have anyway. Drinking water that has been treated with a few drops of bleach and run through a good filter system is healthier than that from a watermaker anyway because you don't have to add chemicals to replace necessary minerals.

There is a good and often-made argument for carrying a hand-operated watermaker in the life raft or in the abandon-ship bag, and this is excellent advice for those of us who are hopelessly paranoid and have big piles of spare cash cluttering up our bank balances. The rest of us need to consider the wisdom of spending $1,000 to $1,500 (the average price of the smallest watermakers; the current lowest price of the Katadyn 6 is $999 from West Marine) on a device that you might need once in every 1,000 circumnavigations. Dying of thirst or starvation while floating around in a life raft is one of those phobic horrors with which advertisers like to terrify us into buying their stuff, but the likelihood of this ever happening is just about the same as being killed by a meteorite.

The degree to which you can make your life safer by buying stuff is limited, and if you really need the kind of security that comes from having gadgets like miniature watermakers in your grab bag, you might want to consider staying at home with the curtains drawn. Me? I'd rather die of thirst while floating around in a life raft any day.

Generating a Question

Vicarious came with an excellent generator, a 3.5-kilowatt NexGen in a sound shield, that was expertly installed in a convenient place. So in spite of being on record stating that generators are an unnecessary nuisance, we have kept it aboard and used it regularly, mostly to charge the battery while at anchor. But the thing cost the previous owner the better part of $10,000 to get it installed properly, and I still contend that is a lot of money for a little convenience. The only boats that really need a generator have air-conditioning, and the only boats that really need air-conditioning are . . . well, we have been there already.

Don't Truster Your Thruster

Long in use on commercial ships, bow thrusters (and less commonly, stern thrusters) became available for pleasure craft some 15 years ago, and quickly became the de rigueur kit for the well-found cruiser. Basically a pair of small electricity-driven propellers housed in a tube set into the bow, bow thrusters are invaluable for guiding a yacht onto a cheek-and-jowl slip at a crowded marina. They also provide emergency steering should you lose rudder control.

But as wonderful as they are, and in spite of accomplished cruisers who tell you "I wouldn't leave the dock without one," a bow thruster should not be on your list of must-have items.

Most of us can cruise for the best part of a year for what it costs to install one, they take up a lot of space, and require heaps of

electricity, and their propensity to get clogged with seaweed or plastic bags makes them hopelessly unreliable. But the worst thing about bow thrusters is the number of cruisers who depend on them to steer the boat and never learn proper maneuvering techniques. Every TowBoat US captain in the fleet can tell stories about the guy who called for help because his bow thruster broke down and he couldn't get his boat back to the dock without it.

Canoes, Kayaks, Bicycles, Pressure Cookers, Scuba Gear, Gas Grills, Sewing Machines, Golf Clubs, and Other Things

All these items can be useful or fun to have aboard, and some don't cost that much to buy. Just go through the checklist above to make sure that you will actually use the item and you have a place to keep it when you aren't.

Guns

If you really want to stir up a firestorm of vitriolic acrimony on any online cruising forum, just post any comment on guns and sit back. Some of these topics generate hundreds of responses. About half come from diehard cowboys who wouldn't think of leaving the bunkhouse without the ol' sixshooter strapped to the hip, just in case some lowdown sneaky skunk tries something foolish. The other half comes from dedicated pacifists who advocate complete submission in the face of any threat with the hope that, after looting everything else on the boat, the aggressor might be kind enough to leave you a pair of clean socks.

Most of the respondents in these forums (and I know this because I have conducted a highly scientific study of the subject) either have a boat but aren't cruising or don't have a boat at all but are dreaming of the day. Most of the actual cruisers whom I have met who have guns aboard and are willing to go through the onerous check-in and check-out procedures—common in every country in the world but the United States—are paranoid macho buffoons (hey, some of my best friends are paranoid macho buffoons) who are more dangerous to themselves than to any potential attacker. The few who hide their guns aboard and don't declare them when they enter a foreign port are paranoid macho-buffoon criminals whose need to have a weapon transcends their fear of losing their boat and everything in it followed by a lengthy stay chained to the wall in some jungle jailhouse where misery and despair would be a giant step up in your quality of life.

I, for fear of violent retribution, refuse to take sides on this controversial issue, but if you are headed for a port where you really might need a gun, you might want to rethink your destination and go somewhere else. Unless, of course, you are a militant gun-nut activist who thrives on mindless violence, in which case you probably ought to forget about cruising and move to Miami.

Holding Tanks and Smelly Plumbing

One promising development in the cruising life has been the availability of compact, self-contained composting toilets that promise to make our trouble-prone holding tanks and flush toilets as outdated as the two-holer we had in back of the house when I was a kid.

Don't get me wrong here. Many of us old timers who can remember cruising in the fifties and sixties when many marinas and anchorages were little more than open sewers are unequivocally supportive of no-discharge laws and their strict enforcement. The holding tank systems used on most cruising boats have worked well for over 50 years, but not without problems. They are dirty, stinky, cantankerous, prone to spillage, expensive, and a huge nuisance. While the United States, Canada, and most of Europe now have excellent pump-out facilities, most of the developing world has a way to go to catch up, and emptying the tank legally can be a problem. Thus, when the first composting toilets were announced, we as full-time cruisers, rejoiced. No more holding tanks, and disposing of waste was as easy as rowing a bag of dirt ashore and dropping it in a dumpster.

Alas, after using one of these devices for nearly two years, we have come to terms with some serious limitations. While they would be excellent for weekend sailing and day-trippers, the capacity is just too small for two people living full-time on a boat. The biodegradation takes several weeks, depending on the moisture and temperature, and two people easily fill the thing in just 10 days. That leaves the problem of dispensing raw waste that hasn't completely composted, putting us back where we started.

On *Vicarious*, we get around this problem by having two spare tanks. As one fills up, we move it to a ventilated locker and replace it with an empty one, and by the time the third one is filled, the first one is ready for disposal. This system works OK for us, but there are a few problems with the stored tanks: they are dirty, stinky, cantankerous, prone to spillage, expensive, and a huge nuisance.

While the technology and the potential of composting toilets for full-time cruisers is great, the reality of today's products leaves a bit to be desired. Until the capacity increases to match the combined output of two adult cruisers, the problem of waste disposal on a cruising boat will remain a . . . well, problem.

Crewing for Your Pets

Of all the many things that you don't need on a cruising boat, a pet has to be near the top of the list. A dog or a cat on board is probably the least cost-effective way to deplete your kitty, and the reasons for forgoing the slobbering obsequiousness of a dog or the arrogant distain of a cat are many. (We won't even consider the various serpents, birds, arachnids, rodents, lizards, and other odd creatures with which many cruisers choose to encumber their lives.)

Both dogs and cats are hairy, very hairy, and the hair gets into everything: your food, your clothing, and into every nook and cranny of your life. They also harbor minute wildlife that persists no matter how often you douse the frivolous creature and the entire boat with toxic, environmentally catastrophic potions. Hosts of tiny insects will eventually abandon your hairy pet and take up abode in your pillow from which they will emerge like vampires sometime after midnight to feast on your ears.

Like most living things, dogs and cats defecate a lot, and they are going to do it whether you like it or not. Cats require a container filled with a special absorbent substance strategically placed where you are sure to step in it or kick it on your way to the head in the (aptly named) wee hours. Of course, in order to defecate, your pet needs food, and it is astonishing how much food even a small animal will require to get it across even a small ocean. A large animal on a small boat crossing a large ocean may even require a support vessel.

Dogs don't require a special container, but they do demand a trip ashore periodically with no regard for the weather or time of day. Thus it isn't uncommon for dog owners to meet fellow travelers while walking the beast on a remote mud bank during a thunderstorm at 3 a.m. or trying to bushwhack their way through a mangrove swamp with the dog leaping about the dingy in excited anticipation of reaching the tiny scrap of beach that he can see through the foliage.

If, in spite of my excellent advice to shun any nonhuman presence on your boat, you decide to harbor one of these atrociously expensive and inconvenient animals, be forewarned

Susan's Cavalier King Charles spaniel, Nelson, is every bit as hairy as he looks, and most of that hair somehow ends upon the bilge-pump strainers. He also eats an astonishing amount of food for a small dog, which entails two trips ashore every day to offload the proceeds of this gluttony. He delights in chasing birds of any kind, and if successful in slipping his lead, he is off like a shot hell bent on catching and ripping to bits anything with feathers while ignoring the hysterical efforts of his persons to stop him. He has never actually caught anything faster than a New Zealand hedgehog (which he regretted immediately), but this humiliating fact just reinforces his determination. This peculiar obsession has caused trouble in several countries with various authorities charged with protecting endangered wildlife from assault by small dogs. But what the heck, he is a cute little guy, and we tolerate his misbehavior because … well, actually, I'm not at all clear why we put up with the little bugger, but we do.

that, while they may start off as cute little kittens or puppies, they grow quickly, and as they grow, they have a bag of tricks that they will use to gradually alter your behavior to suit their perverse needs. It starts like a game with your trying to dissuade your new crew member from turning your polished teak woodwork into a scratching post or from chewing the corners off all your cockpit cushions. In spite of spending most of your day at this game, you will eventually lose, and your pet will gradually assume more and more dominance until, finally, it is firmly in control of your vessel and your life.

Now, your first consideration for every port you plan to visit will be, do they allow pets? What are the costs for quarantine? What about rabies and other inoculations? What paperwork is involved? Do we need advance approval? Is there a resupply of little Twinkle's special ahi-tuna-flavored Gourmet Tabby Treats available? (because little Twinkle refuses to eat anything else).

I know some readers will think I am kidding here, but this is no exaggeration. I personally know several (actually more than several) cruisers who have avoided coming to New Zealand because of the outrageous costs of the quarantine requirements for dogs and cats. These otherwise-sensible cruisers chose to ride out the cyclone season in Fiji or Tonga just so they wouldn't inconvenience the true commander of their vessel. I also know one delightful lady who spent thousands of hard-earned dollars to have her flea-bitten King Charles spaniel flown from New Zealand to North Carolina when she and her husband took possession of their new boat.

I have a lot more to say about all the reasons you should not even consider having a dog or cat on your cruising boat, but more urgent business is at hand. Nelson, Susan's King Charles spaniel, is dancing around the cockpit with that cross-eyed look that says we have about 15 minutes to make the 2-mile trip against the tide to the beach or suffer the consequences of what Susan refers to as an "oopsie." We have already done the trip once today, but when we got there, Nelson had either lost the urge or changed his mind. You would think I would be upset, but no, he is a cute little guy, and when he looks at you as if to say "Sorry for the wasted effort, but while we are here, let me chase seagulls up and down the beach for an hour or so while you try to make me stop before that mean old game warden catches us again and makes good his threat of a heavy fine for letting your adorable pet harass endangered wildlife," what can you do?

OK, you get the idea. If you want to go cruising rather than spend your life at the dock trying to figure out where to put all that stuff you want to take with you or how to get it working in the first place, don't buy stuff that you don't really need and probably won't even use. This concept is so simple it is sophomoric, yet buying too much stuff for a cruise remains one of the top reasons that carefully planned cruises never happen or are terminated early.

12

Commence Cruising: Letting Your Boat Get to Know You

Now more than ever do I realize that I will never be content with a sedentary life, that I will always be haunted by thoughts of a sun-drenched elsewhere.

—ISABELLE EBERHARDT,
THE NOMAD: THE DIARIES OF
ISABELLE EBERHARDT

I have argued (with a great deal of conviction, of course) in the preceding chapters that the type of boat you go cruising in doesn't matter that much but that the purchase of the boat is one of the most important steps on the road to the cruising life and the logical culmination of the planning process. I bared my soul relating the horror story of our near-death experience with *Delphus*, and I have beseeched thee not to buy any boat larger or more expensive than the minimum that will get the job done for you. Now you've gone and done it, and it's too late to look back now. Good cruisers never watch their wake anyway, just the bow and the horizon ahead.

Let's Get Going

OK, so now you have bought your boat, and a beauty she is indeed. True, the gelcoat or the paint is a little dull, and the sails are more gray than white, and the VHF is 10 years old, and the old double sideband isn't legal to use anymore and ought to be donated to a museum. But what the hey . . . you're going cruising.

Now that you have a boat, what are you going to do with it? The surveyor came up with a long list of things that need to be done, like those deck fittings that need to be rebedded and have backing plates installed, the winches that need to be upgraded to a larger size, and the standing rigging that needs to be replaced simply because half the swages are cracked and the wire is exuding a curious white powder in odd places. If there is any money left over, you will be able to get a good roller furler for the jib and maybe even a basic chartplotter or radar, but these things can wait for a while—at least until after you finish upgrading the electrical system. The important thing is that you bought a good solid boat with a sound hull, and that old diesel sounds as if she is good for another 20 years or so.

But before you start fixing stuff, even the important stuff, let's take a few days and just look around.

Don't try to fix anything yet. Before you do anything else, you want to make a complete and meticulous tour of the boat. If you wait few days to do this (just spend some time sitting in the cockpit basking in the glow of a real boat), some of the excitement of new-old-boat ownership will have worn off, a process that can greatly sharpen your vision. Get a notebook, pencil, and a flashlight, and starting at the top, work your way down to the bottom making a note of anything that doesn't look just right or you don't fully understand. Take lots of paper, because, if you are like most of us, you are going to end up with a long list.

Go over the entire boat from the tri-light to the keelson, pausing at every item you encounter. If its purpose isn't obvious at first, put it on your list. Later you can consult your manuals or ask someone who knows about such things. It's not until you are intimate with every screw and rivet and block that you can say the boat is truly yours, and this takes time and study.

There are precious few boats available for less than $100,000 that won't require at least a little work to get them ready to go, and even a brand-new boat will require extensive preparation for a world cruise. Let's assume that your new old boat is structurally sound with a solid hull and a good engine, and revisit some of the areas where most boats will require some attention.

Once you finish your initial tour and have your list of questions and unknowns mostly answered, wait a few days and do the whole thing again. This time take some basic tools with you so you can make any easy adjustments or quick repairs as you go. The routine of this inspection will become your predeparture checklist so it is important to become intimate with everything that might need attention.

The Rigging

Have a trusted ally crank you up the mast in the bosun's chair. Throw away that old board and rope contraption that came with the boat, and get yourself a decent bosun's chair that has a strong crotch strap and a good back support. (West Marine sells a dandy, and the Mast Climber from ATN Products is enthusiastically endorsed by your elderly-and-keen-to-stay-that-way author.) Spend about an hour becoming thoroughly familiar with the masthead hardware. Go over every item one piece at a time until you know what every shackle and bolt is for, what it is supposed to do, and what is going to happen if it fails. On the way down notice how the spreaders are attached to the mast, and pay particular attention to the rubber boots on the ends of each spreader.

If you have an overlapping jib or genoa that can reach the spreaders when fully deployed, make sure that these boots are in good condition and aren't hiding corrosion. If you don't have an overlapping headsail, take them off. Spreader boots seem to be one of those things that boatowners install because they see them on other boats. I frequently see them on the spreaders of mizzen masts where there is no chance of chafe from a tightly sheeted sail. (I'm looking at one on a boat anchored nearby, as I write this.) Superfluous spreader boots don't do much harm, they are tidy, and they may look cool to the uninitiated observer, but they may make you look silly to anyone who knows better. They can also collect water and promote oxidation in a bad place.

Also, while you are up there, check the position of the spreaders relative to the shrouds. In most cases, the spreaders should perfectly bisect the angle of the shrouds. If you aren't sure about the correct position of yours, write it down, then check with a competent rigger. If the spreaders are positioned incorrectly (on many old boats, they are too low) and the wire is in good condition but old (like your ancient-but-robust author), it is probably best to leave them alone until you are ready to replace the wire. There will be a set bend where the wire crosses over the spreaders, and to move the spreaders will leave a kink that looks terrible and can weaken the wire.

Once the spreaders are squared away, check everything else that is attached to the mast to make sure it is bedded and fastened properly. Check aluminum masts for any sign of corrosion, especially galvanic corrosion caused by dissimilar metals such as stainless-steel pop rivets and screws; check wooden masts for any discoloration around fittings that might indicate water incursion. Check every fitting you encounter for any sign of excessive wear or stress, but more important, make sure you know why it is there.

When you buy an old used boat, you can assume that you are also buying old used rigging, and rigging has a few peculiarities that make it worth spending some time on it.

The Standing Rigging

Your surveyor will have gone over your standing rigging, and you, of course, have gone up the mast at least once to get familiar with all the parts and their functions (and to get used to going up the mast, which can be scary if you haven't done it before). If any cracked or corroded terminals or swages are found or if there

Screw-on rigging terminals, like this one from Sta-Lok, have become standard for cruising boats in the past decade or so. Their advantages over swaged fittings are many, but their dependability and strength and the fact that they can be installed by anyone with basic hand tools are the most important. Indeed, the only real disadvantage of these fittings is their considerable cost, which is easily made up for by the fact that they are reusable.

are any broken strands in a shroud or stay, you'll have to replace them right away. Replacing wire that isn't showing any signs of corrosion, doesn't have any strands broken, and is still perfectly round (that is, it hasn't been distorted by overtwisting or untwisting the wire) isn't usually necessary as long as the terminals are sound, but if there is any doubt, check with your rigger.

Inadequate rigging isn't something that you can mess around with in a cruising boat.

It is one thing to snap a shroud while daysailing a few miles from home and quite another to lose that same shroud while hove-to in a gale 500 miles from nowhere. Even if your rigging passes survey without a hitch, you must pay careful attention to its age. Old rigging is like a glamorous movie star grown long of tooth. She can be fixed up to look just fine from a distance, but underneath all those tummy tucks and facelifts, she is still an old movie star. If your standing rigging is more than 20 years old, you have an old movie star on your hands, and you need to pay very careful attention to its condition and replace any parts that are suspect.

Norseman, Sta-Lok, and several other brands of screw-on terminals have gained near universal acceptance among cruisers in recent years, and they are worth considering in spite of their high cost. Installed properly, they are stronger than traditional swaged terminals; they are easy to install using readily available hand tools; they can be disassembled for inspection if they look suspect, then reinstalled; and they make a progressive upgrade of your rigging possible, rather than having the entire boat done all at once by a rigging shop.

It is also a good idea to have a few extra screw-on terminals on hand along with a length of wire equal in length of your headstay (usually the longest wire on your boat) for making emergency replacements at sea or for making an upgrade in a remote spot where these supplies aren't available.

Oversized Wire

Many cruisers have oversized wire installed at the same time they have their standing rigging replaced, believing that this gives them an extra measure of security against rigging failure in heavy weather. I suppose it does do that, but oversized wire also increases windage aloft and adds a lot of weight above the decks right where you don't want it. I personally think it is a waste

of money because most rig failures are caused by broken terminals and hardware, not by broken wire. If you want oversize, spend your money on stronger turnbuckles and thimbles, and use the wire size recommended by your rigger.

You might find that your rigging is made up of wire of two or more sizes. The upper shrouds might be heavier than the lowers, or the mizzen might be rigged with smaller wire than the main. If you have a sloop rig or a cutter, changing all the rigging to the largest size might make sense. For one thing, it will be a lot easier to carry just one size of spare wire and terminals, and you might be able to save some money buying a lot of wire in one size rather than buying smaller quantities of two or more sizes. On a split rig (ketch, schooner, or yawl), however, using the same size wire for the entire standing rigging will result in either the forestay and the upper shrouds' being too small or all the rest of the rigging being ridiculously oversized.

Chainplates

While you're looking at your rigging, be sure to check the chainplates, and if you question their integrity, replace them. Broken chainplates probably account for more lost rigs in the cruising world than any other single factor except turnbuckles, and they are particularly vulnerable in older boats where they are often hard to get at. Chainplates are subjected to incredible force and stress, so even a little surface corrosion can weaken them to the point of sudden failure. Also, some production-boat builders have a tendency to try to save a few pennies on items they think the boat show crowds won't notice, and one of their favorites is skimpy chainplates. That they are just about the most important pieces of hardware on the boat seems lost on them. While you are checking, make sure the clevis-pin hole hasn't become elongated both in the chainplate and the masthead hardware.

My feeling is that chainplates on a cruising boat should be on the outside of the hull where we can keep an eye on them. Of course, most modern rigs use inboard chainplates to allow the jib to be sheeted flat, to allow leaks to develop in the deck right where they will be the biggest nuisance, and to keep them out of sight where you can't see how skimpy they are. If your chainplates are out on the rail where they belong but are embedded in or installed behind the planking or hull, the simplest replacement procedure is to grind off the above-deck portion of the old chainplate and install new ones on the outside. Drill right through the old chainplates, and bolt the new ones in place using the old ones as backing plates. On *Sultana* I was able to simply double up the chainplates so that I didn't have to grind off the old ones. The combined thickness of the quarter-inch original plate and the quarter-inch new one made a plate that is a half-inch thick. Overkill, yes, but I never had to expend a lot of energy worrying about breaking them.

Additional oak or Starboard blocking on the inside of the hull where the chainplate bolts come through is usually in order, and 1-inch by 4-inch oak strips under the new chainplates on the outside of the hull give your boat a cruiserly look while it widens the base slightly, which serves to further strengthen the rig with only a slight detriment to windward performance. Naturally, you would not want to do any of this if the internal chainplates pose no problem and external chainplates would spoil the look of your boat.

Running Rigging

Running rigging is a lot easier to deal with than standing rigging: if it looks like it needs replacing, it does. Frayed lines should be changed right away, but discolored, stained, or weathered lines are usually fine.

The best procedure is to keep a 300-foot spool of the most popular sizes of high-quality braided Dacron on hand and learn how to use a Uni-Fid for splicing. Get the largest size rope you will need; then use this same size for all your sheets and halyards where it will fit through the sheaves. When a cold front moves in and things on deck start to get dicey, big rope is much easier to handle than small rope. Replace all your wire halyards with rope—there isn't any significant advantage to wire with the new low-stretch Dacron rope that is available—and don't worry about color coding your lines. After a few months of cruising, you'll be so familiar with your rig you won't need color coding anyway.

The Electrical System

It's the rare production boat that leaves the factory with adequate wiring. Wiring isn't one of the things that sells boats so it's right up there with skinny rigging as a way for boat factories to save a few bucks. The problem has been made much worse by the way modern boats are assembled from the inside out. A typical production boat is wired before the molded hull liner is installed. Usually the wire is stapled to the liner itself, the liner is dropped into the hull, and then the deck is fastened permanently in place, ensuring that the wiring and other critical components are totally inaccessible.

Rewiring a boat is very expensive even in a foreign port, and hiring a qualified electrician to do this job is usually out of the question for most of us. This means that you must be your own electrician. Even if you can afford to have it done, doing the rewiring yourself will ensure that the job is done right, and you'll end up being so familiar with your electrical system that finding any one component will be as easy as finding the head in the middle of the night. Once again, if you don't feel comfortable with electricity, take a basic course in night school, then read your manual through a few times.

And folks, please pay attention to this: household alternating-current (AC) voltage is the second most dangerous thing on a boat, second only to gasoline and propane fumes. It can kill you deader than a stomped-on squid and just as quick. Until you become a competent electrician and have gained a thorough understanding of what is going on with those little subatomic particles zipping back and forth through their little racetrack circuits, restrict all your efforts to the 12-volt direct-current (DC) systems, and never attempt electrical work on a boat that has any high voltage aboard. Unplug the shore power, and disconnect the inverter every time you do any electrical work. On many inverters, the switch merely turns off the circuit while the unit itself is still live. To be safe, you need to disconnect the 12-volt leads to the set and open the circuit breaker. Even then you will invariably grab onto the right end of the wrong 12-volt capacitor at some point and get a new hairdo out of the deal.

Chasing a Circuit and Checking Voltage Drop

Once you think you have a handle on the basics of electricity, it's time to try a few simple jobs that will put your new skills to work. Get yourself a good digital multimeter (Fluke is recommended as a reliable brand, as are the more expensive ones at Radio Shack) and a test lamp.

First, identify the circuit you want to chase, and what the heck, let's go ahead and replace the wire while we are at it. Select a circuit that is reasonably challenging but not too difficult (leave the masthead light for later). The reading light in the forepeak would be a good starter to learn on.

Before you begin, check the voltage drop at the light fixture. This is a simple matter of subtracting the actual voltage at the fixture

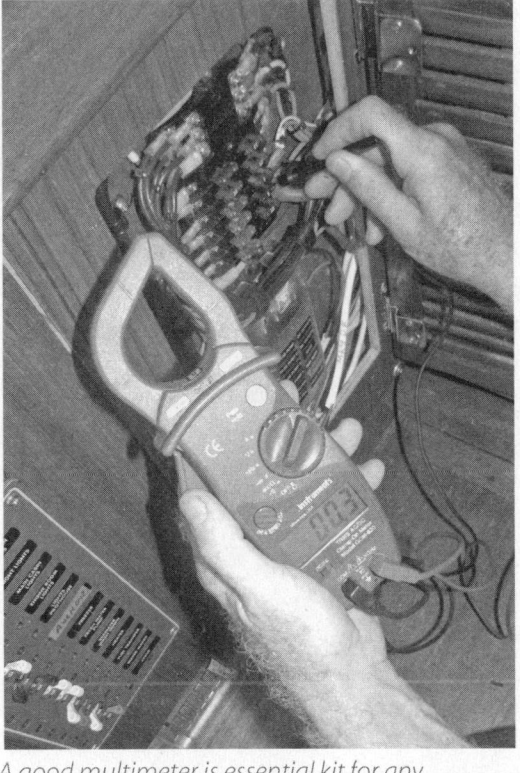

A good multimeter is essential kit for any cruising boat, as is a proficiency with using it. The clamp-on ammeter adds quite a bit to the cost, but it increases the utility of the meter and saves a lot of work undoing terminals when you need to check amperage. It is also safer to use, especially when working on high-voltage circuits.

from the actual house voltage at the battery. Acceptable drops of 3 percent for critical circuits—bilge pumps and such—and 10 percent for noncritical circuits is a good rule of thumb to start with. If you find that the drop is excessive, as you most likely will in any older boat and even in a lot of new ones, you should replace the old wires with new wires of the proper size. The size of wire in a DC circuit is determined by the amperage the circuit is expected to carry and the length of the wire. Thus, a light located on the top of a 50-foot mast that draws 5 amps will need a 10-AWG (American wire gauge; in AWG, the bigger the number, the smaller the wire) wire, while a light in the cabin that draws the same but is only 10 feet from the distribution panel will work fine with an 18-AWG wire.

This is a good point to make sure that the circuit you are replacing is protected by an appropriate circuit breaker or a fuse, as required by the American Boat and Yacht Council (ABYC). On many (probably most) old boats, this important safety feature was ignored, creating a serious danger. Even a half-amp circuit, if shorted, can cause a fire that will destroy your boat.

Chasing the Circuit

Start at your battery (you *have* unplugged the shore power and disconnected the inverter, haven't you?) and chase down the entire DC circuit. Turn everything off at the panel but this one circuit, and use your test light at each terminal. Remove each connector as you come to it, and clean it to bright metal with a small scrap of emery cloth. (I use Susan's disposable nail files when I can get away with it.) Once you have cleaned every terminal on the circuit (don't forget the bases of the lightbulbs and your battery ground connection), check for voltage drop again. You should see an improvement, but it is probably still too high. If it is within limits, replace the circuit with the same size wire that you removed; if it isn't, go up a size or even two.

You will need a 100-foot spool of standard, tinned wire of whatever size you settled on. If you don't have the correct size, it is perfectly OK to use the next larger size, but never use a smaller size. You will also need a terminal kit (Jamestown Distributors has a good one) and a quality crimping tool. The pliers-type crimper that comes with the kit is handy for cutting bolts and stripping wire, but don't use

it for crimps. Get a good ratchet crimper that produces a double compression crimp. You will also need a soldering iron with rosin-core solder, an assortment of heat-shrink tubing, a set of colored electricians' tapes for color coding wires, and a bunch of plastic wire ties of various sizes.

Don't try to buy all the correct colors of wires—there are way too many of them, and the colored tape works just fine. The ABYC specifies over 100 different colors and combinations of colors on wires on a properly wired yacht, but with a minimum of three sizes needed for some colors, such as the orange accessory-feed wires or the dark blue lighting wires, you would need hundreds of spools of wire to do the job properly. Even most professional marine electricians can't keep an inventory of that many wire colors.

Instead, mark the wires with a loop of tape at the beginning and end of each wire and more loops at strategic places along the run, or get a few sheets of the peel-and-stick numbers that electrical supply houses sell for keeping track of circuits. If you use the two-wire insulated and tinned wire sold by Anchor Marine (highly recommended), you can also use a permanent marker to write, at suitable intervals, the identity of the cable run right on the insulation. Use any color wire you happen to have on hand, except green, as long as it is the right size. For your safety, use green wire only for the ground on both high-voltage AC circuits and DC circuits and for bonding circuits. It is also an excellent idea to keep AC circuits isolated and in their own conduits whenever possible. This is to prevent dummies like you and me from getting our cookies fried when we tap into an AC circuit thinking it is part of a DC circuit.

One of the more serious problems with boat wiring color coding has been the use of black for both the hot lead on 120-volt circuits and the return lead on 12-volt circuits.

The ABYC is trying to clear up this dangerously confusing conflict by recommending the use of yellow return wires on 12-volt circuits, but so far it hasn't caught on. Manufacturers continue to use black on 12-volt circuits. The situation will probably improve once inventories of black wires are used up and replaced with yellow.

The only other color of wire that you need to be obsessively concerned with is green, which should be used only for ground circuits and never for anything else. This is for safety, of course, but it also greatly simplifies the often difficult task of chasing circuits.

Double-check to ensure there is no high voltage aboard from any source, then disconnect the 12-volt current by removing the positive leads from all the batteries or by turning the battery switches to Off. Now untie the first bundle of wire that contains the wire you want to chase and replace. This bundle may be tied with string or with plastic loops or, in older boats, with insulated metal loops. (If you find any of these, get rid of them. The insulation on the loop will deteriorate, and the metal can chafe through the insulation on the wire causing dangerous short circuits and fire.) This unbundling can be a challenging job, and if you have a molded hull liner, you may have to cut the wire you want to replace to get it out. Don't leave the old wire in place if there is any way to avoid it. Unused wiring can be a nightmare if any stray voltage should get aboard.

In extreme cases with molded hull liners, you may have to cut access holes to get at the wires. Get used to it; it is the only way to access system components with many production boats. If you have a supply of the small plastic access plates, sold by all marine chandleries, and an appropriate-sized hole saw, the visual damage will be minimal, and you will have easy access next time you need it. (I've seen dozens of these access plates used on older production boats, and done right, they don't look bad at all.)

Next, decide where you want to run the replacement wire. Sometimes you will want to put it right back where you removed the old one, but if you think about it a bit, you might hit upon a direct route that makes more sense. Some builders, in defiance of the laws of nature and common sense, like to run bundles of wires through the bilge as a means of saving a few more pennies, and any you find there should be moved. Naturally, you should make all runs of wire as short as possible (without going through the bilge) because it saves expensive materials and makes the circuit more efficient.

Now cut the new wire to length, and install ring terminals to each end. I'm not really hung up on soldered terminals because I've always had good luck with properly crimped terminals, but soldering is a necessary cruiserly skill that is acquired only with practice, and these first few projects are a good place to practice it. So, if you have the time and want to learn how to solder a terminal, now is the perfect time to do it. Always crimp the terminal onto the wire before you solder it. The crimp ensures a secure connection, and the ABYC does not allow soldered terminals that aren't securely crimped before being soldered. Then put a drop of solder right where the tip of the wire shows through the terminal loop. The solder will flow back up the wires and seal out any moisture in addition to strengthening the terminal. If you have never soldered terminals before, practice on some scrap wire with cheap (automotive) terminals. It is much easier to solder terminals to the wire before you install it, but if the wire must be fished, this is sometimes impossible.

If at all possible, make all cable runs one piece with no intervening splices, and use nothing but marine-grade wire and terminals. Use ring terminals as a standard, but when you encounter a captured screw (one you can't remove), an eared spade terminal is acceptable. Never use flat spade terminals; in fact, there is no reason to have them on your boat. Always use heat-shrink terminals in any delicate or critical circuits.

When possible, avoid the common practice of attaching the old wire to the new one and using the old one to pull the new wire into place. The insulation on adjacent old wiring can be fragile, and it can be damaged by the new one as you pull it through, and it is hard to get a neat job. Those molded hull liners can have razor-sharp unfinished edges in back of the panels where you can't see them, which can strip a wire to bare metal without your being aware of it. Of course in some cases, like when replacing wires inside a mast, pulling the new wire in with the old one makes a lot of sense, but do it carefully.

As you replace the new wire, put a drop of blue Loctite 242 thread locker on the threads of the connecting screw before tightening it. If you want to do the same thing the old-fashioned way (and the cheapskate way—Loctite costs about the same per ounce as certain recreational alkaloids . . . that I have heard about), upset the threads of any screw connectors with the serrated jaws of a pair of Vise-Grips to help ensure that the screw stays in place. Or if you can get at the back of the terminal, a light tap with a spring-loaded center punch right where the male and female threads meet will do the same job.

As each section of wire is replaced, turn the juice back on to check that all is in order. I make it a habit to listen and sniff every time I activate a circuit I have been messing with. If you have a short, you'll often hear it first, smell it second, and see the smoke third. Quick action in turning the juice back off can save a lot of aggravation and extra work. If the light works, turn the juice off again, bundle all the wires, and move on to the next section.

You will find many light fixtures and other electrical apparatus that have been permanently installed or potted leads that are often several

sizes smaller than the recommended wire size. Makers of popular submersible bilge pumps do this as a matter of practice. (They aren't stupid; they just think we are and won't notice.) As mentioned earlier, the appropriate wire size for a given amperage (or "draw") is determined by the distance the wire runs from the distribution panel to the device and back to the panel, and it is beyond me how manufacturers presume to know what this distance will be. While we are grinding this particular axe, I will also mention that not only are these wires too small in most cases but they are also too short, thereby necessitating splices in inconvenient and inappropriate places (like the bilge). Because you can't replace these wires, cut them as short as practical and splice the shortened leads into the new properly sized circuit, and protect it with heat-shrink tubing or, better yet, use the waterproof heat-shrink barrel splices made by Anchor Electric (available from West Marine and most other chandleries).

Speaking of splices, my favorite trick is to forget to put the heat shrink on the wire before I solder it. Susan says that this is because I am getting old, but Sarah thinks it's because my heat-shrink brain has been greatly reduced by constant exposure to the tropical sun.

Naturally, you would never cut or shorten any wire that has been calibrated by the manufacturer as are those on some antennae, depthfinder transponders, and other sensitive monitoring apparatus. In the case of critical components like bilge pumps, a far better practice is to just not use products that come with inadequate leads, especially submersible bilge pumps.

After all the wires in the circuit have been replaced, check for voltage drop once more. See? There it is right within acceptable limits. Doesn't that make you feel like you have accomplished something? And you have a lot more to show for your efforts than more efficient lights in the forepeak. You are now a functioning electrician, and you can use these same procedures to cure at least 90 percent of all your boat's electrical problems.

LED Lighting

While we are on the subject of recreational akalo . . . er, make that lighting, I would like to make one more joint . . . er, I mean point. Consider changing all your bulbs to light-emitting diodes (LEDs) as you replace each circuit. The advantages of this relatively new technology (LEDs have been around since before transistors, but not in the form of afford-able lights) when applied to a cruising boat are huge. LEDs draw just a fraction of the amper-age of halogen or incandescent bulbs; they work fine with a much smaller wire size; they are available in three primary colors (red, blue, green) plus two shades of white, so you don't need light-absorbing globes or filters on your running lights; and they last forever. (OK, so 50,000 hours isn't forever, but it is still a long time.)

The downside of LEDs is their cost, which is about double that of more traditional illumi-nation, but these costs are coming down rap-idly. It is probably a moot point anyway, as the advantages of LEDs are so great that by the time this is printed and read by you, they will have undoubtedly become the industry standard and the cost will have dropped as far as it is likely to drop. Thus, if your new-old boat still has incan-descent or halogen lights, one of your first tasks will be to replace them with LEDs.

We will revisit LED lighting in Chapter 14 with more specifics for their application in a cruising boat, but for now just realize that they are a good thing, and you will probably be, sooner or later, switching to them.

Test for Stray Voltage

Another test you should learn to do with your new multimeter is a stray-current test. When there is an electrical leak into a boat's ground or bonding system, the damage to hardware caused by galvanic corrosion can be catastrophic. Even a tiny leak of a fraction of a milliamp can cause significant damage over time. Fortunately, the test for stray voltage is easy. First, pull all the fuses or turn off all the circuit breakers for every piece of equipment on the boat. With the battery switch or the isolation switch closed so that the battery is connected to the distribution panel, remove the positive battery cable from the battery, and tap the cable end against the battery post. If there are any sparks at all (do it at night when you can see the smallest sparks), you either have a solar panel that you forgot to disconnect (if it's daylight), a piece of equip-ment that is running still connected, or you have a leak to ground somewhere.

For a more comprehensive test, connect a multimeter to the circuit. Leaving the pos-itive battery cable disconnected, place the positive lead on the cable and the negative lead on the battery post, and check for voltage by clicking through the voltage scales from the highest to the lowest. Any reading, even a frac-tion of a millivolt, means there is a leak some-where between the battery and the open circuit breakers or fuses. To find it, you will have to disconnect and reconnect every piece of wire that is connected to this section of the wiring system one at a time until the meter shows a zero reading.

If there is no reading (and there shouldn't be), reconnect the circuit breakers or fuses one at a time for each piece of equipment with the equipment itself turned off and check for voltage. (Don't connect the inverter, though, unless you know for certain just what you are doing.) If there is any reading, first make sure you are not on a memory circuit that is hot all the time (such as is found on bilge sniffers, some GPS and radar equipment, and most AM/FM automobile-type radios), and double-check that the equipment is off. If you still have a reading, you have a leak and will have to break the circuit at each terminal, starting with the one closest to the battery on the negative side, until the meter reads zero and you have isolated the leak.

A few hours spent looking for unwanted voltage drops and checking for stray voltage is a great way to get to know your new old boat and your new multimeter while performing an essential check of your electrical systems. If, after reading this, your manuals, and Nigel Calder's book (*Boatowner's Mechanical and Electrical Manual*), you still don't feel comfortable with DC electrical circuits, either take a course in basic electricity, or ask among the local cruisers and try to find a friendly sparkey (all cruising sparkies are friendly) to show you how to do it. As a last resort, hire a pro, not to do the job but to show you how to do it.

Electrical skills, like cooking skills, are among the most valuable you can have on a cruising sailboat and are well worth whatever it takes to acquire them. Eventually you will acquire the exalted title of "sparkey" yourself. Then, wherever you go, you will find that you are one of the most popular cruisers in the harbor.

Batteries and Charging Systems

This is a subject that deserves its own chapter, and a book could easily be written about your batteries and the various ways of keeping them alive. Come to think of it, there are already several good books out there on the subject, and one of the best is the section on electrical systems in *Boatowner's Mechanical and Electrical Manual* by Nigel Calder, which I've already referred to several times. (No, I don't get a cut on the sale of this book, and I don't even know the guy who wrote it. It's just the best book ever written on marine maintenance.) So,

if you will read this material, you will save me from repeating a lot of stuff that others have already covered a lot better than I could anyway. There are a few details on your 12-volt and charging system that are specific to the cruising life, however, so let's go over them here.

Batteries

The types and sizes of the batteries you have in your boat is another subject that is covered very well in other books you probably already have in your library, so I won't go into the details of the differences between the wet-cell, absorbed-glass-mat (AGM), and gel-cell types of batteries. But there are some general observations I'd like to make.

For active cruising and live-aboard use, you will need a lot of battery power. I'm not going to tell you how much because it will depend on your specific needs, but *Vicarious* carries about 500 amp-hours in the house banks for her modest array of electronics, her refrigeration, and her somewhat greedy autopilot. Our starting battery is a 100-amp-hour heavy-duty (not a deep-cycle) Optimo Bluetop multiuse battery, which is more than enough for our 90-horsepower Beta Marine diesel.

In all our years of cruising, I have never lost a starting battery or had to switch to the house banks to start the engine, which leads me to believe that the traditional battery-selector switch is a vestige of another day when batteries, charging systems, and diesel engines were not as reliable as they are now. Thus, I am removing the selector switches and replacing them with simple two-position isolation switches with no provision for cross-connecting to the house banks other than a handy pair of jumper cables.

A lot of simple and basic boats are out there with no refrigeration or radar or autopilots, and if you can be happy in this category, God bless your Spartan existence. Your need for batteries will be at a minimum, and it is a proven fact that if you can be happy without a lot of electrical gadgets on your boat, you will be a lot happier than those of us who can't be happy without them. It's too late for me, however; I like my autopilot, microwave oven, pop-up toaster, and all the other old familiar simple and basic amenities.

Speaking of microwave ovens and pop-up toasters, these and a coffee pot are the only things we have on *Vicarious* that require 120-volt electricity. And, if it weren't for the hedonistic needs of the skipper for warm bagels and hot coffee, we could (and often do) get along fine without them. With modern 12-volt appliances supported by solar power and a good wind generator, there is really no need for 120-volt service at all on any proper cruising boat. This is, of course, an anathema to many power boaters (and many sailboaters who should be power boaters) who can't seem to survive without "full air" and an "entertainment center" and a huge generator with which to operate them while amusing all the other boats in the anchorage. We aren't there yet, but my goal is to soon have V*icarious* free of any high-voltage electricity (with, perhaps, just a tiny inverter to run my beloved pop-up toaster).

Regardless of your needs, any true cruising boat should have enough battery power and charging capacity to allow you to live comfortably without ever having to plug in to shore power. This means lots of amp-hours in the batteries and in the charging system.

The most appropriate type of battery to use while touring the world in a boat is another controversial subject with experienced cruisers, but I believe that batteries on a cruising boat should be of the wet-cell type whenever possible. Wet-cells are cheaper to buy, last longer, are more reliable, and are more generally available in remote areas than gel-cells and AGM batteries.

On *Sultana* we started with eight 6-volt golf cart batteries for the house bank, then switched to two huge 8D wet-cell batteries in Panama, then switched back to golf cart batteries in New Zealand. The big 8Ds worked fine, but I got too old and feeble to lift the things out of the battery box. I only had to do it twice a year, but moving an 8D is like moving a piano, only the piano is easier to lift. The 6-volt golf cart batteries are lighter than 8Ds, and they are more flexible. If you find you need more capacity, just clamp another pair in series and you've got it.

The drawbacks to the wet cells are the much touted maintenance they require (you have to check the fluid level every so often, which is no big deal) and their bulk and weight (which can be a big deal). However, if you have the room for them, the lower cost and reliability more than offset these rather minor problems.

As much as I like a bank of heavy-duty golf cart batteries as the house bank, on *Vicarious* we have three 4D AGM batteries. Is this hypocritical? Not at all. These are the batteries that were on the boat when we bought it, and I'm not about to toss good batteries on principle. And the battery box is not nearly large enough to accommodate my preferred choice. Until I'm ready to rebuild the battery box (which may happen sometime before the next millennium, but probably not), we are stuck with the reliable-but-expensive AGMs.

Gel-cell and AGM batteries do have their place even if you do have room for wet cells. They are just the thing to have in the forepeak if you prefer a separate battery for your anchor windlass, and because they work well with a solar trickle charger, they are a great idea for part-time cruisers who must leave their boats unattended for long periods and for day-sailors. But if you can fit them in your boat, wet cells are the way to go for cruising sailors.

Whatever type of batteries you decide to use, the trick is to have enough capacity so that with normal use, your solar panels and wind generator will ensure that your batteries will never be discharged to below 12.5 volts. Another thing to remember is that batteries of different types use different charging voltages. Wet cells and AGM batteries charge up to about 14.8 volts, and gel cells charge at about 14.1 volts. Charging gel cells at a higher rate can cause bubbles to form in the electrolyte and drastically shorten their life. While you can mix the types of batteries on a boat, it is better not to, especially if you use a common charger for two banks, as is standard on most cruising boats.

All batteries must be tied down in their own locker separate from the engine compartment. Say that again . . . tied down. Got it? Tied down. There is no excuse for any cruising boat to have batteries, wet or dry, that are not isolated and TIED DOWN.

Series and Parallel Connection

Series connection (the terminals of the two batteries are connected positive to negative) increases the power or voltage of a battery bank by the sum of the voltage of all the batteries so connected. Thus, two 200-amp-hour, 6-volt golf cart batteries connected in series equals one 200-amp-hour, 12-volt battery bank. Parallel connection (the terminals of the two batteries are connected positive to positive and negative to negative) increases the capacity or amperage of a battery bank by the sum of the amperage of all the batteries so connected. Thus, two 200-amp-hour, 12-volt batteries (or two banks of 6-volt batteries connected in series) connected in parallel equals one 400-amp-hour, 12-volt battery bank.

This may sound confusing if you haven't encountered it before, but it is exactly how the battery banks on most cruising boats are wired, so it is important that you understand the principles. It is not really that hard.

Battery Charging

One of the true joys of modern electronic innovation is found in the efficient charging devices that drastically shorten engine-running times even with an increase in battery capacity. In the good old days when we all had automobile alternators and mechanical regulators, the engine had to be run for hours just to keep the light in the head bright enough to find the top to the toothpaste. If you had any kind of refrigeration with the typical underinsulated icebox of the day, engine running was pretty much a full-time deal. Today, we run *Vicarious*'s engine about an hour a day in the tropics, which gives us plenty of power from the Balmar 120-amp alternator with its three-step electronic regulator. If the wind is blowing over 15 knots, the wind generator does most of the work, and once we get our solar panels working, we shouldn't have to run the engine at all, except, of course, on those rare rainy days when the wind doesn't blow.

One good trick on a cruising boat is to get rid of those old three-position battery switches and install three high-capacity toggle switches instead, one for each battery bank and one for the crossover. These switches will give you more positive control than the old battery switch, and you are much less likely to leave the batteries connected by mistake. If you have dual alternators or one dual-output alternator, you can even get away without the crossover switch and just use a pair of jumper cables to start the engine from the house batteries if you have a battery failure (very rare if you take care of your batteries) and need the house bank to start the engine.

Like all electronics, the world of battery charging is changing daily, and there is a wealth of amazing new products available to make the previously arduous process automatic—products like the Blue Sea 7600 CL-Series BatteryLink, which keeps *Vicarious*'s isolated anchor-windlass battery topped up without the knuckle-headed captain never having to think about it (or worrying about the consequences of not thinking about it). This electronic marvel costs less than $100 and feeds the battery on the forepeak through the start battery. And the only maintenance required is an occasional check to see that the terminals are clean and tight.

All other charging functions are controlled through a Heart 2000 interface that is so automated it is easy to forget the batteries are even there. Input from all sources—wind, solar, alternator, generator, and shore—are coordinated, metered, and switched without any need for human interference. Not only does this relieve the captain of the responsibility of the daily battery rituals of the past that we all remember so fondly but it also greatly increases the life of the batteries, especially those batteries in boats captained by lazy louts who often find more entertaining pastimes than dealing with battery issues.

The Engine

Assuming your surveyor has given your engine a clean bill of health, one of the first things you should do is to change the oil and filters. You should have an instruction manual for the engine; if it's missing, you can easily download the manual for most engines, even the obsolete ones, from the Internet. Save it in PDF format, and print out a copy for when your computer takes an unannounced day off. You can also try to get one from the local dealer for the type of engine you have, but they invariably charge for it, sometimes a lot. While you're there, order a shop manual and a parts list. These two things can save a world of grief if you need work done or parts in some faraway place.

The Fuel System

Before you do anything else on your engine, locate and identify all your fuel filters. Start with the primary fuel filter, which should be the first large filter between the fuel tank and the engine. It may have a glass water-separator bowl with a drain on the bottom, and it is probably made by Racor. If it isn't a Racor, consider changing it to one as soon as is practical. Racor filters are effective, and filter elements are available everywhere there are cruisers; elements for other makes can be hard to find. If you don't like Racor filters, and quite a few don't, be sure you have a large supply of replacement elements on hand for whatever filter you do have. Most engines require fuel filters to be changed only once every other oil change. But this can lead to complacency; if you take on a bad load of fuel, it is easy to go through half a dozen filter elements before you get the system cleared.

If your system isn't already fitted with one, consider adding a good vacuum gauge to the outlet side of the filter or anywhere in the line between the primary and secondary filters. Any increase in vacuum reading in this gauge during normal engine running will indicate that the fuel pumps are laboring to draw fuel through the filter, which usually means that the filter is becoming clogged and it is time to change the element. Be sure and get a gauge that incorporates a needle that indicates the maximum vacuum reached and doesn't reset automatically to zero. That way you can easily check the condition of your filters at any time without having to run the engine.

After you have located the primary fuel filter, drained the separator bowl, and changed the element, follow the fuel line until you find the secondary filter. It's usually smaller than the primary and located on the engine itself. It is usually a spin-off type similar to, but smaller than, your auto oil filter. If it is the older canister type with an element inside a fuel-filled reservoir, consider changing the entire filter to the newer spin-on-off CAV type. They're easier to change and less messy, and replacement elements are readily available. While you are at the secondary filter, notice that there are one or sometimes two screws in the top that don't appear to be doing anything. These are usually near the inlet or outlet couplings, and sometimes there is one at each. These are your bleed screws, and we will be coming back to them later.

Continue following the fuel line until it disappears into a little cylindrical protrusion, usually located on the side of the engine block, with a curious little lever on the bottom or side. This is the lift pump that supplies fuel to the injector pump. In newer engines, such as *Vicarious*'s Beta Marine 90, the lift pump is an integral part of the secondary filter. There may be a screen filter in the top of this pump that won't require cleaning unless you experience a major contamination of your fuel (such as when buying it in Mexico), but you should check it now just to get aquatinted with it.

The next item on the fuel line is the injector pump, which supplies fuel under high pressure to the injectors where it is vaporized and exploded into the force that spins the prop and drives you through the water when the winds fail to blow. The only thing you really need to know about this pump is where it is and where the bleed screws are located. Some of these pumps have a separate oil reservoir that needs to be topped off and changed when the engine oil is changed.

You might run into the term "common-rail system" or "common-rail injector pump" in your travels among diesel-knowledgeable cruisers. This is a more sophisticated way of getting fuel into the cylinders under high pressure (like 29,000 psi and more; that's enough pressure to blow a hole through a brick) than the conventional injector pump, and it is becoming increasingly common in light truck engines

that are sometimes converted to marine use. It is unlikely that you will encounter one in any good-old boat that we are discussing here, but if you do, you will now know what they are and not to mess with them. Any work on a common-rail system will require the help of a qualified mechanic.

Bleeding the Fuel Lines

Once all the fuel filter elements have been changed or cleaned, you will need to bleed the system to get every last bubble of air out of the fuel lines. The bleed procedure varies with different engines, but generally it involves cracking the bleed screws—while operating that curious little lever we discovered earlier underneath the lift pump—until the bubbles stop and clear fuel runs out. This is a messy job, and any attempts to catch the fuel are usually frustrated by all the other apparatus that get in the way, but try to catch it anyway. The absorption matts sold by West Marine (and most other chandleries) for about a buck each suck up the fuel while ignoring water and other nonhydrocarbon liquids. These should be a part of every work session that involves fuel or oil.

Start at the Racor filter and work toward the engine. Open the top of the filter case, and fill the reservoir with clean fuel. Then secure the top, making sure there is a good seal at the gasket. Move on to the secondary filter, crack the first bleed screw, and pump until the bubbles stop. Tighten that screw and move to the next one and so on until you have bled them all. If your engine doesn't have bleed screws or if you can't find them, you can do the same job by cracking the coupling nuts at each fitting all the way to the injector pump.

If your boat isn't already equipped with one, consider adding a supplemental electric fuel pump to your system to assist with bleeding the fuel lines and filter. These are particularly useful for engines that are difficult to bleed. Such a pump can also sometimes be used in an emergency to keep an engine with a clogged filter running long enough to get an anchor down or to move out of a busy channel. As an alternative, you can install a bulb-type fuel pump—the type they use on common outboard engine tanks—but make sure it is rated for diesel fuel.

Bleeding the fuel lines should become a second-nature response to any engine failure, so just go ahead and get good at it. It's not that hard.

When a diesel cranks at normal speed but won't start, or when it starts OK, then quickly dies, you can almost bet air is getting into the fuel lines or a filter is clogged. When this happens, first check your fuel system vacuum gauge. Any more than normal vacuum is cause for alarm, but you'll have to learn what normal is by experience as it is different for different engines. The needle should never be in the yellow or red zones printed on the face of most good gauges, and if it is, it indicates a clogged filter or restricted fuel line. If there is no vacuum problem, you probably have an air leak. Make sure that all the filter covers are tight and that the diaphragm in the lift pump isn't leaking. If that isn't it, check that all connections are tight (a cross-threaded connector is another source of air), and if that isn't it, check for restricted fuel lines.

Congratulations! Once you have successfully bled your fuel system, you know enough to fix about 85 percent of all diesel engine problems that you are likely to encounter in the cruising life.

The Oil System

Failure to change the oil and oil filters probably does more harm in more diesel engines than anything else. In fact, if you keep your fuel and oil clean and the engine running at the right temperature, you can expect many diesels to outlast you and your boat.

Changing the oil in a boat engine is essentially the same as changing the oil in an automobile engine except that the oil will usually have to be pumped out because there isn't enough room under the oil pan to drain it through the sump. Many newer engines have a built-in pump for removing the old oil, but most older ones can be pumped through the dipstick port. Several electric pumps are on the market that make this job easier, or you can use most any hand pump with an intake hose small enough to fit into the opening. The best advice is to ask the previous owner how he or she did it, then do it the same way.

How often to change the oil in a marine diesel engine is difficult to determine by reading the popular marine blogs and press. Some self-proclaimed experts will say to renew the oil as often as every 50 hours while others say to go by the manufacturer's instructions, which in the case of *Vicarious*'s Beta Marine 90, is every 250 hours. The difference of opinion comes from the different ways the boating public uses their boats. The average recreational use of a sailboat engine is about 50 hours a season (if that seems low, remember that a large percentage of boats of all types spend most of their lives at the dock or in the driveway on a trailer and many are never used at all), so the oil gets changed once a year, which should be a minimum on any engine.

Active cruisers, however, can easily put 50 hours or more a month on their engines, and changing oil that often would be both arduous and a bit ridiculous. So a little judgment is in order here. In my case, the recommended 250 hours seems a bit long to go between changes, so I do the job every 150 to 200 hours and before every long offshore passage. There is little consequence of changing the oil too often, but not changing it often enough is a formula for disaster, so err on the side of changing it too often.

Change your filter every time you change the oil no matter what the manufacturer recommends. The filter might be fine, but there is often up to a liter of dirty oil in there we want to get rid of. Besides, filters are cheap, but bearings and piston rings are very expensive. There is no excuse for dirty oil or filters on a boat. While you are changing the oil, don't neglect the injector pump if it has a separate oil supply, and check the level of the transmission fluid while you are at it. Oh yeah, don't forget to clean and oil your air-intake filter now too.

The Cooling System

All you really need to know about your engine cooling system is how to check the fluid level, how to change the thermostat, and how to change the engine zincs. If you don't already know how to check the level of the cooling fluid in the header tank, you might want to take a close look at your decision to go cruising or at least look around for a more mechanically inclined crew to take along.

The thermostat is usually a two-bolt-and-gasket affair located somewhere under the header tank. If your engine runs OK but takes a long time to reach operating temperature, it may mean your thermostat is stuck open; if it overheats and runs rough, it could mean it is stuck closed. Stuck open is OK and a nuisance at worst; stuck closed can be dangerous, and it can lead to major repairs. Some cruisers in the tropics remove the thermostat to improve coolant flow, and if your engine runs a bit hot even with a functioning thermostat, this might be worth a try.

Manufacturers delight in making engine zincs hard to find and harder to change. Your boat should have at least two zincs—one in the engine block somewhere where it will protrude into the water jacket, and another in the heat exchanger. There may be a third in your header tank. Check these zincs often, and change them

when they are about 25 percent gone. A rapid increase in the rate of deterioration in these zincs is a sure indication of electrical system leakage, and you must stop everything until you find what is causing it.

Be particularly diligent about your zincs while tied to a marina, even if you are not connected to shore power. Stray current from the boat next door can be climbing all over your boat without your ever knowing about it. The best advice is to avoid marinas altogether and anchor out with the real cruisers. The air is cleaner, the water is clearer, it's quieter, the companionship is more companionable, it's cheaper, you'll be doing what cruisers go cruising to do, and you can always get to the marina bar in the dinghy.

The Raw-Water System

The function of the raw-water system is to cool the coolant in the freshwater system, and on some boats, to cool the oil and transmission fluid. Seawater is circulated through a large, coarse filter by an engine-driven pump, then through the heat exchanger and any other coolers, and then pumped into the exhaust system where it exits the boat through the exhaust pipe. Each of these elements is of critical concern to the cruiser, so let's go over them one at a time.

The Raw-Water Filter

The raw-water filter should be located somewhere adjacent to your raw-water seacock where it is accessible and convenient; it should be fitted with a large glass sight bowl. Some cruisers install two raw-water filters on a Y valve so if one becomes clogged with seaweed, it is a simple matter to switch to the secondary filter without shutting down the engine. It is also important to operate the seacock at least once a month to make sure it's working because when a component in the raw-water system fails, it can sink the boat. Many fine yachts have been lost because a seacock was frozen open. The filter element needs to be cleaned whenever you can see foreign matter accumulating in it.

The Raw-Water Pump

The raw-water pump is located on the engine right where the hose from the raw-water filter attaches. Most of these pumps have a rubber impeller that will self-destruct in about two seconds when the supply of seawater is shut off. It is critical that you keep a supply of these impellers on board and that you become skilled at changing them. If yours is a Jabsco pump, and it usually is (newer engines may have a Johnson pump, which is similar), there will be four to six screws holding a flat plate onto the end of the pump that are removed to expose the impeller. Remove and replace this impeller now just to get familiar with the procedure. I can guarantee that when you really need to change that impeller, you will need to change it quickly, and you won't have time to mess around with an engine instruction manual.

Every time an impeller fails, it may shed a few blades that will be forced downstream to lodge where they can restrict the flow of raw water. You should follow the line and look for traps where these stray blades can hang up. Elbows and sharp bends in the line are likely places; some smaller bits may make it to the heat exchanger. Don't be tempted to leave these broken-off impeller pieces in the system because, even if they are not doing any harm now, they can become dislodged and move to a new address where they will start to raise hell right when you least need it.

The Heat Exchanger

The heat exchanger is the marine equivalent of the automobile radiator, and it works on the same principle except that excess heat is carried away by water instead of by air. Raw water circulates in the exchanger through tubes that are surrounded by coolant from the freshwater system that is being circulated by the engine's water pump.

You already know where the heat exchanger is located because you had to find it to change the zincs. Some heat exchangers have removable plates that give access to the cores that can be cleaned using a bronze cleaning brush designed for cleaning rifle bores. Usually a .30 caliber brush will do the job, but if you have a larger or smaller caliber heat exchanger, the guy at the gun store can help you find the right size.

The only other things you need to know about heat exchangers is that they are critical to an engine's operation and that they are prone to unannounced failure. Heat exchangers are a lot like rigging in that the older they get, the more likely they are to fail when you need them most. They can fail without giving any warning, and a failure can be catastrophic. We had ours let go in the Cook Islands where it soaked the engine compartment with a fine high-pressure spray of seawater. Before we discovered the problem, it ruined a $600 Balmar alternator. After a dozen tries at a temporary patch, we just gave up on the engine and hoisted the sails. We were able to reach Pago Pago although it took a while when the wind died for a solid week. The total bill for replacement parts came to more than $1,000, all because of a pinhole leak that was barely visible when the engine wasn't running. (One good thing about Pago Pago, perhaps the only good thing, is that they have great UPS service from West Marine. OK, so there is a good American grocery store too.)

Many cruisers carry a spare heat exchanger, and it's a good idea to install a new one just before you leave on your cruise, then keep the old one as an emergency spare. That's just what we're going to do—next time.

Sea Trials and Errors: Commence Boat Handling

Chances are you took your new old boat out for a trial sail before you bought it, but it really doesn't matter. I am convinced that unless you are experienced in the type of boat you are buying, the prepurchase sea trial is a classic case of form versus function, and it is not that important anyway. Boats exhibit such a wide variety of behaviors under sail that it is difficult to make any judgment on the sailing characteristics of any one type of boat until you have covered many miles of ocean in it. Your surveyor would have used the sea trial to check out the engine, rig, and the sails and to check for any obvious structural defects—but once around the harbor is plenty of time for most surveyors to do this. Even if you went along, it is doubtful you learned that much. It's hard to spot problems when your eyes are full of stars and your imagination has you dropping anchor next to the ghost of Captain Cook's *Endeavour* in Moorea Lagoon instead of returning to the dock at Podunk Creek.

Once the boat is yours, however, you're going to need to learn how to drive it, and the first thing to learn is how to bring it into dock. Soon after we bought *Sultana*, the crew evolved a foolproof method for docking. Sarah would take the bow with the bow line ready to throw, Phillip would take on the midship rail with the spring line, and Susan would stand next to the pilothouse where she could keep an eye on things. As honorary captain, I was at the wheel. We always began our approach from about a hundred yards out and at a 45-degree angle to the dock. When Susan yelled, "Lookout, we're going to crash," I knew it was time to throttle back and start to lose way. When she screamed,

"Arrrraghhhh," and covered her eyes with her hands, I shifted to neutral and started to turn the bow away from the dock. When she fell to the deck and covered her head with her arms, I put it in reverse, put the wheel hard over opposite the direction I wanted to move the stern, and punched in a good jolt of power. The old boat drifted into the dock as gently as an oak leaf drifts to the ground in an autumn breeze. When the fenders touched the dock, Phillip stepped ashore with the spring line, and Sarah either passed the bow line to a bystander or waited until Phillip could come and get it. I shut down the engine, secured the stern line, then reassured Susan that we had miraculously survived another landing. The crew worked together like a well-practiced drill team, and we never (well, practically never) failed to impress the dockside hangarounders.

This technique worked every time, but it wasn't always that easy. We left a series of gouged docks and loosened pilings from Marblehead to Key West while we practiced. My favorite trick was to forget about the bowsprit, which I couldn't see from the cockpit, and use it to either sweep the dock clear of all bystanders or get it trigged between two pilings. I've even made several attempts at removing dock-side fuel pumps using this procedure. Fortunately, we never did any serious damage to anything more important than the skipper's pride, but if someone had been along with a camera, we would have been a hit on that TV show that features the world's most embarrassing videos.

With our crew grown and gone on to their own adventures, it is just Susan and me on *Vicarious,* and with inside steering instead of the outside steering on *Sultana*, the deck work during docking falls to Susan. Without the crew to rely on, she has overcome her fear of catastrophe, and we are able to execute a simplified form of the docking maneuver detailed above with just the two of us. It is quick, effective, and efficient but not nearly as entertaining for the hangarounders.

Our docking procedure works for us, but unless you have a crew member with Susan's remarkable depth perception, you will have to develop your own technique, and the time to do it is now, not after you get under way. The first thing to do is to motor around the harbor a few times making tight turns to port and starboard. Then try the same thing in reverse and notice how well the bow tracks the stern. You should notice the boat moving slightly sideways while in reverse, depending on which way the prop is turning (to port with a clockwise prop and to starboard with a counterclockwise prop). This is called *prop walk*, and it can be quite dramatic for some boats or hardly noticeable for others. With any amount of prop walk, you can learn to use this movement to great advantage when docking. Once you have a good feel for the boat under power, find a remote dock somewhere where there aren't a lot of bystanders, and practice approaching and leaving. Even if you are an experienced skipper, you will find that all boats respond to the controls in different ways, and you will need practice before you master this important technique.

Once you have mastered the boat under power, you can take her out of the harbor and try sailing. Pick a good day with a gentle breeze and flat seas, and start gradually with a simple reach. If you are new to sailing, it would be a good idea to have a friend who is experienced with your size of boat. A dinghy skipper might be fun to have on board, but he or she isn't going to be a lot of help. If you can get the previous owner to go along for the first few trips, that would be ideal. Sailing a large sailboat is not a difficult thing to learn how to do, there is little need to learn complicated maneuvers, and after just a few trials, you will start to feel like an old hand.

Heavy Weather

One of the important bullets all bluewater cruisers have to bite is learning to handle heavy weather. Our coastal cruising brethren can deal with big waves and high wind by scuttling into port and would be quite foolish not to seek shelter when the weather turns nasty, but you are not always going to have that luxury.

I can recall one instance when we were becalmed after leaving the Tuamotus on a particularly clear and brilliant day and watching a most mammoth and spectacular frontal system approaching from the south. It was a solid wall of ominous black misery that stretched from one horizon to the other. It promised to make a sincere attempt at blowing our socks off, and there was no way we could avoid it. When the front hit, the winds rose from zero to about 50 knots in just a few minutes, and the waves built to the point that they were washing the decks. By the time the first gusts hit, however, we had everything secured, were safely hove-to, and were down below engrossed in a lively game of Monopoly. (Phillip played Monopoly with a ruthless disregard for anything but winning and refused to quit until he acquired every last hotel and property, wiped out everyone, and left the board in a hopeless shambles. We expected him to go into international finance, but he became a counselor for military veterans instead, a much more useful field even if it doesn't require a ruthless attitude.)

As you become more and more familiar with your boat, you should take advantage of every opportunity to learn how she handles when the gales start to howl. Then, instead of scuttling back into port when the winds rise, sail offshore where there is a little sea room and practice your heavy-weather maneuvers. Don't wait until there is a full gale in force, but watch for the small-craft warnings to go up, and start practicing in 20 to 25 knots of wind before you venture out into anything stronger. Foul weather can be a terrifying experience for the uninitiated, and a bad experience in a storm has turned many would-be cruisers into dedicated landlubbers.

There are four commonly accepted methods of handling nasty weather: lying ahull, heaving-to, running off, and lying to a sea anchor or drogue. These are all important enough to warrant our going over them one at a time.

Lying Ahull

Lying ahull is the simplest of the four maneuvers, and depending on your boat, it may be one of the most useful. All you do is take down every scrap of sail, lash the helm in the neutral position, and go below to enjoy the ride. All boats ride differently when left to their own devices. Both *Sultana* and *Vicarious,* like most full-keel boats, tend to ride beam to the sea, which means they wallow a lot if the wind against the rigging isn't strong enough to impart stability. In about 35 knots of wind *Vicarious* lies ahull very nicely with little rolling noticed below. With the wind less than 30 knots, putting up just a scrap of mizzen turns her into the wind and greatly improves the ride even though it could be argued that we are no longer lying ahull. Full-keel boats will often ride better than those of other designs, and deep fin keels can be deadly. Of all the boats dismasted in the notorious 1994 Queen's Birthday storm between New Zealand and Fiji, most were fin-keel boats that broached, tripped on their keels, and rolled.

It is important that you learn how your boat will ride the waves and wind with no sails set, so give it a try in 20 to 30 knots of wind. Make sure you have plenty of sea room, of course, and don't try it in shipping lanes.

Heaving-To

Heaving-to is a little more complicated and a little more work than lying ahull, but it is a much more useful maneuver, is usually safer, and nearly always more comfortable. Once again, each boat will react with its own characteristics, so it is critical that you practice before you leave on your cruise. Generally it involves flying just enough sail to impart stability and keep the boat moving into the wind at headway speed. Usually a scrap of jib is sheeted against the wind (backed), the deeply reefed main or the trysail is sheeted nearly flat, and the rudder is lashed or locked to windward. The idea is to get the boat to move forward, then round gently into the wind until the main stalls enough for the jib to push the bow back to lee, filling the main and starting the cycle all over again. On *Vicarious* this means a backed storm jib and a double-reefed main and a furled mizzen with the wheel lashed hard to windward, but it is bound to be different for your boat. This procedure is nowhere near as difficult as it sounds, and you should have it down pat in one or two practice sessions.

Again, light displacement boats with fin keels are miserable creatures to get to heave-to. They usually respond to attempts to trim the sails by alternately broaching and luffing. If you have one of these boats, you may find that this particular maneuver doesn't work and you will be safer running before the wind, but many experts with more experience with these types of boats than I have argue convincingly that any boat can be made to heave-to with a bit of practice.

The time to heave-to, or lay ahull for that matter, is any time you become uncomfortable sailing the boat or when you need some rest. It is just like reefing. Never wait until the situation deteriorates to the point of being dangerous before you take action to protect yourself and your boat. Even more important, never let yourself get so tired that it affects your judgment.

Running Before the Wind

Running before the wind is just what it says, and it was the favorite foul-weather maneuver with the old square-riggers. All you need to do is take in the sails and steer the boat in the direction in which the wind wants you to go. The trick is to maintain just enough speed to soften the effects of a following sea without the hull surfing down the forward slope of the wave as it passes. Often it helps to drag an anchor or another drogue on a long warp off the stern at least two wavelengths behind the boat (discussed below). Some light-displacement boats don't run well because they are difficult to keep from surfing and broaching in the troughs. We have never used this technique on *Vicarious* because we have never needed it, but I can envision using it as a last resort.

Running off, as it is sometimes called, isn't the same as sailing downwind under bare poles. One (running off) is a survival technique, and the other (sailing under bare poles) is a heavy-weather sailing technique we sometimes use to keep going in moderately challenging downwind conditions when the weather agrees with our destination. The difference is academic because, except for flying the staysail or storm jib for balance when sailing, the technique is the same in both cases. The biggest difference is that the first is scary and the second is fun.

Life's a Drag

Well, not really, but if you want to get a lively discussion going among any group of bluewater sailors, bring up the subject of sea anchors and drogues, then sit back and enjoy the fireworks. The first argument . . . er, discussion . . . will be over the definition of these two devices. One group will maintain that sea anchors are always deployed off the bow, and drogues are always deployed off the stern. Thus a sea anchor deployed off the stern becomes a drogue and vice versa.

The second and equally vocal group will insist it is a matter of size. A sea anchor is large and intended to stop the boat cold, as a normal anchor would do, or as nearly so as possible. A drogue, on the other hand, is much smaller than a sea anchor, and it is intended to slow the boat to manageable speeds and improve maneuverability.

I, of course, as a trained journalist (I took Journalism 101 in college and quite nearly passed) remain completely neutral here even though I do admit to a slight list toward the brilliant arguments of the second group. For our purposes you can deploy a sea anchor anywhere you like, even from the head handle, and it remains a sea anchor. A drogue is a drogue no matter how it's dragged. Deploying a drogue off the bow in anything but moderate conditions (when it will act like a sea anchor and stop the boat) is considered bad form by most bluewater sailors. Without adequate resistance, the small drogue can allow the boat to move backward with the wind, which can impart unacceptable stress to the rudder even at slow speeds.

Regardless of what you call these two devices, they are both designed to either slow or stop your boat under extreme conditions, and the proper use of either involves the highest degree of seamanship and heavy-weather experience.

Sea anchors and drogues are extremely complicated devices, and the dynamics they set up when deployed are often misunderstood even by experienced sailors. Sea anchors and drogues are most often deployed under extreme conditions of high winds and huge seas, conditions that can be terrifying to even an old hand. A novice faced with these conditions and the need to deploy a hundred pounds or so of complicated gear from a heaving wet deck is in a tough spot to say the least. Fortunately, those of us who confine our cruising to the middle latitudes seldom encounter these conditions so we don't need these devices often, and the majority of cruising boats don't carry them. Lightweight high-tech boats (especially multihulls) need them more often than a heavy boat with a traditional full- or semi-full keel.

Right now *Vicarious* does not have either a sea anchor or a drogue aboard, but this deficiency is constantly under review. My problem with them (other than their cost—usually over $1,000 for either a drogue or a sea anchor) is the amount of room they take up in the cockpit lockers. For example, a Jordan Series Drogue for a boat of our size requires a minimum of 100 meters of 5/8-inch line (more is better), a length of 3/8-inch chain, a 25-pound anchor, a buoy, and a trip line. That is a lot of stuff to keep handy when you will probably only need it once every 10 years.

With the above second definition fresh in our minds, let's review these two sea brakes one at a time.

Drogues

Technically, a drogue is anything you can throw overboard secured to a line (warp) that will create drag and slow the boat's progress. A drogue can be one or more long warps of line, your anchor and rode, an unused sail, buckets, or anything else you can induce to go over the side and stay attached to the boat. Commercial drogues are currently available in three general types: the delta drogue, which, as the name implies, is shaped like a triangle; the Jordan Series Drogue, which is a long line festooned with cloth buckets that look and act like underwater windsocks; and the parachute drogue, which is shaped like a small parachute. All three types have their vocal advocates, which leads me to suspect that any of the three types will do the job if deployed correctly.

Drogues are normally streamed from the stern, and the most common use for them is to slow the boat when running before the wind under bare poles. They also are supposed to keep the longitudinal axis of the boat perpendicular to the wave crests, offering minimal surface area to an overtaking wave. The danger is that a boat under bare poles (particularly a light boat with a fin keel) will build speed to the point at which it wants to broach as it races down the face of a large following sea or it wants to jump off the top of a sea that is being overtaken. In either case, the drogue is designed to slow the boat enough to prevent these things from happening.

Drogues pose several dangers over and above the complicated deployment procedures. Unless the drogue is perfectly matched to the boat, it can cause the boat to yaw and sail back and forth on the face of a wave; in so doing, it can actually increase the danger to the boat. Many users of drogues report a loss of rudder control, and I have heard one firsthand report from a skipper who had to cut the drogue free to save his boat when the drogue caused a broach in a heavy sea.

Another obvious problem is that with the stern held into the seas, there is an increased tendency for the cockpit to fill with water. One can only imagine what would happen with the sugar-scoop sterns currently in vogue with the racing set. These two problems point to a third, more insidious, problem: until you practice these techniques, you will have no way of knowing how your boat will react to them, and it is almost impossible to practice because the severe conditions that are needed just aren't encountered that often. Practice under moderate conditions is always a good idea, but bear in mind that your boat is going to take on a whole new personality when the weather gets nasty enough to need a drogue.

There are a few other uses for drogues that don't involve heavy weather. They are a good way to steer a boat that has suffered damage to the rudder. To do so, stream a small drogue from the stern on a bridle so that pressure on one or the other of the lines will direct the boat. Drogues can also be deployed to help hold a position outside a harbor while waiting for the weather to clear or for daylight to enter, and they can be streamed behind a boat being towed to keep it from riding up on the stern of the tow vessel. A great trick when towing a dinghy in a sea is to drag a small drogue (a small plastic pail on a bridle with a short section of chain added for a weight works well) behind the dinghy.

Sea Anchors

Sea anchors are just like drogues only bigger. They are usually shaped like large parachutes. In fact, many boats carry a surplus military or cargo parachute as an economical sea anchor. One popular design is shaped like a deep parachute made of webbing to limit resistance and reduce the shock to the warp. Many products sold as drogues will make fine sea anchors if you simply buy one that is one or two sizes larger than the one recommended for your boat.

Sea anchors are usually deployed off the bow and are large enough to practically stop the boat, or at least slow it to a half-knot or so. Since they are anchors in every sense of the word, all the rules for normal anchoring with your standard ground grabber apply. You will need adequate warp with 100 meters being about minimum. If you deploy with your all-chain rode as a warp, you will need an adequate snubber, and catenary is just as important as when you are ground anchoring in a storm. All the cautions listed above for drogues are true in spades for sea anchors: they are complex devices, difficult to deploy properly, and even more difficult to predict and understand without actually using one in severe conditions.

The big danger in using a sea anchor in severe conditions is that it will not be big enough to stop your boat or slow it to a safe speed. Thus, many boats have found themselves proceeding downwind backward, which can be scary under the best of conditions. The forces on the rudder can break the lashings (the rudder is always lashed in neutral when deploying a sea anchor) or even break the steering mechanism so the rudder slams hard over and causes a broach. Rudders have also been lost, which may just be the more desirable thing to happen under these conditions.

The idea of deploying a sea anchor outside a harbor to wait for tide change or daylight to enter safely is, I believe, another example of cruising mythology that is never (or hardly ever) actually practiced by anyone in the cruising community. Deploying and retrieving a sea anchor is an enormous amount of work, and I can't see anyone doing it just to keep the boat stationary for a few hours—not when there are lots of easier options such as sailing in circles under reduced sail, lying ahull, or just drifting for a while. Deploying close to land with any current running would certainly be a bad idea. Furthermore, if a large ship should come along while you are tethered to a sea anchor off the mouth of a busy harbor, you could find yourself in a dire situation where you had to cut loose a lot of expensive gear to save your boat. I have never heard of such a thing happening, which further reinforces my belief that cruisers simply don't do this sort of thing.

Reducing Sail

OK, so there are five heavy-weather techniques instead of four, but reducing sail is not really a heavy-weather maneuver. You will learn to reduce sail for many reasons, including to slow the boat enough to time the arrival at your destination at dawn so you aren't hanging around the mouth of a dangerous harbor in the dark, or to make the boat a little more comfortable. A boat that booms along with the rail under day after day will get there a lot quicker than one sailed with a more vertically inclined mast, but the crew will be worn to a frazzle by the experience, and the captain might just end up sailing as a singlehander some day.

Although they are becoming increasingly scarce, you may still encounter a boat that hasn't been fitted with roller furling headsails and relies on old-fashioned hanked-on jibs. These require that the headsails be changed every time the sail area must be reduced or increased. Changing jibs can be a dangerous procedure for two reasons. One is obvious to anyone who has ever changed a headsail in a heavy sea and high wind: keeping the thing under control and yourself on board the boat throughout the procedure is a definite art. If the headsail is out at the end of a long bowsprit where it belongs, changing it becomes even more dramatic. Being washed off the foot ropes while working headsails was often the cause of a premature trip through the pearly hatchway for thousands of sailors in the old days, and it can still happen today. Under the best of conditions, fumbling with those little bronze hanks with numb fingers while green water is breaking over the bow is not one of the joys of cruising we read so much about.

For these reasons and others, roller-reefing headsails are almost universal these days. *Vicarious* has both headsails on oversized roller-reefing gear, and it is not uncommon to see boats with three roller-reefing rigs forward of the main mast.

On the big-money boats, motor-driven reefing systems are becoming common even on the main and mizzen. Not that roller-reefing systems don't present their own set of dangers. Once in a mild blow on the way to the Marquesas, we were sailing with *Sultana*'s big genoa reefed down to a nub and a double reef in the main when the reefing line pulled out of its jam cleat, thereby releasing the entire 320-square-foot sail. We got it under control quickly enough, but not without a great deal of excitement, and it could have taken the mast down if the wind had been a little stronger. The lesson here, of course, is to never trust jam cleats—take three turns around a winch, run the reefing line through the jam cleat, then secure the line to a regular cleat. You might need the turns around the winch to help if you need to take in more sail, and if the jam cleat does slip, you will need the winch to get the line off the regular cleat.

The best policy is probably not to reef headsails in heavy weather. *Vicarious* has her 185-square-foot 120 percent Genoa on the forestay and the 175-square-foot staysail on the baby stay. We use the big Genoa by gradually reducing the area until the winds reach about 25 knots, then roll it up and run out the staysail, which, because of its low center of gravity and robust construction, is a good heavy-weather sail. When the winds reach 35 knots, it's time for the storm jib, which laces over the rolled-up staysail. Any increase over 30 knots and it's heave-to time.

When to reduce sail is always a dilemma for cruising sailors, and the old saying that the time to reduce sail is when you first think about it doesn't work for us nervous types who think about it all the time. Reduce sail before the sail reduces you, is a more appropriate way to look at it. Anyway, reducing sail is a pain in the butt, and there is a natural inclination to avoid it until the last minute, which can be dangerous. Of course, if you reduce sail too early and find yourself lolling along at 2 or

3 knots in a fresh breeze, you're going to feel like a fool.

On *Vicarious*, our standard procedure is to reduce sail at the first sign of a rising wind, sit there going nowhere for about an hour, then shake the reefs out just in time to get clobbered by a half gale. On our trip to New Zealand, I had the added problem of what I called the Sarah factor. Sarah likes to go fast, and she firmly believes that the proper place for the sails is up and the normal place for the lee rail is about 6 inches under the sea. Every time I decided to slow down by taking in sails, I had to contend with, "Aw, Dad, what are you doing that for? We were just starting to get going."

Once you get your new old boat in the water and move aboard, get ready for a long period of adjustment and learning before you are comfortable. Be patient, and your boat will eventually learn all your wants and needs and idiosyncrasies and will gradually transform itself into everything you ever wanted a cruising boat to be. It will become your home, and when that happens, you are cruising at last.

13

The Cruising Galley

We can cruise without poetry, music and art;
We can cruise without conscience, and cruise without heart;
We may cruise without friends; we may cruise without books;
But civilized cruisers can't cruise without cooks.

—APOLOGIES TO OWEN MEREDITH, *LUCILE*

The Most Important Part of the Boat

In Chapter 1 of the first edition of this book, I exasperated traditionalists and about 75 percent of active cruisers by stating (and proving by the force of logic) that the cruising boat isn't as important to the cruising life as most people think it is. That being so, what is the most important part of the boat? The engine? Of course not. Lots of boats don't have engines. How about the rig and sails? Close, but wrong again. "The galley," shouts the bloke with the flour-smudged baseball cap in the back of the room—and the cook is always right. No part of any cruising boat is anywhere near as important as the galley because nothing has as much of an impact on our contentment, stamina, mental outlook, and general sense of well-being as the food we eat.

A cruising crew can be wet, cold, tired, and lonely, but if they have recently enjoyed a decent meal, they will be ready to wrestle tigers. Conversely, a crew can be rested, dry, and warm, but if they're hungry, they will be largely worthless. Centuries ago, some military megalomaniac who was fond of coining clichés observed that an army marched on its stomach. We can revise that to say that cruisers float on their bellies, and while it doesn't work as a cliché, it's true.

The quality of your diet will reflect the quality of your cruise more than any other single element of your daily routine. Regular meals of wholesome, nutritious, and tasty food makes cruising—nay, life itself—a joy. And food is much more than mere nutrition.

Mealtimes, or at least one meal a day, should be social events where the crew gathers to discuss the events of the past, to plan and speculate on the events to come, and to confess fears and doubts and ambitions. Eating should be a cultural experience because nothing else you can do, besides learning the local language, will better put you in tune with the inhabitants of the lands you visit than eating the local foods.

The French cruisers you will meet on your journeys have a well-deserved and hard-earned reputation for holding the rest of us in haughty disdain. They are convinced that they are superior to cruisers from any other country because they eat so much better than the rest of us. The most distressing thing about this arrogance is that it's true: the French really are superior to the rest of the world. Eat a few meals aboard a typical French cruising boat, and you'll find out why.

Can the Cans

In spite of the lucid manner in which I present my case, not everyone agrees with my argument that to cruise well, one must eat well, and many cruisers, particularly singlehanders, subsist entirely on canned food. This may be the very reason why singlehanders are singlehanders. Eating from cans is almost a cruising tradition, but it is one that dates back to the days when there were no grocery stores in the jungle, and onboard refrigeration was considered as frivolous as onboard air-conditioning is considered today.

Nearly all the old cruising books and a distressing number of online cruising forums contain extensive narratives about laying in several years' supplies of canned goods, then spending a month or so removing the labels, marking the contents with a magic marker, and even lacquering the cans to keep them from rusting. Then there are usually another few paragraphs about the best ways to inventory the cache of cans and how to store them in the bilge. And while this sort of nonsense may have been necessary in the good-old days, it is mostly a waste of time in these better-new days in which you and I do our cruising.

For short-term cruisers who are too lazy to learn the principles of cooking, and racing crews who love to regale the folks back home with tales of how dreadful the onboard food was, the traditional canned stew, raviolis in that glutinous red syrup they call tomato sauce, and various objects that began life as vegetables are standard fare, but most canned food is dreadfully unhealthy. Even the favorites like tuna fish and corned beef may contain heaps of chemicals and fat with hardly a trace of nutrition—just read the cans. Canned soups, sardines, and beans are handy for quick meals during rough passages; canned tomatoes are necessary for Captain Garlic's World-Famous Spaghetti Sauce (see below); and canned corn, meats (chicken and tuna), mushrooms, and peas add interest to stews and goulash. But beyond that, try to limit the stuff you eat out of cans, and keep the cans you do have limited to basic ingredients rather than prepared meals.

Canned goods are available everywhere, so just buy enough to get you to the next stop, and don't worry about the label falling off. Get rid of any cans that show signs of rust, and always listen for the little puff of air that signals the integrity of the vacuum seal. No puff of air, don't eat the food. It isn't worth taking a chance with botulism and food poisoning.

With 90 percent of all passages lasting less than two weeks, there is no excuse for a crew not having plenty of fresh wholesome produce on board at all times. I'm not saying that canned food isn't a boon to the cruising chef, but to overdepend on it is unhealthy, unappetizing, and unnecessary. Too many cruisers waste too much time learning esoteric things about sailing, such as the relative merits of various brands of chartplotters or watermakers, when what they really need to learn is how to make a good omelet.

Provisioning Myths

Some time ago I read an article in a cruising magazine about the correct way to provision a boat for a six-week Caribbean cruise. The article was illustrated with a photo of all the necessary foodstuffs, more than $3,000 worth, spread out on the dock. It covered all the standard cruising lore about coating your eggs with Vaseline, turning the big ends up, wrapping all the potatoes and onions in newspaper, marking all the cans with a magic marker so the contents can be identified when the labels rot off, and washing all the vegetables in bleach water to rid them of germs and cockroaches.

Unless you are intent on exploring the few remaining areas of the world that are truly remote, none of this is necessary. There are few, if any, areas in the popular cruising routes where good produce and foodstuffs are not available, and many previously primitive areas now sport modern grocery stores. We have bought Skippy peanut butter in the jungles of Honduras and Kellogg's corn flakes on Nuku Hiva, and the closest we have ever come to a food shortage was in Bora Bora when Susan couldn't find any pimento-stuffed olives for my martinis. *Vicarious*'s rule of thumb is to have enough food for any passage so we can be out twice as long as we expect to be without resorting to emergency rations. That means a two-month maximum food supply for the one-month passage from the Galapagos to Nuku Hiva in the Marquesas.

Attempting to have large food stores on a boat guarantees wastage and spoilage that will drive the cost of your meals way beyond what you will save by buying in quantity in the population centers. The exception is for staples such as flour, sugar, baking powder, cooking oil, and such. These should be bought in quantity for convenience and economy, not because they won't be available in the places you will be visiting. Even in the most expensive areas (and the most expensive place on earth to eat has to be French Polynesia) you will not save enough money to warrant the aggravation of trying to lay in supplies for anything longer than the next passage.

One large ketch we met in the Pacific had stocked up on beer and Coke and packed several cases of each in the bilge. A small amount of seawater got aboard, and when the crew reached Atutaki, they had a bilge full of empty cans. The seawater had induced galvanic corrosion that had eaten a tiny hole in each can. All of the liquid had drained into the bilge, where it was pumped overboard without their ever being aware that anything was amiss.

In Rangiroa Lagoon we met a German boat that had stocked up with two dozen cases of beer and several cases of rum in Panama. Halfway across the Pacific, the demons of the night visited the skipper, strongly suggesting that further indulgence in intoxicating liquids would rapidly bring his cruising plans to a halt. He heard the word and swore off the stuff; for several weeks thereafter, he ran a mini-liquor store off the stern of his boat trying to get rid of his cargo—which was a great boon to the cruising community. (Your temperate but thirsty author scored two cases of Heineken out of the deal.) It was also, though, a very foolish thing to do. The French take their import restrictions on alcohol very seriously, and the mind boggles to think of what might happen to any yachtie, not to mention a German yachtie, caught selling illegally imported booze.

A WORD ABOUT ROACHES: YUCK

Cockroaches come in three sizes: little, big, and gigantic. The closer you get to the equator, the more gigantic and more numerous they become. Entomologists tell us that roaches are harmless, intelligent by bug standards, and ubiquitous; they are clean, carry no diseases (unlike mosquitoes); don't eat enough to cause food shortages (unlike locusts); don't contaminate the food on which they nibble (unlike flies); and don't make loud noises that keep you awake at night (unlike crickets). What, then, you might ask, is all the fuss about? If you believed all you read about cockroaches, you would welcome them aboard like old friends and thrill to the sight of their cute little pumpkin-seed bodies scampering around on your countertop, just like a bird watcher thrills to the sight of buntings and finches hopping about on the bird feeder back home.

In spite of the overwhelming evidence that indicates cockroaches should be our friends, we don't welcome them aboard at all. In fact, we will do just about anything short of burning the boat to get rid of the disgusting little vermin. With all their redeeming qualities, they have only one bad one, and that is that they are one of the most revolting creatures on earth. It may be the squishy-crunchy sound they make when you step on them with your bare feet on the way to the head in the middle of the night, or the way they splatter all over your face when you swat one that you mistake for a mosquito that has landed on your nose just as you are falling asleep, or it might even be the guilty and sneaky way they scurry off the leftovers when you flick on the light. I, however, think the real reason we hate and persecute these harmless little insects is a moralistic one. I mean, any creature that can produce 20 to 40 offspring from a single coupling just has to be wicked, amoral, and a poor role model for our children.

Whatever the reasons, all cruisers hate them with a passion bordering on fanaticism, but the sad, tragic fact is that there is nothing you can do about them. They are a fact of the cruising life just like roily harbors and crooked port captains. You can fumigate the boat with noxious chemicals potent enough to destroy all life (except cockroaches) in a 5-mile radius, you can layer the bottoms of your lockers with boric-acid-balls made from secret recipes (which cruisers pass around the way salespeople pass around dirty jokes), you can buy as many Roach Motels as you'll find in the Miami suburbs, and you can repackage everything you buy into sterilized plastic containers before you bring it aboard. But the only thing you can hope to accomplish by all this activity is to keep their multitudes in check. Roaches get onto your boat mostly by hiding in your clothing and flying aboard at night, so short of stripping naked every time you come aboard and enclosing the entire craft in mosquito netting, there isn't much you can do. The buggy little buggers have you beat before you start.

While I'm on the subject of cockroaches, there is one more bit of cruising lore that I must dispense with, and that is the balderdash that you must remove all food from cardboard containers before bringing it aboard. The lore-makers say this is necessary because cockroaches like to lay their eggs on cardboard boxes; therefore, removing the food from the containers will somehow prevent the beastly beasts from getting aboard. I have even read that you are supposed to throw away your cardboard egg cartons.

(continued next page)

209

A WORD ABOUT ROACHES: YUCK CONTINUED

For one thing, the two most common species of cockroach found on boats (the German, which are the little brown ones, and the American, which are the big black ones) both lay their eggs in egg cases that are carried for a while in the abdomen of the female, then dropped. They are loose and never fastened to anything. These egg cases are large enough to be seen with even a cursory inspection, and they are a lot easier to remove from a box than the contents of the box. For another thing, while you are doing all this work, there is probably a big fat cockroach watching the whole process from under your hat brim.

Removing food and other items from cardboard containers is always a good idea when it is convenient and when the container isn't going to be used, but it is a bit silly when it involves boxes of powdered condiments or pancake flour or many other items better left in a box. On *Vicarious* we keep small containers of powdered products in the cardboard container slipped onto a large zip-lock bag with a few sachets of desiccant until we need them. Then we transfer the contents to an air-tight plastic container after we open the box.

Unpackaging merchandise on the dock is a routine part of the shopping ritual that most cruisers follow, but it is to get rid of the trash before it comes aboard the boat, not to get rid of cockroaches.

I'm not saying you should learn to like cockroaches, nor would I expect you to ever get used to finding their crunchy little carcasses in your green salad. But if you could develop a slight toleration for them rather than screeching like a stepped-on cat and trying to swat them with the frying pan every time one comes in sight (as does one person I know rather well but who, for the sake of domestic tranquility, will remain unnamed), you and your shipmates will be much happier.

Eat the Local Food

Cruisers who strive to eat the same diet they eat at home and don't learn about and sample local foods miss a large part of the joy of cruising, and I put these cruisers in the same category as those who make no effort to learn the language of the lands they visit. They are cruisers in body, not in spirit. Anytime you find yourself in a strange and exotic port, you should make every effort to sample the local food no matter how strange and exotic it might appear at first.

There are, of course, some foods that no matter how broad-minded you are, you won't find to your liking, and you will even find some, like trepang, an appalling glop made from sea cucumbers (the French call it *bêche-de-mer*, but that doesn't make it taste any better) and

Chicken McNuggets (have you ever looked inside a Chicken McNugget?) that are quite revolting. This is particularly true in places like China and California where the cultural differences are the most pronounced and where their normal fare may seem strange to your more sensitive palate.

The point is, of course, that the only way to tell which foods you are going to like and which you are likely to leave in the alley gutter is by trying them all. When I was in Japan as a young man in the early sixties, I horrified my American friends by eating raw fish and slurping raw eggs from the shells. I decided to forgo the raw eggs (yuck), but I developed a passion for sushi and sashimi that was 20 years ahead of the trend and is with me to this day.

Meet the Local People

The best way to get aquatinted with the local food in any distant harbor is to separate yourself from the pack of cruising boats and shun the local expat community for an afternoon or so. Then take a walk through the market area or amble leisurely along the streets of downtown. If you visit areas where foreigners are somewhat unusual (avoiding neighborhoods where squinty-eyed dudes with sallow complexions and pencil-thin mustaches stare at you out of the shadows of alleyways and abandoned buildings), you will likely be approached by friendly and curious locals. Often, these will be the more gregarious types who know a bit of English and want to show it off. If you can return their greeting in the native tongue (or a recognizable facsimile), a binding friendship can develop very quickly, and you will find yourself with an expert tour guide with no commercial interest in any of the typical tourist traps.

But communing with local residents of any place you stop will do a lot more than introduce you to the local viands. It will also reinforce your innately human realization that, wherever we roam in our boats, people are wonderful. Of course, if you are lucky, you will meet a few local dirt bags, but this also serves to illustrate how the lads playing *pétanque* on the beach in Vava'u are no different from the kids on the cricket pitch or baseball diamond back home. Of course they eat different food, and they will be happy to share it with you. If you reciprocate by serving up a feed of burgers on the barby, you will have made a friend for life and moved one small step closer to the idealistic goal of international harmony and intercultural tranquility that has eluded humanity from the beginning of time.

A Few Culinary Specifics

In Central America you will find delicacies like iguana and *tepesquintal* (a jungle rodent about the size of a large rabbit) on the menus of the better restaurants, along with more normal viands like *caballo* (horse meat) and a large assortment of unidentifiable seafood. Don't leave Mexico without trying the *cabrito assado* (grilled young goat often cooked on a bedspring suspended over hot coals), and when in the Rio Dulce, don't miss *pescaditos fritos* (a small local fish), a delicacy that is fried to a crisp on oil-drum skillets by street vendors.

The real joy of eating anywhere in the tropics is the assortment of exotic fruits and vegetables you will encounter. Some, like passion fruit and papaya, you will recognize from the desiccated samples that make it to the North American and European markets, but many others will be brand-new. Even familiar foods like pineapples and watermelons will take on new dimensions when purchased fresh from the native farmers who grew them. If you think you know what coconuts and bananas are, just wait until you sample the real thing. The little red bananas that some call *dedos de miel* (honey fingers) in South America, and ladies' fingers in Australia, are seldom found in markets anywhere and are usually given as a gift by the farmer. The milk from an unripened coconut is one of the sweetest nectars on earth. I have read that one can live a healthy if somewhat boring life eating nothing but these two foods.

Ironically, one of the things you won't find very often in the tropics is the tough-skinned, rather tasteless banana that we're all used to seeing in our local supermarkets. These are special export bananas that are picked and shipped green, and the natives seldom eat them. Please, however, don't take this as a slam at imported bananas—they are one of the most economical and nutritious foods around, but they aren't nearly as tasty as the real thing.

Some native foods, like plantains (they look like bananas but taste more like wooden potatoes) and taro (huge black parsnips with warts and varicose veins) are definitely an acquired taste, but you need to try these tropical staples prepared in several ways in order to give them a chance. I find many of these foods to be tedious but tolerable as long as they are served with other more tasty foods and drenched with hot sauce.

Canned New Zealand butter is available nearly everywhere except in the United States and ironically, New Zealand; it is the best butter you'll find anywhere. Ultra-high-temperature (UHT) milk is a cruising standard, comes in 1-liter boxes, and lasts for six months or more. We buy it by the case. It makes the use of powdered milk unnecessary, but if you do need powdered milk, the powdered whole milk available everywhere outside the United States is often better than anything you'll find at home.

Some things such as olive oil, anchovies (for the pizza), and basic spices such as oregano, basil, and whole black peppercorns can be scarce or expensive enough to warrant putting in a substantial supply. Unrefrigerated eggs will last for up to a month if they are kept cool and dry (no need to turn them or coat them with Vaseline). Turning the eggs once in a while may help prevent the yolk from sticking to the inside of the shell, but except for your longest passages in the Pacific, there is no reason to keep them long enough so that this becomes necessary.

Properly stored eggs won't spoil for up to a month or more, but they do go stale very rapidly. Week-old eggs are nutritious and perfectly safe to eat, as is week-old bread that hasn't gone moldy, but the difference in the taste and texture of a fresh egg over an old egg is so profound that you should never buy more eggs than you will use before your next trip to the market, and it is always worth the effort to find the source of the freshest local eggs when you enter a new harbor. The only time older eggs are superior to fresh is if you are going to boil them. Boiled eggs that are not three or four days old can be impossible to peel.

Most of the world outside the United States does not refrigerate eggs, and I'm told that in some European countries, it is illegal to sell eggs that have been refrigerated or washed. My reading indicates, however, that there is a definite advantage to refrigerating eggs in that they will stay fresh much longer. We don't keep eggs in the refrigerator on *Vicarious* (they take up too much room), but if you want to keep your eggs around for a long time, the refrigerator is the place to do it (the idea that refrigerated eggs spoil faster than ones kept at room temperature is yet another cruising myth). Once in the refrigerator, however, leave them there until they are used—they will go bad quite rapidly once removed because the mucous seal that protects and preserves the egg is very fragile, and exposure to refrigeration or any moisture will destroy it, thereby allowing the egg to spoil.

Fishy Fish and Foul Fowls

In any area you visit, the best source of information on local markets and foods is another cruiser who got there a week or so ahead of you. You'll never go wrong buying local produce from a local market and eating what the natives eat. But watch out for the fish and meat, especially chicken. Much of the developing world outside the major population centers doesn't have adequate refrigeration, and many countries we visited (particularly Honduras and Nicaragua) have lengthy power outages. When a power outage causes the meat in the freezer to thaw, most merchants simply refreeze it when the power is restored. A good way to confirm if that's been the case is to check the ice cream freezer. Ice cream becomes crystalline when re-frozen, so if the ice cream has ice in it, you know that the merchandise has been refrozen after a thaw. (In some countries, ice cream that is free of ice crystals is very hard to find.)

Even though frozen fish, poultry, and meat are available nearly everywhere, it is better to buy fish off the fishing boats (or catch your own), buy live poultry, and avoid beef, pork, horse (popular in Panama and often sold to unsuspecting cruisers as premium beef), and goat altogether unless you know the animal was killed that day. The quality butchers in the rural areas of Central and South America often have no refrigeration at all, and they will hang the head of the animal in the window as testimony to its freshness.

This problem with frozen food and refrigeration in developing countries is rapidly becoming less important, especially in the larger cities as more and more merchants invest in portable generators as backups to the municipal power system.

De Facto Vegetarianism

You will meet many vegetarians among the cruising community, and except for having the general appearance of asparagus stalks, they seem to get along quite well on their meatless diets. Although there are many vegetarians who shun flesh for moralistic reasons, most vegetarian cruisers don't eat meat for practical reasons. If you can live on a boat without eating meat, you will simplify your life to an enormous extent. Even those cruisers who don't become dedicated vegetarians, including those aboard *Vicarious*, find that meat becomes an occasional treat or an ingredient in a sauce or stew rather than the focus of the meal.

Most meat in the United States and Canada, especially beef, is hung or aged under moderate refrigeration for about 10 days before it is butchered. This encourages a bacterial process that imparts a lovely flavor and greatly decreases toughness by breaking down natural fibers in the flesh. Aging is not possible in the tropics, however, and most meat in rural areas is eaten or frozen within 24 hours of being slaughtered. Thus, even the best cuts of meat are tough with a strong flavor that most North Americans will find objectionable, and almost all meat, even goat and chicken, is very expensive in most tropical locales, while fresh and wholesome vegetables and fruits are often dirt cheap and readily available.

Another argument for vegetarianism is the tropical weather, which favors a vegetable diet over a meat diet. Your carnivorous author was raised as a bacon-and-egg kind of guy, and even now a slab of fried ham with three sunny-side ups and a side of home fries or grits is my idea of the perfect breakfast. But while cruising, breakfast on *Vicarious* is usually a large bowl of fresh papaya, pineapple, and mango with a sliced banana and a big glop of yogurt on top. If Susan isn't looking, I'll cover the whole thing with honey or raw sugar and mix in some corn flakes, wash it down with two or three cups of good Colombian coffee, and after a hearty belch I'm ready for just about anything the day has to offer.

Galley Layout and Hardware

When you bought your new old boat, you also bought the galley that was in it, and you are pretty much stuck with the basic layout. That doesn't mean, however, that before you start your cruise, you can't redo the existing galley to get it just the way you want it, and there are a few things you can do to greatly enhance the utility of this critical area. Except for the very top-of-the-line boats (Morris and Shannons and such), most galleys in newer boats are designed for weekend and coastal cruising in temperate or semitropical climates. The boat show queens from the major production boat companies will be designed for visual appeal with little regard for practicality. Storage will be inadequate. Half of what space you do have will be taken up by the plumbing for what is either a ridiculously oversized double sink (which apparently has the same boat show appeal as a queen-sized double bed) or a hopelessly inadequate one. The rest of the cabinets are unlikely to have the baffles and partitions necessary to keep food and utensils from shifting around while sailing.

Older boats can be even worse than new boats. They incorporate many of the above sins, and in addition, everything will be outdated and worn-out. In addition to being inadequate, the icebox insulation is likely to be saturated with water, and the countertops might even be covered with linoleum. Fortunately, a galley is a reasonable do-it-yourself upgrade for anyone handy with basic tools. Just try to keep the layout close to the original design, and don't get carried away ("Very easy to do," cries the voice of experience from somewhere near the forepeak) with nonessential doodads that can kill the kitty.

The Icebox/Refrigerator

Unless you are on a strict budget and a devout masochist, get over the idea of going cruising in the tropics without a good icebox. And due to recent developments in 12-volt refrigerators, there is no real reason to go without refrigeration. I know Chichester, Slocum, Uncle Freddie, and the rest of the pioneers didn't have refrigerators or even adequate iceboxes, but that was only because good refrigeration and plastic foam insulation weren't available then. If they could've had 'em, they would've had 'em.

When *Sultana* sailed away from Marblehead Harbor for our never-finished round-the-world adventure, she was equipped with a state-of-the-art compressor, which took up an entire locker in the pilothouse, and a cold-plate freezer installed in a huge icebox in the galley. The two were connected by insulated copper plumbing and charged with freon, a greenhouse gas that does terrible things to the ozone layer.

Unfortunately, the icebox relied on the original 2 inches of fiberglass insulation that the builder had installed in 1958, and changing it would have involved major surgery that we did not have the time nor money to perform until we reached New Zealand.

Thus, we spent three years island hopping in the tropics drinking tepid beer and buttering our toast with an involuntary form of ghee. While the refrigerator was capable of keeping the beer icy cold and the butter solid, and it made ice cubes if asked, it came at the cost of running the engine to replenish the batteries for six to eight hours a day. Naturally, we bought ice wherever we could, but a 20-pound block would be gone in two days, again due to the poor insulation in the icebox.

We solved the problem during *Sultana*'s refit by removing the liner of the icebox, installing 6 inches of foam insulation, and reinstalling a smaller epoxy/fiberglass–covered plywood liner. The capacity was reduced by more than half, but running the engine an hour a day was enough for the crew to enjoy too-cold-to-drink beer and too-hard-to-spread butter when either was fresh from the box.

When we bought her, *Vicarious* came equipped with a full-size chest-type refrigerator and a separate freezer. The previous owners wanted plenty of cold storage, but the combined bulk of the two units took up half the saloon and were a constant drain on the batteries. We got rid of the huge refrigerator and turned down the temperature on the smaller freezer until it was just right for my daily glass of Blue Moon pale ale.

This was my introduction to the Engel line of portable refrigerator-freezers, and I have not looked back. While the 84-quart model (https://www.engel-usa.com/products/ fridge-freezers/portable-top-loading-models/ engel-mt80-ac-dc-fridge-freezer) that we removed was way too big for a 37-foot cruising boat, the smaller 43-quart version (https://www.engel-usa.com/products/fridge-freezers/portable-top-loading-models/engel-mt45-ac-dc-fridge-freezer), which the previous owners used for a freezer, was perfect for our needs when it was used as a refrigerator.

The advantages of the Engel are many. It is a self-contained, plug-it-in-and-sail-away refrigerator. It is designed to be portable, so you could even take it to the beach in the dinghy if you wanted to. The 43-quart version draws 2.5 amps (less than half what the Alder Barber compressor on *Sultana* used), and it will run all day on a 60-watt solar panel; it has very few moving parts so it is as quiet as refrigerators come; and it requires no separate insulated cabinetry. The cost is about the same as an equivalent component product from Alder Barber or Isotherm. But installing a component system can be a major job whereas, providing you can find the room for it, installing an Engle is dead simple.

The Engel refrigerator on Vicarious resides in a compact cabinet where it is easily accessible without sacrificing counter space. It uses less of our valuable battery capacity than any refrigeration system we have ever used except an icebox. Its capacity of 43 quarts is more than enough for two thirsty cruisers who enjoy a glass of cold chablis in the evening and like to chill fresh fish before slicing it up into sashimi. The cabinet overhang makes a convenient spot for Nelson's food and water dishes where I trip over them only five or six times a day.

If you are considering forgoing refrigeration and sticking with a well-insulated icebox, good for you. Using ice will save you a lot of engine time and works very well indeed in areas where ice is regularly available, which is nearly everywhere. If you stick with ice, you won't need to replenish the batteries as often, but you won't save anything on the installation. A proper icebox with adequate insulation will cost about a much to build as a smaller Engel refrigerator, even if you do the work yourself. If you don't do the work yourself, count on it costing about twice as much. We will talk more about ice in the next section.

The low current draw and high efficiency of the Engel is attributed to the patented "swing compressor." I have no idea what that is, but it works. Engel refrigerators have no reciprocating piston to blow seals, and they don't use nasty chemicals. The patented part ensures that you can't yet get the same thing from a competitor.

If there is a downside to the Engel refrigerator, it is the problem you might have in fitting it into the existing space on your boat. But even if you must remove some cabinetry to squeeze it in, there is no longer any need for bulky insulation or special ventilated lockers for an external compressor.

Naturally, if your boat came with a functional component refrigeration system and a well-insulated icebox, you will want to stick with it. We all have plenty of things on which to spend our money without throwing away perfectly good stuff. But if yours is like most new old boats, it will have an out-of-date inefficient compressor with a poorly insulated icebox. In this case give the Engel a close look when it comes time for a new refrigerator.

Ice Is Nice

In the Caribbean, refrigeration isn't as important as it is in other places because ice is readily available, and unless you buy it at the marina bar, it's cheap. The best source of ice in most tropical areas is the fisherman's wharf where, for a few pesos, you can usually get more than you can ever use.

When we got to Isla Mujeres, the first thing Phillip and I did after clearing in was to head to the fish dock for ice. "¿Grande o pequeño?" asked the ice guy. Since the price was only a few pesos and we needed a lot of ice, I figured I'd better get the big block—whereupon the guy disappeared into the bowels of the icehouse to reappear pushing a block of ice only slightly smaller than a Volkswagen bus. We chipped off what we needed, and I gave the rest to the very amused skipper of a nearby shrimp boat.

Naturally, I felt pretty stupid for making such an obvious blunder, but when I related my tale at a cruisers' potluck supper that night, I discovered that just about everyone I talked to had fallen for the same scam. But what the hell, we got our ice, the skipper of the shrimp boat got a few chuckles at the expense of those crazy cruisers, the ice guy made a few extra pesos, the potluck was delicious, and we learned a bit about conducting business in Latin America. It was a small price to pay for a great day.

A warning though: fish-dock ice is often contaminated with giardia lambia and cryptosporidium (the critters that cause gardiasis, better known as Montezuma's revenge or the cruisers' quickstep) and lots of other unpleasant stuff, so don't use it in drinks. Buy a bag of cubes at the bar to use in your martinis. It's probably contaminated too, so add a little extra gin. It won't kill the germs, but it will make you feel better about drinking them. For some reason, outside the Caribbean ice is much harder to find, and a refrigerator really pays off. On *Sultana* we always used ice when we could get it and only ran the refrigerator when we had to.

On *Vicarious*, we have an excellent refrigerator (as explained above) so we don't use ice as much as we did when we were living on *Sultana*.

But we still keep a collapsible ice chest in the lazarette. It stays out of sight and takes up little space, but we can put into service any time that cubes or blocks are available and when the refrigerator is in overflow mode.

The Freezer

The refrigeration we installed on *Sultana* at the refit was capable of making fine ice cubes and keeping a few pounds of meat frozen even in the hottest climates. The problem was that frozen food required too much battery power to keep frozen, and making a few ice cubes for a proper round of gin and tonics required about four hours of engine time. Unless we were motoring for long distances (such as on the Intracoastal Waterway or on days that the wind wouldn't blow), we didn't use the refrigerator at all and relied on ice, even after the refit.

We have met a lot of cruisers over the years who have large efficient freezers, and they seem to manage the power requirements without issues. But our experience indicates the expense of installing and operating any kind of freezer far exceeds any advantage of having one.

Cruisers with successful freezers aboard all seem to be very organized and the sort of folks who can plan meals weeks in advance. Susan and I aren't that sort of folks. Meal planning on *Vicarious* often involves waiting until we are both hungry then checking the larder to see what is available. This leaves no time to thaw anything, much less some unidentifiable block of frozen mystery that we failed to label last year when we put it in there.

If we had a freezer, I'm afraid that I would fill it up with things like fish heads that I *might* use for crab bait someday or with foods that neither of us like that much but hate to throw out because we don't like to waste good food. That means we would leave it in the freezer for about a year, then throw it out, just the way we did when we lived in a house.

Sun-dried fish is a staple with the natives in the Caribbean. It is easy to do on a boat, is delicious, and lasts forever with no refrigeration.

Vicarious had a freezer when we bought her, but as related above, we converted it to a refrigerator when we removed the overly large top-loader that we inherited with the boat. Since then we have sailed without any freezer at all, and we haven't missed it. At times it would be handy to freeze the extra fish we catch, but I have developed a real taste for sun-dried mahi-mahi and wahoo, so it wouldn't be used much even for that.

The Galley Range

A good cruising boat needs a top-of-the-line cookstove with a large oven. In most cases, if you bought a boat that has already been used for cruising, your galley already has an adequate stove, and though it might be a little rusty and worn, if it was a quality unit to begin with, it can usually be refurbished. We replaced the burners, knobs, and burner inserts on the 20-year-old Seaward Hiller Range that came with *Sultana* and got a practically new stove out of the deal. After four years of daily use, the top of the oven rusted through (our own fault for not cleaning up spills right away), and we installed a new three-burner Force 10 for the refit. When we sold *Sultana* 10 years later, the stove was still in like-new condition and ready for another 20 years of hard use.

Vicarious came with a nearly new Force 10 that was the smaller version of the stove we installed in *Sultana*. It has only two burners, which hasn't been a problem, but the smaller oven has been a challenge for Susan who liked the big hot oven in *Sultana*.

I don't cook as often on *Vicarious* as I did on *Sultana*, mostly because Susan does such an excellent job in the galley, but I have always enjoyed making pizza. The larger oven on *Sultana* made excellent pizzas when a proper stone was used, but the little oven in *Vicarious* can't quite manage the task. After a bit of experimentation, I have developed an acceptable recipe for stove-top pizza that is finished under the broiler.

I will share that recipe with you below, but the point is that we have adapted to the smaller stove, for now, and we've given up on the idea of upgrading to a larger one ... for now.

Galley Stove Fuel Types

A favorite topic on all the cruising forums and in most of the popular cruising books deals with the best fuel to use for the galley stove. Butane, paraffin or kerosene, alcohol, propane, and compressed natural gas (CNG) all have their advocates, but today propane has emerged as the fuel of choice for 95 percent of all cruising boats, and the other types of fuel aren't really worth bothering with. Propane is now available just about everywhere; it's cheap, clean, and safe if only the most basic safety precautions are taken.

With any other type of fuel, you are bound to run into supply problems somewhere in the world. Butane is hard to find in French Polynesia, kerosene is expensive everywhere (and may be poor quality in the United States and Canada), and CNG is impossible to find outside of big cities. Propane also burns hotter and cooks better than any of the others.

Denatured alcohol is a popular stove fuel with cruisers in smaller boats and those who don't do a lot of cooking. An alcohol flame burns much cooler than other popular fuel choices, so cooking times for baked goods and complicated recipes become interminable. Even so, the Origo line of unpressurised alcohol stoves is quite popular, and owners of them can get defensive when their stove choice is criticized.

My personal experience with alcohol as a cooking fuel was with our very first boat. It was only a 21-footer, but we covered a good part of the New England coast while we had her. The little two-burner alcohol stove served yeoman duty for three sailing seasons, and we managed quite well with only one frying pan and a small pot. We were young, of course, and consumed with the excitement of visiting exotic places like Cuttyhunk Island and the Isle of Shoals in our new boat. We would have been happy, and quite often were happy, with peanut butter sandwiches and canned tomato soup. Any hot food and a cup of fresh coffee in the morning made it heaven, and the fuel used in getting there was incidental.

If you have a good-quality stove of adequate size in your boat when you buy it, stick with it no matter what fuel it burns. If it is CNG, however, and you are headed for foreign waters, you will make life a lot easier by changing the burners to the propane type. And if it is a pressurized alcohol stove, you should replace it right away as they have a terrible habit of flaring up and setting things, like you and your boat, alight.

You will eventually want to replace your stove, and when you do, you can save yourself a lot of aggravation by sticking with propane.

Range Size

The ideal range size for your cruising boat is the same size as the one you are used to at home, and although this isn't practical, the larger the stove, the happier the cook, and as I said before, the happier the cook, the happier the crew. The more-or-less standard size for cruising ranges is 21 inches wide and 20 inches deep for a full-sized stove (as opposed to 30 inches by 30 inches for your home range). Of course, there are a lot of smaller ones made to fit smaller galleys, and it is amazing what wonderful meals a good cook can produce on these tiny ranges.

Most full-sized ranges built for boats crowd three burners onto the cooktop in such a way that only two are ever usable. Two burners are usually more than enough, but few two-burner stoves have an adequate oven. A broiler is not a necessity, but it is real handy for melting the cheese on your French onion soup and putting an extra crunch in the garlic bread. And it is essential for the frying-pan pizza recipe below.

Stove Safety

Don't buy a stove that doesn't have a good set of fiddles to keep pots and pans from sliding around the cooktop. To be effective, they should grip the pot at least 2 inches above the stovetop. You will also want your propane tanks installed in compliance with the dictates of common sense and the U.S. Coast Guard (even though the two are often at odds), which means they should be enclosed in an isolated locker with an overboard drain and fitted with a remote solenoid shutoff that can be actuated from the galley. The solenoid should be de-energized every time you turn off your stove, and it should include a large red warning light that indicates when the solenoid is activated. Each installation should include a pressure gauge installed between the tank and the regulator.

The gauge is useless for determining the amount of fuel left in the tank (unless the tank is empty), but it is essential for checking for leaks. Every time a tank is changed or whenever any work is done on the propane system, you should charge the system, then shut off the tank and the stove valves, leaving the solenoid and any other in-line valves, such as selector switches, open. Any drop in pressure indicated by the gauge means you have a leak in the line, and all activity must cease until this leak is located and repaired. A little soapy water will usually find the leak in short order, but don't ever be tempted to operate the system until you find it.

Always carry a backup stove on long passages. If you are careful, it is unlikely that you will run out of propane, although that does happen, but if you experience an electrical failure, your solenoid will be inoperative, and rather than attempt to bypass it to get your stove operating, it makes a lot more sense to do your basic cooking on a backup stove until you get the juice turned back on. The Force 10 Seacook is a very popular emergency unit with cruisers, but at around $200, they are a bit pricey. *Vicarious* carries a one-burner stainless camping stove that uses canned butane for fuel. We have needed it only once when we ran out of propane in the Bay of Islands (because New Zealand law forbids the supplier filling our tanks without sending them off to Auckland for a NZ$30 inspection sticker), but it has come in handy many other times for camping on the beach and backpack trips inland. We now also carry a spare solenoid, which we can install if the weather and sea conditions permit.

Stove gimbals aren't necessary on many heavy cruising boats that are capable of standing up to a stiff breeze, and they can be a real nuisance and even dangerous. Light boats that heal and bounce around a lot might need them, but do without them if you can. On a stiff boat it often makes more sense to mount the stove athwartship rather than fore and aft if you have a choice (which you probably don't). The porpoising action of many cruising boats around the lateral axis is milder than the rolling action around the longitudinal axis, and an athwartship-mounted stove without gimbals might be more stable than a fore-and-aft mounted stove with gimbals. Also, if there is a spill, and athwartship stove will tend to dump the contents of a pot to the side instead of slopping hot soup directly on the cook. If you do need gimbals on your stove, make sure a heavy pot placed on the stovetop won't tilt the stove enough to cause a spill, and get the kind with which you can lock the stove in place when they aren't in use.

Microwave Ovens

A small microwave oven is one of those things that can help to make your boat your home. You don't really need a microwave oven, of course, but they're useful and cheap so if you can spare the space, why not have one? Microwaves are useless for any real cooking, but they work fine for a lot of ancillary jobs like melting butter, boiling water, thawing meat, and reheating leftovers. They're also great for putting the steam back in a cup of coffee and can be a lifesaver when you need a quick cup of hot soup on a long cold watch. The smallest one you can buy uses 600 watts, and that is plenty big enough for most boats. The one on *Vicarious* cost about $75 from Amazon.com (including postage).

These little microwaves still draw a lot of power but only for short spurts, and they work fine on modern inverters. A lot of traditionalists and old-timers sneer at *Vicarious*'s microwave; we just sneer back and invite them in for a hot cup of tea: "Be ready in just a second."

THE KITCHEN SINK

In the first edition of this book, I outlined a brilliant plan for replacing the galley sink with a shallow tray made out of solid-surface counter top material like Corian. As brilliant as this system was, it failed to gain the universal acceptance of the cruising community that I expected. If fact, on more than one occasion, I was subjected to ridicule and sarcasm, and chief among my critics was none other than Susan, our chief cook.

Early on, I stopped asking "What would you like for Christmas dear?" because I knew what was coming: "How about a new sink?" Or "Let's walk into the flea market and see what we can find" would bring "Yes, perhaps we can find a used sink."

Thus, I have finally capitulated to the base mentality of the masses and accepted humanity's collective failure to recognize true genius, even when it stands full force in front of them. I have diplomatically refrained from even mentioning the possibility of replacing the sink in *Vicarious* with a shallow tray made from Corian, and domestic tranquility has prospered.

Fortunately, the previous owners of our new old boat had installed an excellent sink with a full-sized faucet and spray nozzle that is perfect for our needs. It is round and deep and big enough to hold all the dirty detritus generated by a party of up to six rambunctious diners. And it makes life in the galley a true joy as I no longer have to answer the inevitable question from every new visitor who comes aboard: "Where's the sink?"

Food Storage

Storage on any small boat is a problem, and storage of foodstuffs in the galley is particularly vexing, especially if you have been used to large and commodious kitchen cupboards at home (which, if you are a normal sort of person, were also jammed to overflowing, no matter how commodious they were). Neat and orderly storage of food and galley gear is one of the devils with which we on *Vicarious* have been wrestling ever since we left Marblehead, and so far the devil is winning. He hasn't quite pinned us to the mat, however, and we are slowly learning how to cope with this problem thanks to a few simple adaptations that I will share with you here.

No Vacancies

Don't assume that the builder of your boat spent a lot of time designing the storage lockers in your boat, particularly those in the galley. Plastic boats with molded hull liners are particularly bad in this regard; I have seen a lot of galley lockers with fancy doors and hardware (visible items), and no bottom so that anything placed in the lockers slides right into the bilge. What few shelves there are often won't have fiddles so when you open a starboard locker while you are on the port tack, you get a face full of whatever was in there. These ills aren't restricted to newer boats either. We found many places where we were able to gain valuable storage room on *Vicarious* with a few minor and inexpensive modifications.

One of the first things you should do is fit every shelf in your boat with a fiddle. Make them from thin (a quarter inch thick is fine) strips of an exotic hardwood like mahogany or bubinga cut about 2 inches wide (it's expensive but you don't need much), then give them a shipshape oil finish. Old oak sail battens, from the good old days when battens were made out of oak and yachtsmen were made out of money,

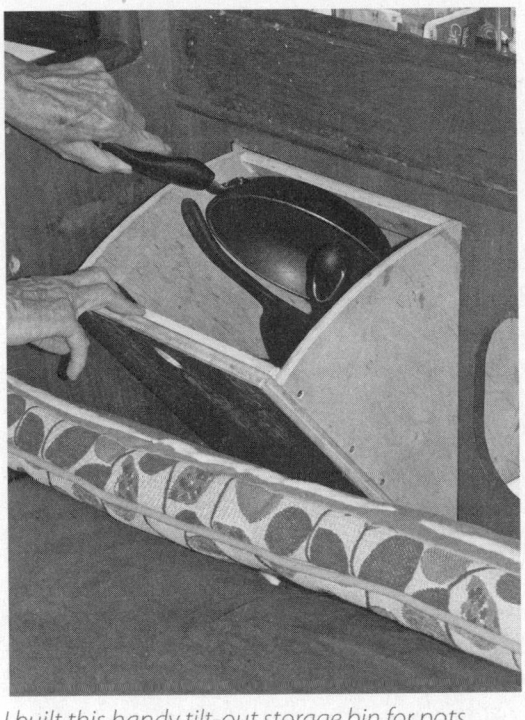

I built this handy tilt-out storage bin for pots and pans in an unused vacancy behind the seat cushions in the saloon. It is right next to the stove and out of sight until a cook pot is needed. A careful investigation will usually reveal usable space behind panels that can be converted into valuable storage with the simple addition of a door or access port.

make excellent fiddles. Many are already finished so all you have to do is trim them to length and fasten them to the front of your shelves with copper or bronze nails. While you are at it, look for wasted space where additional shelves can be added.

Fit bottoms to any lockers that don't have them. Large lockers can be fitted with false bottoms to give you several layers of storage where before you only had one. The trick here, of course, is to store seldom-used materials in the bottom, less accessible tier and the more frequently used stuff in the top tier. While this sounds like a commonsense thing to do, it is much harder in practice than in theory. Somehow, the thing you want right now is always in the bottom tier, and you have to take everything out of the top tier to get at it. Another trick that can help ease access to large lockers is to fit front-opening ones with a hatch through the top and top-opening ones with a hatch in the front, thus giving you a choice of two ways to go wrong rather than just one when you are searching for some critical item.

Make a careful survey of your boat for any unused space behind bulkheads or under the cabin sole where the addition of a simple hatch or port will provide additional storage. Naturally you will want to make sure there is really nothing behind the bulkhead lest you cut into the nearly full holding tank with your hole saw, but I haven't seen a boat yet where considerable new space couldn't be found with a little looking around.

Yet another possibility is to look under and behind drawers, which are another item that sales-oriented boatbuilders like to provide a lot of, but they invariably make them under-sized and put them in illogical places. Drawers that aren't properly constructed waste a huge amount of space—you often can find enough room to store thin flat items under them. Better yet, consider throwing the drawers away, trimming the opening with some of that bubinga left over from the fiddles, and use the entire cavity as a stuff locker.

Be particularly careful about what you store under your floorboards in the bilge. Even a tiny amount of seawater can wreak havoc with anything made out of metal, and if any oil from the engine gets into the seawater, it can make an unbelievable mess of anything stored there. Never store canned food in the bilge, and don't put your extra cans of paint in there either. (If you must carry extra paint, put each can in a plastic gallon milk bottle with a cut-off top.

That way, when the can rusts through, the milk bottle will contain the mess—somewhat.)

Essential Galley Gear

You don't need a lot of pots and pans in your galley, but the ones you do need should be the best money can buy. But this doesn't mean the most expensive cookware is the best. Several years ago, we switched from titanium-plated aluminum sauté pans that were very expensive indeed, to a simple cast-iron skillet and a stove-top griddle. The cast iron cost only a fifth of what the fancy stuff cost, and it actually cooks better on the small stove we use on *Vicarious*. Too many cruisers use worn-out and rejected cookware from home, and while this works just fine for weekend boating, it's a serious mis-take when you are living and cruising on your boat full-time. Good cookware will last forever. Cheap cookware is useless.

Except for two Teflon-coated 8-inch alu-minum sauté pans for omelets and pancakes, we don't use easy-clean coated pots and pans. The inexpensive ones are too flimsy, and even the best lose their coating after a while. Here's a list of the most important items in our galley that has evolved after 20 years of trial and error:

- Two **8-inch aluminum sauté pans,** men-tioned above.
- A **10-inch cast-iron skillet** used to cook anything that needs to be cooked in a fry-ing pan. Conventional wisdom has it that cast-iron cookware doesn't work well on a boat. Most cruising cooks will tell you that it is too heavy and rusts too easily, but I suspect that most of them have never tried it. We have found the heavy iron is a real advantage on a small stove as it distributes the heat evenly, and rust is never an issue if the pan it used regularly and cleaned properly—that is, never in soapy water.

- A **12-inch *plancha*,** which is a shallow frying pan that is a standard item in Spanish kitchens. Ours is made of cast aluminum with a slightly concave bottom like a flat wok. It is perfect for toasting bread and sandwiches because it requires only a tiny amount of butter or oil. The *plancha* makes a wonderful serving dish, and it is the ultimate pizza pan if you like a crisp and crunchy crust. Unfortunately, we had to leave our *plancha* in New Zealand when we moved onto *Vicarious*, and we have substituted a 10-inch cast-iron griddle. It does the same thing as the *plancha*, but it isn't nearly as much fun to talk about.
- A **2.5-quart stainless saucepan** with a cover for soups and stews and sauces. Ours is Farberware, and it seems to be indestructible.
- An **8-quart covered stewpot** with a steamer rack for cooking pasta, steaming lobsters and shellfish, making stews and goulash, and everything else you need a big pot for. This too is Farberware and indestructible.
- A **6-quart stainless mixing bowl** that also doubles as a salad bowl and dishpan. It can also serve as a double boiler by placing it on top of a stewpot. Plastic is OK for this sort of thing, but it does and will melt when you get it too close to the stove—as is bound to happen in the confines of the largest galley. And, of course, plastic doesn't work as a double boiler.
- Two **stainless 9- by 5-inch bread pans,** an assortment of silicon muffin tins, and a popover pan (Susan makes fantastic popovers). We also have two smaller silicone bread pans that I use occasionally. Susan prefers the standard-size 9-by-5 pans, which we haven't been able to find in silicone, so for now, we have both. Unfortunately, the small oven in *Vicarious* can't quite handle popovers as they require a very high heat, but we are holding on to the popover pan anyway, just in case the tooth fairy (or some other equally benevolent entity) brings us a new stove someday.
- A **10-inch chef's knife.** A good chef's knife is outrageously expensive—our Henckels costs about $100—but you need only one per lifetime, and when you really need a knife, you don't need a cheap one or a dull one. A good sharpening steel is also expensive, but get one anyway. A good way to spot a quality knife—besides the price—is to look at how the blade is ground. Cheap knives are usually hollow ground; quality knives are usually flat ground. If you don't know the difference between the two grinding methods, don't feel bad, but if you can see a hollow where the knife was sharpened at the factory, it's probably a cheapo.
- A **good paring knife.** It won't be as expensive as a chef's knife, but it will still cost a few bucks. A good one will make a world of difference in your cooking, however, so spend the money.
- A **pepper mill.** Nearly all spices and herbs taste much better fresh than preground or dried, but nowhere is the difference more dramatic than with black pepper. The preground stuff is just about tasteless, and there is little reason to carry any, but freshly ground pepper makes a world of difference in many dishes. Salt mills are also popular, but there is little reason to have one unless you favor sea salt finely ground. Sea salt has a unique flavor reminiscent of Cape Cod in the summer at low tide. It comes in flakes that are fine just the way they are, and I see no reason to grind them up.
- **Cookbooks.** When we left Marblehead, we had more than 100 cookbooks in our kitchen library, on *Sultana* we had a grand

total of 4, and on *Vicarious*, we have 2. Susan favors the *Joy of Cooking* by Irma Rombauer and Marion Rombauer Becker because it contains nearly everything a cookbook needs to contain, and it gives precise and detailed instructions on hundreds of fantastic recipes. My favorite is *The Fannie Farmer Cookbook* by Marion Cunningham because it is simple and basic and easy for a simple and basic cook like me to understand. We also have a dozen or so cookbooks on Kindle, including the *Boat Galley Cookbook,* by Jan Irons and Caroline Shearlock; the *One-Pan Galley Gourmet,* by Don Jacobson and John Roberts; and *Beard on Bread,* a classic by James Beard. The Kindle books are read more for inspiration than for recipes, and both the *One-Pan Galley Gourmet* and the *Boat Galley Cookbook* are full of informative tips on galley cooking, food storage, and everything to do with eating well on a boat.

No-Pressure Cooking

Before we left Marblehead on *Sultana,* we read all the cruising books and magazine articles on how best to reinvent ourselves from weekend coastal cruisers to full-time world voyagers, and one of the things that all the experts agreed on was that we had to have a pressure cooker. So we bought one, a shiny aluminum one with a big rubber seal and a little wobbly thing on top that danced around in an amusing manner while our food cooked inside.

Alas, after five years of trial and error (lots of trials and a great many errors), we gave up and donated the thing to a family in Fiji who needed a new pot. In wasn't that it didn't do all the things that the experts said it would. It did. It cooked vegetables in half the time of conventional methods, you could bake bread (of sorts) in it, and you could preserve food in it for weeks and weeks if you liked. But in the end

we decided that, like the generators and watermakers that experts also classify as essential to happiness afloat, the advantages of pressure cookers weren't worth the effort of using them, even after factoring in the entertainment value of the little wobbly thing on top.

My problems with pressure cookers are many. For one thing, you don't really save that much time. Once you finish cooking in the damn things, you must deal with a quantity of dangerously hot water under high pressure. You can release the pressure by removing the little weight from the top, thus filling the boat with steam, which is not what most boats cruising in the tropics really need most of the time. Or you can wait around for the thing to cool off, which takes more time than if you just cooked whatever is in there the normal way.

The big objection I have to cooking in the pressure cooker, however, is the taste of the food that comes out of them. Vegetables cooked under pressure are invariably overcooked, mushy, and tasteless, while most of the nutrients get thrown out with the water. A simple steamer rack on the bottom of your kettle cooks vegetables better and faster with less water than a pressure cooker, especially if you stop cooking them while they are still nice and crunchy instead of being as soggy as an overboard jelly donut.

Another favorite use of the pressure cooker is to make soups, stews, and goulashes that can be cooked in about 20 minutes rather than the two hours or so that a real stew needs to simmer. It does save a lot of time, but the problem is that the tough meats that make the best stews just get tougher and lose their flavor when cooked quickly over high heat. Stews and soups need to be cooked for a long time over very low heat, and the pressure cooker just doesn't make it. Besides, soups and stews are great while cruising in the fjords of Norway or in the Falkland Islands where you need a lot of calories just to stay warm, but we spend most of our time in the tropics where a cold tomato bisque is much more welcome than a beef stroganoff and is much easier to prepare.

Many cruising books talk about using the pressure cooker as a way to preserve food. The idea is that you cook the food in the pressure cooker, then leave the food hermetically sealed in the pressure cooker for a week or so until you are ready to eat it. This looks good in principle, but everything is dependent on there being a perfect seal between the lid and the pot, and there is no way of checking the integrity of this seal without breaking it. Thus, you won't know if the food in the pressure cooker has spoiled or not until you go to use it, and you may not even know then because many bacteria, including botulism, don't give off any odor. Who needs to take the chance?

If you really need to preserve food without refrigeration, pack it in salt and hang it in the sun for a week or so the way the Central American Indians do (any one of them can show you how it's done in about 10 minutes). Most foods preserved this way will last longer than a false rumor.

Pressure cookers work just fine in high-altitude places like Denver and Innsbruck and Guatemala City where the reduced atmospheric pressure gives them a definite advantage, but if you plan to do most of your cruising down here at sea level, like most of us, you might find that you can do very nicely without one.

Galley Gadgets

There are a lot of other things you'll need in your galley, of course, but try to keep them simple, basic, and stainless, and you can't go too far wrong. Although I have to admit to a weakness for esoteric kitchen tools, avoid collecting gadgets if you can. I fell in love with a tortilla press I bought in Mexico even though it takes up a lot of room and we hardly ever use it.

And then there is the coffee filter that we used to have. Before we left Marblehead, I bought a gold-plated guaranteed-for-life coffee filter so we wouldn't have to buy hundreds of those cone-shaped paper coffee filters. It cost a lot of money, but I figured, what the hell, at what we were paying for the paper filters, we'd break even in less than 20 years. I can still remember the day I threw it overboard with the dishwater. It was beautiful how the gold plating caught the light and reflected the sun and how long it stayed in sight as it drifted away into the depths.

Electric Galley Gadgets

With modern inverters and battery systems, if you want electrical gadgets in the galley, there is no reason not to have them. Don't waste your money on 12-volt kitchen appliances because they tend to be poorly made, flimsy, and usually cost three or four times what the standard 120-volt household appliances cost. Most of the ones sold in your local department store will work just fine, particularly with the trend away from using metal or casings and other external parts. The plastics revolution is truly a boon to the cruising chef.

Here are a few gadgets you will find in *Vicarious*'s galley:

- **Toaster.** Toast on a boat is a problem. The little camp gadgets that go over your stovetop burners don't work very well, and even the stainless ones rust away in a few months. You can make excellent toast on a *plancha* or under the broiler if your oven has one, but *plancha* toast is really fried bread and not very healthy, and making toast in your oven isn't energy efficient. The best bet is a small inexpensive toaster from a discount store. We bought ours, a compact Hamilton Beech two-slice, from Amazon. com for about $20. Like microwave ovens, toasters draw a lot of juice but only for short periods. However, make sure your inverter will handle heating elements—many of the old square-wave inverters won't.

- **Coffee grinder.** All coffee snobs know that freshly ground coffee is the best, and while those hand grinders with the little wooden box on the bottom make great planters for your ivy at home, they don't grind coffee beans worth . . . well, worth beans. Get a simple 120-volt electric one from a discount store. Just make sure that it grinds with a burr and not with whirling blades like a blender, or the coffee snobs will sneer at you.

- **Hand blender.** Not a Cuisinart or a "food-processing station," but a $20 hand blender. Perfect for making bread crumbs, soups, milkshakes, frozen banana daiquiris, and about a zillion other things you can't make any other way.

- **Hand mixer.** This simplest and smallest one you can find will be fine for whipping cream, mixing batters, and dozens of other things better done manually. There is no question that a hand whisk is better that an electric mixer for many culinary tasks, but flailing about like a monkey trying to catch a butterfly in the confines of a galley takes too much effort, and I never do it unless Susan or someone else whom I am trying to impress with my culinary expertise is watching.

Sharing the Chores

Cooking on a boat can either be an ordeal or a creative joy, and there is no reason why it should be anything but the latter other than the attitudes and prejudice of the crew. Anyone can become a passable or even a passionate cook if the task is approached with a positive attitude and a bit of diligence.

I recall the first time I cooked for a dinner party at my apartment on Beacon Street in Boston. There were six of us including Susan, whom I had just met and was quite anxious to impress. The menu included roast duck with orange sauce, and while the duck was pretty straightforward and came out of the oven in fine shape, the sauce was a disaster. It started out OK, and I never did figure where I went wrong, but I ended up with a black goo that resembled road tar—it even smelled like road tar.

With about 20 minutes until my guests were to arrive, I literally ran to the all-night grocery on Newbury Street and bought one bottle of everything I could find that was made from oranges. I bought a quart of orange juice, a jar of orange marmalade, a small jug of Cointreau, and a tiny bottle of grenadine. Back at the apartment with no time to spare, I threw the lot into a saucepan over high heat and stirred up what was to be my very first culinary triumph. Everyone agreed that it was indeed one of the most unusual orange sauces that they had ever tasted, and we're talking serious epicures here. Unfortunately, up until now it has remained my only culinary triumph, but that one experience gave me the confidence to keep trying, and I've come close to triumphing again on several occasions.

Today, Susan and I share the cooking aboard *Vicarious*, although I remain in the category of the adventuresome dilettante, and her refined and sophisticated cooking skills make my efforts look like those of . . . well, an adventuresome dilettante. Regardless of our relative prowess in the galley, we both enjoy cooking and respect each other's tastes and techniques; as a result, the crew of *Vicarious* is one of the best fed in the fleet.

A Few Fantastic Recipes from Vicarious's Galley

I must confess that the hundred or so cookbooks mentioned above (now packed away in a storage bin in New Zealand) were purchased by me, not Susan. I am an unrepentant cookbook freak and buy and read them like some people buy and read detective novels. My all-time favorite is *Beard on Bread* by the late James Beard, and my least favorites are any of the many that expend more effort on glossy photography than on refining the recipes, a prejudice that may have come from the years I worked as a slick food photographer. My driving ambition is to someday write my own cookbook to share some of the wonderful recipes I've collected that work well in a cruising galley.

As a preview to this coming opus, I've given in to the clamor of public demand and share below a few samples of what to expect. The following few recipes are selected for their simplicity, versatility, and adaptability to the cruising life. None of these are original, but all have an original element or twist that makes them particularly useful on board *Vicarious*. I offer them with the hope that you will find them as useful as we have. All the following recipes are designed to feed four ravenous crew, which Susan and I find just right for the two if us (we always eat more on a boat than ashore). Adjust quantities to fit your circumstances.

NOW A WORD ABOUT GHEE: IT'S PRONOUNCED "GEE"

Some years ago, while we were still on *Sultana*, I got a tip from a fellow cruiser (the very best kind of tip because you know it is going to work) on a way to reduce the workload of the onboard refrigeration by clarifying all the butter. Once all the corruptible solids and water have been removed from the butter, it can be stored at room temperature indefinitely, even in the tropics. I tried it; it worked well; and I have been clarifying the butter ever since.

The one flaw in my friend's tip is that, where he used it as a substitute for butter, I find that it isn't up to being spread on toast or used in sandwiches. It tastes OK, but it melts at a very low temperature and makes the toast (pancake, crumpet, muffin, or something else) soggy. That's not a problem if you keep a stick of regular butter in the chiller for your toast and use the clarified stuff for everything else.

Then, sometime later, I learned from another food-savvy cruiser that clarified butter is used extensively in Indian cooking. It is called *ghee* in Hindi and Sanskrit, and, he assured me, it is exactly the same thing as clarified butter. Since *ghee* sounds much more worldly than *clarified butter* (or even *drawn butter*, the term used in New Zealand and other former British colonies), and since I am always trying to enhance my standing with food snobs, I started calling my clarified butter *ghee*.

Ghee making in Fiji

While cruising in Fiji, I was taught to make ghee properly by these two delightful Hindu ladies. Unfortunately they spoke only Hindi so while the demonstration was fascinating, I am still a bit unclear on the actual procedure. Real ghee has a nutty brown color that comes from cooking the butter solids until they are dark and crispy and delicious.

(continued next page)

NOW A WORD ABOUT GHEE: IT'S PRONOUNCED "GEE" CONTINUED

That is, until we got to Fiji where, after a 45-minute lecture from a Hindu taxi driver cum tour guide named Rakesh, I learned that ghee is definitely not the same thing as clarified butter. After the lecture, Rakesh took us to his home to meet his mother and sister both of whom shrieked with laughter when told of my faux pas. The two ladies then further enlightened me on the art of making ghee with a demonstration and a detailed explanation in Hindi (neither lady spoke a word of English), which lent an authentic air to the discussion but left me a bit vague on the details.

I came away re-indoctrinated and chastised. But not enough to stop calling my clarified butter *ghee*. The coolness factor and the obvious impression it makes with food snobs is just too great to relinquish for mere technical accuracy. Besides, I do use real ghee when I can get it and can afford it (it is about twice the cost of butter in most places) because it has a delectable nutty flavor, and for our purposes, it is interchangeable with clarified butter. So, for the sake of coolness and snobbery, and to enhance my reputation as a *bon viveur*, let it be ghee for the remainder of this treatise.

How to Make Ghee

The admittedly inauthentic (but still delicious) form of ghee we use on *Vicarious* is dead simple to make. First melt a pound of butter in a saucepan over very low heat (in the tropics, just leave it out on the counter for an hour or so), then transfer it to a plastic tub with tapered sides (to facilitate removal), and pop it into the refrigerator/icebox until it settles into three layers and solidifies. The water will be on the bottom; the solids will float on top of the water; and the butterfat will be on top. With a large spoon, transfer the butterfat to another container, leaving the water and solids where they were. The solids are delicious spread on toast, so don't throw them away.

Water, of course, is not a natural part of butter. It is added by the manufacturer to make us think that we are buying a pound of butter when we are actually buying 14 ounces. But don't blame the U.S. food industry. They sell us adulterated butter (and bacon and ham and lots of other things) for our own good because they know that if they only put 14 ounces of butter in a package, we might think we were being cheated (wouldn't want that to happen, would we).

(The difference between ghee and clarified butter, in case you are interested and don't already know, is that the solids and water are cooked away in preparing ghee while they are skimmed off in making clarified butter. Ghee purists will natter on about using only buffalo butter and cooking it in a hand-hammered copper pot over a donkey-dung fire, but as far as I'm concerned, none of that has any snob appeal at all.)

A Simple, Foolproof Way to Cook Pasta, Rice, Eggs, and Other Boiled Things

This isn't a recipe as much as a clever method for cooking anything that needs to be boiled, including most pastas, oatmeal, grits (a personal favorite), rice, garbanzo beans, and boiled eggs, while conserving fuel and without wasting a drop of precious water. It was actually given to me by my grandmother many years ago when I was just a young lad, but I have never forgotten it. And it is one of the few ideas that I haven't encountered in any of the cooking tips listed on any of the cruising blogs or in the popular cookbooks.

It is quite simple, really. Anytime you want to cook spaghetti, noodles, elbows, bowties, rice, boiled vegetables, or hot cereal, put the item in a pot (just about any pot will do as long as it has a tight cover), and add enough cold water to cover the food to a depth of half an inch. This should equal a ratio of about two parts water to one part food. Potatoes, carrots, or any other large veggies need to be diced, of course; large (lasagna) or long (spaghetti, linguini, and so on) pasta should be broken up enough to form a layer on the bottom of the pot, and both should have about an inch of water to start. Just use clean fresh water, and save any salt or other seasoning for later. Bring the pot to a frolicsome boil, turn off the heat, and cover with a tight lid. Now go do something else for a half hour or so, and don't touch the pot or remove the cover. When you come back, your food will be perfectly cooked.

In the case of rice and other cereals, all the water will have been absorbed. Pasta will have some water remaining, and most of the water used to cook vegetables will still be there. Vegetable water can be saved for stock for gravy and soups or for any recipe calling for added moisture.

Oatmeal and grits will require a bit more water than rice does, depending on your desired consistency degree of doneness. Pasta will be stuck together in a large glop. (The reason all Italian recipes say to cook pasta in gallons of water is to remove the external starch that makes it sticky. You don't have to do this because starch is a complex carbohydrate that is nutritious for active cruisers who aren't following fad diets or who haven't been ordered to avoid them by a genuine medical professional—as opposed to, say, a diet guru.) Get rid of the sticky by drizzling with olive oil or ghee and stirring, or you can just mix in the sauce before serving.

The beauty of this system, besides the obvious savings in fuel and water, is the simplicity and imprecision of applying it. You don't need any particular pot; most any old pan will do as long as the lid fits tightly. You don't need to measure anything; just pour a quantity of whatever into the pot, and cover it with cold water (room temperature is fine, but it doesn't work with hot water) until it is about a half inch over the food. If you insist on measuring, just touch the food lightly with the tip of your index finger, and fill with water to your first knuckle. Experience (and the length of your finger) will dictate the exact amount of water, but even if you get it wrong, the food will be perfectly edible and delicious, if not exactly to your desired specifications.

Naturally, you will need to experiment a bit to get it right. Just adjust the boiling time and amount of water for each type of food until it suits your taste. For me, the rice is turned off as soon as the pot boils, potatoes and carrots are boiled for about 30 seconds (depending on the size of the dice), and spaghetti is boiled for about a minute for al dente. Larger or thicker types of pasta will require a little more water than the thinner or lighter types, as will brown rice in place of white rice.

Save the seasonings until the cooking is finished because salt especially lowers the boiling point of water and affects the cooking times.

OK, as I said, I have not seen this method of cooking boiled foods on any cruising forum or in any cookbook (most cookbook authors will cringe at the lack of precise measurements and cooking times), but Granny gave it to me over 50 years ago, so it has been around for a long time. I am sure to get emails saying "Everyone knows about that" or "My Aunt Milly invented that back in 1906." So here is a twist that makes it even more useful on a cruising boat and has up to now, as far as I know, been privy only to the crew of *Vicarious*.

Just about everyone likes hard-boiled eggs, in salads or just as a convenient snack, and this method works perfectly for cooking them. (If you want soft-boiled eggs, just remove them from the water sooner.) But while it uses less fuel to cook eggs this way, it doesn't save any water. To fix that, simply add a few eggs to every pot when you use this method, then pop them in the icebox until you need them. You will have a steady supply of cooked eggs on hand, you will not have used a drop of additional fuel or water to cook them, and you don't even have to adjust the cooking times to do it.

For example, if you are cooking rice, just nestle one or two eggs into the rice so they rest on the bottom of the pan and aren't touching, then cover with water to half an inch over the rice. It doesn't seem to matter if the eggs aren't completely covered; they come out evenly cooked anyway. Bring the pot to a boil, cover, and go away for a half hour. When you return, the rice will be cooked just the way you like it (assuming you like it sticky), all the water will have been absorbed, and the eggs will be done to perfection.

Recipes

Susan's Linguini with Clam Sauce

I'm forever embarrassing Susan by telling our friends I married her because of this recipe. Susan always blushes and everyone always laughs, but the funny thing is that they all think I'm kidding. This recipe originated in *The Silver Palate Cookbook* by Julee Rosso and Sheila Lukins, but Susan has made a few modifications that make the dish tastier and make preparation on a boat a little easier.

¼ cup olive oil
1 cup chopped fresh clams, conch, cockles, squid, periwinkles, or any other similar tough-bodied creature you find while snorkeling. Canned baby clams work just fine.
6 to 12 cloves of garlic depending on taste, chopped fine but not squished to death in a garlic press. (Chopped garlic retains its flavor better than pressed garlic. Fresh garlic is best, of course, and we seldom encounter any trouble finding a ready supply, but garlic preserved in olive oil will do in a pinch.)
2 to 3 tablespoons fresh chopped chives (Dried chives are a poor but acceptable substitute, and parsley will also work.)
1 pound (approximately) dried linguini
1 tablespoon (approximately) ground pepper
Fresh parmesan cheese (or any other hard cheese)

1. Place the oil in a sauté pan, and let it get just hot enough so that it doesn't smoke.

2. Add the clams and cook while stirring for 2 minutes (longer if you are using squid or conch). If you are using canned clams, just heat them through.

3. Add the garlic and the chives, and cook just until the garlic starts to turn color—about 1 minute—but not long enough to cook the flavor out of it. It is perfect if it retains just a hint of raw garlic bite.

4. Pour the sauce over the cooked pasta, and add the pepper and cheese. Serve with fresh *plancha* bread (see below), an inquisitive white wine, and a fresh salad. Now sit back and enjoy a trip to heaven.

Captain Garlic's World-Famous Spaghetti Sauce

My friends all know me as a humble man, but when it comes to this sauce, I don't mind saying that it's the greatest sauce ever concocted in the history of humanity. I have this habit of inviting large numbers of fellow cruisers aboard for dinner and neglecting to tell Susan that they are coming. This is not one of the best routes to a harmonious cruising relationship, but I can usually smooth things over a bit by doing all the cooking, and the thing I cook the most is my world-famous spaghetti sauce. It takes only about an hour to make, has several uses as leftovers, and rarely fails to make a hit. The following feeds four with some left over, but multiply the recipe to make as much as you can—you're going to need it for some of the recipes that follow.

2 tablespoons olive oil
1 large green onion—the larger and greener the better
2 cans (10-ounce) whole Italian plum tomatoes (Or whatever other kinds of tomatoes you might have aboard—fresh are OK too.)
8 ounces tomato paste
1 cup water
½ teaspoon salt
1 pound ground beef (also called *carne molieda* in Spanish or *mince* in English; if you are in Mexico try it with *carne cabria* [goat meat] for extra flavor) or fresh Italian sausage. (I prefer hot sausage, but it is best to defer to the taste of your crew and guests, especially if they're wimps.)
Garlic, finely chopped (Use as many cloves as you think your guests can tolerate—I seldom use fewer than a dozen.)
2 to 3 large bay leaves
1 teaspoon habanero pepper (Available in a little spice store in Zona Diez in Guatemala City that is licensed to sell explosives. It is worth every minute of the five-hour bus ride with the pigs and chickens to get some. If you don't have habanero peppers, ahi peppers, fresh hot chilies, or ground red pepper will do just fine.)
½ teaspoon salt

2 tablespoons olive oil
1 tablespoon (approximately) freshly ground black pepper (Equals about 50 grinds from a pepper mill.)
2 tablespoons crushed oregano (Use fresh if you can get it.)
2 tablespoons crushed basil (Ditto on the fresh.)
2 tablespoons butter or ghee
1 tablespoons sugar

1. Place the olive oil in a large saucepan or small kettle, and heat.

2. Chop the onion fine, and sauté it in the oil until translucent.

3. Add the tomatoes (undrained) and the tomato paste, and stir, breaking the tomatoes into bits. Stir in the water and salt, bring to a boil, and reduce the heat to a simmer.

4. Brown the *carne molieda*, sausage, or any other meat you want to throw in by crumbling it into a hot frying pan; add it to the sauce.

5. Add the garlic, hot pepper, oregano, basil, and the bay leaves, and simmer for an hour or so. If the sauce starts spluttering, add some more water until it stops. If you add the garlic at the end of the recipe instead of sautéing it with the onion (as in most inferior recipes), it will retain much more of its flavor.

6. Stir in the butter and sugar, and serve over heaps of spaghetti with *plancha* bread or crusty French bread, a fresh garden salad, and lots and lots of cold beer.

Soups and Stews

Soups, stews, and casseroles form the basis of many cruising meals, especially in the high latitudes, and all of the culinarily capable cruisers you meet will have numerous recipes that they believe are special and will be eager to share with you. One of my favorites is the macaroni and cheese recipe in *The Fannie Farmer*

Cookbook, and Susan makes a killer potato scallop from *The Joy of Cooking*. There is little point in repeating these recipes here, but here are two others that are unique.

~~~~~~~~~~~

Captain Garlic's World-Famous Chili

One way to prepare this zesty dish is to take the leftover spaghetti sauce and add some pinto beans and an extra measure of chili powder. The oregano in the spaghetti sauce won't hurt the chili a bit. Of course, real Texas chili lovers will protest that this isn't real Texas chili, but that's because we haven't done much cruising in El Paso. What follows tastes better anyway. If you want to make a from-scratch version that's quick and easy, here's how. Serves six to eight.

Garlic finely chopped (Use as much as you
 think your guests can tolerate—I seldom
 use fewer than a dozen cloves.)
1 large green onion
2 tablespoons olive oil
2 cans (10-ounce) whole Italian plum
 tomatoes (Or use whatever other kinds of
 tomatoes you might have aboard—fresh
 are OK too.)
8 ounces tomato paste
1 cup water
1 can (16 ounces or 450 grams) pinto beans,
 drained
1 pound *carne molieda* or fresh Italian sausage
 (optional)
2 tablespoons fresh chili powder (Chili powder
 loses its kick real quick in the tropics, so
 use a fresh lot whenever you can.)
1 teaspoon habanero pepper (Or use ahi
 peppers, fresh hot chilies, or ground red
 pepper.)
½ teaspoon salt
Freshly ground black pepper (about 50 grinds
 from a pepper mill) and salt to taste

2 tablespoons oregano
1 large Spanish or Bermuda onion, chopped
Grated longhorn or sharp cheddar cheese

1. Chop the garlic and the onion together, and sauté in the oil until translucent.

2. Add the tomatoes and the tomato paste with the water, and stir, breaking the tomatoes into bits. If you have any fresh tomatoes, peel a few and chuck them in.

3. Add the drained beans.

4. Crumble the meat into a frying pan and brown until it sticks to the pan, then scrape it off and brown some more—you want the meat to be crisp, almost burned—and add it to the pot.

5. Stir in the chili powder, and simmer for an hour if you can wait that long.

6. Serve in bowls with the chopped onion and grated cheese sprinkled on top. Make sure there is plenty of crusty bread and butter and cold beer on hand.

Believe it or not, this makes a terrific dish for a hot tropical evening; it will sure take your mind off the heat in a hurry.

~~~~~~~~~~~

Captain Garlic's Spicy Bean Soup

OK, so it's just the leftover chili with a little water thrown in to thin it out a bit, but it's simple, easy to prepare, and incredibly delicious. I wonder why no one seems to like it much? Could it be that because by the time we get to the soup, everyone's pretty sick of Captain Garlic's World-Famous Spaghetti Sauce? (Naw, that couldn't be it.)

Onboard Bread

Bread is one of the most basic of foods, and the ability to turn out a decent loaf from the ship's oven is one of the most useful of all the nautical skills. Aboard *Vicarious* we make no attempt to bake all of our own bread. To do so would take too much time away from other more cruiserly activities and would preclude us from sampling breads from the local ovens in the lands we visit. In all our cruising, I can recall only one boat with a crew that claimed to bake all their own bread, and that was an exceedingly thin German couple who appeared to have a limited appetite.

We do bake a lot of bread, however, but usually it is for a special treat, to provide fresh bread on a long passage, or to provide variety when the local fare becomes limited and tedious.

Cuban Bread

My favorite bread recipe is the one on the side of the King Arthur flour bag. In the Caribbean it is known as Cuban bread, and it's about as simple a bread recipe as you can find. If you are new to bread making and you want a whole-some, nutritious, and easy place to start, this is the first recipe you should try.

1 tablespoon or one packet active dry yeast
2 teaspoons sugar
1 1/4 cups warm water
4 cups bread flour or all-purpose flour
2 teaspoons salt
1/4 cup melted ghee

Set aside 1 cup of the flour to use while kneading and half the ghee to brush on top while baking.

Mix everything remaining in a bowl until a wet dough forms. Turn it out onto a flour-dusted bread board (one of those roll-up plastic sheets is perfect), and dust with the reserved flour.

Knead the dough for 15 or 20 minutes until the consistency is just right. You can read all you want about making bread, but *just right* comes only with experience. After you have done it a few times, you will recognize *just right* as soon as it happens.

Return the dough to the bowl, cover with a clean dish towel, and leave it alone until it rises to double its original volume. Many novice bread makers go wrong here by letting the dough rise too much, but you need some life left in the yeast for the second rising or for baking. (Yeast, as you know, is a eukaryotic microorganism related to lichens and mushrooms, only more mobile and therefore a lot more fun—sort of like cruisers.)

Form the dough into a loaf shape and place it (gently) into a loaf pan. Set it aside until it doubles in volume a second time. Brush the top with the leftover ghee, slash the top in an artistic manner with a sharp knife, and pop it into a preheated oven. Personally, I prefer a more traditional free-form loaf with this recipe, but I have not been able to achieve an acceptable one in the small oven on *Vicarious*. Until I figure it out, or get a bigger oven, the loaf pan works fine.

Now comes the hard part. All the bread recipes in print will give you a specific temperature (usually around 350 degrees) and a specific baking time (usually 45 minutes). But none of this works on a boat, especially one with an undersized anemic oven. Just get your oven as hot as you can, using a pizza stone if you have one, place the loaf pan as close to the center of the oven as you can get it, and bake it until it is done. This is usually about an hour on *Vicarious*, but I remove the loaf after 45 minutes and tap the bottom of the loaf for the characteristic hollow sound. If it seems to need more baking, I pop it back in the oven without the pan and check it again after 10 minutes. It's a lot like kneading; you get to know when it's just right.

OK, the purists are right; this isn't real Cuban bread, the official rations of the CRMF (Conch Republic Military Force—when you get to Key West, you'll learn all about it—whether you want to or not), but it is close, and

English muffins, flat bread (pizza base), and a loaf of basic white bread all from the same basic recipe. Crude by sophisticated bread-making standards? Perhaps. Delicious and nutritious? Definitely.

"Cuban bread" sounds way cooler than "basic white bread."

English Muffins

English muffins are a favorite of the entire crew but they are often hard to find and sometimes expensive. You can, though, make delicious English muffins on the galley stove using the basic bread recipe. Roll out the dough to about ½ inch thick, and cut out rounds with the floured rim of a large water glass. Set the rounds aside to rise until they are 1 inch high, then cook them in a frying pan or on your *plancha* set over a medium flame. Cook one side until it is browned, then flip the muffin over and cook the other side. Store the muffins in a ventilated container (never wrap or store homemade bread in plastic) until you are ready to use them.

Pizza à la Plancha

Making pizza on board *Sultana* was a straight-forward exercise not that much different than making it in a house-sized oven. But because of the smaller not-so-hot oven that came with the new boat, we have a few extra hoops to jump through before we can enjoy this Italian delicacy on *Vicarious*.

When we first moved aboard our new old boat, I tried everything I could think of to get the oven to produce an acceptable pizza, and as Susan will tell you, my standards aren't that high. Edible is really all that I was asking for; anything above that on the culinary scale of excellence would be a bonus. So when my first attempts came in at the barely edible level, I knew it was time to either make sure we did our cruising in range of a Pizza Hut or come up with a new recipe. I enjoy a pizza-shop pizza as much as anyone, but decent pizzerias tend to be scarce in some of the areas we frequent, so it was back to the mixing bowl in a trial-and-error effort that came up with the following perfect-pizza-producing procedure.

The basic bread recipe, called Cuban bread above, makes an excellent pizza base if you add an extra tablespoon of ghee or olive oil to the dough, and a *plancha* (which as mentioned above, on *Vicarious* is a 10-inch cast-iron griddle; any heavy flat cook surface will do as long as it will fit into your oven) makes a perfect pizza pan. Captain Garlic's World-Famous Spaghetti Sauce makes an fine pizza topping so there is little point of repeating those recipes here. Besides, cruisers who start making pizza aboard quickly come up with their own versions of both base and toppings, so consider the recipes here as your start up the culinary mountain to your own pinnacle of pizza perfection.

This method works best if you have a broiler in your oven, and I realize that not all small marine stoves have one. If you don't have a broiler, just follow the procedure with the oven as hot as you can get it, and you will be fine. The broiler is better, but the oven is OK.

Follow the above recipe for Cuban bread to the first rising. After the dough has doubled in size, tear off a fist-sized piece and form it into a ball. Punch it down with your fingertips into to shape of a pizza until it is as thin as you can get it. A quarter inch thick is fine, but thinner is better. It will puff up a bit as you cook it. Using your fingertips seems to work a lot better than rolling it out with a rolling pin because it is easier to keep the round shape and it improves the texture of the crust.

While you are forming the dough, have the *plancha* heating on the largest stove burner to a medium heat. Then transfer the round dough to the hot pan. This is a bit tricky as the dough is very thin. I find folding it into quarters then unfolding it on the pan works well even if it is

at the risk of burned fingers. When the dough is slightly browned on the bottom, flip it over, and cook the other side until brown spots appear. You can do several of these in advance and set them aside as they will keep for a day or so.

What we have, of course, is a form of leavened flat bread that is quite delicious all by itself. Try drizzling on a little garlic-infused ghee or olive oil, add some dried basil (or fresh if you have any) and salt for a quick and tasty white pizza.

To make a traditional tomato and cheese pizza, place your *plancha* in the oven, and preheat to its highest temperature. Once it is hot, turn off the oven and start your broiler. Remove the *plancha* from the oven, and place the cold base dough on it. Then add your sauce and toppings. Naturally, mozzarella is the favorite, but try different cheeses or combinations. Any cheese that will melt works well. I usually just grate up all the bits and pieces of whatever cheese is leftover, after slicing off the green bits, of course.

Pop it back under the broiler, and keeping the door open so you can see what is going on: get on your knees and watch the pizza top. I use a small flashlight as it is dark in there even with the broiler going full blast. When the cheese starts to bubble and brown spots start to form, you are all done. Remove your fresh-baked pizza from the oven, and try to wait until it cools enough to eat without burning the inside of your mouth, which is the hardest part of the whole procedure.

~~~~~~~~~~

Susan's *Plancha* Bread

This is the classic recipe for a delicate Italian bread called *foccacia* that has been adapted to life on the high seas and cooked on the *plancha* instead of in a brick oven. It was given to Susan by another cruiser to whom we will be forever indebted, but we have completely forgotten who it was. It makes a lovely light bread for sandwiches, makes marvelous toast, and is one of those rare breads that is even better a few days after it is made (though it rarely lasts that long on *Vicarious*) than when it is fresh. The secret is in the extra gluten, but if you can't find any, don't worry about it; the bread will taste fine—it just won't be as chewy.

1 ¼ cups tepid water
2 ½ teaspoons dry yeast
1 ½ cups all-purpose flour
1 tablespoon sugar
2 teaspoons gluten
3 tablespoons olive oil
½ teaspoon salt

1. Put the tepid water in a glass measuring cup, add the yeast and sugar, and let it sit until it foams—usually about 10 minutes.

2. Mix the dry ingredients in a large mixing bowl; then add the oil and the yeast mixture a little at a time.

3. Stir into a sticky, wet dough.

4. Turn onto a floured board, and knead for 10 minutes. Try not to incorporate too much flour in the kneading process—you want a thin, light dough.

5. Put the dough back into the bowl, and let it rise until it has doubled in bulk; then punch it down.

6. Smear the surface of the *plancha* with ghee, butter, or oil, and place the dough in the center. It should be thin enough to form itself into a round flat loaf.

7. Let the dough rise once more, then place it in a hot (375°F) oven for about 20 minutes.

Genuine foccacia is baked with little holes punched into the top and filled with olive oil; the top is sprinkled with sliced black olives and salt. You can do that if you like, or you can cook it in a normal loaf pan or form it into small round rolls. It also makes a dandy pizza crust if you find the basic bread not to your liking or if you just need a change of pace.

A crew that eats well feels well, and a crew that feels well is well. The galley isn't only the most important part of the cruising boat. It's the center of the cruising universe. The trick is to realize that simple, basic, and fresh food is the best food and to make sure that there is plenty on board at all times.

14

Electronics

Electronic Marvels

Nothing has changed the cruising environment in recent years as much as the electronics we use to communicate with each other and the world, to locate ourselves on the surface of the globe, and to summon assistance should we do something stupid or just run into a bit of bad luck. Communications, navigation, and life on a boat today are much easier than they were just a few short years ago and miles ahead of what the cruising pioneers of a few decades ago experienced. But the big news isn't what has happened so far but what is to come. All phases of marine electronics are still under intense development, and the technology now exists for profound advances that will dwarf the ones we have seen to date.

In the first edition of this book, when radar and 406 emergency position-indicating radio beacons (EPIRBs) were being used on less than a quarter of cruising boats, I asked the reader to imagine an integrated onboard system consisting of electronic charts, onboard transponders, encoding 406 EPIRBs, depthfinders, satellite communications links, weather-faxes, electronic winches, autopilots, radar, and Global Positioning System (GPS) data. I stated, "All this technology exists right now, and everything mentioned above is not only possible but very likely. The only obstruction to full implementation at the moment is a rather cumbersome price tag."

And, sure enough, all that was predicted has come to pass; well, almost all. (We have electric winches, but those electronic ones are still a ways off.) Many cruising boats now have a multifunction display with chart-plotter, radar, depth, weather-fax, GPS location, course and speed data, automatic identification system (AIS) data (which is a transponder-based system), and digital selective calling (DSC), which duplicates the function of the 406 EPIRB for short-range emergency calls (see the discussion of DSC later in this chapter).

I don't claim to be a visionary (that job falls to Susan who always seems to know what I am about to say), and I can make these predictions only because the trends in electronics are easy to recognize. But, you may well ask, what new technological miracle is coming to the cruising community as an encore to the multifunction display and portable navigation apps? In their ceaseless efforts to extract even more of our scarce cash from our ever-thinning wallets, what new essential gadget will the electronics folks come up with next?

Well, imagine if you will, a chartplotter so thin and flexible that you can roll it up and store it in a tube much as we once did with our paper charts; a satellite-AIS (S-AIS) system that constantly tracks our position, speed, and course no matter where in the world we travel; the inclusion of satellite television in extreme high definition (EHD) on your mul-tifunction display that is now built into the surface of your chart table (or you can move it to any surface you want and even adjust the dimensions), allowing continuous streaming of *Beverly Hillbillies* reruns with ads targeted so precisely that they will direct you to the nearest MaxiBurger restaurant or Walmart megastore (which will soon have so many locations in the United States that you will never be out of sight of the nearest—oh wait, I think that has already happened).

How about replacing your boat's batteries with nano-carbon-powered supercapacitors that are the size of your fist and wirelessly

charged by invisible solar cells built into your decks; powerful boat engines driven by electric-ity or perhaps natural gas instead of diesel fuel; and automatic weather routing that monitors atmospheric and sea conditions to plot your best course to any destination in the world?

All of this stuff is either here or is under serious development, but don't throw away your trusty diesel engine just yet. New technology will always be expensive, and when these new marvels finally do arrive, they will be buggy and unreliable at first, just like the first radar, GPS receivers, and chartplotters were (and sometimes still are).

Fortunately, it will take a long time for all these advances in cruising technology to filter down to basic cruisers like you and me and even longer for the price to be anywhere near affordable, but a significant number of items have already filtered down. They are here now, and most are affordable for even crotchety old skinflints like your thrifty-but-practical author. Some of these new items are true boons to the cruising life, and others are not. So let's take a look at a few of the ones that are also here now, and we'll worry about what is coming when it gets here. (Later in this chapter, I discuss "Electronics That Enhance Safety at Sea.")

LED Lighting

One important change in the cruising lifestyle that is here now, even though very few cruis-ing authorities saw it coming, is a minuscule, extremely efficient, and powerful source of artificial light.

We discussed these new lights briefly back in Chapter 12, but they are important enough to revisit here, because . . . of all the stunning developments in the technology applicable to the cruising life, none can equal the shift to light-emitting diode (LED) lighting for the way it slipped in, unheralded and unnoticed.

The technology of creating an efficient source of light by stimulating photons in a semiconductor has been around for about 50 years now. It is used in all sorts of industrial applications; in remote-control devices; in the numbers in digital readouts and on digital watches; and as indicator lights to let you know that your toaster is toasting. But until recently, LED lighting has been too expensive to be practical for cruising boats. When LED replacement bulbs were first offered to boaters, around 2002, the average cost was well over $70 per bulb. That's a lot of money to spend on a lightbulb on a small boat, so most of them remained on the dealer's shelf, and it was rare to see one on a yacht that wasn't some rich guy's toy.

But now the price per bulb has dropped to around $10 each, and while that is still a lot compared to incandescent bulbs that cost about a buck each, it is now cheap enough to consider as an option. There are several important advantages to LED lights on a boat that may make it worth spending the extra money, and these advantages go far beyond the cost of the bulb itself.

Diodes, as we know from our basic electricity course, are semiconductor devices that act as check valves so that electrons can flow in only one direction. We also know that as electrons move, they create heat, and a byproduct of heat is light (or sometimes it's the other way around—but let's not get overly theoretical here). Light-emitting diodes are simply diodes made up of materials that emphasize the emission of photons when stimulated with an electrical current. The difference is academic but important. When the filament in an incandescent bulb is electrically stimulated, heat is created, and the light is a byproduct. Thus, about 90 percent of the energy used to light your boat with incandescent bulbs is wasted as heat. This is fine for those few of us wintering over on the Kamchetka Peninsula (last count there were approximately none), but all that extra heat is unwelcome for the rest of us. LEDs are designed to produce very little heat so the proportion is reversed: 10 percent of the energy goes into heat, and 90 percent goes into light.

The implications of this reversed proportion are profound. Instead of using 50 watts to power the light in the galley with an incandescent bulb, we can get the same illumination with only 6 watts. Without the destructive heat working on a fragile element, the LED bulb will last so much longer (up to 50,000 hours of continuous burning) than an average incandescent bulb that it almost makes up for the higher cost all by itself. In fact, if that new LED bulb in your head is used an average of two hours a day, it is probably going to last longer than you are.

LED bulbs can also be produced in just about any color by altering the components in the semiconductor matrix. This means that colored lights, such as your green-to-starboard and red-to-port running lights no longer need a lens or filter to achieve the desired color. Filters on an incandescent bulb work by absorbing all the colors in the spectrum but the one desired, a process that can easily reduce the intensity of an incandescent bulb by 90 percent. LEDs, in contrast, are formulated to emit only one color so your running lights no longer need to shine through intensity-killing filters. Thus, your running lights and masthead tricolor light can be a tiny fraction of the wattage required to achieve the statutory 2-mile visibility required by international treaty.

But the LED advantage doesn't stop with the bulb. LED light fixtures no longer need to be designed as heat sinks to absorb the wasted energy of the incandescent bulb, so they can be smaller and lighter or even nonexistent. And the wire that feeds the old 20-watt anchor light on the masthead no longer has to carry nearly 2 amps, so it can be a lot smaller. Where a 20-watt bulb on the end of a 60-foot run (remember to measure the entire circuit—both the positive and negative leads all the way back

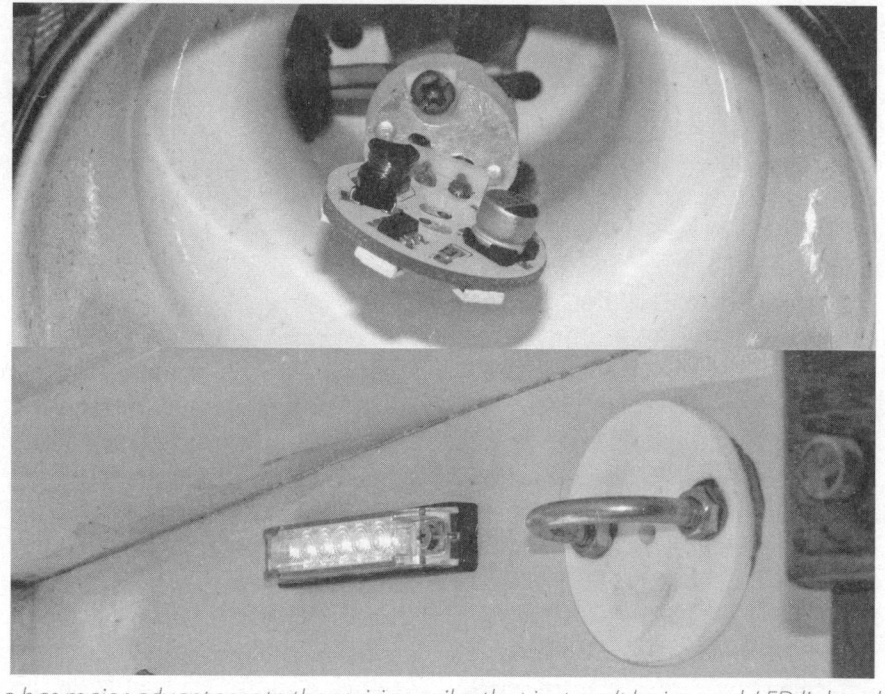

LED lighting has major advantages to the cruising sailor that just can't be ignored. LED lights glow bright with minuscule amounts of current while producing very little heat, and they last just about forever. LED replacement bulbs are available to retrofit incandescent fixtures (as in the top half of the photo) although they don't look anything at all like light bulbs. And they can be bought as dedicated fixtures for dozens of applications. The waterproof LED fixture in the bottom half of photo is one of two that illuminate Vicarious's cockpit. These bulbs draw a half amp each so we can leave them on all night with the anchor light (another half amp) and never have to worry about the battery being depleted in the morning.

to the fuse) needs a 12-gauge wire; a 6-watt bulb will burn bright at the end of a 24-gauge wire and still achieve a voltage drop of under 10 percent. (The actual drop using $V = IR$ would be 9 percent. We don't have to be too pedantic with lightning, but for safety most cruising electricians use a minimum of 18-gauge wire on all lighting circuits save instrument lights.)

Now, if we have our entire boat converted to LEDs, instead of using 400 amp-hours, we are only using 40. That means we no longer have to worry about draining our battery to the limit by leaving the anchor light on all night, and our batteries are going to last much longer than before, or we can just use smaller batteries.

When you add all this up (longer bulb life, no filtration required for colors, smaller fixtures, smaller wire size, and reduced battery stress), LED bulbs at $10 each are a bargain. But it isn't over yet. LED technology is still in its infancy. Lighting consumes more energy in our society than all other nonindustrial uses of electricity combined, so it won't be long before LED lighting sends the incandescent bulb to the same museum shelf to which the transistor sent the vacuum tube back in the fifties.

LED Problems

As with everything else on a boat, there are a few drawbacks to LED lights. First, of course, is the cost. An LED replacement bulb still costs about 10 times what an equivalent incandescent bulb costs, and the dedicated LED fixtures are also more expensive. A traditional anchor light, for example, is about $300 in the LED version at this writing and about $200 in the incandescent version. The cost differential has narrowed considerably just in the past year or two, so we can expect this price disadvantage to steadily shrink until it all but disappears entirely. Interestingly, as LED prices are coming down, the prices of incandescent fixtures are going up.

The only other real problem with LEDs is in the color of the light. Some users report having difficulty getting used to the harsher brilliance of LEDs. This is the same problem many users complain of with florescent bulbs, and for most of us, it is just a matter of getting used to the new experience. As mentioned, LEDs can be produced in just about any color of the spectrum, but right now the most available for marine use are cool white, warm white, red, green, and blue. Using the warm white for reading and interior lighting seems to mitigate the problem a bit, and the cool white is quite harsh and should be used only for exterior lights.

LED Warnings

What could possibly go wrong with such a wonderful new product like LED lighting? Well, two incidents from personal experience come to mind.

The first is the distressing tendency of novice electricians to install small LED lights on circuits that aren't protected by a proper fuse. They will either tack the new circuit onto an existing circuit, which may or may not be protected, reasoning that the new addition is going to draw less than half an amp, so what's the big deal? This attitude springs from the notion that a fuse is installed to protect the device on the end of a circuit and a half-amp draw isn't worth

worrying about. But the primary function of a fuse is to protect the circuit itself, and a short in any unfused circuit can destroy your boat no matter what the draw is in normal operation.

The second problem with LED lighting is illustrated by an experience I had with a boat we were considering buying. The owner had converted all the lighting to LEDs and had spent about $35 each on about 18 LED replacement bulbs and over $150 each on five dedicated LED fixtures with dimmers. When the boat didn't sell for over a year and the seller was forced to lower the price, he tried to cut his losses by changing all the expensive LED lights back to the less costly halogen bulbs, and being in a hurry, he didn't bother to check their function. While I was looking at the boat for the second time, I turned on a light in the pilot-house. The halogen bulb glowed briefly, then a puff of smoke emitted from the side of the fixture, and it went dark. Thinking that this was a bit odd, I turned on another light in the galley, and the same thing happened.

At this point, we decided that this wasn't the boat for us, and we left to keep looking. It took a while for me to nut out just what had happened. The first light I tried was a dedicated LED fixture with a dimmer that worked through a transistor, and transistors are very sensitive to current flow. When I turned on the light, the recently installed halogen bulb drew about 10 times the upper limit for the transistor, and it disintegrated in a puff of smoke. The second light didn't have a transistor because it didn't feature a dimmer, but the owner had installed it as an LED even though it used a standard incandescent fixture. When I turned it on, the small-gauge wire that worked just fine with the LED couldn't handle the current draw of the large-wattage halogen bulb, and it burned up, fortunately without igniting the boat.

When I finally figured out what had happened, we were three states away looking at another boat. I rang the broker to advise him to not let anyone turn on any lights until the proper bulbs were installed and the circuits properly fused, but it was too late. All five of the expensive dimmer fixtures had been destroyed. In trying to save $50 in lights, the owner lost over $700 worth of fixtures. The point here is that once you install a circuit for an LED light, you must have a proper fuse for every fixture. And if you size the wire run for the low amperage of the LED, you can't convert back to incandescent by just replacing the bulb. You must replace the entire circuit with the correct size wire and fuse.

Electronic Navigation for Budget-Busted Cruisers

I am of two minds about electronic navigation. First, the enormous benefits of the Global Positioning System (GPS), used with an autopilot, electronic charts, and a multifunction display, cannot be denied. While at times it took Slocum and Chichester hours to locate themselves within a 10-mile radius of ocean, most cruisers today have multiple GPS receivers, one or two of which will be on constantly giving a location that is precise to within a few meters. *Vicarious*, for example, has three permanently wired GPS receivers (one on the chartplotter, one on an independent depthfinder for backup, and a Garmin antenna for VHF and SSB DSC); a Garmin eTrek handheld, which we use ashore and carry in a grab bag on passages; and three more on iPads. There is even a GPS receiver built into my camera so I can no longer fail to recall exactly where a particular photo was taken, no matter how badly I want to forget it.

But in spite of the high level of reliability that has been designed into satellite navigation over the years, there are problems with overreliance on GPS. Although your satellite signal may be unerringly accurate, the charts you are using aren't. Every waterfront pub where cruisers congregate is alive with tales of close calls caused by inaccurate charts. *Vicarious* has encountered several instances of reefs, atolls, and even entire islands that are far enough from where they are supposed to be to be a hazard to navigation. Many are in the South Pacific, and the Haí Paí island group in Tonga is full of them. More recently, as we approached the well-marked entrance to the anchorage at Providencia Island in the Western Caribbean, we discovered that the electronic charts were off by over a quarter mile. This wasn't a problem with good buoys and clear weather, but if the buoys were missing or off station (as they often are) or if it was the middle of the night and stormy, it would have been a different story. This error is called *offset,* and most chart displays have a provision for correcting it. Unfortunately, while offset compensation works fine when you go to the same areas repeatedly, it doesn't help much when you travel from place to place as cruisers do.

Of course, using a sextant or dead reckoning doesn't make charts (even the electronic ones) any more or less accurate than they already are, but when we relied on our instincts and eyeballs as the primary means of offshore navigation, we were aware of the inherent inaccuracy of the instruments we were using, we were more alert and cautious about fixing our position, and we were always skeptical of the result once we did get a fix.

Most of us can easily recall the famous Sandy Island, originally charted by Captain Cook in 1774 between New Caledonia and Australia, which after appearing on the charts for over two centuries, turned out not to exist at all. Here is what Wikipedia (http://wikipedia.org) says about it:

Sandy Island remained in global coastline and bathymetry compilations used by the scientific community and was still there when the R/V Southern Surveyor *sailed toward the Coral Sea in October 2012. The erroneously reported island persisted because it was included in the World Vector Shoreline (WVS) Database, a data set originally developed by the U.S. National Imagery and Mapping Agency (now the National Geospatial Intelligence Agency, NGA) during the conversion from physical charts to digital formats, and now used as a standard global coastline data set. Inconsistencies in this data set exist in some of the least explored parts of Earth, due to human digitizing errors and errors in original maps from which the digitizing took place.*

Today, many of us will accept the GPS readout without question and without regard to external reference (such as looking over the bow at what is coming), which is, of course, potentially dangerous. When we rely on a GPS fix and electronic charts, we need to employ the same caution and skepticism that we once applied to the celestial fix. Instead of a knee-jerk acceptance of a hopelessly unanalytical digital readout, we must realize that the very pinpoint accuracy of GPS can be a hazard when the charts aren't spot on.

So if GPS is such a wonderful thing, what are we to do about that remote but niggling possibility that it might fail just when we need it most? When I first learned navigation, the axiom was that you always fixed your position with three independent observations (which today we call "inputs"). With an increase in vessel traffic and a general decrease in navigation skills, not to mention the number of people sailing around without enough inputs, this rule is even more important today than it was in the past. Every time you take a GPS reading off of your multifunction display, you should reinforce that reading with two other unrelated observations.

Under normal conditions, and using the GPS on your chartplotter as your primary navigation

tool, how do you get three inputs when you are on the high seas and there is nothing around you but water? Your first input is your GPS position; the second is your dead reckoning fix, which will happen subconsciously after you do it enough; and the third comes from a pair of the most marvelous inputters ever invented, of which most of us have two mounted on the anterior of our skulls somewhat north of our noses. They are called "eyeballs." If you are in an area where there is supposed to be an island on the distant horizon, open 'em up and confirm that an island is there, or as in the case of Sandy Island above, isn't there. At the same time, scan for traffic.

This sounds sophomoric, I know, but you must develop the habit of keeping your eyes open and using inputs other than electronic readouts. Imagine my embarrassment when, halfway between Panama and Tahiti, in an area of ocean I thought devoid of all humanity, I heard a hail on the VHF and looked up to see a previously unnoticed yacht a hundred yards off our starboard beam. Three days out of Nuka Alofa while sailing on flat seas in light winds on the way to New Zealand, I did a visual scan of the horizon and was startled to see an island where I didn't expect one. It wasn't an uncharted island; it's just that it was printed so small on the chart I was using that I hadn't noticed it. It was only a tiny island, but I have it on good authority that even a smallish island can make a biggish hole in your boat if you hit one.

Yet another problem with the GPS on your chartplotter is that on most boats it is always on, informing the skipper and crew of their exact position every minute of the day. This may be fine on a tricky coastal passage fraught with natural hazards, but on an ocean passage, particularly a long one with no intervening hazards, knowing right where you are all the time can raise anxiety levels and become a significant psychological drag on your self-confidence and feeling of well-being.

How can this be? The average speed of most cruising sailboats is equivalent to a fast walk or maybe a slow jog for a really fast boat, and when considered on a global scale, as on a world cruise or a long passage, this is almighty slow. So slow that to realize just how slow it is can be psychologically debilitating, especially for new cruisers accustomed to a frantic shoreside life.

For example, when you are halfway between Hawaii and the Marshall Islands and the weather is clear and your boat is sailing well (making a hundred miles a day or more), it is perfectly OK to know you are halfway between Hawaii and the Marshalls and let it go at that. But if you regularly check your position and make little Xs on your small-scale chart, with even daily fixes those little Xs are going to practically touch each other and you are going to get the idea that you aren't going anywhere at all—a depressing feeling in any kind of travel. It is much wiser to use your GPS just as we once used our sextants. Check your position twice a day, once a day, or even (when the conditions are ideal) once every other day, then turn off the GPS and enjoy sailing.

I can hear the armchair traditionalists, including the author of the following statement (taken from a popular boating manual), bellowing in sanctimonious dismay: "A [good sailor] always knows his or her exact position so that in the case of emergency that position can be reported to the appropriate rescuing agency."

This is bunk. It is pure bunk with sugar on top. While sailing on the high seas, you are in one of the safest environments on earth; statistically, you are safer in a cruising sailboat that is not in a shipping lane and is clear of land than a baby is in its mother's arms. That's about a thousand times safer than you were in your car driving to work and back when you indulged in such perilous activities. On the odd chance that you do get into trouble out on the open sea, there will be plenty of time to get a

position from your GPS, and your 406 EPIRB (that most marvelous of all electronic marvels) is going to report your position with unerring accuracy anyway.

In case I haven't made myself clear . . . the problem with GPS is the enthusiasm with which a large segment of the cruising community embraces it as the only means of navigation. Many seasoned cruisers have sold their sextants in the belief that they will never need them again. The new cruiser who devotes the time and energy to becoming a competent navigator with a sextant and timepiece is the rare exception.

Before we depart from this already overdone subject, here is another bit of anti-electronics cruising heresy for you: your GPS and chart-plotter should be used to fix your position and nothing else. All those other features (way-points, cross-track error, time to go, miles to go, miles made good, and so on) are great for racing tacticians and computer geeks, but they are useless for a skilled cruising sailor, and for the less experienced skipper, they are detriments to acquiring important navigation skills. As soon as a position is fixed on a chart, an experienced navigator will automatically, instantly, and often even subconsciously calculate all of these things without referring to any instruments. Overdependence on GPS readouts will help ensure that you will never develop these important skills and the self-confidence that goes with them.

The only exception to the above is the altitude function that comes as an integral part of the GPS system. When you are sailing somewhere near to nowhere in a favorable wind on gentle seas and you are on watch at the helm reading a Dirk Pitt novel or just basking in the camaraderie of the stars and the sea birds, you will want to refer to the altitude function of your GPS often, just to make sure you haven't died and gone to heaven.

Radar

I don't know where it came from, but I seem to have developed the reputation among all my friends for being anti-radar. Both of them tell me that I am constantly putting down radar and advising budding cruisers not to buy one. This is unfair and untrue. Yes, I did remove the perfectly good radar that was installed on *Sultana* when we bought it, but that was because the thing had a masthead unit that weighed more than 80 pounds and a CRT screen that took up half the cabin, and it sucked the juice out of a battery bank the way politicians suck the money out of a congressional budget.

It is also true that *Sultana* had no radar when we sailed to New Zealand, and we suffered no particular issues where radar would have been a deciding advantage, but we did install a compact Furuno 16/21 during her refit. On the way to Fiji, when the refit was complete, we ran into a storm in the Cook Straight and the famous mountains of water the natives call the Cook-Straight ripple. We turned back into Tasman Bay, and on a pitch-black night we were able to safely anchor in Mutton Cove to await better weather. This was our first of many experiences where the radar proved its worth. Without it we would have been forced to stand off until dawn. This wouldn't have been a problem, but a night spent in a cozy bunk is always better than a night standing watch while going nowhere.

I have never advised anyone not to buy a radar, but I have always preached to all who will listen the same message of caution and restraint that I preach about GPS and all other electronics. Radar is a wonderful device, and to deny its many useful functions would be foolish. For tracking shipping in busy channels, for locating major above-the-waterline hazards, for tracking storm cells, and as a navigation tool, radar is unsurpassed for use at night. It is marginally useful in inclement weather, and it can be a big help in fog. In clear weather and in daylight, it is much better to switch your radar off and revert to your Parallel Ocular Range-finding and Tracking System (PORTS)—a.k.a. your eyeballs—a much more accurate and reliable navigation device.

To use radar as a tool is fine, but to rely on it to the point where you consider it as essential to a safe passage is foolish and dangerous.

Radar No-Nos

Like all electronics, radar is a source of information and nothing more. And it is the single most unreliable source of information that you have. Radar will happily tell you that there are massive objects looming right off your bow when there is nothing but clear ocean, and when there is a massive object right off your bow, it can blithely ignore it. Radar can be blanked out by rain or fog or breaking waves or even your own rigging just when you need it the most, and in rough seas or when the boat is heeled at a healthy sailing angle, it will lose some measure of accuracy, unless, of course, you have one of those fancy (and expensive) gimbaled antenna mounts, which most cruisers don't.

Even the new more efficient sets use a lot of electricity (the Raymarine RD418RD on *Vicarious* with the C140W MFD consumes about 100 watts when operating and 60 watts on standby). So unless you have a substantial reserve of battery power, you will not be able to turn it on except for short periods while sailing without your engine or generator running.

Radar Technology

Vicarious's Raymarine radar will squirt out 4,000 watts of pure power at a frequency that approaches 9,500 MHz (1 MHz is 1 million cycles a second) at a rate of 500 to several thousand pulses a second. All this energy comes from a magnetron that is just like the one you use to cook frozen tacos in a microwave. When this massive jolt hits an object, a tiny fraction (about a millionth of a watt) is bounced back to the reflector where it is detected in the tiny interval between the outgoing pulses. This information is relayed through the processing unit to the screen where it is displayed as a blip (or a "target" in the jargon of the radar elite—which seems to be an odd thing to call something we most often want to avoid). As technology goes, radar is every bit as remarkable as a transistor or a microchip, and it is one of the things that has changed the way cruisers and shoresiders alike live.

The effective use of radar requires extensive training and years of practice in interpreting echoes. It is one thing to look at a blip on a radar screen and announce in an authoritative voice, "We have a target, Captain," and it is another thing to have any inkling of what that target is. Is it a large ship bearing down on us? Is it two or three small fishing boats going away from us? Is it a reflection of our own boat bouncing off a distant sea wall? Is it a small storm cell? Or is it just our radar itself being mischievous and playing little tricks on us? There is no way to tell for sure—not with the tiny yacht-sized radars we are talking about here. If your radar shows a target where there is supposed to be a distant mountain or a close-in buoy, then it is most often a safe assumption that is what it is. But there is no way to tell for sure what a blip on your screen represents. For this reason, radar is never a substitute for a lookout on the bow using those eyeballs we talked about earlier. Radar tells us that there might be something out there. Eyeballs tell us if there is really anything out there and if so, what it is.

The efficiency and effectiveness of radar are determined to a large degree by the width of the beam pulse emanating from the magnetron into the parabolic reflector, properly called a *radiator*. That beam width is determined by the length of the radiator. Thus, a really good radar is both large and expensive, just the opposite of what you and I are looking for—a radar that is small and cheap. The most effective big-boat radars use a beam pulse that is 1 minute of angle (MOA) or less in width, but this requires a radiator that is about half as long as the average boat's main boom—5 feet or so. The radiator on most small radars is less than 1 foot long, and the beam is usually more than 5 MOA wide. That is one big fat beam, and when that beam gets out there a half mile or so, it is hundreds of feet wide—more than 350 feet wide in fact. Anything that it hits within that football-sized arc is going to show up as a target (if it shows up at all) regardless of its size or shape. It could be a cargo ship or an exposed reef, or it might just be a figment of your radar's imagination.

Another result of a short radiator and a wide beam is a phenomenon called *side-lobe error*. Side lobes are caused when some of that energy from the magnetron spills out of the sides of the short radiator. These side lobes are much less powerful than the main beam, but if they hit a target, it can show as a blip just like the main beam. Because the side lobes are directed off to the sides, the blip on the screen will be in a different place than the main blip, and in the worst case where multiple side lobes are bouncing off a single object, your boat can look like it is surrounded by targets when there is really only one. You can get rid of most side-lobe ghosts by detuning the set with the gain control, but in so doing, you risk detuning the main target.

There are lots of other ways for the inexperienced operator to go wrong with radar: multiple echoes when a signal is bounced back and forth from a target several times resulting in multiple blips; false targets where there is a strong blip and nothing there; and blind sectors where a target is blanked by a mast or other physical obstruction are just a few. But the biggest failing of radar is in the head of the person using it—the feeling of false security that a blank screen imparts. Radar shows us what is above the water, when it is what lies below that is of primary interest, and it shows us what *might* be out there when it is what is *really* out there that can sink our boat.

Radar for small boats gets better with each new generation. The new sets are more efficient than the older ones, the displays are sharper, side-lobe error and spurious emissions are less of a problem than before, and there is no question that radar is a useful navigating tool. But please remember that radar is not essential to a safe or enjoyable cruise nor does it deserve even a part of the fanatical loyalty that it seems to engender in a large part of the cruising community. There are many of us who will terminate a cruise when the radar malfunctions and even more who won't leave the dock without one. If you can afford radar, great, get one. If you can't afford one, that's fine too—go cruising anyway, and don't worry about it.

OVERRELIANCE ON ELECTRONIC MARVELS

If people tell me that they will not sail without their radar (or GPS or autopilot), they are telling me that either they have not developed their fundamental navigation skills, or they have not developed confidence in those skills to the point where they can make a major passage safely. Some will say that they can't make a passage at all unless they have a full complement of electronics on board. To that misconception I reply, "Precisely, my dear Watson, and that is the problem."

Not long ago, Les Powles, a well-known British singlehander who was 70 years old at the time, was feared lost when all attempts to contact him failed about a week after he left New Zealand. Three months later he sailed blithely into Lymington Harbor on the south coast of Britain looking for a berth, a hot bath, and a good meal. He had lost his engine, his radio, and all his electronics while under way in heavy weather, so rather than stop in some remote port where repairs were inefficient and costly, he simply broke out the sextant, hunkered down, and sailed the 9,000 miles to his homeport.

That was in 1996 at the beginning of the current shakeup in marine electronics. The question that arises, of course, is how many of today's active cruisers could duplicate that feat, or even come close to it, and how many would panic, set off the EPIRB, and abandon ship? The number of documented cases of cruisers who took to the life raft while their deserted boat was recovered, weeks or months later, intact and still sailing, is a moot answer to that question.

No, I don't recommend that any cruiser in such a predicament simply sail home, but I do recommend that all cruisers acquire the skills to do just that before they undertake a serious voyage. How do you acquire these skills? You go cruising. Start with coastal cruising, then try a few overnight passages. When you feel confident enough, try a few two- or three-day passages. Except for your depthsounder and VHF radio, leave your electronics turned off, and use them only when you sense danger or when your self-confidence starts to flag and your ego needs a boost.

(continued next page)

OVERRELIANCE ON ELECTRONIC MARVELS CONTINUED

When Susan and I set out to become full-time cruisers, we had 10 years of coastal cruising experience behind us, much of it aboard this antique powerboat. While this experience gave us solid background in seamanship and navigation, it also gave us the confidence to finally extend our cruising ambitions to the far horizon. What it didn't give us was the ability to live year-round in a space smaller than our kitchen had been before we left home. We had to learn that the hard way.

At the end of a year, you'll be sailing the way Slocum, Chichester, Robin Lee Graham, and Tania Aebi did it—with your eyeballs, your brain, your sextant, and your good judgment. Then, if your multifunction display decides to take the day off and you drop your backup handheld GPS overboard, you can sail on without a care in the world, and the ability to do that will set you head and shoulders above less-skilled cruisers.

Electronics That Enhance Safety at Sea

I have spent a lot of time trashing the consumer society and the profusion of pointless products it foists off on innocent cruisers. Perhaps I can redeem myself in the eyes of manufacturers and advertisers alike by recommending some expensive products that you really should have on board before you depart. Yes, even I will admit that technology has come up with some products that you must have on your boat. GPS is one, of course. A satellite telephone, once they are generally available at a reasonable price, will be another no matter how much curmudgeonly old cruisers bemoan their coming.

There is a lot of hypocrisy about safety, and we all like to bandy about such slogans as "One thing you can't compromise on is safety" or "If you can't do it safely, don't do it at all."

Of course, if we followed these maxims, we would never get out of bed in the morning much less do anything as foolish as crossing the street or going cruising on the ocean in a sailboat. The fact is, many cruisers compromise safety. They do it quite consciously and with the full realization that they could someday get in trouble for it. Many boats are sailing without life rafts aboard because of the amount of space they take up and because they cost so much to purchase and maintain. These people know full well that they would be safer with a life raft, but they have decided that the risk of going without one is worth the savings in space, money, and aggravation.

The same goes for most other expensive gear that is dedicated solely to safety. Most of us carry a good selection of outdated flares; most cruisers today do have a 406 EPIRB on board, but they are far from universal; few boats carry sea anchors in the low and middle latitudes; and even SSB radio equipment is not found on all cruising boats, but a VHF radio equipped with *digital selective calling* (DSC) is nearly universal even if few of us bother to activate it (see the following). Dedicated safety gear is a lot like insurance in that many of us would like to have it, but we are not going to let our inability to get it or pay for it deter us from going cruising.

On our three-year voyage to New Zealand, *Sultana* carried the following safety equipment: a four-person Avon life raft, SSB, 406 EPIRB, and a double complement of updated parachute flares, but this is primarily because we had children on board. The full complement of safety gear helped assuage the considerable guilt associated with exposing our kids to the slight but undeniable dangers of sailing a small boat on a big ocean.

Digital Selective Calling (DSC)

Most of us who have been around boats for a while are familiar with the operation of a basic VHF radio, and many of us who venture offshore know our way around the single-sideband system. But if you have a newer set, one bought in the past 10 years or so, you may have noticed (and have probably ignored) a curious red button marked with the initials DSC. It is there for two reasons: since 1999, it has been contrary to the provisions of the International Convention for the Safety of Life at Sea (SOLAS) to manufacture a VHF radio without one, and one day it could be one of the most important buttons on your boat.

The most profound function of the DSC system is to allow anyone aboard a vessel in distress, no matter how unfamiliar he or she may be with radio protocol, to send the equivalent of a Mayday call simply by pushing a button. When the guard shield is lifted and the DSC button activated, a digital signal is automatically transmitted over VHF Channel 70 to the U.S. Coast Guard and to any vessel equipped with the proper receiver that is within range. The message is repeated until reception is confirmed by an answering station.

The importance of this automatic distress call will be immediately obvious to anyone who has ever been in a Mayday situation. In over 50 years of boating, I have called a Mayday only once. It happened in Boston Harbor when the gasoline engine in a powerboat I was piloting burst into flames and quickly engulfed the entire engine compartment. It is one thing to theorize a Mayday call according to the book (call "Mayday" three times, state the nature of the emergency, give the vessel name and position, stay calm, stand by the radio and listen for two minutes before repeating) and quite another to send a coherent message when the flames are licking at your shirt tail and your vessel is adrift.

In my case, I was forced overboard after a very brief and probably incoherent Mayday call and an abbreviated position (2 miles east of Boston Light) report. The Coast Guard heard

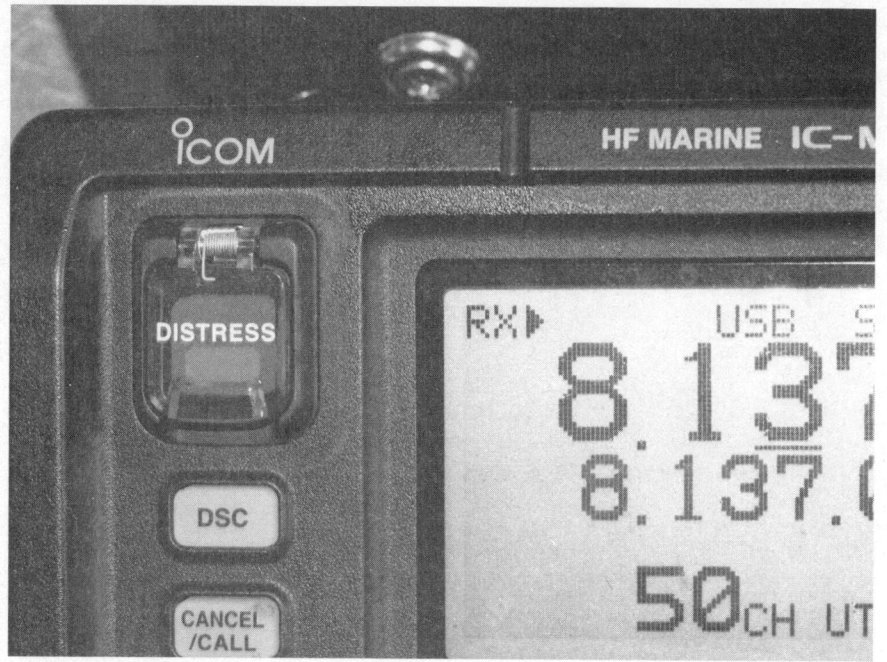

All VHF and HF marine radios, except handhelds, are required to have digital selective calling (DSC) capability. It is the little red button prominently located on the front of your set. It is there for emergencies and substitutes for or reinforces a Mayday call. DSC can also be used to expedite regular intership communications and works much like a cell phone. But you do have to take the trouble to install it properly and learn how to use it. Most cruisers don't, and they are missing a useful and free tool.

the call, but when they responded on Channel 16, I was busy emptying the three small fire extinguishers I had aboard in a futile attempt to control the flames. By the time I realized my efforts were in vain, I had to abandon ship with no time left over for chatting with the Coasties.

The boat would have surely been a total loss, but in a brilliant burst of good luck, the chief of the Danvers, Massachusetts, fire department was fishing only a hundred yards away, and being a fire chief, he never went anywhere without an industrial-size CO_2 fire extinguisher aboard. He also knew just how to use it and quickly had the fire under control. The Coast Guard, to their credit,

arrived in record time, but they would not have been quick enough to save the vessel.

If the boat in the above situation had been fitted with DSC, I could have nonchalantly pushed the little red button, then busied myself with the more mundane tasks of emptying fire extinguishers, panicking, rushing madly about trying to save my most treasured items, then diving gracefully off the bow with a suitably dramatic flourish just in case there was a camera crew passing overhead in a helicopter, and the episode was destined for the evening news. (There wasn't, and it wasn't, which is just as well as news watchers would have thought it odd to see a grown man tumbling overboard backward with an armload of photography gear, three bottles of Havana Club rum, and 27 Jimmy Buffett tapes.)

When you install a new VHF, the DSC function is ready to transmit a distress signal right out of the box, and new radios will have the GPS function programmed right into the radio. This saves a lot of annoying electrical work that was necessary with the original DSC sets, plus it offers yet another backup to your primary GPS. Unfortunately, the receiving station will not know anything about the nature of the emergency or the vessel sending the signal. They will know where you are, but they won't know who you are. Nor will they know if it is a real emergency or just some clown who couldn't be troubled to read the instruction manual and is trying to figure what the little red button is for. (It is a well-known fact that among the male half of the population, it is egregiously uncool to read the instructions before installing anything in a boat. This is pure human nature and something we all just have to learn to live with, a fact that I have been attempting to explain to Susan for the past 40 years without even a hint of success.)

In order to get your DSC working properly, you need to do two things after you install the radio. If you plan to go more than 3 miles offshore, you will need to get a radio station operator's license from the FCC or whatever bureaucratic agency is responsible for such things in your country. In the United States you can submit FCC Form 605 (you can do it online by going to http://transition.fcc.gov and clicking on the "online filing" link). When you receive your license, it will have, in very small print, your personal *marine mobile service identification* (MMSI) number. The easiest way to get your head around this number is to think of it as a cell phone number for your radio because, well, that's just what it is.

If you never plan to venture offshore or visit a foreign country (including Canada, Mexico,

and the Bahamas), BoatUS has a handy service that will assign you an MMSI that will work within U.S. waters and doesn't involve applying for a station license. You can get full details on their website at http://boatus.com/mmsi/.

Once you have your MMSI number, it remains useless until you program it into your radio. How you actually do this critical step will vary slightly with different brands of radios, but it is most often a straightforward procedure involving pushing a lot of buttons in painfully exact sequence.

DSC is a major improvement in marine safety. It simplifies the mission of agencies around the world charged with looking after roaming yachties who drift onto the rocks, wander into hurricanes, or stumble into other situations in which survival becomes problematic. If this is so, and it is, how come fewer than 40 percent of DSC-equipped radios are ever programmed with an MMSI number? According to U.S. Coast Guard figures, 60 percent of the buyers of new VHF radios never apply for an identification number (MMSI), and very few of those who do ever take the trouble to program in into their radios.

I don't actually know the reasons for this low level of compliance, but I will hazard a guess anyway. ("Here we go again," says Susan.)

The reason for the low compliance for the use of DSC VHF radios is the proliferation of cell phones. There is a pervasive idea among coastal cruisers that cell phones duplicate and can replace normal VHF radio communications. After all, if the boat is sinking and Uncle Dave has fallen overboard, it takes only a few seconds to dial 911 and help is on the way.

The sad fact is that, as a means of marine communication in an emergency, cell phones are notoriously inadequate, and the Coast Guard has been pleading with us for years to not rely on them for distress calls (or any other calls where VHF is available). In addition to frequent dead spots where there is no reception at all and range limitations, cell phones are chronically susceptible to salt air–induced malfunction, and they are practically guaranteed to pack it in when you need them the most.

Cell phones are fine for making reservations at the next posh marina down the ICW, if you are the sort of cruiser who indulges in that sort of behavior, and for ordering pizzas delivered to the anchorage dinghy dock. But of you have a VHF radio on board and it is equipped with a DSC button, get the button operational before you venture out of the harbor. You and your loved ones will be able to relax knowing that, should catastrophe raise its ugly head and look you in the eye with its cynical grin, you can grin right back because help is just a push button away.

You can save your cell phone battery power for the really important stuff like making sure that there is double cheese on the deep-dish regular and to *puulllease* hold the anchovies on the extra-large Italiano Extravaganza.

Nonemergency DSC

There are other reasons to activate the DSC button on your VHF, and they don't have anything to do with getting rescued or being safe at sea. Your MMSI number is unique to your boat (if you have more than one radio aboard, all of the radios should be programmed with the same MMSI number), and as we discovered above, it works just like a cell phone number. Thus you can call up any boat that is in range by looking up its MMSI on the contacts list that you store in your radio's memory. As we said—just like a cell phone, only more reliable.

This hailing function doesn't use the little red button; that sucker is reserved for legitimate emergencies. The way hailing works differs a bit with each brand of radios. But basically, you program the MMSI of the boat with which you wish to chat into the radio with the keypad,

indicate the com channel you want to use, and push the go button. You will get a message that your request has been transmitted and another when the message is received. Then your radio will automatically switch to the chatting channel when the request is acknowledged. All you have to do is pick up the mike and start talking.

No more waiting for half the boats in the harbor to do their radio checks on Channel 16 while the Coast Guard admonishes them not to do that anymore. And no more secret codes ("copy that *Mother's Mink*; up two and down three") in a futile attempt at a private conversation. In fact, if you communicate a lot with buddy boats, if you are involved in racing or any other group activity, or if you just want to simplify your life (which we hope is why you bought this book), then getting the DSC system operating is well worth the effort even if you are so upbeat on life that you can't imagine a situation from which you might want to be rescued.

There is one more amazing feature of DSC that makes it worth the time it takes to program your radio. You can, with a simple menu call, discover the exact location of any vessel for which you have an in-range MMSI number. Not only does this help you keep up with boats who have friends aboard (and perhaps avoid other boats who don't), but it is a boon to parents cruising with kids who are old enough to take the dinghy by themselves. (Sarah got her dinghy pass when she was 12, and Phillip was tagging along when he was 10; until you experience it, the amount of responsibility cruising kids can handle at a young age is quite surprising.)

It works like this. First get the kids their own handheld VHF making sure that it has DSC (not all handhelds do; only permanent sets are required to have DSC). Then register it to the dinghy, and get the dinghy a radio station license. This will give the dinghy a unique MMSI, and the location of that MMSI can be checked with a simple menu call on the ship's main station without the kids' knowing that their mom and dad are checking up on them. You can also ring the kids for a chat any time you want, and they can ring you. As I've said two or three times already: just like a cell phone only better. No contract fees; no dead spots; no salt-sensitive SIM cards, automatic worldwide coverage; and if you drop it overboard, it floats (just make sure you get the floater model).

EPIRBs (and PLBs)

As the name indicates, emergency position-indicating radio beacons (EPIRBs) are small radio transmitters that, when activated, send out a signal beacon on which rescuers can home in and trace to the victim. EPIRBs were developed for aviation search and rescue, and all aircraft have been required to have them aboard ever since the early seventies. There are two basic types most easily identified by the frequencies they use.

The first is a general-purpose EPIRB that, when activated, will broadcast a beacon on 121.5 MHz that can be picked up by passing aircraft, a rescue party with a receiver tuned to this frequency (any radio direction finder will work), or under ideal conditions by a passing National Oceanic and Atmospheric Administration (NOAA) Search and Rescue Satellite Aided Tracking (SARSAT) satellite. These EPIRBs are compact enough to be kept handy at all times, and they are economical enough so that every offshore boat should have one. The drawbacks to these basic units are their low power (less than a tenth of a watt), the fact that satellite reception is incidental (the SARSAT satellite must be right overhead, and atmospheric conditions must be perfect), and the high number of false alarms they generate. Thus, 121.5 EPIRBs are now used only for personal locator beacons (PLBs) and as a part of a larger search-and-rescue (SAR) effort.

In many respects, the 406 EPIRB seems to duplicate the function of the DSC-equipped VHF and SSB radios discussed above. But the major difference is that the DSC system is strictly a terrestrial technology, and there are no plans, that I know of, to adapt it to satellite transmission. This relegates DSC to a local environment where it is very useful for distress calls and social contacts to shore stations and vessels that are within range of a terrestrial antenna, but it limits its versatility to only those areas where there is likely to be a receiving station within 25 miles or so. But there are many areas of the world that are practically deserted and where another radio within calling range of the DSC is unlikely. It is to these areas that many cruisers are drawn, so the worldwide, satellite-link functionality of a 406 EPIRB and its all-weather reliability makes it a required kit for any vessel venturing into remote anchorages in faraway places.

In the most recent versions, the 406 EPIRBs incorporate several improved features over the older sets, some of which please cruisers, some of which make retailers and manufacturers very happy, and one that is a huge relief to armchair sailors everywhere. We who cruise in offshore sailboats welcome the new smaller size of the 406 transmitters and the slightly lower price (new units are about half the price of the original sets when inflation is considered). But new or old 406 EPIRBs are the most important advances in marine safety since the life jacket.

With a direct satellite link that locates an activated set to within a 2-mile radius, worldwide coverage, and a reliability that is nothing but remarkable, a distressed vessel can count on rescue within hours of activating the EPIRB in most areas. Even in the most remote corners of the globe, rescue efforts can be organized and executed within a day or so. The reliability of these units is such that you can safely cut back the emergency rations and other supplies packed in your life raft and in your abandon-ship bag.

Retailers, advertisers, and manufacturers are happy with 406 EPIRBs because they are essential gear (if you don't have one at departure, you should work just a few more weeks and get one), and they are, at about $600 each, not very expensive—a combination that puts them close to consumerist nirvana, making them candidates for the essential-product hall of fame.

And what about the armchair cruisers (that's all of us, isn't it)? We have all read the life raft sagas about some boat that is sunk by some whale in some remote area of ocean and the crew floats around for several months in a life raft eating raw seagulls. Now I don't want to sound insensitive here, and my heart goes out to those who have suffered through this ordeal, but after reading two or three of these epics, they get a bit . . . well, tedious, and the very best thing about the advent of the 406 EPIRB is that we will never have to read another one.

Automatic Identification System (AIS)

One recent addition to the International Convention for the Safety of Life at Sea (SOLAS) has been the requirement that all vessels over 300 gross tons be equipped with a transponder broadcasting position and identification data to the world. This requirement was a major improvement in technology for shipping companies, large commercial vessels, and anyone interested in predicting departures and arrivals in major harbors around the world. The AIS also improves safety by broadcasting a vessel's exact position to anyone with a properly tuned AIS receiver.

When AIS sets first became available in 2002, they were far too expensive to be anything but a curiosity to cruising vessels, but by 2006 compact receivers were available at a price attractive to owners of private yachts.

The current versions of AIS are receiver-only sets that will display the position of any commercial vessel equipped with an AIS transponder, either in alphanumerical format or as an icon overlay on your chartplotter and radar screen. These receivers will also broadcast the name of the ship and other voluntary data that the captain chooses to add, such as ports of origin and destination. Most ships broadcast only the statutory speed, course, and position data that is required by the treaty, but this is a major advantage to cruising yachts trying to stay out of the way of approaching shipping.

As this is written, the AIS is still in its early developmental stages with lots of changes coming and coming fast. AIS data is now transmitted over marine terrestrial radio facilities and data links between ships and shore stations and then, when necessary, retransmitted over conventional airways. This limits the capacity of the system, but we will soon have satellite tracking (S-AIS) that will be capable of handling millions of signals simultaneously. We can also expect full functioning sets that are cheap and compact enough to be attractive to yachts and other small craft. These will automatically broadcast your position and speed data to anyone in the world who is interested enough to tune in.

The downside of the S-AIS is obvious to those of us who treasure the ability to sail into anonymity whenever we get the urge. Even those of us who have no reason to disappear and never will can value the ability to do just that if ever we wanted to. That S-AIS is an invasive technology is obvious, and as smaller and cheaper sets become available, governments (being governments) will be hard-pressed to resist making them mandatory. But speculations of this nature are best left to the political pundits while we get on with our simple and basic cruising lives remaining blissfully oblivious to such distressing possibilities.

The Masthead Tri-light

Running lights have been used on boats since Phoenician times, of course, but the advent of the masthead tricolor running light with built-in anchor light has been a quantum leap forward in marine safety. Bright lights on the tip of a mast are far more visible than conventional running lights mounted at deck level, they are more obvious to the crew on the bridge of a large vessel, and they can be seen for a greater distance.

When outfitting your boat for departure, you should consider mounting one of these units as an adjunct to your regular running lights, not as replacement for them.

If the budget allows, get the LED version (for all the reasons listed above, with an integral strobe even though it just about doubles the cost to about $600). Technically, the strobe is to be used only in emergencies when the crew requires rescue, but when craft and crew are in danger, it is my personal philosophy to remove them from that danger by whatever means is expedient and to sort out the legality of my actions later. This means turning on the strobe any time there is imminent danger of collision with shipping in any condition of limited visibility.

One of the first upgrades we made after we bought *Vicarious* was to install an LED tri-light on the masthead. But instead of getting one with an internal strobe, we mounted an independent strobe on the mizzen. This limits the visibility of the strobe slightly, but it gives us redundancy should anything happen to the mainmast. It also cost quite a bit more to do it this way, especially when the extra wiring was considered, so if we ever do it again

"Tropic birds"

The waterfall at Daniel's Bay in the Marquesas Islands is a popular side trip for cruisers visiting this remote anchorage. We hiked for hours through jungle and copra plantations surrounded by the vestiges of the ancient civilization that flourished here many centuries ago. The trip takes a full day during which we had the valley to ourselves and shared it only with the multitude of wild goats that call it home. When we first visited here in 1994, Sultana had no radar, autopilot, or chartplotter, and only a rudimentary GPS. Vicarious has all these things and more, but electronic aids are no more a requirement today than they were 20 or 50 years ago. Don't let the absence of modern electronics on your boat keep you from the cruising life. Learning to navigate the old-fashioned way will make your cruise safer and more enjoyable even when you do have the luxury of modern electronics.

(unlikely), we will go back to the version with the integrated strobe.

There are few of us senior cruisers (Susan prefers the term "curmudgeonly old farts") who refuse to use the better features that all these new electronic doodads offer, no matter how much we talk about resenting the way they make sailing so easy that "any moron with a credit card can do it" and how much the mystique of cruising the world in a boat is diminished with their coming.

This is the apogee of hypocrisy, I know, but hypocrisy is part of what becoming a curmudgeonly old fart is all about, and I plan to enjoy it to the fullest while I am able. Now, if I can only find my astrolabe and cross-staff, I'll show these kids a thing or two about navigation.

15

Staying in Touch and Surfing the Web While Cruising the Seas

Cruising the high seas in a boat is one of life's safest pastimes. Sinking, though, is very dangerous.

—ANCIENT CRUISING WISDOM

Of all the myriad social changes that have affected those of us who choose to float afar on boats, nothing since the Gutenberg Bible has had the impact of the Internet. This is true, of course, of society in general, as the smartphone and the tablet computer not only have become a part of our lives but are starting to dictate how we live them. On a recent foraging trip on a bus destined for Vero Beach, Florida, I observed a good half of the 30 or so passengers with their faces plastered to the screens of smartphones. The remarkable thing about this scenario is that it is no longer remarkable. The zombielike stare of smartphone-transfixed teenagers as they ride their bikes or stumble through shopping malls is no longer relegated to teenagers; throngs of stressed-out adults are joining the trend.

In our recent travels, we have met cruising families who won't venture outside of cell phone range, sometimes to appease teenage crew members but just as often because they themselves get anxiety attacks if the 4G signal falls below two bars. There is even a name for this phenomena: it's called *nomophobia*. And as this insidious infliction reaches epidemic proportions, it has been shown through studies scientific to be responsible for lowered efficiency and performance in classrooms and in offices across the land. The ironic implication is that smartphones are making us stupid, and the associated fallout most certainly has an effect on the cruising life.

Keeping in Touch

But this chapter isn't a treatise on the detrimental effects of cell phone addiction—you can find plenty of that on the Internet. It is a celebration of the advantages and benefits that the Internet and wireless technology have brought to ocean voyaging and how it has so greatly simplified our lives afloat. No, Internet access is not required for successful cruising any more than a chartplotter or a GPS, but even more than modern electronic navigation, tablet computers and smartphones have become an indelible part of the cruising kit of practically every boat venturing onto the blue.

Here the alert reader will notice that I discuss smartphones and tablets, and laptop computers in the same breath. This is because the technological differences between voice communications (4G technology) and data transmission (Internet technology) are, except for legal and proprietary considerations, indistinguishable; talking on your cell phone, surfing the Internet, and emailing your mates all work the same way and are essentially the same thing. And with the switch to digital TV, you can toss that into the pot as well.

However it is done and whatever it is called, the ability to communicate electronically has had a major impact on all of us. Even if you are among the few remaining curmudgeonly holdouts trying to exist without a cell phone, you are rowing upstream against a strong tide. In the old days you could count on finding a pay phone on nearly every street corner of every town large enough to have streets. Occasionally, you might even, on the first try, find one that actually worked. Of course pay phones are with us still, mostly in airports and museums, but just try finding one when you really need it.

The upshot is that the percentage of cruising boats that don't have some sort of Internet access on board is probably way down in the low teens and shrinking as we speak. The number of cruising boats without a cell phone on board is so small that we won't even waste our time talking about it. It is conjecture (that's Norwegian for dumb-assed guess), but I suspect that there are more boats without GPS than there are without a cell phone aboard. (Oops, there I go talking about not having a cell phone when I said I wouldn't . . . damn, there I go again.) And the reason for this virtually universal acceptance is that, while not yet indispensable, cell phones and tablet computers (or laptops, if you prefer) make life aboard so much easier that it is only the most rugged traditionalists who try to get along without them. Let's just look close up at a few of these reasons to make that rather substantial investment in digital communications.

(The alert reader will recall that back in Chapter 6 I advised anyone who was trying to build a kitty to get rid on the smartphone, and I stand behind that in spades, especially if your cruising plans will take you to destinations in developing countries or in remote areas, as they should. It isn't the smartphone I object to but the contract that goes with it. In the United States the average contract was over $100 a month [personally, my last smartphone contract was costing well over $300 a month], and the total cost of the phone over the life of an average two-year contract can easily exceed $3,000. That's a lot of money that rightfully belongs to your kitty. So keep in mind that when we talk about cell phones in the flowing discussion, we are talking about your garden-variety, distinctly uncool, and very cheap, flip phone, not a smartphone.)

Telephone

In the old days, one of the most difficult adjustments we had to make when we forsook the shoreside life for the wandering life aquatic was the difficulty of staying in touch with friends and relatives. Those who were closest to us were often the most skeptical of our decision to embrace what they viewed not as a lifestyle but an irresponsible and frivolous pastime. The resulting lack of any contact save an occasional postcard, often from some forlorn island that civilized people had never even heard of, did nothing but reinforce that impression.

In 1994, when we spent the hurricane season hiding in Guatemala's Rio Dulce, *Sultana* had all the up-to-date communications we could cram aboard. These included a state-of-the-art single-sideband (SSB) and ham radio; a very high frequency (VHF) radio with a high-gain antenna; a handheld GPS (one of the first) that talked to up to three satellites simultaneously and usually gave you a fix within a half hour of turning it on, at which time you had to change the eight AA batteries; a new Pactor terminal for translating weather-fax signals through the SSB to our new third-generation Macintosh computer (with an amazing 1-megabyte hard drive and little 3-inch floppy discs that were quickly devoured by a humorless-but-voracious green slime); and a Motorola portable phone that was so small it came with a shoulder strap so you could carry it around with you.

All of this stuff cost thousands of dollars, of course, but the only things that ever worked were the ham radio and the VHF. The GPS was rendered obsolete by changing technology, which didn't matter as we pretty much knew where we were at that point and were going broke buying batteries anyway. The portable phone looked cool, but without a signal to receive, talking on it was nothing more than a good way to impress other cruisers. And the Pactor weather-fax never did work in spite of consuming dozens of hours of the combined expertise of every radio-savvy cruiser on the river.

Making a phone call on the Rio was a study in ease and simplicity. First, you rowed ashore in the dinghy and made a reservation at the telephone office in the little frontier town of Fronteras; then you sat (on a very hard bench with no back) and waited to be summoned for your call. If all went well, you were eventually ushered into a booth with a phone where after considerable multilingual negotiations with the operator, a connection of sorts was made with your party— sometimes with the party you wanted to speak to, sometimes not. (I once had a delightful conversation with a lady in Germany named Greta just because I was so glad to get through to anybody that I didn't want to hang up.) Often (no, usually) the connection was lost right after the pleasantries, and you started all over again.

If all *didn't* go well, you made your appointment, then sat for several hours only to be informed that there was no telephone service that day, but it might be restored by the end of the week . . . or maybe next week.

At the time, I was working against a deadline on the final draft of a project for International Marine, and I didn't have the luxury of waiting a week to make a call . . . maybe. The alternative entailed an entertaining two-hour bus trip over dirt roads through the jungle to the slightly larger town of Morales, which boasted of a somewhat more reliable telephone office.

This trip was, of course, via the famous Guatemala chicken busses, which no matter how stuffed with humanity, could always find room for one more passenger. I made many of these trips jammed between jolly Guatemalan ladies going to market and more than one with steely eyed *campesinos* with razor-sharp machetes strapped to their backs, but the most memorable trip was with a pretty teenage girl holding a squeally piglet in a basket while sitting on my lap. I didn't mind the girl, but the pig . . . well, come to think of it, I didn't mind the pig either.

As you might expect, all this has changed, at least as far as communications for cruisers are concerned. The chicken busses still are jammed to capacity with happy humanity, but the roads are now paved, that little girl is now a grandmother, and the piglet was long ago rendered into *manteca* and pork chops. But talking to the folks back home is now as easy as it was when you used to live just down the street or in the next town.

The problem with using cell phones while cruising is that you can use them only within range of a signal. That sort of makes sense, and it is a big improvement on talking from the end of a wire. But as cell phone coverage gradually becomes universal, even in developing countries, it is still limited in utility for active cruisers who spend a lot of time on long passages and anchored in remote harbors around the world. It can also be expensive and confusing as you travel from country to country, changing SIM cards and servers with resulting changes in numbers, and the costs can be a major stress generator for some cruisers whose needs for back-home contact are stronger than the need to conserve cash. Of course, there are wireless companies that offer worldwide roaming service, but these tend to be expensive, and you still need tower coverage to use them.

Texting

The ability to send messages between telephones by typing them out on a telephone keyboard was not something even the most far-sighted science visionary was able to predict (another unpredicted scientific advance was the now-universal digital readout), yet cell phone texting has become one of the most important means of transmitting superficial information ever invented. Legions of teenagers and pre-teenagers do it pretty much full-time, while post-teenagers (up to about age 99) only do it a lot. I once watched in amazement a young lad in New Zealand texting his mates on one cell phone and talking on another while zooming downhill through traffic at breakneck speed on a skateboard—an act worthy of the Cirque du Soleil for sure.

Anywhere there is a cell phone signal, texting has become a boon to the cruising sailor. As a quick and efficient means of transmitting short messages, it is hard to beat. The only problem with texting messages is the same one we have with cell phones: you need to be within range of a transmission tower to use it, and there is no such thing and never will be over 90 percent of the Earth's surface.

Satellite Telephone

Satellite telephone service would seem to be the answer to every cruiser's communications dream. The new-generation phones are almost as small and as handy as normal cell phones: they offer worldwide coverage without the bureaucratic hassles and inconvenience of SIM cards and number changes; they work fine as far offshore as you can get; they interface with email, weather-fax, and gridded information in binary (GRIB) charts; and they could be a lifesaver if you ever need to take one into the life raft with you. The only downside of satellite phones continues to be their high cost, even after decades of steadily lowering calling fees.

Of the three most popular satellite telephone services available (Inmarsat, GlobeStar, and Iridium), the only one I am familiar with is Iridium, which in spite of its higher cost (for both initial and monthly service) seems to be the most popular with cruisers, probably because, as of this writing, it is the only one with true worldwide coverage.

There is a fundamental difference in technology between Iridium and the other two. Without going into too much detail, which I'm not qualified to do anyway, Iridium uses a lot of satellites going very fast in a low orbit while the other two use only a few in a high stationary (geosynchronous) orbit. This results in near-universal coverage for Iridium but at a much higher cost, while Inmarsat has coverage issues in low-population areas and no coverage at all over the poles.

The current price for a basic Iridium Model 9555 phone set is about $1,000 plus a minimum of about $50 per month (or you can buy prepaid time cards for about $1.40 per minute). Inmarsat phones start at about $600 with monthly service available for about $35 per month. GlobeStar is competitive in price with Inmarsat at this writing, but it has a much more restricted service area. The company is in the process of playing catchup with a bunch of new satellites to be launched soon, so like everything electronic, this could change a lot real fast.

Email

I don't remember my first email, but I suspect it was in Guatemala City using one of the early versions of the Internet café. At first it was nothing but an amusing novelty, but email communication quickly became an essential ingredient in the cruising life, and it remains so today.

Two or three paragraphs above, I recalled my adventures trying to write a book from the jungles in Guatemala before the Internet was generally available. I didn't mention the galley proofs that had to be sent from Camden, Maine, to me via fax, then sent back with corrections noted. There were also contracts to sign and other important documents that were also sent by fax. Those of us ancient enough to remember Thermofax paper and mechanical printers of the day will appreciate the mostly illegible and always incomplete nature of these transmissions into the humid and hostile-to-electric-stuff rainforest.

Some years later, in early 1999, I found myself anchored off the docks in Savusavu on Vanua Levu Island in Fiji, working as rewrite editor for another book, also for International

Marine. This time the entire project was completed on the Internet via email. Not from the boat, mind you, we hadn't gotten quite that far yet, but from the new Internet café that had opened there just across the street from the dinghy dock. The difference was astounding. Instead of the smudged and unintelligible copy of the fax that took hours and hours of effort to get transmitted successfully, we enjoyed instant two-way communication that was just short of the convenience of a long-distance phone conversation at a tiny fraction of the cost. A project that would have taken six months to finish doing it the old way was completed to everyone's satisfaction in a matter weeks. It would have been even faster if it weren't for the 12-time-zone difference that separated us: a regrettable inconvenience for which technology has yet to find an answer (but I bet they are working on it).

That was in 1999. Today I am writing this from the cockpit of *Vicarious* while anchored in a quiet cove along the south rim of Lake Okeechobee in Florida with nothing to distract me from my keyboard but the distant grunting of alligators and the insalubrious croaking of the great blue heron in the dead cyprus over my head. When this chapter is ready, I'll simply touch a certain spot on the computer screen, and it will instantly fly away, via email and the wonders of the 4G data network, to my editor in Camden. Then to be returned an instant later with a sticky message announcing, good try, but no, it isn't really ready yet.

The above esoteric example of the maritime Internet in action is unique to me, but the principle applies to just about every cruiser cruising. Email is by far the easiest, cheapest, most reliable, and the most universally available means of communication for the world-wandering sailor that there ever was. Emails can be sent from computers and tablets using the Internet and from smartphones via 4G any time you are in range of a signal. From the high seas, or anywhere else out of range of a transmission tower, emails can be sent directly from an SSB or ham radio using a Pactor III modem (which is so far ahead of the original Pactor that we couldn't get to work in the Rio Dulce, that it isn't even comparable) and SailMail or WinLink2000 stations. Or, for a less costly option for remote emails, you can use your smartphone or iPad to send and receive via a Delorme InReach device, which also functions as an emergency beacon of sorts. And most satellite phones now come with email and texting capability.

From just about anywhere you can go on a boat you will be able to communicate by email of some sort. Sometimes the length of the message is limited by bandwidth or other technical issues and sometimes the cost is higher than we would like, but email remains the most reliable and efficient way to let the folks back home know that yes, we are still alive, no, we haven't drowned or been eaten by sharks, no, we have not come to our senses and are not giving up and coming home, and yes, we do realize the strain that our selfish refusal to act like grownup normal people places on everyone who cares about us.

Weather Reports, Online and Off

Weather reports have been the essential material of ocean voyages ever since humanity's first paleolithic proto-cruisers set out for the horizon in their hollowed-out logs. And the absence of reliable prognostications on the behavior of the planet's weather has led to the demise of multitudes of unhappy sailors and their ships.

Today we no longer must rely on the degree of discomfort experienced by the tribal shaman's arthritic hip (although joint pain is still used today by a flotilla of Maine lobstermen, and the

throbbing of a bunion on a big toe was used to good effect by my Uncle Freddy) or the pattern of entrails spilled from an eviscerated fish to get an idea of what we can expect on tomorrow's tide. We have weather satellites by the hundreds, special-purpose buoys by the thousands, computer models by the score, subscription services for weather reports of every variety, GRIB charts, weather-fax, animated frontal-data playback, personal weather-routing advisors (who work just like personal trainers do with our shoreside brethren), minute-by-minute replays of what weather we have had and what we can expect for the next few hours or the next 10 days, and an army of esoterically trained scientists working overtime dissecting, analyzing, and coordinating the data from all these sensors into a comprehensive prediction of what is going to happen to you and your boat if you persist in sailing into that line of little pointy triangles that is headed your way.

All this amazing technology and expertise results in amazing weather predictions available to all of us from a multitude of sources. And the most amazing thing about all this amazing technology is how amazingly wrong it can be with such amazing frequency. Who among us hasn't spent hour upon hour pouring over a collection of weather data that convinced us that, yes, this is the time to boogie across the bay only to get our Topsiders handed to us the next day by a force 8 gale? Sometimes it is enough to make us revert to Uncle Freddy's lumbago or to consult a gutted fish.

But wait. Let's not digress into a negative tirade on the inadequacies of the world of weather reporting. We can leave that to other publications who delight in obsessive negativity (the *National Inquirer* is perhaps right after: *Real Cannibal Zombies Discovered in Mexico*). That dog has already been kicked to death anyway. It is true that the weather reports that we rely on so heavily are often wrong, but they are

Vicarious carries an impressive array of electronic gadgetry, mostly because I work on the boat but also because I like electronic toys. But even with a top-of-the-line multifunction display radar, two chartplotters, depthfinders, several iPads, laptops, and a host of other paraphernalia, our electronics inventory is only about average for an up-to-date cruising boat. The old Acer computer on the left has been retired from active service and now does duty as our entertainment center—Netflix when we can get it and DVDs when we can't.

usually right, and in the short term, they are almost always right.

Accurate weather reports are as essential to successful and safe cruising as they have ever been. The big difference is that today they are available from many reliable sources. On *Vicarious* we check the weather at least daily and sometimes, when a storm is approaching or when we are about to leave on a passage, hourly. When we have 4G or WiFi access, we check any number of online sources. A favorite of ours (as it is with most cruisers we meet) is Passage Weather (passageweather.com): a free website that offers current and predicted worldwide weather patterns in a variety of useful and easy-to-understand formats. Another

is Intellicast (intellicast.com), an excellent and complete Internet source of weather for North America. Intellicast is not a dedicated marine weather site, but the iPad app does have a useful marine component available for a small fee (the basic service is free to download).

International weather is available from hundreds of websites, but the one we rely on most is The Weather Channel (weather.com), a huge site that is searchable for about anything on the globe related to weather. The Weather Channel (TWC) approaches climatic variation as an entertainment medium so you must keep this in mind when consulting their broadcasts. To them, every low-pressure area is a potential category 8 hurricane, and every raincloud threatens a torrential downpour. If you can keep this sensationalism in mind and allow for it, TWC can be useful, but watch out that you don't overcompensate. When TWC predicted that tropical storm Sandy would turn into Superstorm Sandy, many of us accustomed to the predictable exaggeration laughed it off only to get plastered by, you guessed it, Superstorm Sandy.

When the Internet isn't available, weather reports get a little trickier and a bit more costly. We rely heavily on the Sirius weather system, which has excellent satellite coverage of North America and has the added advantage of being a constant source of classical music (or any other kind for that matter). At $35 per month, this service is expensive, but to us the reliability and the quality of the reports is worth it. The Sirius system uses a dedicated antenna that passes the signal to the multifunction display so no radio signal is involved. Unfortunately at this writing, coverage is limited to the quarter of the globe centered on North America.

Once we venture outside of North American waters, we need to come up with another source. We also get weather-fax through the SSB via a simple audio interconnect with our laptop computer. On *Vicarious*, we use an app from Black Cat Systems (blackcatsystems.com) on the iPads, and on the laptop we use JV Comm 32 (jvcomm.de). This is a subscription service, but it does offer a fully functional demo version that is free. We do not have Pactor III at this point as the modem costs around $1,000 and the SSB connection we do use works so well, but Pactor is a possibility when the time comes because we would like the high-seas email. Another possibility, especially for a backup system, is weather-fax, email, and GRIB charts through a satellite phone.

Another source of offshore weather is through one of cruiser's nets that are available anywhere cruisers congregate. These nets are transmitted on SSB, ham, and VHF depending on the location and the intended audience, and they are a reliable source of firsthand weather data that is bound to be more accurate than anything you can get from a shore station. If you are enjoying ideal conditions but the boat sailing 200 miles ahead of you is getting pounded by wind and seas, it is probably time to lock up the cat and tie down the deck chairs.

Navigating the Seas of Life: Other Internet Sites That Are Worth Your Attention

I have already recounted our adventures day-sailing off the coast of Maine in the fog with a boat full of nautically challenged friends when we lost all our electronics due to an electrical fault, so I won't repeat it here. Nor will I indulge in a further discussion on the wisdom of relying on electronic charts as a sole method of navigation, as that deceased nag has also been adequately flogged. But, since this chapter dwells on the wonders of the Internet, I will restate that there are a great many downloadable navigation programs available online that are both economical and useful.

One of the most popular of these is the Open CPN system (opencpn.com), and it is an open-source (that is, free to all) program that installs a reliable chartplotter on your computer and makes charts for just about the entire world available for download. The plotter and the charts are saved in the computer memory so there is no requirement for an Internet or satellite link, although a GPS unit is necessary for full functionality. The downside of Open CPN is the same as for all other computer-based navigation systems: they are only as reliable as your computer, and because marine computers are not practical for most cruising boats and regular computers are venerable to the constant vibration, salt air, and humidity that are a part of the cruising life, this can preclude their use as a primary electronic navigation tool.

We don't use Open CPN on *Vicarious,* but we do have it on the hard drive just in case we need it. The two that we do use are the Garmin Blue Charts and the iSailor apps on the iPad. On the laptop we use The Captain from Landfall Navigation: an excellent program but one that costs about $400 to buy (we were given a copy with a bunch of charts by a friend) so it isn't an economical option. It also requires a GPS dongle that adds another 50 bucks to the price.

Blogging Your Way to Fame and Fortune

Are you thinking of starting a blog about your adventures on the high seas once you finally get going? Of course you are. Nearly everyone who isn't already posting a personal blog is thinking about it, and for good reason. Blogs are dead easy to do; they are an excellent way to share stories, photographs, and videos; they are an efficient way to let a large number of people know just what exactly is going on in your new cruising lifestyle; and they are one of the best ways there is to share your knowledge and expertise on sailing a boat to distant lands.

Types of Blogs

There is really no hard classification for the types of blogs, and the possible subject matter is endless, but for our argument, let's focus on three specific to cruising: the logbook blog (or logblog), the how-to-do-it blog, and the philosophical blog.

Of the three, the *logbook blog* is the most popular by far. This is just what it says it is: a daily review of what is happening to you, your crew, and your boat in the cruising life for the past 24 hours. Not only does the logbook blog give you a semipermanent record of your trip and everything that happens on the way but it also keeps everyone who cares about you up-to-date and informed of everything from your location to your mental state. I say "semi-permanent" because of the ephemeral nature of electronic data. If you want a permanent record, keep a hard copy of your blog, or maintain a traditional handwritten parallel log.

You can, of course, write anything you want into your logbook blog, but keep in mind that your followers may not want to be informed of every dolphin you see playing in the bow wave or what you had for breakfast every day of your cruise, unless, of course, you feast on eggs-mc-*escargots* in Genoa one morning and *brouillade-de-truffes* the next morning while under way to Savona. Personal observation and a dash of philosophy are fine and help to keep followers interested, but keep focused on your subject. Digressions can be saved for a separate blog or posted in a separate file.

How-to-do-it blogs are among the most helpful on the Internet. There are hundreds of them dedicated to educating the cruising sailor, and if you are about to work on your boat, there is a good chance that you can find one that covers the specific project that you are about to undertake. Cooking on a boat, creative stowage tips, and just general living-afloat advice are all popular with cruising bloggers.

If you want to start a how-to-do-it blog, it helps a lot if you know a bit about your subject. But it isn't necessary to be an expert or even an accomplished amateur. In fact, some of the most interesting and useful blogs are posted by complete klutzes who are honest and know how to write in complete and interesting sentences. I recently encountered one such blog where the blogger was recounting his adventures in replacing a plastic glazing in a portlight. It was his first attempt at a glazing project, and it didn't go quite as planned. He ended up with black polyure-thane sealant all over himself and the boat, and the cleanup took more time than completing the job. In the end, the project was finished to satisfaction, and it was documented in full detail including all the mistakes he made and how he corrected them. In all, it was a very entertaining and informative post. (Please note that I am not giving specific references to blogs here because of the transitory nature of the genre. They come and go on a whim, and the average age of cruising blogs is under two years. Interestingly, this is about the length of an average cruise.)

With *philosophical blogs* there are no rules. This is where you can let your hair down and let it all hang out. I just came across one blog written by a macho powerboater who says anyone with a boat that can't do 30 miles per hour is a sissy and sailboats are for wimps, as is anyone in a powerboat who slows down for them. I suspect he has a lot of followers on the ICW in Florida where waking sailboats seems to be becoming the state sport. It was kind of a cool site, really, but I declined the invitation to "like" on Facebook and posted something to the effect that $10 per gallon marine gasoline wouldn't be such a bad thing for these guys.

There are many more basic types of blogs than these three, of course, but while it is possible to create a general, do-everything sort of blog, it is advisable to focus on one subject rather than try to cover several topics. You might have a logbook-style blog, for example, and try to include how-to-do-it instructions on tying useful nautical knots. The problem is that such a multisubject blog risks losing the reader who isn't at all interested in knots while also alienating the other readers who don't know you well enough to care a fig about the daily machinations of your voyage; they just want to learn how to ties knots. When you want to cover more than one subject, it is better to do it with a separate blog or with a separate file on your parent blog. You can always link the two so that readers who are interested in both can switch back and forth at will.

Starting Your Blog

All you really need to start your own blog is an Internet connection, some sort of computer (more than one blog is run from a smartphone), and a general idea of what you want to blog about. But the first step should be to get on the Internet and check out as many blogs as you can find. You don't have to restrict your blog surfing to cruising or sailing topics because there is a lot to learn from blogs of just about any genre. There are hundreds of blogs telling you how to knit sweaters or play bridge (both useful cruiserly pastimes), and if you are a movie fan, you will find bloggers dissecting every aspect of the film industry from the technical errors in *Captain Ron* (one diligent blogger with a lot of time on his hands has counted 14) to "what were the fools thinking of when they cast Marlon Brando as Fletcher Christian in *Mutiny on the Bounty*?"

As you read through blogs, you will quickly learn to separate the good ones from the over-abundance of mediocre ones, and this will give you a feel for what you want your blog to look like and how you want it to function. But before you commit yourself to a specific format, you should decide on where you want your blog hosted. In geek-speak that means the server, website, or Internet service provider (ISP) that will display your blog and make it accessible to the world. While it is possible to host your own blog on your own server, which is the most economical and flexible way to do it, it is also the most difficult. Operating a server on a boat would be a challenge because it requires skill with scripting languages, a lot of time, and a dedicated computer that is more or less stationary, so we will skip right over this one as being impractical for budget cruisers.

The next blogging option in complexity is to use a blogging software on a host of your choice. There are a great many of these easy-to-use programs with names like Joomla (joomla.org) and Drupal (drupal.com), but the most popular and the easiest to use is WordPress (wordpress.org). These three and many more like them are scripting platforms that differ considerably in complexity. All three are fairly easy to use on the basic level, and they are free to start, but they become progressively more complex and costly as your skills and needs evolve.

This is the best option if you want a commercial site associated with your blog. Lots of cruisers turn a buck or two by selling photographs, calendars, books they have written, handicrafts, and tons of other stuff on the Internet. Logistically, this can get complicated: you will need some PHP (a scripting language that makes it easy to have on online store), and probably a link to a commercial market basket, the most popular of which is PayPal (paypal.com/webapps/mpp/shopping-cart/).

To build a blog using one of these scripting platforms you will first need to select a host for your blog, and of the hundreds available, the most popular is Bluehost (bluehost.com); you will need some basic scripting skills with at least html and css (plus PHP if you want a commercial site), and you will need to know how to use an FTP (file-transfer protocol) site. None of this is difficult on the entry level, and it should be within the capabilities of any computer-literate cruiser. But unless you already have at least a moderate (advanced amateur) proficiency with basic code, you might want to take a pass on using scripting software such as Joomla.

The danger is that you will spend so much time becoming proficient with the code that you will forget the purpose of your blog is cruising and not blog building. Thus it is best for us to leave Joomla and the like to the cruising supergeeks and turn to the last and best option for simple and basic cruisers like you and me.

Probably 90 percent of the cruising blogs that you have looked at are provided through either WordPress (wordpress.com [as opposed to wordpress.org, which is the more complex and expensive version discussed above]) or Google Blogger (blogger.com). These are click-and-go blogging services that make it easy for complete amateurs with no scripting skills to build professional-looking blogs with just a few clicks. Blogs built with WordPress and Blogger can do just about everything that the more sophisticated programs can do, but both of them are free to start and are so simple to use that anyone who can turn on a computer can have a blog going in a matter of minutes.

The drawbacks (the price you pay for "free") to these programs are fairly minor for most of us, but they need to be considered before you commit yourself to a blogging platform. If you choose to build your own blog using Joomla or something similar through a host you select, you will own your domain name and you will have your own URL (a cumbersome abbreviation for "uniform resource locator" designating the address of your blog). If you go through Google Blogger or wordpress.org, your blog will be appended to a massive Internet network as a subdomain. Thus, if you select your own host, you might become http://my-wonderful-cruising-blog.com, and you would own that URL for as long as you paid the yearly fee for it. If you use wordpress.org, your URL would be http://my-beautiful-cruising-blog.wordpress.com, and if you used Blogger your URL would be http://my-beautiful-cruising-blog.blogspot.com.

There may also be restrictions on any commercial activity on the free blogging services, and you will probably have to tolerate advertisements placed on your blog by companies you never heard of and probably wouldn't even like very much if you had.

If you think you want to start a blog, first give it some thought. One of the biggest problems with cruising blogs is the number that are started, then abandoned. Blogging is a lot of work, and it should be considered a commitment. Once you establish a working blog with a loyal cadre of followers, you have a moral responsibility to maintain it and let your fans know what is going on in your life. And writing a regularly updated blog with interesting content is one of the best ways there is to build a healthy list of dedicated followers.

A Forum on Forums

One of the more entertaining ways to spend time on the Internet is by reading through the multitude of forums that dissect and analyze just about every topic known to humanity. If you are interested in any subject, no matter how obscure or ridiculous, you will be able to find a forum that covers it in excruciating detail. There are blogs on beekeeping, how to run a whorehouse, and how to start a revolution. But since our topic here is sailing big oceans on small boats, we still concentrate on cruising forums.

If you are a contentious sort of person with strong views about sailing and the cruising life, the cruising forum is the best way to express your views. The more controversial your topic and the more vituperative your argument, the more vitriolic will be the responses. The advantages of light, go-fast boats for long ocean passages over traditional heavy, full-keelers; firearms on board for defense; the best anchor for mud bottoms; and the disgraceful disrespect for yachting traditions among the younger cruisers are all subjects guaranteed to generate an endless variety of posts, counterposts, and comments, not to mention lots of name-calling and speculation on the intellect and moral standing of anyone with opposing views.

As a reader, all this can be hugely entertaining as long as you remain aloof from the emotionalism and don't get drawn into whatever argument is being promulgated. I once got sucked into a discussion on the merits of a do-it-yourself marine toilet made from a standard household commode with the bottom somehow filled with cement. I forget the exact details of this preposterous device, but after posting my objective opinion of the thing (something to the effect that it was the stupidest idea I had encountered in a lifetime of being bombarded by stupid ideas), I was roundly castigated by the regular forum participants as being inflexible and closed minded. I have many faults (just ask Susan), but inflexibility and closed mindedness are not among them, and I refuse to even consider that possibility—case closed—no further discussion allowed.

Forums are like blogs with one overriding difference: where blogs express the opinion and observations of one or two individuals with comments and feedback from followers whose contributions are usually heavily edited, forums are platforms for anyone with an opinion or observation to express themselves, usually with only rudimentary editorial interference for such things as foul language and offensive commentary and very frequently no editing at all. Participants can, and do, say anything that they want with no requirement to be either morally responsible or factually accurate, all from behind the anonymity of a "user name."

I have a friend in New Zealand named Dave (a.k.a. The Sprocket Rocket) who takes his participation in an international bicycle-racing forum very seriously, to the extent that he maintains three cyber identities so he can participate in the forum as three separate people. He has great fun arguing with himself and often threatens to punch himself in the nose if he gets a chance. If you think this is extreme, consider that each of his identities has thousands of posts (posts are collected by forum addicts like power pods are collected in a video game), and he spends an average of four hours a day at it.

As you read through the cruising forums, you will quickly become familiar with the regulars who are there for every query and post daily. Many of these regulars provide a very useful service because their posts are full of insight and logical good advice. My favorite forum is called, appropriately enough, the *Cruiser's Forum* (http://cruisersforum.com), and three of the regular posters that I actively look for have the user names of *David Old Jersey*, *Seaworthy Lass*, and *Atoll*. There are lots more posters on this forum who are genuinely concerned with helping you and me to find answers to our questions and solutions to our problems, but these are three of my favorites.

The insidious danger in forums is the very openness with which they welcome new posts without regard to accuracy or validity. There is a ton of wrong information dumped on the forums every day, and sometimes it can be difficult to separate the gems from the gravel. There are many prolific posters who feel compelled to let us all know their feelings on every topic and their position on every argument, no matter what their experience or expertise. This misinformation is almost always countered by other more knowledgeable members of the forum who correct the miscreants right away. Thus it is important to read everything with skepticism (advice that applies to everything written about cruising, except this book, of course) and to read entire strings instead of just the individual posts.

Here is an example of a ridiculous post and a moderating response, the sort of thing that makes forum following so much fun. The thread was about the suitability of using firearms to scare away suspicious-looking boats that come too close. This poster, who most assuredly isn't

an active cruiser, proposed blasting them with a flame thrower:

There is a [shotgun] round called Dragon's Breath which turns the 12-gauge into a 100-yard flame thrower. After using it, people tend to choose fighting a fire over having a fire fight; sometimes they even want to become your friend if they have to abandon ship.

This response was from *Cat Man Do*, another of my favorite posters:

Exaggeration in a gun thread? Who would have thought.

Then he includes a quote from Wikipedia:

A Dragon's Breath usually refers to a zirconium-based pyrotechnic shotgun round. When the round is fired, sparks and occasionally flames shoot out to about 15 meters (48 feet); beyond 15 meters, the round's already limited effectiveness is drastically reduced.

Two other forums that I follow regularly are *CruisingAnarchy* (http://cruisinganarchy.com) and *SailNet* (http://sailnet.com). Naturally, there are hundreds of other forums that concentrate on sailing and cruising, and each of them is different with an interesting diversity of opinions and viewpoints. Check out as many as you can, and you will soon develop your own set of favorites. But watch out and don't become a forum addict like my friend Dave. Forums take a lot of time to just read, and participation in them can become all-consuming if you aren't careful. Sharing our opinions with others via the forums is a fine way to pass some time and to learn a thing or two, but it can quickly develop into a passion. If we are ever to get our new old boat in the water, we must keep that goal foremost in mind and take care not to allow forum reading, or anything but getting the bottom wet, to become obsessive.

Epilogue

So far, I have successfully shattered a few cruising icons, demythologized a few cruising myths, and debunked some cruising bunk. I have tracked the dragon of misinformation to its lair and slain it with the golden arrow of truth. Unfortunately, the demise of the dragon will not be met with a universal uproar of praise from the traditionalists. There are those in the cruising community who will continue washing their dishes in nothing but that certain brand of dishwashing detergent, who will sneer at any boat that does not have softwood plugs wired to all the seacocks, and who will continue to try to wash a 10-inch pot in a 9-inch sink. But, as Gloria Steinem said, "Truth never harms a cause that is just" (or was that Gandhi?), so not only will we stand tall in the shadow of our slain dragon but we will also continue the pursuit of false doctrine, and like medieval monks searching for heresies, we will smite them as we find them.

Writing this second edition of *The Cruising Life* has been a fun trip. It started when we were in North Carolina having just recently taken possession of *Vicarious*. From there we sailed north to Maine where we spent the summer in Robinhood Cove while I roughed out the first five chapters. Then, as the autumn leaves on the trees that lined the shore were donning their tourist-greeting colors, we sailed south to Florida where I spent several months roughing out another five chapters, dodging bullets, and getting *Vicarious* rewired, reprogrammed, and renovated for a long-anticipated trip across the Atlantic. Alas, we waited too long for the Atlantic crossing, so instead of a late start east, we turned south to Cuba and Mexico, where I finished the first draft before heading south once more to Bocas del Toro on the Caribbean side of Panama, where this Epilogue is being written.

The purpose of an epilogue is to inform the reader of events that have transpired since the original manuscript was written. If a writer were to try to update a volume of this size as it progressed, it would never be finished. And indeed a lot has happened in the past year. As the long and tedious Great Recession that tormented much of the world for seven years recedes into history, boatyards everywhere are getting busy again. And ancillary services like upholstery shops and sail lofts that survived the dismal economy (many did not) now have a backlog of work where only a year or two ago they were considering closing up and finding honest work in more lucrative trades. Unfortunately for us, this new found prosperity, with its increasing demand for nautical services, is driving the cost of nearly everything ever higher, making it even more imperative that aspiring cruisers on a budget become do-it-yourself adept and go-it-alone self-sufficient.

The good news for those of us looking for a boat to fulfill our cruising ambitions is that the prices of fine used vessels remain favorable while the inventory of unsold boats remains high. The big change here is that the good deals on used boats are being snapped up a lot more quickly than they were just a year or two ago. Where great boats would sit patiently awaiting interested buyers for years (*Vicarious* had her for-sale sign dangling from her bow pulpit for two years before Susan and I came along to rescue her), a clean cruising sailboat in good condition listed at a fair price will now sell in just a few months.

Just one other little thing I'd like to mention before I turn to other less interesting but nonetheless imperative tasks. I hereby claim the honor of penning the very first cruising book to not even once quote Kenneth Grahame's *Wind in the Willows*. It's not that I'm not a great fan of Grahame's, mind you—I am—and *Wind in the Willows* is one of my all-time favorite books, but that particular quote is a tad overcooked, and I refuse to perpetuate the travesty.

With that, friends, a book, like a long ocean passage, has to come to an end sometime. We have gone far in the last couple of hundred pages, and I hope you have enjoyed the journey as much as I have. If you are still determined to try the cruising life after all that has been said, welcome aboard, Godspeed, and fair winds. And if in your travels you drop the hook in some remote lagoon next to a tattered old ketch with a tattered old skipper and a still-young old lady sitting in the cockpit, hop in the dinghy and row over. Sit and share a yarn or two and maybe a brew, but no matter what you decide to do with your life, just remember this: "There is *nothing*—absolutely nothing—half as much worth doing as simply messing about in boats." Ooooops . . . damn!

Index